THEATER
OF THE WORLD

THEA
TRVM
ORBIS
TERRA
RVM

THEATER
OF THE WORLD

The Maps that Made History

BY THOMAS REINERTSEN BERG

Translated from the Norwegian
by Alison McCullough

Little, Brown and Company
New York Boston London

For Fredrik and Erlend,
With the hope that you'll
see much of the world.

———————————————

Little, Brown and Company
Hachette Book Group
1290 Avenue of the Americas, New York, NY 10104
littlebrown.com

First North American Edition: December 2018
Originally published in the Great Britain by Hodder and Stoughton, September 2018

Little, Brown and Company is a division of Hachette Book Group, Inc.
The Little, Brown name and logo are trademarks of Hachette Book Group, Inc.

The publisher is not responsible for websites (or their content)
that are not owned by the publisher.

The Hachette Speakers Bureau provides a wide range of authors for speaking events.
To find out more, go to hachettespeakersbureau.com or call (866) 376-6591.

ISBN 978-0-316-45076-8
Library of Congress Control Number: 2018958395

10 9 8 7 6 5 4 3 2 1

LSC-C

Printed in the United States of America

CONTENTS

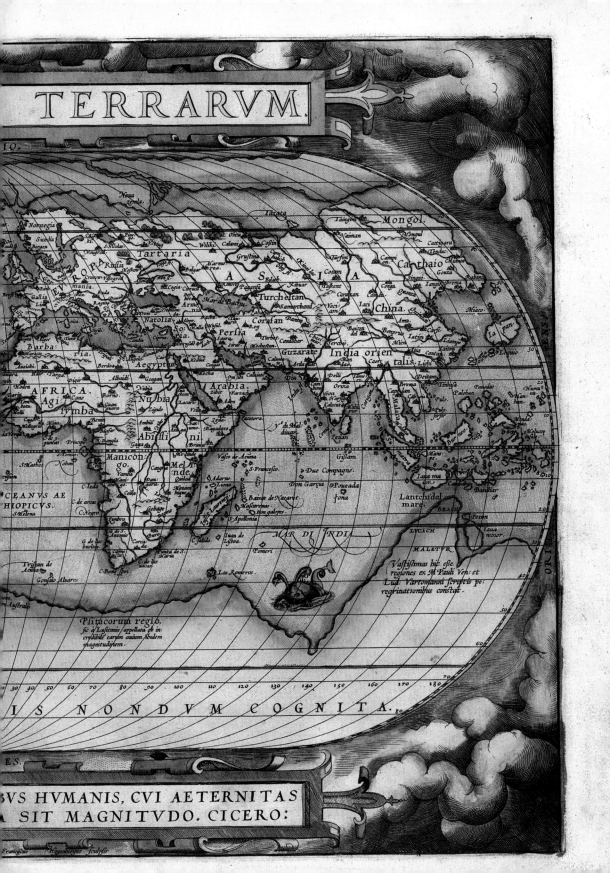

Preface

All the world's a stage

Oslo, Norway
59° 56′ 38″ N
10° 44′ 0″ E

Human beings took a bird's-eye view of the world long before learning to fly. Since prehistoric times, we have drawn our surroundings as seen from above to better understand where we are – rock carvings of houses and fields provide early evidence of this need. But it is only relatively recently that we have been able to see how everything really looks. On Christmas Eve 1968, the three astronauts aboard *Apollo 8* orbited the Moon and became the first humans to see the entire Earth at once. 'Oh, my God! Look at that picture over there! Here's the Earth coming up. Wow, is that pretty! [. . .] Hand me that roll of colour quick, will you,' said astronaut William Anders, before taking a photograph of our planet hovering beautiful, lonely and fragile in the infinite vastness of space.

Apollo was the Greek god who rode across the sky in his chariot each day, pulling the Sun behind him. When Flemish cartographer Abraham Ortelius published the world's first modern atlas in 1570, just 400 years before *Apollo 8* orbited the Moon, a friend of his composed a tributary poem in which Ortelius sits beside the god in order to see the whole world: 'Ortelius, who the luminous Apollo allowed to speed through the high air beside him in his four-horse chariot, to behold from above all the countries and the depths that surround them.'

Ortelius's atlas opens with a world map, with clouds drawn aside like stage curtains to reveal the Earth. With the book open before us, we look down on *Noruegia, Barbaria, Mar di India, Aegyptus, Manicongo, Iapan, Brasil, Chile* and *Noua Francia*. Ortelius called the book *Theatrum orbis terrarum – Theatre of the World –* because he believed the maps enabled us to watch the world play out before our eyes, as if in a theatre.

Regarding the world as a theatre was common in Ortelius's time. The year after *Theatrum* was published, English playwright Richard Edwardes had one of his characters say that 'this world was like a stage,/ Whereon many play their parts' – a formulation so admired by William Shakespeare that he used it in *As You Like It* some years later: 'All the world's a stage,/And all the men and women merely players;/They have their exits and their entrances.' Shakespeare also named his theatre the Globe.

Ortelius was no original cartographer. Nor was he an astronomer, geographer, engineer, surveyor or mathematician – in fact he had no formal education within any discipline. He did, however, know enough about cartography to understand what made a good map and what made a poor one, and with his sense of quality, thoroughness and beauty – in addition to a large network of contacts and friends, who either drew maps themselves or knew others who did so – was able to collate a refined selection of maps for inclusion in the world's first atlas.

Writing a book about the history of maps is somewhat reminiscent of Ortelius's work with *Theatrum*. This book also builds upon the work of many others, and I have studied a considerable number of books, texts and films to identify the most important and interesting material. It has also been necessary to make certain choices – no map can cover the whole world, and no book can contain cartography's entire history, since the history of maps may be said to be the history of society itself. Maps are of political, economic, religious, everyday, military and organisational significance, and this has necessitated some difficult decisions about what to include. The hardest decisions to make have been those relating to material closest to our present time, since scarcely any aspect of society is unaffected by cartographic questions.

Throughout history, the creation of maps has been guided by value judgements as to what is worthy of inclusion. Maps have always given us more than geographical information alone – as illustrated by the clear contrast between an Aztec map of the city of Tenochtitlan, which only provides details of the rulers of each district, and *Norgesatlas* (*Atlas of*

Norway) from 1963, where the publisher, Cappelen, due to social considerations, has 'chosen to include too many place names, rather than too few.' The Aztec map reflects the hierarchy of a strictly class-based society, while the *Norgesatlas* represents the golden age of social democracy in which everyone must be included. Both maps were influenced by the values of the age in which they were created.

The same is also true of the writing of this book. I have chosen to give significant attention to the mapping of the northern areas of the world throughout the text – not because the peoples of these areas play any greater role in the history of maps than the Americans, Arabs, British, French, Greeks, Italians, Chinese or Dutch, but simply because this is where I come from and the part of the world in which I live. To the best of my ability, I have attempted to show how broader historical developments – those concerning improved surveys and new methods, new measuring instruments and a greater understanding of the ways and areas in which maps may be used – eventually reached this corner of the world and were taken into use by a poor country with a vast and difficult geography. Norway is characterised by mountains, plateaus, great forests, 25,148 kilometres of coastline and 239,057 islands, and was a Danish colony from 1380 to 1814. The country was also part of a union with Sweden between 1814 and 1905. A number of changes have been made to the original Norwegian text to make the book more accessible to an English-speaking readership.

In 1969, American cartographer Waldo R. Tobler formulated what is known as the First Law of Geography: 'Everything is related to everything else, but near things are more related than distant things.' When looking at a new map, the first thing most people seek out is their home town. 'Some will perhaps search this theatre of ours for a performance of a particular region (since everyone, because they love their place of origin, would like to see it among the rest),' wrote Ortelius in his preface to *Theatrum*, so the phenomenon is an old one. And yet once we have found our home town, many of us experience a thrill as we journey through an atlas – pausing to look at Takoradi, Timbuktu and Trincomalee; running our finger along the route taken by the *Orient Express*, the Silk Road, the Western Front and the boundaries of ancient Rome – and realise that we are just as equally an exotic and inevitable part of the world as any other.

Distance and nearness are relative. Seen from space, the Earth must have seemed like the home town of all humanity. As astronaut William Anders said: 'We came all this way to explore the Moon, and the most important thing is that we discovered the Earth.'

The oldest surviving map from the Middle Ages was drawn in the late 600s or early 700s. At the top, Christ is shown ruling over the globe, his arms outstretched. Africa is named *Cam* for Noah's son Ham, who was said to have travelled south after the Great Flood, while Europe and Asia are named after Noah's other two sons, Japheth and Shem, although this is difficult to see here. South of Africa is a large *Terra inhabitabilis* – uninhabitable land. The two longest sets of lines represent the Mediterranean Sea and an unknown sea south of Africa, which cross the Don River and the Nile. The diagonal lines represent the Sea of Azov. Read more on page 74.

SCA

Virgo israhel reuertere

Sca maria. succurre miseris

TERRA
... ...
... ... EUROPA

ASIA ... BO

CAM

abcdefg hiklmnopqr stuxyz
abcdefg hi klmnopq
abc
Abc

bbb
lb. bbb. xxbb

Acknowledgements

There are many people I would like to thank for helping me through the process of writing this book. First, editor Trygve Riiser Gundersen, who pulled the text in the right direction; Benedicte Gamborg Briså at the National Library of Norway for inspiring lunches, discussions and general enthusiasm, and librarian Siri Røsbak Glosli for sending me maps; Bjørn Ragnvald Pettersen for all the articles he sent me about modern surveys of Norway; designer Dimitri Kayambakis for giving the book such an attractive appearance; Astrid Sverresdotter Dypvik and Tor Ivar Østmoe for translations from the German and Latin; Erling Sandmo, an exceptional consultant and source of information about Protestant sea swine; the Norwegian Polar Institute for their help and friendly responses to my enquiries; Ellen Giilhus and Sidsel Kvarteig at the Norwegian Mapping Authority; and my parents, who gave me a world atlas when I was eleven years old – an atlas I still use to this day. But most of all I would like to thank my partner, Maria, who has patiently listened to an endless range of more and less interesting cartographical anecdotes, given me time to write and read through my work in progress.

All errors – whether these be a city listed at the wrong latitude, an omitted name, the size of a lake given incorrectly or a river running out into the sea at the wrong location – are of course my own.

As a father, I have an excellent vantage point from which to observe my sons as they gradually map their world. Once tiny tots who surveyed the rooms of our apartment, from one bedroom to the next and from living room to kitchen, as they have grown their geography has expanded to include their kindergarten and school, the local shops, bakery and playground and the homes of friends. Over the coming years they will continue to explore the vastness of our world. This book is therefore dedicated to them.

The first images of the world

Bedolina, Italy
46° 02′ 00″ N
10° 20′ 29″ E

Val Camonica is a fertile valley in northern Italy, where people have lived for several thousand years. Today it is located somewhat off the beaten track – route E45 and the railway line weave their way from south to north through Verona and the Alps slightly further east. But the valley is a cradle of cartography – home to the 3,000-year-old Bedolina Map.

The map is carved in stone, high up on a mountainside with a good view of the valley. A large, advanced rock carving measuring 4.3 metres wide by 2.4 metres high, it depicts people, animals, warriors and deer in addition to houses, footpaths and rectangular dotted fields – a total of 109 figures representing a village and agricultural landscape as seen from above. But who created this map so long, long ago – and why?

The Romans called the area *Vallis Camunnorum* – Valley of the Camuni – after the people who had lived there since the Iron Age. Graeco-Roman geographer Strabo mentioned them in his *Geographica* around the year 1 BC: 'Next, in order, come those parts of the mountains that are towards the east, and those that bend round towards the south: the Rhaeti and the Vindelici occupy them [. . .]. The Rhaeti reach down as far as that part of Italy which is above Verona [. . .]; and [the] Camuni belong to this stock.'

The Bedolina Map, carved in stone, probably from around the year 1000 BC. If you make the trip to Val Camonica in the Italian Alps north of Brescia, to the western side of the mountain just past the small town of Capo di Ponte, you can see it for yourself. The area contains several thousand rock carvings, and is therefore protected.

Around 2,500 years ago, the Camuni came into contact with the Etruscans, a people who lived further south, from whom they learned how to write alphabetic characters. The rock faces near the map feature over 200 textual inscriptions, although nobody has ever managed to decipher and read them. But we can therefore say with some degree of certainty that this was indeed a map, carved into the stone around 3,000 years ago, although we have no written sources to confirm this.

The Bedolina Map is not a geographically correct map – it can't be used to find the route from one place to another. So then what was its purpose? Italian archaeologist Alberto Marretta believes that the map should be understood in purely symbolic terms – according to Marretta, it represents a crossroads in the history of the people who created it: the transition from a hunting society to an agricultural one. Other rock carvings and archaeological findings from the area show that the Camuni had a landowning aristocracy, and the purpose of the map, Marretta believes, was to show the symbolic power the aristocracy held over the landscape. Maps are always created to fulfil a need, and many of the oldest maps we know of were made to demonstrate ownership of certain areas. Others are more elaborate, and fulfil a religious need to show the place of human beings within the cosmos.

When encountering prehistoric rock carvings and cave paintings, we have to ask ourselves what a map actually *is*. What distinctive qualities distinguish a map from other motifs? How can we recognise a map when we know little of the society in which it was created? In their preface to the classic work *The History of Cartography*, editors J. B. Harley and David Woodward provide the following definition: 'Maps are graphic representations that facilitate a spatial understanding of things, concepts, conditions, processes, or events in the human world.' This definition therefore includes even the most primitive representations of space, and 'the human world' refers to our surroundings in the broadest possible sense – including cosmic space and the afterlife. But what constitutes a map ultimately remains a question of interpretation.

Norwegian archaeologist Sverre Marstrander studied rock carvings across the Scandinavian peninsula. In his book Østfold's *jordbruksristninger* (*Østfold's Agricultural Rock Carvings*), published in 1963, he described 'some strange, irregular, grid-like patterns,' which he believed were 'primitive schematic depictions of a specific type of field complex used in Bronze Age agriculture.' There could 'no longer be any doubt,' Marstrander asserted, 'that these formations depict ancient fields.'

But Marstrander decided not to call these depictions of fields maps. Instead, he viewed them in the context of the fertility rites intended to ensure that the fields would bear crops. Might another archaeologist have interpreted them along the lines of maps indicating land ownership?

Modern maps are always equipped with explanations – legends that clarify the symbols depicting roads, cities, footpaths, schools and ski trails. Of course, no such explanatory material is available to us when we encounter what we suspect may be a prehistoric map, so we are forced to guess and make interpretations – and anyone who has ever attempted to navigate the icons on an unfamiliar mobile phone knows how difficult this can be. Maps can never be fully translated, and societies have a tendency to simplify symbols to an ever-greater extent, until they ultimately become completely incomprehensible to outsiders. Hidden, symbolic and coded messages are first revealed when cartographers have studied not only what they believe to be a map, but also the entire society that surrounds it. And studying a map created by people who lived thousands of years ago is a demanding exercise.

But on the other hand, we can compare prehistoric works with each other. Minusinsk, Russia, is home to a large rock carving similar to the Bedolina Map, which also features houses, people and animals scattered across a large area almost ten metres in length – this too is a representation of a village. Here, however, the stonecutter was more interested in reproducing the houses than showing how they were situated in relation to each other, and everything is drawn in profile. It is also difficult to say whether the rock carving was created as a single picture; whether the houses were drawn together, or whether new ones were simply added where there was space to draw them on the rock. The comparison suggests that the rock carving at Bedolina is a map, while that in Minusinsk is an image.

MAPS IN THE MIND | The ability to communicate geographical information was developed by certain species long before the age of modern humans – the most widely known of these techniques is the dance honey bees perform to tell each other where flowers can be found. The bee moves up the honeycomb while waggling its tail, before turning to the right in a semicircle, back to the starting point, and beginning the dance again. Then the bee turns down to the left. If the flowers it has found are in the direction of the Sun, the bee dances straight up the honeycomb; if the other bees must fly to the left or right of the Sun to reach the flowers, the bee marks the exact angle in the dance. The further forwards the bee dances, the further away the flowers are; the more intensely the bee waggles its tail, the more enthusiastic it is about its findings. Aristotle noticed that bees must be able to give each other directions: '[…] each bee on her return is followed by three or four companions,' wrote the Greek philosopher in his *History of Animals* over 2,000 years ago.

The dance of the honey bee has a clear function – the hive gets richer when bees who know where food can be found share this information with the others. The same must have been true of prehistoric peoples – those who were able to communicate where prey, plentiful fruit or fresh water could be found ensured that the community would grow fat and survive. The early humans were nomads, and while our closest relatives, the other apes and Prosimians, lived mainly in the forests, we spent much of our time out on the plains. This resulted in us developing better sight than our predecessors, along with a different relationship to distances, space and direction. Spatial awareness was probably the first part of our primitive consciousness.

Humans also acquired four additional traits that were central to the development of our ability to think in maps. First, the ability to go on exploratory expeditions; second, the ability to store acquired information; third, the ability to abstract and generalise; and fourth, the ability to know what to do with the information. While our ancestors were generally only able to talk about what was happening in the here and now, humans learned to link events in terms of the past, present and future – and to physical space.

Putting the world into words – *this* tree, *that* lake and *that* mountain – makes the world simultaneously larger and smaller, and more comprehensible. It facilitates the dissemination of information, and it is therefore easy to see how the development of spatial awareness and language have helped each other. Because they wished to articulate the maps they had in their heads, prehistoric peoples may have built up a vocabulary to express long and short distances, directions, landmarks and the time it takes to reach a specific location. They may then have created the first maps from sticks and stones, using sand, earth and snow, and making marks with their fingers or a brush on cave walls.

PREHISTORIC MAPS | Humans began creating representations of the world around 40,000 years ago – or at least, the oldest images we know of – depictions of animals painted in black, red and yellow on the walls of the Cave of El Castillo in northern Spain – are from this period. The cave-dwelling peoples here used the pigments they found in clay and soot, and mixed them with fat, wax, blood or water. Rock carvings discovered in Australia are also estimated to be around 40,000 years old.

What is believed to be the world's oldest map is carved into the tusk of a mammoth. Estimated to be somewhere between 32,500 and 38,000 years old, it was discovered in the Alb-Donau-Kreis region of Germany, and according to German professor Michael A. Rappenglueck is a celestial map of Orion. Rappenglueck also claims that a 17,300-year-old painting discovered in the Lascaux Caves in south-west France, which depicts an ox, a man with a bird's head and a bird, is a map of the stars Vega, Deneb and Altair, also known as the Summer Triangle – the first stars to become visible on Nordic summer evenings. Rappenglueck illustrates this by drawing three lines between the eyes of the figures.

Not everyone is convinced by Rappenglueck's theory, but it is logical to think that humans created maps of the stars before creating maps of the landscape – it's much easier to obtain an overview of the sky than the

Next pages | An illustration of the Bedolina Map, which makes it easier to see what the carving represents. The map depicts six houses and around thirty fields, all connected by small paths, in addition to a ladder, animals and people, all viewed from above. Not until 1934 did anyone begin to wonder whether the carving might be a map.

terrain. The stars hang above us, arranged into formations as if stretched across a canvas or a wall, and are easy to represent using dots. Celestial maps may have played an important role in the earliest agricultural societies – the emergence of certain constellations continues to be used today as a sign of when crops should be sown. But not all prehistoric dot formations are celestial maps.

Rævehøj, on the island of Fyn in Denmark, is situated on a ridge that houses a hidden burial chamber from the Stone Age. Carved into one of the load-bearing stones is an elegant pattern of dots, and in 1920 Danish historian Gudmund Schütte argued that these represented the Plough, Virgo, Gemini, the Tropic of Cancer, Boötes, Leo, Canis and Auriga. But the problem with this theory, as Schütte himself admitted, is that the distances between the various constellations are incorrect, and the carving features more dots than there are stars. It's easy to see why Schütte was so convinced – the pattern of dots has a striking resemblance to a celestial map. But today's archaeologists believe the dots form a sun cross – an equal-armed cross within a circle.

In 1967, British archaeologist James Mellaart published a book about the excavations undertaken at the 9,500-year-old city of Çatalhöyük in Turkey, in which he claimed that one of the discovered wall paintings was a map of the city featuring the Mount Hasan Volcano in the background. The map quickly became famous – with many supporting Mellaart's interpretation.

'The oldest town plan in existence,' wrote Jeremy Harwood in *To the Ends of the Earth: 100 Maps That Changed the World*; 'The oldest authenticated map in the world,' wrote J. B. Harley in the *UNESCO Courier*; 'The oldest known [map],' wrote Catherine Delano-Smith in *The History of Cartography*; 'The Catal Huyuk map [...] is perhaps 2,000 years older than the oldest known writing system,' asserted James Blaut in *Transactions of the Institute of British Geographers*. But was the painting really a map? In 2006, archaeologist Stephanie Meece wrote an article in which she argued that the 'houses' are geometric patterns, which have also been found at other locations in Çatalhöyük, and that the 'volcano' is actually a leopard skin. Seven years later, a team of geologists tested the map theory by investigating whether Mount Hasan might have erupted around the time at which the map was created. Rock samples showed that the volcano had in fact erupted around 8,900 years ago – and the eruption would have been visible from the city. Does this ultimately prove that the painting is a map? Not necessarily. but it does illustrate how hard it can be to find clear answers to questions about historical artefacts from so long ago.

Our view of prehistory also influences how we view maps from the period, and may result in the under- or overestimation of their existence. First, it was common to underestimate the presence of prehistoric maps – as late as 1980 only four maps that could be said to be from prehistoric times had been properly studied. Then followed a period in which new theories arose around prehistoric religion, the Stone Age people's way of thinking, the role of symbols in primitive society and the significance of rock carvings. This resulted in the discovery of a number of 'new' maps – when the first edition of *The History of Cartography* was published in 1987, the chapter on prehistoric times in Europe, the Middle East and north Africa concluded with a list of fifty-seven possible maps. Several of these have since been refuted, while others continue to be debated today.

At Talat n'Lisk, in the Atlas Mountains in Morocco, is a round cave painting measuring one metre in diameter. Inside the circle is a painstakingly crafted image, thought to show a broad valley flanked by two mountain ranges, and between them a wide river and tributaries as well as two dots, one small and one large, symbolising settlements. The painting is around 6,000 years old.

In the North Caucasus mountains, a 5,000-year-old silver vase was discovered, engraved with two rivers running down from a mountain range to meet at a lake or sea. This may have been an attempt to represent the mountains of the Caucasus region, and two of its rivers.

Another vase, from Tepe Gawra near Mosul in Iraq, features a motif depicting hunters in a wide valley containing a river and tributaries, flanked by high mountains. Some believe the design was painted with a specific landscape in mind, while others believe the image to be more schematic and illustrative of a general phenomenon – hunting – rather than a particular place.

The Cangyuan region of south-west China is home to yet another rock carving reminiscent of the Bedolina Map. At its centre is a village, featuring houses constructed on stilts. That the stonecutter's aim was to denote space, distances and the positions of these houses is evident from the fact that the houses furthest away are painted upside down, to indicate that their stilts are located against the outermost fence. Towards the village run dotted lines – roads – along which people and animals walk.

Another village is reproduced in stone at Lydenburg in South Africa. The rock carving is large – 4.5 by 4 metres – and with its depictions of round settlements within a network of roads is also not unlike the Bedolina Map.

Along the Yenisei River, at Mugur-Sargol in Mongolia, are rock carvings that provide a bird's-eye view of the local shepherds' tents and enclosures. Mongolia is also home to many maps of grave sites, some of which illustrate both our world and that of the afterlife.

MAPS OF THE DEAD | Historians estimate that humans first began to imagine the existence of a world other than our own around 100,000 years ago, and graves from this period have been found to contain objects that the dead wished to take with them to the next world. But it was long believed that prehistoric peoples would have been unable to produce maps of anything other than their immediate surroundings – that representing their position relative to the Sun, Moon, stars, realm of the dead and abodes of the gods was far more advanced than their capacity allowed. 'As a rule [...] the maps of primitive peoples are restricted to very small areas [...] their maps are concrete [...] they cannot portray the world, or even visualise it in their minds. They have no world maps, for their own locality dominates their thought,' wrote historian of cartography Leo Bagrow in 1964. More recently, however, maps that illustrate how humans viewed themselves in relation to the rest of creation have been discovered. These often feature labyrinths, circles, ladders and trees, and several of them present the various levels that make up the universe, including the heavens, Earth and kingdom of the dead.

A rock carving found in the Sahara depicts a human-like figure surrounded by a pattern of ovals, waves and rectangles, with an opening at the bottom thought to represent the path to the kingdom of the dead.

A small stone statue in Trioria in Italy features a motif comprising the Sun at the top, the Earth in the middle and a ladder leading down to the underworld. In Yorkshire, England, rock carvings have been discovered that depict ladders leading from one circle to the next – perhaps in an attempt to show a connection between the Earth, stars and planets.

A painstakingly crafted cave painting found in Madhya Pradesh, India, shows a sea with rushes, fish and birds at the very top, and a sun surrounded by various geometric patterns at the centre. It is thought that this might be a map of the universe, as understood by the map's creators.

There is much evidence to suggest that maps were also used in ritualistic contexts. Shamans among indigenous populations in both Australia and Siberia, who have preserved all or parts of their religion over thousands of years, paint maps on the drums they use to enter a trance. These maps prevent the shamans from getting lost when they visit the spirit world.

In the early 1700s, Norwegian missionary Thomas von Westen drew a map taken from a Sami ceremonial drum, with clear cartographic features from both the old beliefs and the new Christian faith. Two lines divide the Earth from the heavens and the heavenly gods from the earthly ones; the Sun is included, and along the Christian road (Ristbaiges) are a horse, a goat, a cow and a church. The kingdom of the dead (Jabmiku di aibmo) features yet another church and a Sami cabin. A fishing lake and the Sami people's earthly residence are also represented on this cosmic map.

Maps are images of the world – representations of a world view. Religious narratives are related to maps in the sense that they seek to describe what the world is like. They are ways of imposing order and structure on a world that is seemingly endless and difficult to comprehend, and we therefore find *cosmogonies* – stories about how the world came to be – and *cosmologies* – theories describing how the world might have been created – in almost all cultures throughout all ages.

The current dominating cosmology – the scientific theory that the universe was created by the Big Bang 13.8 billion years ago – is not particularly old. It was first suggested by the Belgian priest and physicist Georges Lemaître as recently as 1927 – before this, scientists believed the universe to have existed in an eternal and generally unchanging state. But the Big Bang theory was not readily accepted by all astronomers and physicists – that everything had been created in this way sounded far too religious; it reintroduced God as a primary cause, it was said – but the theory has since gained a strong foothold, not least due to astronomer Edwin Hubble, who in 1929 proved that the universe is expanding. But it was not until 1964 and the discovery of cosmic microwave background radiation thought to be left over from the Big Bang that the theory was finally taken seriously in scientific circles.

The Big Bang theory is also embraced by many who hold a religious world view. Hindus believe that their Hymn of Creation, in which everything is described as being interwoven and initiated by heat under unclear circumstances, describes it:

> At first there was only darkness wrapped in darkness.
> All this was only unillumined cosmic water.
> That One which came to be, enclosed in nothing,
> arose at last, born of the power of heat.

The Quran states 'that the heavens and the earth were of one piece, then We parted them,' while in 1951 Pope Pius XII declared that the Big Bang theory is not incompatible with the Christian theory of creation.

Every place and time has its own stories of creation and ways of seeing the world. A Finnish creation story tells of an egg that divided to become the Earth and the heavens; in Hawaii people told of how the slime on the seabed gave rise to the Earth. The Inuit believed the Earth fell from heaven; the Greeks told of Gaia, who gave birth to the heavens, great mountains, beautiful valleys and Oceanus – the endless sea. These stories sometimes vary within the same culture at different times and locations, and their mythological descriptions do not always correspond to the geographic knowledge people possessed. This tells us that creation narratives should not necessarily be taken literally. 'That which at some points in time is regarded as history becomes mythical at others, and the stories regarded as myths today may be considered truths tomorrow, or may have been regarded as such in the past,' write Tor Åge Bringsværd and Jens Braarvig in the book *I begynnelsen: Skapelsesmyter fra hele verden* (*In the Beginning: Creation Myths from Across the World*).

What the early cosmologies generally agree upon, however, is that the Earth we live on is situated somewhere in the middle, and that there is also a realm of the dead and a supernatural place where the gods reside.

The Old Norse religion provides a good example of such a world view. At the centre of the world is Yggdrasil, an ash tree. 'This ash is the best and greatest of all trees; its branches spread over all the world, and reach up above heaven. Three roots sustain the tree and stand wide apart,' says one of the characters in medieval Icelandic author Snorri Sturluson's narrative *The Fooling of Gylfe.* Around the tree's trunk is Asgard – home of the gods – and surrounding this is Midgard – the home of humans. At the tree's roots are Niflheim – in Norse mythology the deepest region of the realm of the dead – and the serpent or dragon Nidhogg, who belongs to the dark powers. Encircling Asgard and Midgard is the great ocean, where the Midgard Serpent poses a great threat.

The 13th-century *Eddas* and *Sagas* provide no account of how the tree named Yggdrasil came into existence, but describe how the world itself was created from a primordial being. The *Prose Edda* gives the following version:

Of Ymir's flesh
was earth created,
of his blood the sea,
of his bones the hills,
of his hair trees and plants,
of his skull the heavens;
and of his brows the gentle powers
formed Midgard for the sons of men;
but of his brain
the heavy clouds are all created.

Next pages | A ceremonial drum confiscated by Norwegian missionary Thomas von Westen in the 1700s. The drawings form a map of the Sami view of both this world and that of the spirits. 'Let there be an end to devilish shaman arts, with wands, sorcery and magic drums,' said von Westen, threatening villages with the bailiff or district sheriff if they refused to hand over their shamanic objects. He collected almost 100 ceremonial drums using this method.

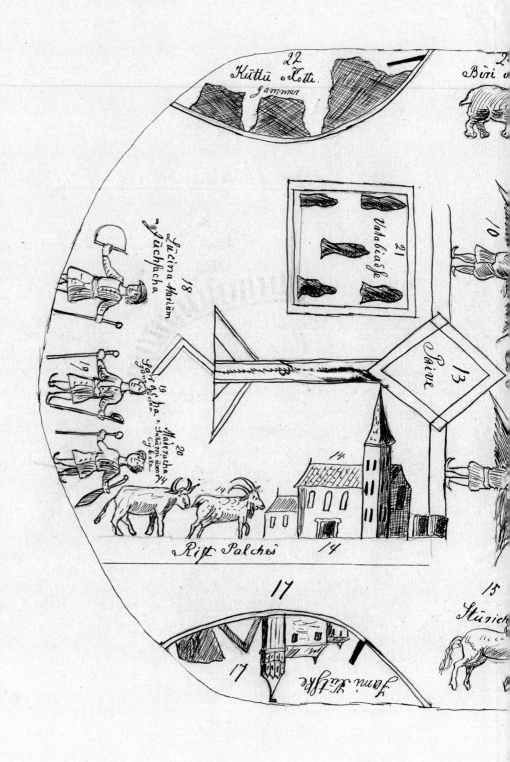

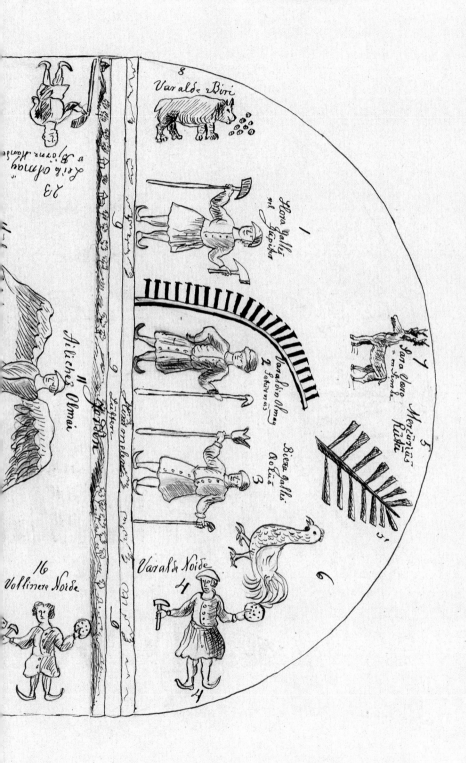

Ymir was a giant, who in prehistoric times came into being in the waste-land of Ginnungagap, between the scorching-hot realm of Muspelheim to the south and ice-cold Niflheim in the north. One day, the waters of the Élivágar rivers ran so far from their sources that they froze in the northern regions of Ginnungagap. Upon encountering the sparks flying from Muspelheim, the ice melted and began to drip – these drips were given life by the sparks and formed Ymir.

As he slept, Ymir began to sweat; a man and a woman grew from un-der his arm, and his feet produced a son – these were the ancestors of the giants. Ymir was nourished by Auðumla, the cow – she too was cre-ated from frost and ice, and fed on salted ice-blocks: 'the first day that she licked the blocks, there came forth from the blocks in the evening a man's hair; the second day, a man's head; the third day the whole man.' This man was named Buri, and he bore a son, named Borr. Borr took Bestla, a giantess, as his wife, and they had three sons: Odin, Vili and Vé.

A power struggle then ensued in Ginnungagap. Borr and Bestla's three sons killed Ymir to put a stop to the stream of giants he continued to sweat out. In *The Fooling of Gylfe*, Snorri retells the story of how the brothers fashioned the Earth from Ymir's body – adding that his blood became a sea 'in a ring round about her [the Earth]; and it may well seem a hard thing to most men to cross over it.'

The Egyptians also believed the world of the living to be surrounded by a vast, chaotic sea; above and below this was the invisible part of the universe, where the Sun, Moon and stars resided when they were not vis-ible in the sky – humans and animals were also believed to travel here when their earthly lives came to an end. An Egyptian map from the year 350 BC shows Egypt and its surrounding areas, with the south at the top. The goddess Nut arches over the world like a bridge, with her hands in the west and her feet to the east. At other times, Nut is represented as ly-ing below the Earth, extinguishing the Sun in the evening to birth it again the next morning.

The *Iliad*, the Greek epic first written down some time in the ninth or eighth century BC, describes a similar cosmology featuring a world sur-rounded by sea. While war raged between the Greeks and the Trojans, the Greek fire god Hephaestus was tasked with forging a substantial shield for the Greek warrior Achilles. The description of the imagery with which Hephaestus decorated the shield is also a description of the Greek universe:

> There earth, there heaven, there ocean he design'd;
> The unwearied sun, the moon completely round;
> The starry lights that heaven's high convex crown'd;
> The Pleiads, Hyads, with the northern team;
> And great Orion's more refulgent beam;
> To which, around the axle of the sky,
> The Bear, revolving, points his golden eye

Hephaestus hammered depictions of the world into the metal, including images of cities, people and animals, warriors and estate holders, and finally the sea, which defined the shield's outermost edge:

> Thus the broad shield complete the artist crown'd
> With his last hand, and pour'd the ocean round:
> In living silver seem'd the waves to roll,
> And beat the buckler's verge, and bound the whole.

Our view of earlier times also influences how we translate their texts. In the Norwegian translation of the *Iliad*, the Greek *Gaia* is translated as '*jordskiven*' – 'earth disc'; it assumes that the ancient Greeks believed the Earth was flat.

A similar problem can be found in the translation of the Bible's creation narrative. In the King James Bible, Genesis i, 6 reads: 'And God said, Let there be a firmament in the midst of the waters, and let it divide the waters from the waters.'

The problem here is that 'firmament' is not necessarily a correct translation of the Hebrew word *raqiya*. The new English Standard Version of the Bible from 2001 instead uses the word 'expanse' – 'Let there be an expanse' – something that spreads outwards. It is therefore not necessarily the case that the early Jews regarded the heavens as a kind of solid bell jar curving above the earth.

The Book of Genesis provides certain hints as to how much of an overview the writers of the Bible had of the world. Genesis ii, 10–14 states: 'A river flowed out of Eden to water the garden, and there it divided and became four rivers. The name of the first is the Pishon. It is the one that flowed around the whole land of Havilah, where there is gold. And the gold of that land is good; bdellium and onyx stone are there. The name of the second river is the Gihon. It is the one that flowed around the whole land of Cush. And the name of the third river is the Tigris, which flows east of Assyria. And the fourth river is the Euphrates.'

Havilah probably refers to the Hijaz Mountains in western Saudi Arabia, where several thousand years ago a river system, now dried up, ran westwards to the Persian Gulf. Cush was a kingdom situated at the current border between Egypt and Sudan, also known as Nubia, and the Gihon has been said to be the Blue Nile. The Tigris is the river that runs from eastern Turkey, down through Iraq and out into the Persian Gulf, and the Euphrates also runs through Iraq.

Adam and Eve's son Cain killed his brother, Abel, then 'went away from the presence of the Lord and settled in the land of Nod, east of Eden.' But since *nod* is the root of the Hebrew word meaning 'to wander', Nod is not usually understood as a specific country or region, but rather to imply that Cain began a nomadic life.

At the centre of the Bible's world is Jerusalem. Ezekiel v, 5 states: 'Thus says the Lord God: This is Jerusalem. I have set her in the centre of the nations, with countries all around her.' The temple in Jerusalem was constructed like a map of the cosmos – the outer courtyard represented our visible world, with its countries and seas; the holy space within was an image of the visible heavens and God's garden. The innermost space represented the invisible Kingdom of God.

The belief that the world has a central point is found in many cultures. It may have arisen because, over time, people noticed how the stars rotated above them, and therefore assumed that they must be turning around something. Naturally enough, people generally tended to regard the centre of the world as somewhere close to where they themselves lived. Home is the place that people know best; it is constructed and cultivated, while everything at a distance is unknown, representing chaos, night and death. The location regarded as the centre of the world was often an elevated place where earth met sky, such as a mountain, tree or temple.

The Japanese viewed the holy Mount Fuji as the centre of the world. In North America, the Cheyenne people viewed Moʻóhta-voʻhonáaeva – the Black Hills in South Dakota – as the world's centre. For the Pitjantjat-jara people in Australia, Uluru/Ayers Rock was central. The Greeks had the oracle in Delphi; Chinese Taoism describes Kunlun as 'the mountain at the centre of the world.' China has also gone a little further than most when it comes to claiming to be the world's central point: in Mandarin the country's name is Zhongguó – the Middle Kingdom.

THE SUMERIANS AND BABYLONIANS | Babylon is at the centre of the oldest world map ever to be discovered – a 2,600-year-old clay tablet found in the Babylonian city of Sippar, south-west of modern Baghdad. Measuring just 12.5 by 8 centimetres, the tablet isn't large, and was at first of no particular interest; it was among 70,000 other tablets that were sent to the British Museum following excavations undertaken in 1881. But today, the tablet has a prominent position among the museum's collections as the Babylonian Map of the World.

The map consists of a small ring within a larger one. The innermost ring contains several other small circles, rectangles and curved lines, and around the outermost ring are eight triangles. The tablet only became comprehensible as a map when the ancient text on the back was deciphered and understood.

This text tells us that the outer ring is *marratu*, 'the salt sea', and represents the great sea that surrounds the inhabited world. Within the inner ring is a rectangular shape that starts at the top of the ring and extends down past its centre – this is the River Euphrates. Its source is represented by a circle to the north marked 'mountain', and ends in a horizontal rectangle to the south representing a 'canal' and a 'swamp'. The rectangle that crosses the Euphrates is Babylon; circles represent the neighbouring areas of Susa (southern Iraq), Bit Yakin (Chaldea in southern Iraq), Habban (Yemen), Urartu (Armenia), Der (eastern Iraq) and Assyria.

The triangles that stick out from the other side of the sea are labelled *nagu*, which translates as 'region' or 'province'. Certain ancient Babylonian heroes are said to have been to these areas, and the accompanying text describes the region where 'the Sun is hidden and nothing can be seen' – a sign that the Babylonians may have heard of the lands to the north and their dark winters. Another region is labelled as being 'beyond the flight of birds'. Exotic animals are also mentioned, including chameleons, apes, ostriches, lions and wolves. These regions are the unmapped regions – the remote, mystical areas beyond the Babylonian knowledge of the world.

Why the map was created is unclear. The text states that the map's creator was a descendant of Ea-bel-ili from the city of Borsippa, situated directly south of Sippar – and that's as much as it tells us. But this is not the only map to have survived from this time and region.

Before the Babylonians, the Sumerians were the leading people of the Iraqi plains. The world as they knew it extended from Turkey and Caucasus in the north to Egypt in the south, and from the Mediterranean, Cyprus and Crete in the west to India in the east. Their closest neighbours to the east were the Elamites, a rival people with whom the Sumerians were often at war, while in the west wandered the Martu, a Semitic, nomadic people who lived in tents and kept sheep and goats. In the north lived the Subartu, a people the Martu often pillaged in order to obtain timber, other raw materials and slaves; to the south was Dilmun (Bahrain), a trading post that became associated with both the creation narrative and the land of the dead.

The golden age of the Sumerian people lasted from around 3500 to 2270 BC, and they left us two things that we continue to use when creating maps today: script and mathematics. The modern method of dividing maps into 360 degrees of longitude and 180 degrees of latitude is based on the Sumerian number system – although their system was based on the digits 6, 12 and 60, rather than 5, 10 and 100.

There are several theories as to why the Sumerians developed such a system. One posits that it is easy to count to twelve when using your thumb to count the tips and joints of the hand's four fingers: 1–2–3 on the index finger, 1–2–3 on the middle finger, 1–2–3 on the ring finger and

1–2–3 on the little finger. And if you then lift a finger on the other hand for each time you count to twelve, you have sixty once you have counted five times twelve.

Sixty is also a useful number in that it can be divided equally by eleven other numbers: 1, 2, 3, 4, 5, 6, 10, 12, 15, 20 and 30; this makes it easy to create smaller units such as halves, thirds, quarters and tenths. The Greeks maintained this number system when building upon Sumerian and Babylonian astronomy, geometry and geography, and this is why we continue to use it today.

The Sumerian writing system – the earliest writing system we know of – made it possible to record geographical information. Advancing armies, and merchants who travelled from place to place to collect metals, stone and timber, created lists that stated how far it was from one city to another and how long each journey would take. One such example is a military travelogue detailing the route from the southern part of Iraq to the city of Emar in northern Syria. All the listed stopping points are around one day's journey from each other, between twenty-five and thirty kilometres, and if the troops spent more than one night in a location, they recorded for example that this was 'where the chariot broke down' or 'when the troops rested for two days.'

Around the year 3000 BC, the Sumerians developed units of measure, and 200 years later used geometry to survey arable land and calculate taxes. They used a measuring rope and a peg that was driven into the ground to hold the rope – a method known as triangulation, so simple and effective that it continued to be used right up until the present day. To triangulate an area, you first measure a baseline on the ground. You then find a point a couple of hundred metres away, such as a house or a tree, which becomes the last corner of the triangle. You then walk to one

---

Next pages | A papyrus map from the time of the pharaohs, probably from around the 1100s BC, which shows the quarry in Wadi Hammamat – the Valley of Many Baths – in Egypt's Eastern Desert. The map was found in the early 1800s in a grave near the city of Luxor. Over the years the original map, which was 210 centimetres wide when created, has broken into several pieces. On the most well-preserved it is possible to make out four houses, a temple to the god Amun, a water reservoir, a well and the mountain where the Egyptians mined gold.

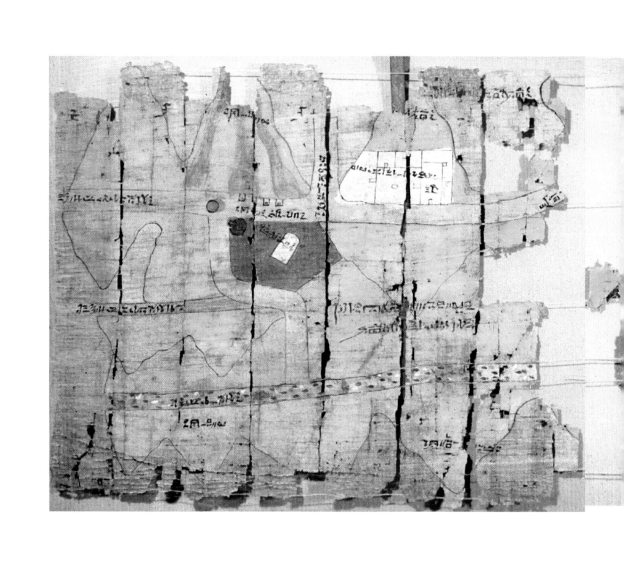

end of the baseline and measure the angle between this and the point, before doing the same from the other end. The length of the baseline and the size of the two angles gives you all the information you need to calculate the distance to the point.

A 3,500-year-old Sumerian map shows a landscape with several fields and canals at a location where the river makes a sharp turn. A map of the holy city of Nippur from the same period shows the city's most important temple, a park, the Euphrates, two canals that run through the city and seven gates – all of which have names. But what is possibly unique about this map is that it may be the first to have been drawn to scale – that is, the various elements are reproduced in the same relationship to one another as in reality. Numbers given beside several of the buildings also specify their size, and modern excavations of Nippur have resulted in claims that the city looked exactly as it appears on the map. The accurate reproduction of this fortified city may indicate that the map was of military significance.

Occasionally, the Sumerians also attempted to create maps of places situated greater distances from each other – a map discovered in Nippur depicts nine cities along three canals and a road.

The Babylonians built upon Sumerian mathematics, developing it further, and surviving tablets provide evidence of a high level of skill – particularly within geometry. The Babylonians also developed specific units for indicating distances and lengths, which were based on the time it took to reach the location in question. The main unit was the *beru*, the 'double-hour' – around ten kilometres.

The Babylonians used this mathematical knowledge to create maps of estates, territories, houses, named streets, temples, and rivers and canals – sometimes even using wavy lines to denote the water. One fragment of a city map is thought to show a temple in Babylon and the surrounding streets; another shows the city of Uruk and a building within it.

The importance of the Babylonian Map of the World has already been noted, but equally important in cartographic history is the first map to indicate the cardinal directions east, west and north, with east at the top. This was discovered close to the city of Kirkuk in northern Iraq. The map was created around the year 2300 BC, and shows a valley with a river running through it. Text in the bottom left corner states that the map is of a place called Mashkan-dur-ibla. At its centre is an area of land specified as measuring 354 *iku*, or around 12 hectares, and its owner is named as 'Azala'. Most of the text is otherwise unreadable.

If the Babylonians were indeed the first people to indicate compass points on a map, and the Sumerian map of Nippur was created to scale, then two of today's most important cartographic principles were already being used in ancient Mesopotamia.

THE GOLD MINE MAP | Like the Sumerians and the Babylonians, the ancient Egyptians were a people who undertook agricultural activities beside a great river – they were dependent upon the Nile flooding its banks each year to produce fertile mud for them to cultivate. The floods also resulted in frequent changes to the landscape, and meant that the ancient Egyptians – like the Sumerians and Babylonians – needed to survey their lands.

In his *Histories*, written between 450 and 420 BC, Greek historian Herodotus wrote about the Egyptian pharaoh Sesostris, stating that he 'divided the country among all the Egyptians by giving each an equal parcel of land, and made this his source of revenue, assessing the payment of a yearly tax. And any man who was robbed by the river of part of his land could come to Sesostris and declare what had happened; then the king would send men to look into it and calculate the part by which the land was diminished, so that thereafter it should pay in proportion to the tax originally imposed.'

The age of the pharaohs began with the unification of Upper and Lower Egypt in 3100 BC, and the first Egyptian maps were created during this period. Decorations discovered in tombs feature elements of landscapes and buildings drawn both from above and in profile along strips representing the horizon, and may be said to be simple forms of pictorial map. The difference between cities and the countryside is denoted using trees.

The *Book of the Dead*, a collection of ancient Egyptian funerary texts composed on papyrus around the year 1400 BC, includes a drawing of a garden in which the dead may work. The garden is rectangular and divided by canals, and the use of colour strengthens the impression that the image is a map. Other maps associated with the realm of the dead have been discovered painted inside coffins from around the year 2000 BC, and show a landscape with two paths: one is blue and runs via water, while the other is black and crosses the land. Both paths lead to the god Osiris, ruler of the afterlife.

A map from around 1300 BC shows the military conquest procession of Seti I as it travels past watering holes and boundaries along the desert road to Canaan, where Israel, Palestine and Lebanon are situated today. Seti I's successor, Ramesses II, attacked a fort in Kadesh, where the Orontes River meets a smaller river near Homs in what is now Syria, and a graphic reproduction of this battle has clear cartographic qualities. The rivers encircle the city, separating the two armies.

Around the year 1150 BC, the Egyptian bureaucrat Amennakhte created one of the most beautiful maps to survive from the ancient world, showing the way to gold mines and a stone quarry in eastern Egypt. In addition to being a topographical map depicting mountains, roads and waterways, it is also the world's oldest geological map, as it indicates which types of stones and metals are present in the area. The map was created for Ramesses IV's expedition to obtain stone for use in creating new statues of the king.

Two wide roads pass through a pink mountainous area. These are drawn horizontally across the papyrus, which is almost three metres long, and connect to a third road that crosses the papyrus and leads to a fourth. The road at the bottom features gravel depicted in various shades of brown and white, and sparse, green vegetation, typical of a dried-up river bed. The writing on the map specifies where the roads lead, and even explains the pink mountains: 'the mountains in which gold is worked, they are coloured pink.' Beside the gold mine are four houses where the workers lived, a temple to the god Amun, a water reservoir and a well.

In modern times, the map has been compared with the place it is intended to replicate – a fifteen-kilometre stretch of the Wadi Hammamat dry river bed – and has been found to be accurate. Archaeological surveys have also shown that gold was mined here during the period. The area runs parallel to the main road, which extended from Qift, by the

Nile, through the eastern desert to the port of Quesir, by the Red Sea. From here, the Egyptians embarked on trading expeditions to a country to the south, which they called the Land of Punt. The country's exact location continues to be debated by historians today.

This map may have been created as a result of the distance calculations performed for purely logistical reasons, which Amennakhte then expressed visually. The question, then, is whether this map was the only one of its kind, or whether other Egyptian cartographers also painstakingly crafted maps that were later lost – or which now lay hidden in a cracked clay pot somewhere out in the desert, awaiting discovery.

FOUNDATIONS | Like those of our own time, prehistoric and ancient maps were influenced by the age in which they were drawn, and designed to fulfil the needs of that age to the best of their creators' ability. The Sumerian and Babylonian maps illustrating land ownership – and that discovered in Bedolina, if it is true that this map also depicts the possession of property – anticipate our modern economic map series by several thousand years. Religious representations of the world and the universe fulfilled the need to understand one's place in the bigger picture.

Our view of the past and its peoples influences our interpretations of how *they* viewed the world. The fact that we have long believed people before Columbus thought the Earth was flat – which is incorrect – has influenced translations of texts from before Columbus's time, and our belief that creation narratives and cosmogonies were intended to be taken literally has also had peculiar consequences. We interpret old maps and texts through the fog of history – but sometimes the prehistoric terrain might just correspond to the maps we draw of it.

C. de Bichieri.

Farion.

Alessadria, Vechia.

Alessandria.

Roseto.

Porto Vechio.

Atacon.

Turbet.

Caliz

E G

Calizene de Ataco.

MAGNVM D

abi.

T

Turamania.

Deruti.

Michale.

Acatos f.

Leonton.

Zuga.

Demerio cuti.

Nacaria.

Munusi.

Moeridis laco.

Derat.

Subsir.

Narnit.

Farson.

Sibenit.

B

T

Sachil.

Ca

Nitriotu.

Barbare pirani.

Nilu

SAYT
INTERIOR.

Meser.

Buli.

Menuia.

Exiclese pira mide.

Cofer.

LIKE FROGS ABOUT A POND

Alexandria, Egypt
31° 12′ 32″ N
29° 54′ 33″ E

During antiquity, Alexandria could be seen from around sixty kilometres away when arriving by sea. On the narrow island of Pharos, just north of the city, stood a lighthouse measuring over 100 metres in height – one of the Seven Wonders of the Ancient World. To guide travellers along the seemingly monotonous Egyptian coastline, with its hidden sandbanks and rocks, a fire was lit in the lighthouse at night, and the Sun's light reflected using a large mirror during the day. But the lighthouse was more than just a landmark to navigate by – it also informed travellers that they had arrived in one of the great metropolises of the age. Julius Caesar was impressed when he visited the city in the year 48 BC, calling it 'a tower of great height, of marvellous construction.'

Alexandria had been founded around 300 years earlier by another builder of empires – Alexander the Great. One of Alexander's Macedonian generals, Ptolemy, was appointed governor of Egypt, and succeeded Alexander as Ptolemy I Soter in 304 BC. Alexandria then became the country's capital, and it wasn't long before the city became known as the greatest and most important in the Mediterranean. With its position on Egypt's northern coast, Alexandria sits at the centre of a cultural inter-

A map of Egypt, featuring Alessandria – Alexandria – on the coast, based on Ptolemy's co-ordinates from antiquity. Drawn by Girolamo Ruscelli in 1561, it is one of many Italian Ptolemaic maps published during the Renaissance. The image shows a section of the original map.

section. Here, Africa and Asia meet; Indian, Arabic and African ships sail the Red Sea to the south-east, and Europe is just a short voyage north across the Mediterranean.

As travellers sailed through the strait that led into the harbour, with Pharos on the right, the city with its 'building[s] upon building[s]' would come into view, as geographer Strabo described the experience while living in Alexandria just before the birth of Christ. The area around the harbour was dominated by the royal quarter, and as soon as the ships docked they would be boarded by bureaucrats tasked with finding out whether any scrolls were aboard. All books brought into the city were borrowed so that scribes could make copies of them.

Demetrius of Phalerum, a former student of the philosopher Aristotle who had been greatly inspired by Aristotle's library, advised Ptolemy I Soter to collect books from all the peoples of the world. The thinking behind this was simple: trade generates wealth, wealth pays for knowledge and knowledge stimulates more trade. Just a few years later, the library in Alexandria was established as the Mediterranean's most important knowledge centre.

The books were transported from the ships to the palace area, where the museum and its library were located, and the copies made of them later returned to the boats. The library – the first attempt to collect, categorise and catalogue all available knowledge of the world – appreciated originals.

Alexandria not only housed the world's largest collection of books – possibly as many as 700,000 when the collection was at its largest – but also acted as a meeting place for scholars from three continents. The Egyptian kings offered food and lodgings, pay and – best of all – access to the library. The city was consequently visited by astronomers, geographers, engineers, literary scholars, mathematicians and physicians, and it was in Alexandria that modern cartography was born.

Around the year AD 150, astronomer and mathematician Claudius Ptolemy began searching the library for material so that he could write a book about geography. The result was his *Geographike Hyphegesis* (*Geographical Guidance*), later simply referred to as the *Geography* – a three-part work containing the longitude and latitude values for over 8,000 locations in Africa, Asia and Europe; instructions for how to best represent the round globe on a flat surface; and a discussion of the role of astronomical calculations and other forms of collated knowledge in the study of geography. Never before had anyone written such a comprehensive book on the subject.

We can imagine Ptolemy wandering between the worn colonnades overlooking the museum's park, a papyrus scroll from one of the library's many bookshelves tucked under his arm. He's on his way to the *exedra*, the large, crescent-shaped stone bench that forms part of the park's walls, where his colleagues can almost always be found reading or deep in discussion.

Ptolemy is now around fifty years old. On this particular day he's carrying volume IV of the encyclopedia *Naturalis Historia* from the year AD 77, written by Roman officer and historian Pliny the Elder, who served in Germania from AD 42 to 52 and while there heard rumours of large islands recently discovered in the northern regions. Ptolemy opens the scroll:

> In their country is an immense mountain called Saevo, not less than those of the Riphæan range, and which forms an immense gulf along the shore as far as the Promontory of the Cimbri. This gulf, which has the name of the Codanian, is filled with islands; the most famous among which is Scatinavia, of a magnitude as yet unascertained: the only portion of it at all known is inhabited by the nation of the Hilleviones, who dwell in 500 villages, and call it a second world: it is generally supposed that the island of Eningia is of not less magnitude. Some writers state that these regions, as far as the river Vistula, are inhabited by the Sarmati, the Venedi, the Sciri, and the Hirri, and that there is a gulf there known by the name of Cylipenus, at the mouth of which is the island of Latris, after which comes another gulf, that of Lagnus, which borders on the Cimbri. The Cimbrian Promontory, running out into the sea for a great distance, forms a peninsula which bears the name of Tastris.

The immense mountain called Saevo is probably Norway, and the Cimbrian Promontory and Tastris Peninsula are the Danish mainland. The Codanian Gulf is a combination of Skagerak, Kattegat and Østersjøen, and according to Pliny the most famous island here is Scatinavia –

the Romans did not understand that Scandinavia is a peninsula. 'Hillevi-ones' is probably Pliny's collective term for the Scandinavians.

Using these kinds of texts, Ptolemy pieces together an image of the world. He reads travelogues, geographical treatises and astronomical calculations, and studies old maps – all from among the great library's many scrolls. He also talks to seamen who have travelled to distant harbours: 'But there is a consensus among those who have sailed there and visited the places over a long period, as well as among those who have come to us from there, that [Simylla] is just south [and not west] of the mouths of the river, and it is called "Timoula" by the natives,' he writes in his Geography.

Ptolemy had previously written the Almagest or Syntaxis Mathematica, a work about the stars and planets, and at the time of its writing his knowledge of the world was little greater than that possessed by those who had lived 300 years before him. He believed Sri Lanka was the southernmost country known to exist, and knew nothing of Africa south of today's Ethiopia, nor anything of what lay east of the Ganges River other than Serica – the area of China that marked the end of the Silk Road. Towards the end of the Almagest, Ptolemy laments the lack of assured coordinates for the world's most important cities, 'but since the setting out of this information is pertinent to a separate, cartographical project,' he stated, this work would have to wait. But it was this project – a catalogue of the latitude and longitude values of the world's most important cities – that was the seed that gave rise to the Geography, and soon Ptolemy's aim was to reproduce 'through drawing [...] the entire known part of the world together with the things that are, broadly speaking, connected with it,' including rivers, gulfs, large forests 'and the more noteworthy things of each kind.'

As he worked on the Geography, Ptolemy's knowledge expanded, the world he would eventually present to us becoming bigger than that described in any other work from classical antiquity either before or after him. It stretches from 16 degrees south of the equator, from Agisymba and Kapp Prasum (Mozambique and Tanzania), east to Sinai (China) and the cities of Zabai and Kattigara – probably in today's Cambodia – north to the Cimbric Peninsula (Jutland) and the island of Thule – probably Norway – and west to the Fortunate Isles somewhere out in the Atlantic Ocean. Ptolemy used eight scrolls to describe the world, and when the work was finished had summarised several hundred years of Greek, Hellenic and Roman thinking regarding the Earth's appearance. For his part, Ptolemy was modest – rather than claiming to have produced a pioneering work, he emphasised how he had built upon the works of those who had gradually and laboriously gathered geographical knowledge before him. The foundations for his *Geography* were laid 700 years earlier, when the first natural philosophers began to doubt the mythological narratives about the nature of the world.

THE FLOATING WORLD | The ancient city of Miletus is a good example of the fact that any geography is only a temporary truth. When the city was founded, it was situated on the outermost point of a promontory that stretched into a bay, but this was gradually filled by sediment from a river, which caused the coast to move further and further from the city. The city's inhabitants moved accordingly, and today Miletus lies abandoned and in ruins, around ten kilometres from the sea.

Miletus was a beautiful city in its time. It had a theatre with capacity for 15,000 people, a town hall, a stadium, two large squares, a gymnasium and public baths – and all this despite the fact that the city was often afflicted by war. Around the year 600 BC, the neighbouring kingdom of Lydia attempted to destroy Miletus, while at the same time the city's ruler abolished the aristocracy. This resulted in the city's two communities, the Aeinautes and the Cheiromaches, coming to blows in a revolt that lasted for two generations.

Amidst all this, Miletus became the most important cultural centre in the Greek world. The city is situated in modern Turkey, within range of Babylonian mathematics and astronomy, and these played an important role in the development of Greek philosophy and science, which started here. With these disciplines came new thinking regarding what the Earth must look like – philosophers were dissatisfied with mythological explanations;

Next pages | In the 1800s, it was popular to draw world maps based on what various authors had written during antiquity. Here we see the world according to Hecataeus, Herodotus, Strabo and Eratosthenes – as presented in *Cram's Atlas of the World* from 1901.

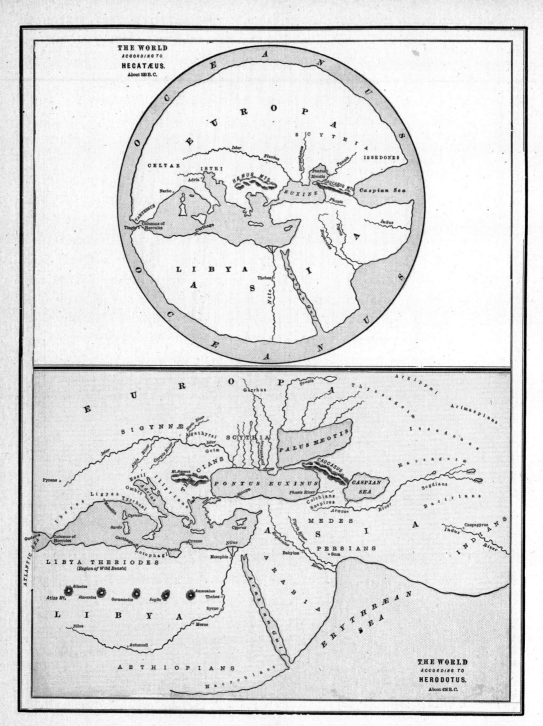

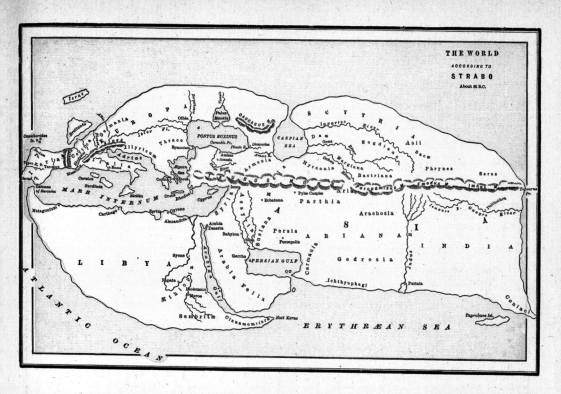

THE WORLD
ACCORDING TO
STRABO
About 25 B.C.

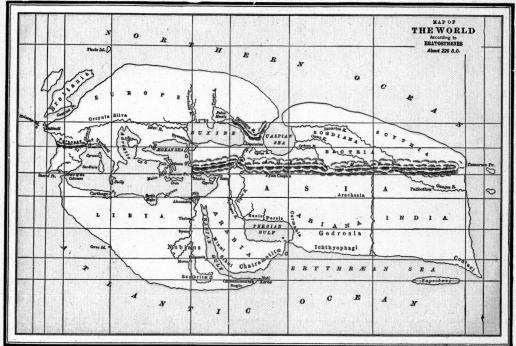

MAP OF
THE WORLD
According to
ERATOSTHENES
About 225 B.C.

571

they asked more systematic questions, gave explanations other than the supernatural for what they observed around them, and attempted to describe the Earth and heavens in accordance with scientific principles.

Later Greek writers gave much of the credit for these advances to Anaximander (610–546 BC), who rejected the Babylonian, Egyptian and Greek notions of the Earth floating on water and was the first to imagine that we are living on an object floating in empty space. In Anaximander's model we float, unmoving, at the centre of infinite space, without anything to support us. The Earth is shaped like a cylinder, 'a column of stone', and on one of the two end pieces is a land mass surrounded by sea. How Anaximander managed to imagine something so completely unlike the views of everyone else at the time is shrouded in the fog of history, but his model marked the beginning of modern cosmology. A floating earth opened the possibility that the Sun, stars and planets might be floating *around* us, not just above us, and paved the way for Greek astronomy. A supposition made by the astronomer Anaxagoras 100 years later – that the Moon shines because it is illuminated by the Sun – would not have been possible without the concept of a floating earth.

Anaximander was also 'the first to draw the outline of the sea and the land', and 'published the first geographical map [*geographikon pinaka*],' wrote biographer Diogenes Laertius around the year AD 200. In Anaximander's time, the Greeks had no specific term to describe a map, but began to use the word *pinax* – a tablet or metal plate used for writing or drawing – around the third century BC.

Unfortunately, nothing that Anaximander drew or wrote himself has survived, but based on what we know of his beliefs and from later Greek maps, we can deduce that his map must have been round, and that he placed either Miletus or the Oracle of Delphi at the centre of the world. Three continents must have been situated around the Aegean Sea – Europe, Asia and Africa – and around these Oceanus, the great river encircling the world. Europe would have been separated from Asia by the Black Sea and the River Tanais (Don), and from Africa by the Mediterranean. Africa would have been separated from Asia by the Nile.

The Greeks called these three continents *oikoumene*. The word stems from *oikeo*, 'to dwell', and means 'the inhabited world'. *Oikou-*

mene stretched from Gibraltar in the west to India in the east, and from Ethiopia in the south to the mystical Hyperborea in the north.

Hyperborea means 'beyond the north'. Boreas was the Greek god of the north wind, depicted as a bearded and dishevelled man with ice in his hair, and father of Chione, goddess of snow. He ruled over the Riphæan mountain range to the far north, and beyond these mountains was Hyperborea, a land with a pleasant climate because the sun shone twenty-four hours a day, and whose inhabitants lived for ever, without illness or hunger.

Another Greek myth tells of Callisto, who had a son with the god Zeus. Zeus's furious wife then turned Callisto into a bear as punishment. Later, when Callisto's son grew up, he came close to killing his mother the bear while out hunting, but Zeus prevented the tragedy by lifting them up into the sky as the constellations Ursa Major and Ursa Minor – the Great Bear and Little Bear.

The Greeks believed that the Riphæan mountains were located directly below Boötes, the Great Bear and Little Bear, because these constellations are always seen in the skies to the north. The northern regions were named the Arctic because *arktos* is the Greek word for 'bear'. The Pole Star is the brightest star in Little Bear.

The Strait of Gibraltar, the westernmost area known to the Greeks and where the Mediterranean Sea met a great, unknown ocean, was also shrouded in myths. One of these tells of how the brawny demigod Hercules had to perform twelve tasks after killing his wife and six sons. One of these tasks was to steal cattle from a giant who lived on the mystical island of Erytheia out in the sea to the west of Africa. Instead of climbing over the Atlas mountain range in modern Morocco, Hercules used his strength to smash through it, opening the strait between the two continents. One part of the destroyed mountains formed the Rock of Gibraltar; another the Jebel Musa mountain in Africa. The Greeks therefore named these two formations the Pillars of Hercules.

What lay beyond the great Oceanus was uncertain. Perhaps there was an unknown country there, or mythical islands such as the Hesperides, Erytheia or the Fortunate Isles – a paradise for the heroic dead.

Hecataeus of Miletus (550–476 BC) is thought to have significantly improved Anaximander's map when he wrote the world's first geographical treatise. *Periodos ges* (*Journey Around the World*) was divided into two parts: one about Europe, and one about Asia and Africa – Hecataeus was probably the first person to think about the world as being made up of different continents. The book was written as a travelogue, first describing Europe from east to west, mainly along the Mediterranean but with a detour up to Scythia – the region north-west of the Black Sea. The section about Asia and Africa stretched as far west as the Atlantic, and to India in the east. Hecataeus described cities, distances, borders, mountains and nations, occasionally taking a detour up a river. Attempts to reconstruct his map in retrospect have revealed that unlike Anaximander, Hecataeus included the Red Sea, linked Africa and Asia at Suez, and was aware of both the Indus River and the Caspian Sea.

It is difficult to say with any certainty who first had the idea that the Earth is round. Some have argued for philosopher and astronomer Thales of Miletus (624–546 BC), stating that since he knew about the stars he would probably have deduced that the Earth is a sphere; others believe that Anaximander actually described a spherical world, rather than a cylindrical one. But we can point to mathematician Pythagoras (570–495 BC) and his students with more certainty.

Pythagoras came from the island of Samos, which was an arch-enemy of Miletus, but settled in Croton in southern Italy and founded a school there. In the eyes of the Pythagoreans, the circle and the sphere were the most perfect of geometric shapes. Everything in the universe, the Pythagoreans believed, was made up of spheres – including the stars, the heavens and our globe – and everything moved in circles. This theory was reinforced by the observation that the stars circulated around a fixed point during the night. Diogenes wrote that Pythagoras believed that the Earth, round like a ball, was inhabited 'all the way round', and that antipodes existed, for whom 'our "down" is their "up"'.

One of Pythagoras's students, Parmenides (515–460 BC), is thought to have been the first person to divide the earth into different climate zones: two ice-cold, uninhabitable zones in the far north and south, a scorching hot and equally uninhabitable zone around the middle, and two temperate zones between the hot and the cold.

HERODOTUS LAUGHS | Historian and author Herodotus (489–425 BC) was critical of Anaximander, Hecataeus and others who drew round maps, and the Pythagoreans' belief in perfect circles. In his *Histories*, he pointed out that it was not in the least proven that the land mass was circular and surrounded by sea:

> And I laugh to see how many have before now drawn maps of the world, not one of them reasonably; for they draw the world as round as if fashioned by compasses, encircled by the Ocean river, and Asia and Europe of a like extent.

According to Herodotus, Asia was only inhabited up to India – further east was nothing but a great desert: 'thereafter, all to the east is desolation, nor can anyone say what kind of land is there.' Nor had anyone 'obtained knowledge of Europe's eastern or northern regions, so as to be able to say if it is bounded by seas,' and 'concerning those [countries] in Europe that are the farthest away towards evening,' wrote Herodotus, 'I cannot speak with assurance.' Herodotus claimed that the Caspian Sea was not a bay in northern Oceanus, as Hecataeus believed, but a lake, thereby giving the land mass a new area that extended to the north-east, into the unknown. But Herodotus refused to create a map of the inhabited world while so little was known about its outer edges. He criticised the theoretical cartographers who based their ideas on geometry, arguing instead for an experience-based cartography grounded in travel and discovery.

Democritus (460–370 BC), a contemporary of Herodotus, was the first to assert that the inhabited land mass was oval-shaped, not round, and that it was therefore best reproduced on an oval map. This is the format we still use when creating world maps today, and it was during this period that the theoretical and religious view of the land mass as a perfect circle with a defined centre, whether Babylon or Delphi, was gradually forced to make way for an oval with an uncertain outer boundary.

Although much of the Greek cartography during this period was somewhat theoretical, and mostly debated by mathematicians and philosophers, Herodotus understood that maps were about to become widespread. In his *Histories*, he described their dawning practical significance

– how Aristagoras, ruler of Miletus, once came to Sparta around the year 500 BC to use maps in the war against the Persians: 'as the Lacedaemonians report, he brought with him a bronze tablet on which the map of all the earth was engraved, and all the sea and all the rivers.'

Herodotus's reference is important because it shows that at this time, maps could be engraved on portable bronze tablets – that several world maps were probably created in ancient Greece, and that these were more informative than the simple Babylonian map created at the same time. The account is one of the earliest examples of maps being used for political and military purposes – using the map, Aristagoras was able to show the Spartans the route they should take to reach Persia:

> (This he said pointing to the map of the earth which he had brought engraved on the tablet.) 'Next to the Lydians,' said Aristagoras, 'you see the Phrygians [...]. Close by them are the Cappadocians, whom we call Syrians, and their neighbours are the Cilicians, whose land reaches to the sea over there, in which you see the island of Cyprus lying [...]. Next to the Cilicians, are the Armenians, another people rich in flocks, and after the Armenians, the Matieni, whose country I show you. Adjoining these you see the Cissian land, in which, on the Choaspes, lies that Susa where the great king lives and where the storehouses of his wealth are located.'

A scene in Aristophanes' comedy *The Clouds* from 423 BC also indicates that maps were widespread. The protagonist, a farmer named Strepsiades, has been forced to settle in Athens due to war, and the following scene occurs when he attends the philosophical school:

> STUDENT: This is a map of the world. Look, here is Athens.
> STREPSIADES: Don't be stupid, that can't be Athens. Where are all the jurors and the law courts?
> STUDENT: I'm telling you, this area is clearly the region of Attica.
> STREPSIADES: So where's my deme then? Where's Cicynna?
> STUDENT: I don't know. Over there somewhere. You see here, that is Euboea, the long island lying off the coast.

STREPSIADES: Yeah, me and Pericles really laid those revolting bastards out. Where's Sparta then?

STUDENT: Right here.

STREPSIADES: That's far too close! You need to move it immediately! You had better reponder that one, mate!

STUDENT: But it's simply not possible just to . . .

STREPSIADES: Then you'll get a beating, by Zeus . . .

The scene illustrates that theatre audiences in Athens during this period knew what a world map was, and Strepsiades' ignorance emphasises the fact that he comes from outside the city.

In *Phaedo* by the philosopher Plato (429–347 BC), we meet Socrates (470–399 BC), who marvelled at both the Earth's size and its appearance:

'Secondly,' said he, 'I believe that the earth is very large and that we who dwell between the pillars of Hercules and the river Phasis live in a small part of it about the sea, like ants or frogs about a pond, and that many other people live in many other such regions [. . .] The earth when seen from above is said to look like those balls that are covered with twelve pieces of leather; it is divided into patches of various colours [. . .] one part is purple of wonderful beauty, and one is golden, and one is white, whiter than chalk or snow.'

THULE | Some time between 330 and 320 BC, the Greek explorer Pytheas travelled between the Pillars of Hercules and north across the Atlantic towards the white part of the Earth. He was sent from the Greek colony of Massalia (Marseille) to see where the goods purchased by the colony – tin from Britain and amber from the Baltic Sea – came from. Upon returning home, Pytheas wrote a work titled *On the Ocean*, but sadly this has not survived. We therefore only know of the book's contents and Pytheas's travel route from the works of others who wrote about Pytheas in retrospect.

Pytheas put Norway and the northern regions on the map for the very first time – or at least made these areas a part of world geography.

In his descriptions, Pytheas mentions the island of Thoúle or Thule, 'six days' sail north from Britain and near the Frozen Sea'. Out there, he believed, he'd been to the edge of the world.

Since antiquity, debate has raged over where Pytheas travelled to, and whether he ever made it there at all. In fact, two of the most important sources of the details of his journey, Strabo and Greek historian Polybius (200–118 BC), were both keen to brand him a liar. Polybius believed that it was simply impossible for human beings to live anywhere as far north as the imaginary island of Thule, and set *oikoumene*'s northern border at 54 degrees north – at the Baltic coast.

Not only was Pytheas an explorer, but he was also an outstanding astronomer – the first in history to use astronomical calculations to determine a location on Earth. Using the shadows cast by a sundial, he managed to locate the market square of his home town of Marseille at a latitude of 43 degrees and 13 minutes north. A more accurate measurement would not become available until modern times, and this calculation became the starting point for the measurements Pytheas took on his travels.

The locations of the lines of latitude are determined by the height of the Sun at the equinox. At the equator, which is situated at 0 degrees, the Sun is directly overhead at the equinox. At the North Pole, the Sun is around 90 degrees further down, around where our noses point – just over the horizon. The North Pole is therefore located at latitude 90 degrees north. At the lighthouse at Lindesnes in Norway, the Sun is 57 degrees, 58 minutes and 46 seconds below zenith at the equinox, and this is therefore the lighthouse's latitude.

Minutes and seconds are used for greater precision because it is a long way from one latitude to the next – just over 111 kilometres on average. A latitude minute is almost equal to a nautical mile, 1,852.216 metres on average, while a latitude second is around 30 metres.

After passing between the Pillars of Hercules, Pytheas sailed north alongside Spain and France, around Brittany and out to Cornwall on the south-west coast of England. From here he probably sailed up the Irish Sea to the northern tip of Scotland, and from here, Norwegian polar explorer and researcher Fridtjof Nansen asserts in his book *In Northern*

Mists, Pytheas must have travelled north to the Orkney and Shetland Islands, then on to western Norway and up to the Arctic Circle. Nansen deduced this from the astronomical observations Pytheas is said to have made according to the astronomer Geminus of Rhodes. Geminus wrote that Pytheas described places where the night lasts no longer than two hours – so this is as far north as 65 degrees north. Geminus also quoted Pytheas as stating that 'the Barbarians showed us the place where the sun goes to rest'. Pytheas may therefore not only have heard about Thule, as some have claimed, but have actually been there himself. Other descriptions stemming from Pytheas state that Thule extended all the way up to the Arctic Circle, and the writings of Strabo, Eratosthenes and Pliny the Elder all feature quotations that show that Pytheas described Thule as the land of the midnight sun. In his *Naturalis Historia*, Pliny wrote:

> The farthest of all, which are known and spoke of, is Thule; in which there be no nights at all, as we have declared, about midsummer, namely when the Sun passes through the sign Cancer; and contrariwise no days in mid-winter: and each of these times they suppose, do last six months, all day, or all night.

It is thought that Pytheas reached the Norwegian coast somewhere around Møre or Trøndelag, where he encountered a people who, according to Strabo's account, lived on oats, vegetables, wild fruits and roots, and who made a drink from grain and honey – a kind of mead. He also described how they threshed corn in large buildings due to sudden rains and the lack of sunlight. To Pytheas, the threshing of corn in barns instead of outside in the Mediterranean sunshine must have seemed rather strange and exotic.

But why did so many intellectuals try to brand Pytheas a liar? If his narrative is accurate – if it is true that he not only travelled as far into the

Next pages | A Renaissance map, based on Ptolemy's coordinates. Note how the Nordic region, depicted with countries such as Norvegi, Gottia, Dana, Pilapelant and Tile, pushes beyond the frame of the map north of 63 degrees north. Ptolemy either did not believe there to exist, or did not know of, lands further north. Printed by Nicolaus Germanus in Ulm in 1482.

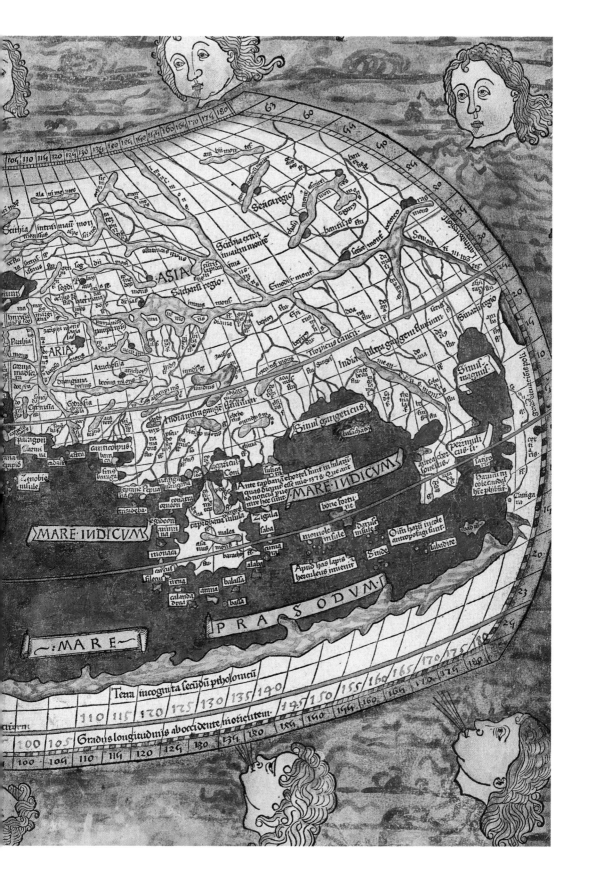

unknown as the islands north of Scotland, but then onwards over the unknown North Sea to discover yet another country – he pushed the limits of Greek knowledge of the world from the south coast of England all the way up to the Arctic Circle, an entire 16 degrees of latitude northwards. It must have seemed simply unbelievable to many.

Nansen, himself a far-travelling explorer of northern regions, did not find it in the least bit strange that Pytheas chose to travel so far: 'There is nothing intrinsically impossible in the supposition that this remarkable explorer, who besides being an eminent astronomer must have been a capable seaman, had heard in the north of Scotland of an inhabited country still farther to the north, and then wished to visit this also. We must remember how, as an astronomer, he was especially interested in determining the extent of the "œcumene" on the north, and in seeing with his own eyes the remarkable phenomena of northern latitudes, in particular the midnight sun.'

We don't know whether Pytheas believed that Thule was an island, but this seems likely. Travelling as he did, northwards from one island to the next, and then setting out across the sea from Shetland to reach a country even further north, he must have found it difficult to imagine that he had arrived at the mainland. In any case, Thule was drawn as an island on all later maps.

This mystical country to the north eventually became an established part of the geography. 'Still further above these is Thule,' writes Ptolemy after describing the Orkney Islands, and locates Thule at 63 degrees north – possibly because Roman historian Tacitus identified Thule with Shetland in his *Agricola* from the year AD 77.

THE EARTH'S CIRCUMFERENCE | Aristotle (384–322 BC) summarised the classical period of Greek geography. Through simple facts, such as that the shadow the Earth casts on the Moon is circular, and that the Pole Star climbs higher and higher in the sky as one travels north, he determined that the Earth must be round. Aristotle believed the universe to be symmetrical and in balance. It is the nature of earth and water to pull in towards the universe's centre, he claimed, since these are the heavy elements, and overall the Earth's mass will therefore stay the same distance from this centre. Aristotle also believed that it was possible to travel to

India by sailing westwards from the Pillars of Hercules – 1,800 years before Columbus set out on his voyage.

Aristotle also ascertained that the Earth consisted of five climate zones. 'There are two inhabitable sections of the earth: one near our upper, or northern pole, the other near the other or southern pole,' he wrote in *Meteorology*. The known and inhabited world, which stretched from Gibraltar in the west to India in the east, and from Ethiopia in the south to the Sea of Azov in the north, was according to Aristotle longer than it was high in the ratio 5:3. It was therefore logical that maps should be oval: 'They draw maps of the earth in a laughable manner; for they draw the *oikoumene* in a very round form, which is impossible on the basis of both logic and observed facts.'

Aristotle tutored Alexander the Great, the Macedonian who in 334 BC set out on a military raid all the way to India, taking with him not only soldiers but scholars who collected data about local flora and fauna, culture, history and geography as they travelled, and measured the distances between the places at which they stopped. Alexander had learned from Aristotle's method, which placed greater emphasis on observations than on theories – on the importance of noticing the world around oneself. This military expedition marked the start of an era in which cartography was based less on theories, and more on experience. Later geographers made extensive use of the descriptions of Alexander's journey to create maps of Asia, and a more detailed world map.

Alexander's conquests resulted in a shift in the Greek culture from small city-states to a number of dynasties spread around the Mediterranean and Asia. The political geography changed, and during the Hellenistic period Greek culture and power reached their peak, while simultaneously starting to absorb elements from north African and west Asian cultures. The library in Alexandria was not only founded on the model provided by Artistotle's school and library in Athens; it was also part of the tradition established by the pharaohs and Mesopotamian kings, and particularly King Ashurbanipal's library in Nineveh, northern Iraq, which Alexander is thought to have visited.

Around the year 250 BC, Greek mathematician Eratosthenes (275–194 BC) was asked to come to Alexandria to take over the running of the library. With his *Geographika*, he established geography as an independent discipline, bringing together all previous attempts to describe the Earth's appearance, size and history. He was also the first to use the word 'geography', created from the words *geo*, a variant of Gaia, the name of the Earth, and *graphia*, which means to write or draw.

Using a simple experiment, Eratosthenes also managed to calculate the Earth's circumference with staggering accuracy. First, he assumed that in Syene (Aswan) in southern Egypt, the Sun was at its zenith at the summer solstice. Then he estimated that Alexandria was on the same longitude as Syene. Finally, he estimated that the distance between these two cities was 5,000 *stadions*. At the summer solstice, he measured the shadow cast by a sundial in Alexandria. Since this covered around a fiftieth of the dial, he multiplied 5,000 by fifty, and deduced that the Earth's circumference was therefore 250,000 *stadions*. He later increased this to 252,000 *stadions* so that the figure would be divisible by sixty – a nod to Sumerian and Babylonian mathematics.

But how long was the *stadion* used by Eratosthenes? If he used the Egyptian *stadion*, equivalent to 157.5 metres, he calculated the Earth's circumference at 39,960 kilometres, which is only 1.6 per cent from the actual length of 40,075 kilometres. If he used the Athenian *stadion* of 185 metres, however, he calculated the Earth's circumference as 46,620 kilometres – 16.3 per cent from the correct answer. Eratosthenes also based his calculation on misconceptions – in Syene, the Sun is not at its zenith at the summer solstice; nor is the city situated on exactly the same longitude as Alexandria.

Ultimately, however, the question of the *stadion*'s length and these geographical blunders are insignificant. Eratosthenes knew that the calculated distance between Alexandria and Syene was approximate – it was based on the time it took to travel between the two cities by camel. The important thing was that he had something he could use as a unit of measure.

With knowledge of the Earth's circumference, Eratosthenes was able to find out just how much of the Earth was covered by the *oikoumene*. In his *Geographika*, he described the relationship between the size of the Earth and that of the *oikoumene*, illustrating it on the first map we know of to feature lines of latitude and longitude.

Eratosthenes probably used eight circles of latitude. The northernmost was situated at Thule, the second at the mouth of the Dnieper River in Russia, the third at the city of Trake in northern Greece, the fourth – the major circle of latitude – at Athens and Rhodes, the fifth at Alexandria, the sixth at Syene, the seventh at the city of Meroë in modern Sudan, and the southernmost at Sri Lanka and the Land of the Kinnamomom (cinnamon) Bearers, which the Greeks thought lay somewhere south of Khartoum.

Eratosthenes' main line of longitude stretched from Ethiopia in the south to Thule in the north, and passed through Meroë, Aswan, Alexandria, Rhodes and the mouth of the Dnieper River. East of this he placed three lines of longitude that passed through the Euphrates, the Caspian Gates and the Indus River, respectively. To the west, one line of longitude passed through Rome and Carthage, another through the Pillars of Hercules and a third through the west coast of Portugal.

Lines of longitude can be placed anywhere one pleases – unlike north and south, which start and end at the poles, east and west don't begin or end anywhere. The placement of o degrees east and west – the prime meridian – is therefore a matter of taste, and over the years cartographers have located this at Jerusalem, Alexandria, Rome, Paris, Copenhagen, Kongsvinger, Trondheim, Bergen, Kristiansand and Oslo. Highly political negotiations resulted in the official prime meridian being located at Greenwich in 1884 – France was particularly dissatisfied at this, and continued to use the country's own Paris meridian long afterwards. But the prime meridian is simply a point from which we start counting, and while the distance between the degrees of latitude is determined by the height of the Sun in the sky, we count degrees of longitude using time. The Earth rotates once – 360 degrees – every twenty-four hours, and 360 divided by twenty-four is fifteen. The Earth therefore rotates 15 degrees of longitude in an hour.

Next pages | Two pages from Jacopo d'Angelo's translation of Ptolemy into Latin. To the left is Ptolemy's first projection, which he was least satisfied with, while to the right is his second – which was more accurate, but also more complex. Printed by Nicolaus Germanus in Ulm in 1482. See pages 98–99 for more information about d'Angelo's translation.

sexaginta & vuo. Vicesimũ primum horis octo differre distãte gdibꝰ sexaginta & tribusꝗ per tyle scribitur. Notabitur & alius versus meridiẽ post eqnoctiale cõtinẽs differentiã bore dimidie: ꝗ p raptũ promontoriũ & cattigara describitur: ferme p ꝯequales cũ oppositis distans ab eqnoctiali gradibꝰ octo cũ tertia ac duodecima.

Qualiter in plano terra designetur.

ODVS scribendi in tabula plana vltimos paralellos eosdeꝗ ꝯequales vero situi talis erit. Faciemus tabulã rectorũ ꝗtuor angulorũ vt AB CD. & sit AB ferme in duplo maior ꝗ AC & supponatur qd latus AB ĩ superiori situ locatũ sit. ꝗ erit plaga septetrionalis. Deinde AB diuidamus in partes eꝗles & ad angulos rectos & sit ea linea. EF cui regulam ꝯequale ac rectã ita adaptemus. vt p eandẽ media linea ꝗ ẽ EF boc ẽ recte p ipius longitudine crescat linea vsꝗ G & diuidatur EG in triginta & ꝗtuor tales ptes ꝗlium ẽ. G F centũ & triginta vna & tertia ac duodecima & p centrũ G & p punctũ ĩ recta ipius linea ꝗ distet a centro ptibꝰ septuaginta & noue circulũ describemus ꝗ babeatur p paralello p rbodũ vt H K L Circa vero longitudinẽ ꝗ ex vtraꝗ pte centri spacia sex borax cõtinebit. sumentes distã ꝗ est in K E linea meridionali ꝗtuor sectionũ seu partiũ in paralello p rbodum. p quinꝗ diuisam cũ maximis circulis sit sere epitetartus ad ipm: ac taliũ dece & octo sectiones ab vtraꝗ pte centri signantes in H K L. circũferentia babebimus puncta p ꝗ ducẽdi erunt meridiani a cẽtro G quoꝝ ꝗlibet ab altero distabit tertia pte vnius bore. Quare meridianos babebimus terminantes vltima. G H M atꝗ G L N Deinde notabitur paralellus p tyle in linea G F ꝗ distet a cẽtro G. sectionibus quinquaginta ac

duabꝰ ut O P Q. Eqnoctialis vero describetur distans a cẽtro G ptibꝰ centũ & ꝗndecĩ vt R S T. Paralellꝰ aut ꝗ ẽ vltimus versus austrũ & oppositis paralello p meroẽ notabitur. distans a centro G ptibꝰ centũ & triginta & vna cũ tertia & duodecĩa vt M V N. Colligitur etiã ratio. R S T. circũseretiẽ ad circũferentiã O P Q. in eadẽ esse ꝓportione in ꝗ centũ & ꝗndeci sunt ad ꝗnꝗginta & duo iuxta rationẽ paralellorũ ꝗ in spera sunt. Cũ ꝗlium ptium supponitur. G S esse centũ & ꝗndeci taliũ ẽ. G P ꝗnꝗgita et duarũ. Queadmodũ eni se babet linea G S ad G P se babet circũferentia R S T ad circũferentia O P Q. Relinꝗtur ergo distantia P Q. meridiani: boc ẽ ea ꝗ itercipitur a palello p tyle & paralello p rhodũ ptiũ viginti & septẽ. Distãtia vero K S. ea scilicet que a paralello rodbensi eqnoctiale attingit: similiu ptiũ restabit trigita & sex. Deinde S V. boc ẽ distantia ꝗ sit ab eqnoctiali ad palellũ oppositũ paralello p meroem. Relinꝗtur ptiũ similiũ sedeci cũ tertia ac duodecĩa. Preterea ꝗliũ ptium ẽ. P V. in latitudine ꝯgniti nostri orbis septuagita & noue cũ tertia & duodecĩa. aut vt ad integra veniamꝰ partiũ octuaginta taliũ erit. H K L. media longitudinis distãtia centũ ac ꝗdragita & quatuor babita eorum ratione que supponuntur. Eãdem enim ferme proportionẽ babẽt

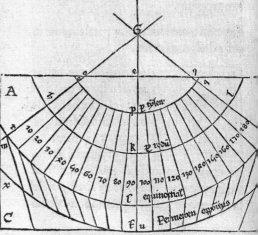

Ab F auté cum quatuor & femis cum tertia in eifdé ipis. Poft hec fcribétes p tria pű-
cta diftantiax equipollentium circúferétias
q̃ erūt p reliq̃s meridianis velut tminantes
totam longitudinem fcilicet. S T V & X y
Z. fupplebimus circúferétias p ceteris pa-
ralellis a cétro qdé L p ptes vero notatas i
F K. fcdm diftatias ipax ad ipm eqnoctiale. Qd aut modus hic magis fit fimilis fpe-
re q̃ alius hinc clare patet· Cum illic manete
fpera nec circúducta qd tabule cótingit ne-
cefíe é cũ afpectus in medio defignatióis fi-
gitur vt vnus qdé meridianus: q̃ medius é
& fub axe noftri afpectus cadit. imaginé recta linee pbeat. Reliq̃ vero q̃ ex vtraq̃ pte
iftius fint · omes vertantur ad húc i ipox
curuatóib; & magis q̃ ab ipo plus diftetit
qd hic aiaduerteretur cũ deceti curuationũ
xportione· Preterea coeqtione circúferentia-
rũ paralellox inuice nó folũ ad eqnoctiale
& ad paralellũ p tyle qúeadmodũ illic é p
pria ratióe habere· fed etiã in aliis q̃ maxi-
me poffibile fit veluti intueri fas é. Inde to-
tius etiã latitudinis ad tota lógitudiné neq̃
fola in paralello p rhodũ vt ibi fed fere in
omibus· Si eni hic pducamus. S & V recta
qúeadmodũ in priori pictura. H. & circúfe-
rentia minore ratióe habebit ad F S & K
V· quã oporteat i pfenti figura cũ cópreha
fa hic fit p tota H T. Qd in eqnoctiali piter
accidit G M. Si vero coeq̃lem hanc faciem9
ad K F. latitudinis fpaciũ cũ. F S & K V·
maiores erũt q̃ coeqtiones ad F K· veluti
K T. Si aũt F S· & K V· feruemus coeq̃les
H. & mior erit ad K F. q̃ coeqtio veluti H
T. Ex his igitur mod9 ifte melior habetur
q̃ pmus fed ab illo etiã deficiet in facilitate
defignatóis· cũ illic ab vnius regule circum
ductóe· defcripto vno paralello diuifoq̃ lo-
cari poffit q̃libet locus· Hic aũt nó fimiliter
cótingit ob meridionaliũ lineas ad media
flexas. Omes eni circulos infcribere fingilla-
tim oportebit & locox fitus inter palellos
incidentes ex vtrorumq̃ ratóib; coniectare

His aũt fic habitis magis & hic tenendũ é·
qd fit equius qdq̃ feriofius· q̃ id qd debili9
faciliufq̃. Vtreq̃ tamé forme feruãde funt.
ob ea q̃ facilius in opere adducuntur.
Qualiũ é eqnoctialis q̃nq̃ taliũ é p meroem
q̃tuor & femis cũ tertia. Vnde ratióe habet ad ipm q̃ triginta ad viginti & noué·
Qualiũ é eqnoctialis q̃nq̃ taliũ é p fyene q̃-
tuor & femis cũ duodecia· Vnde rationem
habet ad eũ q̃ fexagita ad q̃nq̃ginta & q̃n-
q̃ hoc é quã duodeci ad vndecim·
Qualiũ é eqnoctialis q̃nq̃ taliũ é p rhodũ
q̃tuor. Vnde ratióe hét ad ipm epitetarti·
Qualiũ é eqnoctialis q̃nq̃ taliũ p tyle duo
cũ quarta. Vnde ratióe habet ad ipfum q̃
viginti ad nouem·

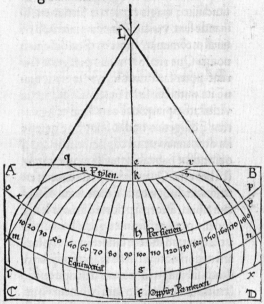

Claudij ptolomei cofmographie liber pri-
mus explicit.
CLAVDII PTOLOMEI VIRI AL-
LEXANDRINI COSMOGRAPHIE
LIBER·SECVNDVS·HEC HABET·
Eiufdé tractatus· expofitioné plage magis
occidétalis Europe iuxta bas puintias feu
fatrapas. Britaniã. Ifpaniã. Galliã· Germaniã
Retiã· Vindelicos. Noricũ· Pannoniã· Illiri-
cos. atq̃. Dalmatiam.

Eratosthenes placed his 7 degrees of longitude where he saw fit – the distances between them varied, and it would be fair to say that they were little more than a system of artificial lines that helped him to place the various cities on his map. They were based on assumptions, wild guess-work, and some surviving solar observations and documents from Alexander the Great's military campaign.

Eratosthenes' *oikoumene* was 78,000 *stadions* from west to east and 38,000 *stadions* from north to south, and therefore took up around a quarter of the Earth. Eratosthenes believed there was a good chance that three other continents also existed, and that they too were inhabited. Using mathematics, he confirmed the Greeks' suspicion that they were aware of only a small part of the world.

Shortly after this, Crates of Mallus created a globe based on Eratosthenes' calculations of the size of the Earth and *oikoumene* – the first globe that we know of with any certainty. It was huge, with a dia-meter of around three metres, and showed the part of the world known to the Greeks together with three other, unknown parts. Directly south of the equator is *antoikoi* ('those who live on the other side'), on the other side of the northern hemisphere *perioikoi* ('those who live nearby') and south of this the *antipodes* ('those with their feet the other way'). The continents were thought to be islands without any contact with each another.

Not everyone accepted Eratosthenes' calculations. Hipparchus of Nicaea (190–126 BC) wrote a treatise in three books titled *Against the Geography of Eratosthenes*, in which he criticised his predecessor's lack of astronomical observations when drawing maps. 'Hipparchus,' Strabo wrote, 'shows that it is impossible for any man, whether layman or scholar, to attain to the requisite knowledge of geography without a determina-tion of the heavenly bodies and of the eclipses which have been observed.' Hipparchus, the Greek who knew most about Babylonian mathematics, developed the modern system that uses 360 degrees of longitude and 180 degrees of latitude, and showed how eclipses of the Sun and Moon help us to determine the degrees of longitude. His major work was a cata-logue of the exact positions of 850 stars.

THE STARS | In the library in Alexandria, Claudius Ptolemy can find no better geographical calculations based on astronomical observations than those performed by Hipparchus. He is 'the only one,' Ptolemy writes, to have given us accurate coordinates – despite the fact that Hipparchus' text was 300 years old at the time of his reading it. Ptolemy was first and foremost an astronomer, and therefore shared Hipparchus and Strabo's view that astronomical observations were the key to geographical knowledge, while reconnaissance at sea and on foot provided inadequate results. Unfortunately, he was far too ahead of his time to be able to follow this principle – simply too few observations had been recorded. 'If the people who visited the individual countries had happened to make use of some [astronomical] observations, it would have been possible to make the map of the *oikoumene* with absolutely no error,' Ptolemy laments.

Ptolemy was well aware that he had insufficient knowledge to create a complete world map – just as 'all subjects that have not reached a state of complete knowledge, whether because they are too vast, or because they do not always remain the same, the passage of time always makes far more accurate research possible; and such is the case with world cartography too,' he writes. 'For the consensus of the very reports that have been made at various times is that many parts of our *oikoumene* have not reached our knowledge because its size has made them inaccessible, while other [parts] are themselves different now from what they were before because features have ceased to exist or have changed.'

This is why Ptolemy highlighted the necessity of using the latest available surveys, claiming that he had little to offer in terms of new knowledge of the world. As he described it, his work was to use the latest information to update and correct the work others had done before him – first and foremost that of Marinus, a geographer from Tyre in modern Lebanon, who probably died around the time Ptolemy was born. We know of him from no source other than Ptolemy's *Geography*. 'Marinus of Tyre seems to be the latest [author] in our time to have undertaken this subject, and he has done it with absolute diligence,' Ptolemy writes, never attempting to conceal the fact that the geographical data in his *Geography* is for the most part taken from his predecessor.

But Ptolemy's work on how to best reproduce a spherical globe on a flat sheet of paper was pioneering. This challenge – which continues to tax us today – was first taken up by Democritus 450 years earlier, when he drew the land mass as oval-shaped instead of circular, and later by Eratosthenes with his artificial lines. Others must also have tried to find solutions to this issue, as Ptolemy writes that Marinus of Tyre had criticised 'absolutely all' previous attempts to create flat maps, but information about these has not survived.

Ptolemy proposes two different map projections, and common to both is that they bend in different ways to simulate the curvature of the Earth.

The first projection has completely straight lines of longitude that meet at an imaginary point beyond the North Pole. Across these, Ptolemy arranges curved lines of latitude, which get longer the closer they get to the equator. The ratio between the equator and the northernmost line of latitude, which passes through Thule at 63 degrees north, is correct, and at the centre is a line of latitude that passes through Rhodes. 'Above all, the semblance of the spherical surface will be retained,' Ptolemy wrote of this projection, but was still somewhat dissatisfied as it has an inherent error. In reality, the lines of latitude become shorter the further north or south of the equator they are – but here, they get longer south of the equator. To resolve this, Ptolemy makes the southernmost line of latitude, 16 degrees south of the equator, the same length as the equivalent line of latitude in the north, causing the lines of longitude to buckle. He regards this as a minor error, however, since his map doesn't extend so far south, but it would result in greater problems as areas of the world further south were discovered. The projection does not lend itself particularly well to expansion.

Ptolemy therefore created another projection that he was more satisfied with. Here, the lines of both latitude and longitude are curved, and almost all the lines of latitude are in the correct ratio. 'It is immediately obvious how such a map is more like the shape on the globe than the former map,' he writes, but admits that it is much more difficult to draw than his first model. He concludes that there is a need for both a simple and a more accurate projection.

For decades, cartographic historians have discussed whether Ptolemy drew the map that was included in the first edition of the *Geography*, or whether this was drawn by someone else. Nowhere in any of his works does Ptolemy ever refer to any included maps. It is also likely that there was no practical need for a world map in the year AD 150 – the Romans were more interested in maps they could use in military campaigns and colonisation. Many therefore believe that the maps included in the Byzantine copies of the *Geography* from the 1300s are the first to be drawn based on Ptolemy's meticulous records. Others argue it is unlikely that Ptolemy could have possessed so much geographical information and prepared such advanced projections without ever drawing a map himself.

THE SCANDIAN ISLANDS | To look at maps drawn in accordance with Ptolemy's instructions is to look at maps we can understand. North is at the top, and the Mediterranean, Europe, north Africa, the Middle East and parts of Asia are recognisable. America and Oceania, southern Africa and eastern Asia – of which Ptolemy knew nothing – are not included. The same goes for the Pacific Ocean and most of the Atlantic. The Indian Ocean is an enormous lake, because southern Africa extends far west, to link up with the Malay Peninsula.

Ptolemy's *oikoumene* extends across a far greater part of the world than it should because he underestimated the Earth's size. He chose to use the calculations performed by the Syrian mathematician Posidonius (135–50 BC), which claimed that the Earth had a circumference of 180,000 *stadions*, instead of Eratosthenes' more correct estimate of 252,000 *stadions*. This meant that the eastern part of China, which led into terra incognita, was located just 40 degrees of latitude from what we

Next pages | Petrus Bertius's map of the Nordic region, included in his 1618 edition of Ptolemy's *Geography*. There are islands correctly located to the east of Cimbrica (Jutland), if one too many, but southern Sweden and Scandinavia in general have been demoted to the island of Scandia. A striking feature of Bertius's version is how far north Albionis (Britain) stretches.

Albionis *pars*

OCEANVS

Banacia

Rpa alta

insu

Bogoria
æstuarium
Aluana flu.
Victoria
Tina flu.
Tina æstuarium
Deua flu.
Celnius flu.
Vedra flu.
Vararextra
rium
Tuesis æstuarium
Taizalum prom

Cimbrico

Saxonum insu
læ tres

Dunum sinus

Sigulones

Gabrantuicorum
portuosus sinus
Oceli promont ,
Abupus flu

Sabalingij

Albis flu.

GERMANICVS

Saxo.
Treua nes
Cauchi maiores

Lirimiris

Tecelia
Phabiranum
Cauchi minores
Longidni flu.
Phileum
Marionis

Phrisij
Siatutanda
Marmaniis portus
Busactores maiores
Ascalingium
Tuliphurdum
Lephana
Laccobardi

Gesoriacum
nauale

Medola
Lanium
Visurgis flu.

Angriuarij

Caritium promont
Iciun promont

Taruanna

Lugodinum

Batauodurum
Vlpia
legio 30
Ascihurgium
Longobardi Sueui
Mesuium
Dulgumnij

Mesuium

Busactores minores
Chemę
Tulisurgium
An gi li Sueui
Trophea Drusi Cher

Gal
Iia
Origiacum
Atuacutum
Castellum
Vetera
Sicambri
Munitium
Melibocus n
Semana silua

Cæsaromagus
Bagacum
Tenchteri
Bogadium
Sterenontium
Pheugarum

Belgica
Agrippinensis
Alesum
Ingriones
Niesium
Amasia
Casuari
Nertereæ

Augusta Ro
manduorum
Bonna legio pri
mia
GE
Matriacum
Candium
Turoni
Bicurgium

Augusta Tri
uerorum
Traiana le
gio 22
Intuergi
Vargiones
Melocabus
Grauonarium
Marouingi

Augusta Vesso
num
Neomagus
VANG
Mogontiacum
Borbetomagus
Artaunum
Locoritum
Bergium
Menosgada

Durocottorum
Rufiniana
Caritni
Budoris
Olinobij
Segodunum
Curiones

Lutetia
TRIBO
Breucomagus
NVM
Argentoratum
Vispi
Deuona
Setuacotum
Chetu
Marobud

Augustomana
Elcebus
Argentuaria
Torodunum
Meluei
orum
eremus
Arę Flauię
Cantiobis
Bubacum
Alcimoennis
Brodentia

Diuodurun
Augusta Rau
ricam
Riusiaua
Parmę
campi

Tullum
Nasium
Danubius flu
Artobriga
Phabiana
Beodurum
Aredata

Andomatunnum
Gannodurum
Rhenus flu
Dracuina
Viana
Carrodunum

Visontium
Forum Ti
berij
Taxgetium
Ret
ia
Augusta Vinde
licorum
Gesodi

Noric

38 40 e 42 44 46 f 48 50 g 52

Phauonae

Chedini

Scandia proprie dicta

Leuoni Phiresij

insula

Gutæ Dauciones

SARMA

TICVS

a

58

Insulę Scandię quatuor

OCEANVS

Venedicus sinus

b

56

Cimbri

Charudes

nesus

hali

Laeburgium

Sideni

Rugium

Pharodini

Bunitium

Alisus

ones

Auarpi

Vritium

tuia

Viruni Virunum

Bug untę

Susudata

Colancorum Lincę

Sueui

Corconti

Budorigum

Batenı

Lugidunum

Calegia

Bonochęmę

Chatte

Stragona

fordum

Tubantı

Hegirmatia

Nomisterium

IA

Cogni

edintuinion

Budorgis

euriochęmę

Visburgij

Casurgis

sylua

Streuinta

ra sylua

Meliodunum

Eburum

Quadi

urcomanni

Pheliria

Ferri mi

nera

Racatę

Teracatriæ

Medoslanium

Anduetium

Iuliobona

Panno

Rhispia

nię

Pretorium

Rutíclij

Scurgum

Gythones

Aeluæones

Aseaucalis

Luti Omanni

Setidaua

Ascibur gius mons

Luti Diduni

Calisia

Leucaristus

Arsonium

Luti Burí

Carrodunum

Sidones

Vistula fluuius

Ve ne dę

Venedici montes

Phinni

c

54

Medius meridianus 36, reliqui
ad hunc inclinantur iuxta ra
tiones parallelorum 49 & 55.
Qua ratione Scandiarum insu
larum maximam maiorem de
lineauerim q̃ numeri exempla
riorum exhibent, in tabulæ hui⁹
fronte annotatum habes.

52

d

50

Hercinia sylua

Parienna

Arsicua

Singone

Carpatus mons

e

Iazyges

Rhucmium

Docirua

Chrpis

Parca

Celmantia

Anabum

Salua

Aquincum

Candanum

Vlpanum

Salinum

Curta

Lussonium

Daubana fluuius

Pessium

Tibyscus flu.

Dacię pars

f

48

Sacarbantia

Carnus

Valina

Serbinum

Vacontium

Lugionum

Partiscum

Ziridaua

46

38 e 40 42 f 44 46 g 48

now know as the west coast of America; and here, perhaps, is the seed of Columbus's voyage west: Columbus also believed the Earth to be smaller than it is. Supported by a 1487 edition of Ptolemy's work, Columbus believed it was just 2,400 nautical miles from Portugal to China. Had he known that in reality this distance is 10,000 nautical miles – ignoring the fact that America is in the way – he might never have set out on his journey.

The Sun sets over the sea and the Libyan desert. At the museum in Alexandria, supper is served to the lodging scholars. Ptolemy rolls up Pliny's encyclopedia and walks back along the colonnade. In the evening he sits in the flickering candlelight of his room and writes down several more place names and coordinates:

> East of the Cimbrian peninsula there are four islands called the Scandian islands, three of them smaller, of which the one in the middle has the following position:
>
> 41°30 E 58°00 N
>
> But one of them very large and the most eastwards at the mouth of the river Vistula; its ends are located
>
> to the west 43°00 E 58°00 N
> to the east 46°00 E 58°00 N
> to the north 44°30 E 58°30 N
> to the south 45°00 E 57°40 N
>
> It is properly called Scandia itself; and its western region is inhabited by the Chaedini, its eastern region by the Favonae and the Firaesi, its northern region by the Finni, its southern region by the Gutae (Gautae) and the Dauciones, and its central region by the Levoni.

Over the coming centuries, all the Ptolemaic splendour will fall to ruin, drowning in the Mediterranean at Alexandria's port. Even in Claudius Ptolemy's time, the city is not what it once was. Two hundred years earlier, Caesar had set fire to the ships in the harbour while battling Ptolemy XIII; the fire spread, destroying a great number of the library's books. Caesar's adopted heir Augustus took control of Egypt after the death of Cleopatra in the year 30 BC, and Alexandria was demoted from the capital of Egypt to a provincial Roman town. The library slipped into a state of gradual decline.

Ptolemy belongs to the region's last golden age. His books are among those that survived and were passed on – but only thanks to the random copies and translations created over the centuries, as it seems the *Geography* was largely forgotten after Ptolemy's death. Quotations from it occasionally pop up in Latin texts, and the Arabs translated parts of it and improved some of the coordinates, but in Constantinople (Istanbul) around the year AD 1300, Maximus Planudes wrote that he 'discovered through many toils the *Geographia* of Ptolemy, which had disappeared for many years.'

In the year AD 1323, as Ptolemy is being rediscovered and gradually attaining his rightful place in cartographic history, an earthquake destroys all that is left of the great lighthouse that cast its light over Alexandria's glory days. But Ptolemy's *Geography* travels onwards with an Italian monk who, after visiting Constantinople to learn Greek in AD 1395, takes a copy of the book home to Florence, and ten years later publishes the work in its first Latin translation – giving the Europeans an alternative to the view of the world they have held over the more than 1,000 years since the *Geography* was first published.

WESTWARDS | Greek natural philosophy built upon Sumerian and Babylonian astronomy and mathematics – these ideas travelled west to Miletus, where new thoughts about the Earth's place in the universe took shape and resulted in both airy philosophising and concrete maps. Scholars also began to use astronomical observations to cast a net of latitudes and longitudes across the world, making it easier to say exactly where a given place was located. Around the year AD 150, Claudius Ptolemy began to compile all available Greek knowledge of the world, combining it with information provided by travellers to Alexandria to publish his *Geography*, antiquity's greatest work about *oikoumene* – the inhabited world. The work looks back in time, to the knowledge of all Ptolemy's predecessors, but also forwards – towards a time in which the Europeans would forget much of the Greek geography.

'Ptolemeo de gli Astronomi prencipe' – 'Ptolemy, prince of astronomy, who diligently and accurately observed the heavenly bodies' in Giacomo Gastaldi's edition of the *Geography* from 1548. This was the first edition to be published in Italian, as well as the first edition of Ptolemy in handy pocket format. It was also the first edition of the *Geography* to feature engraved maps of the American continent.

Ptolemeo de gli Astronomi prencipe, dili-
gentißimo inuestigator & osseruator del-
li moti celesti, uisse in Egytto nel
tempo di Adriano & Anto-
nino Imperatori.

SOno alcuni che pensano l'auttor di questo libro non esser
stato quel medesimo, che compose de moti, & iudicij de

HOLY GEOGRAPHY

Reykholt, Iceland
64° 39′ 54″ N
21° 17′ 32″ W

Snorri Sturluson paces back and forth across the dirt floor of the farmhouse at Reykholt as he speaks. A scribe, perhaps his friend Styrme, is sitting at a nearby table, taking notes on calfskin using a goosefeather quill. Snorri is writing a book about Norse mythology and minstrelsy, and like any good medieval Christian he starts his work with an account of God's creation. After describing Adam and Eve, the Great Flood and the glory of God, he describes the world:

> The world was divided into three parts. From south to west up to the Mediterranean was the part known as Africa, and the southern portion of this is so hot that everything there is burned by the sun. The second part, running from west to north up to the ocean, is called Europe or Énéa, and the northern half of this is so cold that no grass grows there and it is uninhabited. From north to east and down to the south is Asia, and these regions of the world have great beauty and magnificence; the earth yields special products like gold and precious stones. The centre of the world is there also [...].

A medieval map included in a prayer book from around the year 1250, with the east at the top. London is marked in gold leaf, since this is where the book was created, but the religious emphasis on the east means that Europe occupies a humble location down in the bottom left. Norwegia is a peninsula connected to Saxonia.

At around the same time that Snorri is writing his book, the *Edda*, an artist in London is drawing a map in a prayer book. Here, Christ is shown lifting his right hand to bless the Earth below him; in his left he holds a globe to demonstrate his dominion over the world. He is standing in the east, as this is the holy cardinal point and the part of the world in which Christianity originated, while two dragons mark the entrance to hell down in the west. The world is divided into three parts – Africa, Europe and Asia – and at its centre is Jerusalem.

Snorri grew up in a literary home, studying Latin, theology and geography, and he and the anonymous English cartographer probably read many of the same books about the nature of the world. In the Middle Ages, the word was mightier than the image. Eight hundred years before Snorri, one of the early church fathers wrote: 'I shall now wander with my pen through what man knows about Europe.' Scholars preferred textual descriptions of the world to images, which were better suited to the illiterate masses, and so in a medieval sense, Snorri's description is a perfectly adequate map – albeit a somewhat brief one.

At first glance, it isn't necessarily obvious that the map in the prayer book is a world map. Unlike the maps drawn by Ptolemy – or if not by Ptolemy himself, by others but based on his work – this map does not resemble the world as we know it. This is a medieval *mappa mundi*, and the name is taken from the Latin *mappa*, meaning 'a sheet of cloth', and *mundus*, meaning 'the world'. The map provides an image of the world as it would have appeared to a European Christian in the mid-1200s, and reproduces the theological, cosmological, historical and ethnographic notions of the age. The aim is not to represent the world as accurately as possible – more important is to explain how the divine permeates geography. Here, stories from the Bible are illustrated alongside medieval legends and geographical knowledge from antiquity. As on the earliest Greek maps, the land mass is round and surrounded by an ocean containing a smattering of islands and peninsulas – including Norwegia, far to the north on the left of the map – and decorated with biblical motifs such as the Garden of Eden, Noah's Ark, and the parting of the Red Sea as Moses and the Israelites flee the Pharaoh's soldiers.

ROMAN MAPS | The Roman conquest of Egypt, and the dominating position the Romans achieved across the Mediterranean, not only diminished Alexandria's position as a seat of learning; it also resulted in Latin superseding Greek as the dominant written language among European, north African and west Asian scholars. Nor were the Romans particularly interested in translating the Greek geographers' elaborate explanations of the world's appearance – they took a more practical approach to maps. It is characteristic that the only Roman world map to have survived, the *Tabula Peutingeriana*, is almost 8.5 metres long but only 34 centimetres high, as it describes the world by reproducing 104,000 kilometres of roads spanning from Britain, Spain and Morocco in the west to Sri Lanka and China in the east. Marked along the roads are posting stations, baths, bridges, forests, distances and the names of countries and peoples. The only copy of the map to survive is from the Middle Ages, but it is believed that the original was created during late antiquity, some time between AD 335 and AD 366.

Roman maps were generally used in connection with the establishment of new colonies, the construction of roads and aqueducts, court cases, education and propaganda. City maps were also a Roman genre – the Severan Marble Plan, which hung on the wall of the Temple of Peace in central Rome, consisted of 150 stone slabs engraved with the capital's network of roads and buildings. *Orbis terrarum*, the round globe, was generally only drawn to show that new emperors had been granted the gift of the world from a god, and then in extremely stylised form. Countless Roman coins show emperors and gods with a symbolic globe in their hand or under a foot.

We know of only two geographical treatises written in classical Latin. The first is *De situ orbis* (*Description of the World*) by Pomponius Mela, a slim volume that mainly builds on the work of Greek geographers; the second is the *Naturalis Historia* by Pliny the Elder, who added his own observations from northern Europe to the knowledge of the Greeks. Pliny's world stretched from the Iberian Peninsula and Britain in the west to Serere (China) in the east, and from the Scandinavian 'islands' in the north to Ethiopia in the south. Both Mela and Pliny were important sources of geographical knowledge for medieval scholars.

In the *Republic*, Cicero (106–43 BC), a lawyer who had studied under Greek philosophers, provides a rare Roman view of the world when he describes a dream in which the Roman general Scipio is lifted up to the stars so that he may see how diminutive the Roman Empire is in a broader context. The vision is reminiscent of Socrates' associative thinking and the Greek maps that divided the Earth into five climatic zones:

> Look at all the different zones enveloping the earth; the two most widely separated from one another, at opposite poles of the heavens, are fixed with an icy cold, while the midmost zone burns with the heat of the sun. Only the two zones between these extremes are habitable. The zone which lies south of yours has no connection or means of connection with your zone, because they are prevented from crossing the midmost zone. If you look at your own northern zone, you can't help but notice how small a section of this region can be regarded as yours. The territory you occupy, your vast Empire, is nothing more than a small island, narrow from north to south, a bit wider east to west, surrounded by the sea which is known as the Atlantic. In spite of the grand name given to this stretch of water, mark how small it really is.

The Roman orator Eumenius took a more traditional approach to maps, conquests and propaganda when, in the year AD 290, he presented a map of the Roman Empire to his students and said: 'For now, now at last it is a delight to see a picture of the world, since we see nothing in it that is not ours.' Such panegyric speeches, given both with and without the use of accompanying maps, and in which the speakers reeled off the names of countries belonging to the Roman Empire, were a form of propaganda used in the same way as the exhibiting of looted treasures and captured prisoners. The map that opens every *Asterix* comic book, which features a staff topped by the Roman eagle planted firmly in the middle of Gaul, is a fairly accurate interpretation of the Roman use of maps (with the exception of the magnifying glass highlighting the indomitable Gaulish village, of course).

World maps played such an important role in Roman propaganda that they could only be created with approval from the state. Any private person found to have created a world map was assumed to be plotting against the emperor – as Mettius Pompusianus soon discovered after drawing a world map on his bedroom wall. Pompusianus was executed – Emperor Domitian (AD 81–96) took the world map as a sure sign that Pompusianus had plans to take the throne.

AUGUSTINE OF HIPPO | Christianity, however, took another view of geography. The story of creation taught that the Earth belonged to the people and should therefore be used by them, and that since God had come down to the world through Jesus and told the apostles to go out and make disciples of all peoples, anyone could retrace the routes the apostles had taken to convert others to Christianity. Reproductions of the world were no longer reserved for the ruling classes. But geography was not regarded as a discipline in its own right – it was merely an aid to help people better understand creation and history. Information about the world was a part of *scientia*, knowledge of human matters, and must be used to support *sapientia*, knowledge of the holy.

Around the year AD 400, in his work *De Genesi ad litteram* (*The Literal Meaning of Genesis*), Algerian church father Augustine of Hippo wrote that a Christian should know at least as much about the Earth, heavens and other parts of the universe as a non-Christian, in order to avoid misunderstanding any of the Bible's higher truths due to a lack of knowledge about more worldly matters. One must study the Earth alongside biblical history in order to better understand divine creation. In his book *On Christian Doctrine*, Augustine wrote that if 'any competent man were willing in a spirit of benevolence to undertake the labour for the advantage of his brethren [...] he might arrange in their several classes, and give an account of the unknown places, and animals, and plants, and trees, and stones, and metals, and other species of things that are mentioned in Scripture.'

Jerome (AD 347–420) took up this challenge when he published the *Liber de situ et nominibus locorum hebraicorum* (*Book on the Sites and Names of Hebrew Places*) around the year AD 390. This was a topographical dictionary featuring the names of over 1,000 biblical sites, written because anyone 'who knows the sites of the ancient cities and places and their names, whether the same or changed, will gaze more clearly upon Holy Scripture.'

The Bible, however, was both lacking and contradictory in its provision of geographical information. Augustine's advice was to do as the Israelites had done when they 'plundered the Egyptians' before setting out for the Promised Land – in other words, to use the knowledge stemming from the heathen Romans and Greeks.

When writing his *Historiarum adversum paganos* (*History Against the Pagans*), Paulus Orosius (AD 385–420) did as Augustine recommended. 'Our ancestors divided the whole world, surrounded as it is by the belt of the Ocean, into three rectangular blocks, and called these three parts Asia, Europe, and Africa [...]. Asia is surrounded on three sides by the Ocean and extends across the entire East. To the West on her right she borders Europe, which begins at the North Pole, and to her left Africa [...].' Orosius then gives a secular description of these three parts of the world – Jerusalem isn't mentioned, nor is Bethlehem, Jericho, Nazareth nor any of the other cities from biblical history, confirming that Orosius consulted Roman sources. Palestine is only mentioned in passing as one of three Syrian provinces, but nevertheless, Orosius was frequently used as a source for the remainder of the Middle Ages.

ISIDORE OF SEVILLE | Over 200 years later, a Spanish bishop would unite classical and Christian geography. Legend has it that his story starts on the day he ran away from home as a young boy, no longer able to withstand the beatings he received from his older brother, who had taken over his care after his parents' deaths and shocked many of the family's acquaintances with the physical punishments he so generously doled out. Fleeing into the forest outside Seville, the boy finally managed to evade the blows, but never quite managed to escape the feeling of being stupid, rejected and a failure.

Isidore of Seville was born in the city of Cartagena in southern Spain around the year AD 560. These were turbulent times – the Roman province of Hispania had been taken by the Germanic Visigoths over 100 years earlier, and in AD 557 the Byzantines had taken control of Cartagena and the south-eastern part of the province. This is probably why Isidore's family moved west to Seville. His mother was of Visigothic stock, possibly aristocratic, and his father was from a distinguished Spanish-Roman family. Both Isidore's parents died not long after the family had relocated to the new city, and the responsibility for his education therefore fell to his older brother, who educated Isidore accordingly – although Isidore didn't learn as quickly or as much as his older brother felt he should.

Out in the forest, Isidore noticed water dripping onto a stone not far from where he sat. The drops individually appeared completely power-less, seemingly unable to have any impact on the hard stone – but Isidore could see that, over time, they had created a depression in the rock. He thought that perhaps the same might be true of his studies – that bit by bit, hard work would result in great knowledge.

Isidore of Seville is now regarded as one of the most learned men of his time. He was the first Christian author to attempt to write a *summa* – a compilation of all available knowledge. His major work, *Etymologia-rum sive originum* (*Etymologies*), is a kind of combined dictionary and encyclopedia in twenty volumes, which he worked on from the year AD 621 until his death. The work covers everything from grammar and medicine to agriculture and shipping. Book 14 covers the Earth and its var-ious regions ('*de terra et partibus*'). Isidore emphasised that he presented the knowledge 'according to what has been written by the ancients and es-pecially in the works of Catholic writers.' For him, the universe and all its natural phenomena were an expression of God's divine work. Isidore cit-ed John i, 10 as evidence that 'the world was made through him,' compared the Sun with God and the Moon with the church, and stated that the seven stars that make up the Plough symbolise the Christian virtues.

Isidore described the world in the traditional way, writing that it 'is divided into three parts, one of which is called Asia, the second Europe, the third Africa.' His Christian faith influenced his description of Asia:

Next pages | Two sections of the long road and world map *Tabula Peutingeriana*, drawn by cartographer Petrus Bertius in 1619 and based on a reproduction started by Abraham Ortelius the year before he died. To the bottom left of the map is Constantinopolis (today's Istanbul), marked by a stately woman. The many branches of the Nile Delta can be seen in the south, and east of this is Sinai, where according to the map the children of Israel wandered for forty years, while Hierusalem has been placed at an insignificant location even further east.

ARMATE

Lupiones. Sarmate. Ad aquas. VENADI

esia inferior.

MA CEDO DO

lepirum. novum.

SINVS MACEDON

SINVS CORINTHVS

ACHAIA

Arcadia

MILASCO

H A D R I A T

Garamantes. Natio. Selor.

MANIRATE Saurica. Cannate. Psaccani.

Tanasis. Galatie Serace. SARDETAE. Aspur

ROXVLANI. SARMATE

LACVS MEOTIDIS

SINVS AVXINVS PON TO

BITHINIA

BYZANTINI Constantino polis

SINVS HERACTICVS

Ceronesos. SINVS NICOMEDICVS

VS   VAECTVM MARE

Insula. Cretica LACASSON

Montes. Cyreni.

Fl. Nilus qui diuidit Asiam et Libiam.

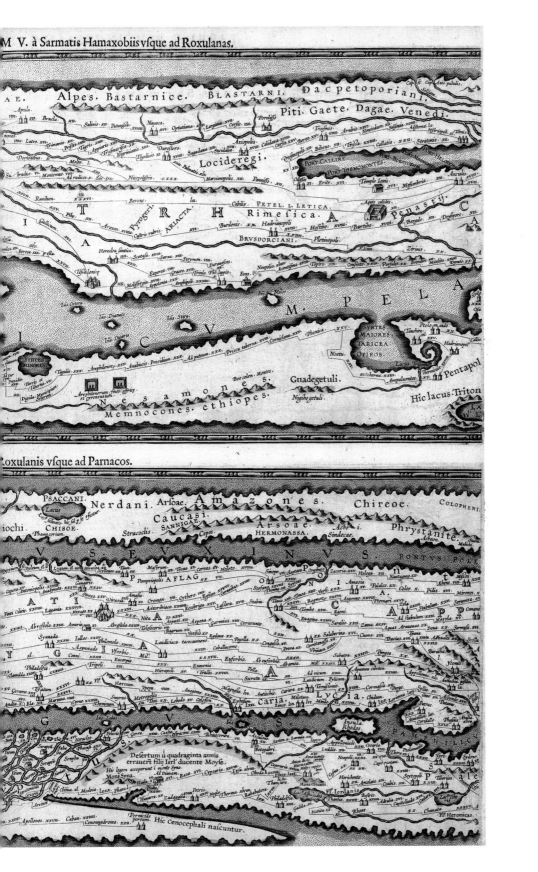

Asia is named after a certain woman who, according to the ancients, had an empire in the east [...]. It has many provinces and regions, whose names and locations I will briefly explain, beginning with Paradise. Paradise is located in the east. Its name, translated from Greek into Latin, means 'garden'. In Hebrew in turn it is called Eden, which in our language means 'delights' [...]. Access to this location was blocked off after the fall of humankind, for it is fenced in on all sides by a flaming sword, that is, encircled by a wall of fire, so that the flames almost reach the sky. Also the Cherubim, that is, a garrison of angels, have been drawn up above the flaming sword to prevent evil spirits from approaching, so that the flames drive off human beings, and angels drive off the wicked angels, in order that access to Paradise may not lie open either to flesh or to spirits that have transgressed. India is so called from the river Indus, by which it is bounded on the west.

For Isidore, there is no marked crossing from paradise to India – for him they are neighbouring regions. But he was unsure whether other regions and peoples existed in the unknown southern part of the globe.

Greek mathematician Pythagoras had the idea that people lived on the other side of the globe – those with their feet facing the other way – long before Isidore; the Greeks and Romans such as Plato and Cicero simply took it for granted that there must be people living on the other side of the world. But in his *City of God*, Augustine of Hippo dismissed this idea: 'But as to the fable that there are Antipodes, that is to say, men on the opposite side of the earth, [...] that is on no ground credible.'

For the Christians of the Middle Ages, the question of whether inhabited countries existed on the other side of the Earth, separated from the world they knew by either burning heat or a great ocean, was not just a geographical question; it was also a theological one. The Bible teaches that all peoples stem from Adam and Eve – so how could any of their descendants have ended up in a region it was impossible to reach? Why was nothing written about these descendants in holy scripture? How would the apostles fulfil the Great Commission to convert all peoples to disciples if there were peoples whom it was simply impossible to get to? Were the antipodes damned? Or had Jesus visited them separately? Augustine admitted that, yes, there might be dry land on the other side of the Earth, but 'though it be bare, [it does not] immediately follow that it is peopled. For Scripture, which proves the truth of its historical statements by the accomplishment of its prophecies, gives no false information.'

In Book 9 of the *Etymologies*, which describes the Earth's kingdoms and languages, Isidore writes that 'the people called Antipodes [...] are on no account to be believed in.' But in Book 14, after describing Asia, Europe and Africa, he writes: 'Apart from these three parts of the world there exists a fourth part, beyond the Ocean, further inland toward the south, which is unknown to us because of the burning heat of the sun; within its borders are said to live the legendary Antipodes.'

This self-contradiction may be due to the fact that Isidore had several church fathers with differing views to consult. At the same time as Augustine, Jerome and Orosius, Macrobius – a man we know little about – was also writing a commentary on the Dream of Scipio, the description of the world from Cicero's *Republic*. He accompanied his commentary with a map, which illustrated the world with the North Pole, South Pole, equator and two inhabitable zones, as described in the dream. Macrobius read the dream as a reminder to powerful men that achieving fame on our little planet is unimportant – in line with Jesus' teaching not to store up treasures on earth, where moths and vermin will destroy them. The map and commentary gave the church fathers a tangible way to express the smallness of humanity; an account of the entire world harmonised with the religious idea of transcendence – the idea of leaving one's body and rising above the Earth in a moment of spiritual insight to witness just how small human beings really are in a cosmic context. The inclusion of the antipodes on medieval maps was therefore permitted – despite Augustine's recommendation to 'let us seek if we can [...] the city of God that sojourns on earth among those human races who are catalogued as having been divided into seventy-two nations and as many languages.'

Here, Augustine is referring to the genealogies described in the Book of Genesis. Noah had three sons, Shem, Ham and Japheth, who after the Flood gave rise to seventy-two different peoples. The Graeco-Roman tripartite vision of the world was woven more tightly into the Christian mentality when the three sons were said to each have populated a different part of the world: Shem was said to have travelled east to be-come the forefather of the Asians and Ham to have journeyed south to Africa; Japheth, forefather of peoples on distant shores, became the European among them. Isidore elaborated on this narrative, asserting that Japheth's son Magog was the forefather of the Goths, i.e. the Swedes of Götaland. But other than this, the Nordic region was barely part of Isidore's geography, and was lumped together with Great Britain, Ire-land and the Gorgades – a group of islands inhabited by strapping, hairy women with wings – in a chapter about islands:

> Ultima Thule is an island of the Ocean in the northwestern region, beyond Britannia, taking its name from the sun, because there the sun makes its summer solstice, and there is no daylight beyond (ultra) this. Hence its sea is sluggish and frozen.

Isidore's *Etymologies* was used as a source of knowledge over the next 900 years. It was the most popular book in medieval libraries – almost 1,000 handwritten copies of it have survived, and we can safely assume that Snorri Sturluson read it. Around the year AD 800, a copy of the *Etymologies* could be found in every cultural hub in Europe. It paved the way for similar books that were written and published in other parts of the world.

The cover of one edition of the *Etymologies* features a map that attempts to illustrate the geography the book describes. The book is from the 800s, but various studies have concluded that the map is from the late 600s or early 700s, making it the oldest surviving medieval map we know of. The map is simple – it looks like something a student might scribble down while listening to a lecture given by a tutor – but it none-theless says something about the direction in which cartography was moving. Asia is marked with the name of Shem, Africa with Ham and Europe with Japheth; the map is oriented towards the east, with the Med-iterranean extending up from the bottom to branch out into the River Nile to the south and River Don to the north. From the very top, Christ rules over all below him, his hands pierced by nails and his arms spread wide above the globe to signal his protection of it.

CHRISTIANISATION | This religious shift became even clearer when the Spanish abbot Beatus of Liébana drew a map for inclusion in a book about the coming apocalypse – the year AD 800 was looming perilously close when he started his work. Theologians at the time believed that doomsday would arrive that year because 6,000 years had passed since the Earth's creation. Every thousand years that passed was equivalent to one of the six days God used on the creation of the world, and on the seventh day – 7,000 years – after God had defeated Satan and condemned living and dead to heaven and hell, the world would enter a state of eternal Sunday peace.

Beatus counted all the years in the Bible – from the creation to the Flood, from Noah to Abraham, from Abraham to King David, from David to the Babylonian exile and from Babylon until the birth of Jesus – and concluded that 5,987 years had passed since God created the Earth. The end was therefore only thirteen years away. His map was intended to illustrate biblical history from creation to doomsday; in the east he drew Paradise with Adam and Eve, where history began, and the twelve apostles in the areas to which, as legend would have it, they had travelled – Matthew in Macedonia, Thomas in India, Simon in Egypt and John in Spain – to illustrate that doomsday would come when all the peoples of the world had been converted to Christianity.

Augustine and Orosius had presented a view of history that moved from east to west. The creation had taken place in the Far East, but after the fall history moved further and further west, via Babylonian, Assyrian and Macedonian empires, to the Roman Empire and its conquests of Spain, France and Britain – the world's westernmost outposts, where the Sun set over the sea. Now, history had no more geography upon which to unfold. Soon, everything must come to an end.

The dragons at the very bottom of the map in the English prayer book, in the west, are a part of this history, and Beatus was the first person to present this history using a map. He used a Roman map as the basis for

Next pages | A third of the Catalan Atlas from 1375, in a restored version from 1959. It was probably created by Cresques Abraham in Mallorca, although this is not known for certain. The map is reproduced here in the correct orientation – it should be read from east to west. Norway is a mound of rocks down in the north.

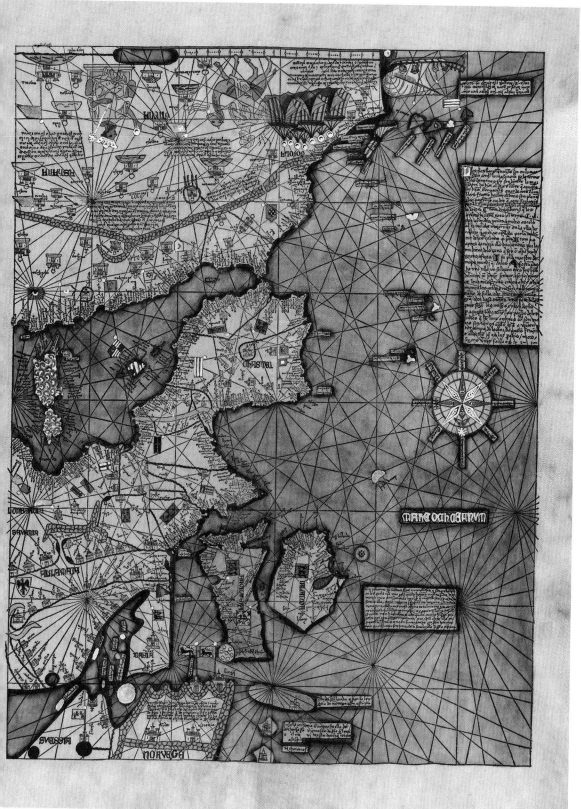

his own, layering the events of biblical history over it, and thereby started the tradition of filling maps with increasing references to the word of
God, the Tower of Babel, Noah's Ark, the Red Sea, the Sea of Galilee, the
crucifixion and the Day of Judgement. From the 800s, the biblical narrative included on maps was supplemented with secular information about
other peoples, zoology, botany and legends from classical antiquity. The
maps were similar to illustrated encyclopedias, and people who were unable to read could obtain a visual overview of the medieval knowledge of
the world by looking at them in churches, prayer books and textbooks.

But few *mappae mundi* could present new geographical knowledge based on exploration. Since the decline of the Roman Empire's infrastructure, travelling had become more difficult for the Europeans,
and reports of the Norse expeditions rarely reached the scholarly, Lat-
in-speaking cartographers on the continent. Those who travelled were
missionaries, pilgrims, crusaders and certain traders – few travelled for
travel's sake. In the greatest literary work of the Middle Ages, the *Divine
Comedy* by the Italian poet Dante Alighieri (1265–1321) – a theological
travelogue from hell, purgatory and heaven – we meet the Greek seafarer
Ulysses in hell. Ulysses tells of how he set out on a final journey, because
he wished to explore the world. He sailed west towards unknown waters,
through the Strait of Gibraltar, 'Where Hercules his landmarks set as
signals,/That man no farther onward should adventure,' and said to his
crew: 'Consider ye the seed from which ye sprang;/Ye were not made to
live like unto brutes,/But for pursuit of virtue and of knowledge.' Dante,
however, had little time for Ulysses' desire to learn – he saw this as a kind
of vain curiosity. Only towards the end of the 1200s did eyewitness accounts start to make a systematic mark on European maps.

NORÐWEG | Like Ulysses, the Norwegian seafarer Ohthere of Hålo-
galand set out to explore the outer edges of the world. He set sail some
time towards the end of the 800s, with the intention of travelling as far
north as he possibly could. Some years later, he described his journey to
King Alfred the Great of Wessex. King Alfred must have enjoyed the story,
as he had it written down and added to the Anglo-Saxon translation of
Orosius's *Historiarum*, which only described the world south of the Alps.

Ohthere told his lord, King Alfred, that he lived the furthest north of all Norwegians. He said that he lived in the north of Norway on the coast of the Atlantic. He also said that the land extends very far north beyond that point, but it is all uninhabited, except for a few places here and there where the Finnas have their camps, hunting in winter, and in summer fishing in the sea. He told how he once wished to find out how far the land extended due north, or whether anyone lived to the north of the unpopulated area. He went due north along the coast, keeping the uninhabited land to starboard and the open sea to port continuously for three days. He was then as far north as the whale hunters go at their furthest. He then continued due north as far as he could reach in the second three days. There the land turned due east, or the sea penetrated the land – he did not know which.

Ohthere sailed to the White Sea in Russia, and then home again. To King Alfred, he described Norway as a long, narrow country – 'broadest in the south, and the further north it goes the narrower it becomes.' Alongside the southern part of the country, on the other side of the mountains, was Svealand, and alongside the northern part the land of the Kvens. Ohthere was a merchant, and often travelled south to Skiringssal, a market town not far from where Larvik is situated today. From there, he travelled on to Hedeby in Denmark to exchange furs for luxury goods and textiles:

> From Sciringes heal [Skiringssal] he said that he sailed in five days to the trading-town called Hedeby, which is situated among Wends, Saxons and Angles and belongs to the Danes. When he sailed there from Sciringes heal he had Denmark to port and the open sea to starboard for three days. Then two days before he arrived at Hedeby he had Jutland and Sillende and many islands to starboard. The Angles lived in these districts before they came to this land. On the port side he had, for two days, those islands which belong to Denmark.

So ends the oldest existing description of Europe's northern fringes. This is also the oldest description that is dated and features the name form 'Norway' – *Norðweg*. Over 100 years later, an anonymous Briton drew a world map that to some extent combined geographical information from both Orosius and Ohthere – the *Cottoniana* or 'Anglo-Saxon map' exhibits a strong Nordic influence, since Neronorweci, Island, Dacia and Gothia are included, if not particularly accurately located or reproduced.

The links between the Nordic region and the rest of Europe were strengthened when the region was Christianised and began to learn Latin. Initially, before Lund, Nidaros and Uppsala became archdioceses, the Nordic region came under the administration of Bremen and Hamburg, and around the year AD 1070 clergyman Adam of Bremen wrote the *History of the Archbishops of Hamburg-Bremen*. The book was the most detailed description of the Nordic region to be written in Latin, and describes Norway as follows:

> As Nortmannia is the farthest country of the world, so we properly place consideration of it in the last part of the book [...]. It begins with towering crags at the sea commonly called the Baltic; then with its main ridge bent toward the north, after following the course of the shore line of a raging ocean, it finally has its bounds in the Riphean Mountains, where the tired world also comes to an end.

Nidaros became an archdiocese in the year AD 1154, around the same time that the *Historia Norwegiæ* – a work describing Norway and the northern regions – was written by an anonymous Norwegian author. Here, Norway is described as a large country, although mostly uninhabited due to extensive forests, mountains and extreme cold, and located as follows:

> It starts in the east from the Great River, but bends towards the west and so turns back as its edge circles round northwards. Full of fjords and creeks, it is a country that pushes out countless headlands, and along its length encompasses three habitable zones: the first and largest is the seaboard; the second is the inland area, also known as the mountain region; the third is wooded and populated by the Finns, but there is no agriculture there. To the west and north, Norway is enclosed by the Ocean tides, to the south lie Denmark and the Baltic Sea, while to the east are Sweden, Götaland, Ångermanland and Jämtland.

The Christianisation of the region resulted in prominent Scandinavians and Icelanders sending their sons off to study on the continent. Many returned home with both transcripts and books they had purchased, containing the scholarly, Latin literature of the age, and much of this was translated into Icelandic. From the 1100s we have the *Landafræði* (*Geography*) – clearly influenced by Isidore of Seville and others: 'Paradise is located in the eastern part of the world [. . .]. Then Noah divided the world into three parts between his sons, and gave names to all the parts of the world that previously had no name. He called one part of the world Asia, another Africa, and the third Europe.' The book's geographical origins reveal knowledge of the northern regions: 'The country from *Vegistafr* in the north – where Finnmark is situated by Gandvik – to the Göta älv river in the south, is called Norway. This country's boundaries are Gandvik to the north and the Göta älv river to the south, Eidskog to the east and *Engelsøysundet* to the west. The main cities in Norway are the market town of Trondheim, the resting place of King Olaf II of Norway; the next is Bergen in Hordaland, the resting place of Saint Sunniva; the third is to the east of Vik, the resting place of Saint Hallvard, kinsman of King Olaf.'

Vegistafr was the northern boundary of the old, Norwegian kingdom, probably the Russian Cape Svyatoy Nos on the western side of the White Sea, while Engelsøysundet is the Menai Strait between the island of Anglesey and the Welsh mainland. In other words, Norway extended to the west coast of Britain. *Landafræði* was probably written by Níkulás Bergsson, the first abbot at the newly established Benedictine monastery at Munkatverå in northern Iceland in AD 1155, and who also wrote the travelogue *Leiðarvísir* (*Guidebook*) about a journey from Iceland to Jerusalem. Níkulás crossed Europe on foot after travelling first to Norway, and then on to Denmark. 'Thus pilgrims travelling to Rome may expect the journey from Aalborg to Viborg to take two days [. . .]. Another way to Rome is to travel from Norway to Frisland, to Deventer or Utrecht, where one may collect one's staff and bag, and be blessed prior to the journey to Rome.' From Rome, Níkulás journeyed down to Brindisi, and from there to Venice, Greece, Turkey and Cyprus by boat, before coming ashore at Acre and from here travelling up to Jerusalem – 'This is the finest of all the world's cities.'

In setting out on his journey, Níkulás set himself apart from other Benedictines. Upon admission to the monastery, the monks made a vow to stay in one place – *stabilitas loci*. Through reading descriptions of journeys to the Holy Land, however, it was possible to embark on a *peregrinatio in stabilitate* – a pilgrimage undertaken without moving. Matthew Paris, a British Benedictine monk, created a map for this purpose around the year AD 1250 – it extends across several pages of a book, and by turning from one page to the next, monks could 'travel' from the monastery to London, Dover, Calais, Paris, Rome and Otranto, where they boarded a ship and travelled to the Holy Land and Jerusalem – all while sitting at a desk.

Books such as *Landafræði* and *Leiðarvísir* were written at the dawn of Norse penmanship and literary culture – when the Old Icelandic language, which would later be used to compose the *Sagas*, was coming into being as the conveyor of literature. The Icelandic written culture took shape when the domestic and the European stimulated each other, and it was during this time and in this environment that Snorri Sturluson grew up.

HEIMSKRINGLA | Snorri has completed his book about Norse mythology and minstrelsy, and is now starting work on a larger work about the Norwegian kings. In the *Edda*, he had already told of how the Asians are 'most richly endowed with all gifts, with wisdom and strength, with beauty and with all knowledge' compared to other peoples, and how chieftains from Troy in Turkey had travelled north to become the start of the Nordic royal lineage. Now, Snorri aims to provide a more detailed description of their history and where they came from. The Old Norse kings' sagas open with a long description of the world:

> It is said that the earth's circle (Heimskringla), which the human race inhabits, is torn across into many bights, so that great seas run into the land from the out-ocean. Thus it is known that a great sea goes into Njorvasound, and up to the land of Jerusalem. From the same sea a long sea-bight stretches toward the northeast, and is called the Black Sea, and divides the three parts of the earth; of which the eastern part is called Asia, and the western is called by some Europe, by some Enea. Northward of the black Sea lies Svithjod the Great, or the

Cold. The Great Svithjod is reckoned by some not less than the Saracens' land, others compare it to the Great Blueland. The northern part of Svithjod lies uninhabited on account of frost and cold, as likewise the southern parts of Blueland are waste from the burning sun.

Snorri's place names are not immediately understandable to a modern reader. 'Njorvasound' is the Strait of Gibraltar, and the sea that stretches to the land of Jerusalem is the Mediterranean. The country to the north of the Black Sea is Russia, but Snorri uses the Norse name for Sweden, Svithjod, instead of Gardarike, which was the common name for Russia in the sagas. Perhaps he confused Svitjod with the Greek Skytia, a kingdom located in south-eastern Russia during antiquity. The 'Saracens' land' is the area that stretches from southern Iraq to Morocco – the Arabic countries – while 'Blueland' is the rest of Africa, named for the blue-black skin of the country's inhabitants.

Like Greek Herodotus, Roman Pliny and church father Isidore of Seville, Snorri describes the Tanais River (Don) as the dividing line between Europe and Asia, but claims that this was previously known as the Vanaquisl:

> The country surrounding the Vanaquisl was therefore known as Vanaland or Vanaheim, and the river separates the three parts of the world, of which the easternmost is called Asia and the westernmost Europe. The country east of the Tanaquisl in Asia was called Asaland or Asaheim, and the chief city in that land was called Asgard. In that city was a chief called Odin, and it was a great place for sacrifice.

Vanaheim, writes Snorri, was where the Vani lived – a group of gods who fought the first ever war against Asgard and the other tribe of gods, the Æsir. Snorri uses the similarity between the Norse word 'Æsir' and the word 'Asia' for all it's worth, thereby linking the pagan Norse religion to Asia, the holy part of the world, and giving the Norwegian kings a noble, Asian descent. In fact, Odin is forced to flee northwards due to the war, and his son, Sæmingr, becomes the forefather of the Norwegian kings. Snorri reinforces Norwegian royal power using geography, by incorporating it into a map that emphasises noble origins.

Around the same time, King Henry III of England used geography to bolster his power when the barons revolted in 1258. In a chamber in the Palace of Westminster, where he had both living quarters and meeting rooms, he had a large *mappa mundi* painted on the wall behind the chair in which he sat as a signal of his knowledge and power. The strategy worked only up to a point – five years later the map was destroyed in a fire during the Barons' War. Matthew Paris had created a copy of the map, however – and although the copy has also been lost, it is probable that the map in the English prayer book is a copy of this in turn. The enormous amount of information included on this small map may indicate that it is based on a larger original. The 145 inscriptions on a circle measuring only 8.5 centimetres in diameter make the map a highly detailed medieval reference work.

The image of Jesus included on the map has its roots in the classical tradition. Here, Jesus is holding a globe in the same way as the Roman god Jupiter, to show that he rules over the world. The globe he is holding is divided into three parts, as is the Earth below him. The gesture he's making with his right hand, with his index and ring fingers bent, dates back to how Roman orators would signal their right to speak. The twelve winds that encircle the world have classical names; the north wind, *septentrio*, is named after the seven oxen (*septem triones*) the Romans saw in the Plough, and *septentriones* became the Roman name for the north.

The creatures in the southern part of the world are mostly taken from the Roman author Gaius Julius Solinus and his book *De mirabilibus mundi* (*The Wonders of the World*). Here we see cannibals munching on legs, headless people with their eyes, nose and mouth on their torsos, an individual with a single, large leg, a person with only a small hole for a mouth drinking through a straw, someone eating a snake, a person with six fingers and another with two pairs of eyes. North of Norwegia is the island of the Hyperboreans, a people who according to the Greeks lived where the north wind started, and even further north the island of Aramphe, also a feature of the far north in Greek myths.

At the very top, furthest east, is the Garden of Eden. Within a ring of mountains that symbolises how difficult the garden is to access, we see Adam, Eve and the tree of life. From the mountains, the four rivers of

Paradise join the Indian River Ganges – the easternmost place the cartographer knew of, apart from the Garden of Eden. A third of Asia is the
scene of biblical events, and south of Jerusalem, Bethlehem is marked.
East of the city is the Sea of Galilee, drawn with a large fish in the middle – a reminder that it was here that Jesus fed the five thousand with
five loaves of bread and two fish – and in Armenia we see Mount Ararat,
where Noah's Ark lies stranded. In the south-east is an enlarged Red Sea,
parted as Moses and the Israelites flee.

Turning from the map to the next page in the prayer book reveals
yet another map – a round, text-based map divided into the three continents and featuring the names of the most important kingdoms and cities in Africa, Asia and Europe. For the reader who wishes to learn about
geography, the two maps complement each other. The image-based map
provides a simple overview of our place in creation, the world and biblical history, while the text-based map can be studied to learn the names of
countries and various locations.

The *mappæ mundi* reached a highpoint with the creation of the English Hereford Mappa Mundi around the year 1300. Like the map in the
prayer book, it depicts a round land mass with Jerusalem at the centre
and strange beings living on its outskirts – including people with dog
heads not far from Noreya, where we see the world's first drawing of a ski
trail – but this map is much larger and far more detailed. The Hereford
Mappa Mundi is drawn on a large piece of calfskin measuring an entire 159 by 133 centimetres, and features Paradise, Noah's Ark, the Tower
of Babel, Moses receiving the Ten Commandments at Mount Sinai, the
Red Sea, the Dead Sea, Jordan, Jericho, Sodom and Gomorrah, Lot's wife
turned into a pillar of salt, the Mount of Olives, the crucifixion and – at
the very top – the resurrected Jesus allowing the Day of Judgement to

Next pages | One of the most beautiful maps in the world – Fra Mauro's world map, dated
1460. In many ways, the map marks the end of the medieval, biblical map tradition and the
start of a more modern, scientific tradition. For example, Fra Mauro did not wish to place
paradise somewhere in the Far East because he could not be certain that it existed there –
he had read about the travels of Marco Polo. Fra Mauro therefore situated paradise beyond
the edge of the map.

come down. Two rows of people to the right and left of him represent the recently deceased on their way to their designated final destinations. The Hereford Mappa Mundi is a theatre of the world, in which all of history is played out, from start to finish.

NAUTICAL CHARTS | While *mappæ mundi* were being painted on the walls of palaces and cathedrals and in prayer books, textbooks and geographical works, another entirely different type of map was also being developed across medieval Europe – nautical charts presenting with striking accuracy the stretches of coastline along the Mediterranean, Black Sea and Atlantic Ocean north and south of Gibraltar. These maps cared little for inland areas – almost all the included place names are those of coastal cities – and only the mouths of rivers are added. None of the religion, history, ethnography or zoology presented by the *mappæ mundi* is found here – all the geographical information included on the nautical charts has a purely practical function.

The oldest of these maps to survive is the rectangular *Carta Pisana* from around 1275. This map, along with two others from around the same time, is so highly developed that many others must have been created before it. But nautical charts are particularly vulnerable due to their use – they are liable to get sprayed with seawater or lost overboard.

The *Carta Pisana* features as many as 927 place names, from Lebanon in the east to Morocco and England in the west. One wind rose, which indicates the orientation of the cardinal directions, is drawn to the west of Sardinia, another south of Rhodes, and from these extend several geometric figures that specify wind directions and travel routes. The map also features a scale for calculating distances, and isn't oriented with any particular direction at the top – all the text is written at right angles to the coastline, and the navigator must turn the map to read it while sailing along.

The *Carta Pisana* is probably originally not from Pisa but from Genoa, since the first reference to a nautical chart was found onboard a Genoan ship, and many cartographers lived in the city. But how anyone was able to draw it is unclear. Who explored all these coastlines? What instruments did they use? How was all the information collated onto a single map? One answer is that the cartographer may have combined several regional maps, which may explain why the scales for the Mediterranean and Black Sea are different on several of the later nautical charts. The first nautical atlas was produced in the early 1300s, when someone had the idea of binding several nautical charts together. This offered a more practical and durable format than a long map that required rolling out and in, and also provided space for greater detail.

Despite the Italian clergy's complaints that nautical charts failed to show the world's most important aspects, the nautical charts began to influence the *mappæ mundi*. The merchant class – frowned upon during the Middle Ages because they neither worked, waged war nor served God – was growing, particularly in the city-states of northern Italy, and had the resources to create secular maps for practical purposes. The influence of the nautical maps made the *mappæ mundi* less schematic, and more detailed.

But the *mappæ mundi* also influenced the nautical charts, which were improved and expanded as the Italians, Spanish and Portuguese began to travel both over greater distances and more often, and eventually began to feature cities, mountains and rivers within the coastal areas. A map from 1339 shows an African king, the queen of Saba in Arabia, a large area of Africa to the south and Asia in the east, and features explanatory texts in the manner of the *mappæ mundi*. The added decorations indicate that the nautical charts no longer had a solely practical function – they had also become objects of status, bearing witness to discoveries and power.

The most extravagant of all these maps is the Catalan Atlas from 1375 – a gift from the king of Aragon to the king of France, consisting of six calfskin vellum leaves mounted on wooden panels. The first two panels consist of geographical and astronomical texts and diagrams, while the map occupies the next four panels, providing an overview of the known and not-so-well-known world from the Canary Islands in the west to Sumatra and China in the east, and from Norway in the north to the Sahara in the south. The map is elaborately decorated with sumptuous gold leaf and illustrations of cities, animals, kings and flags. Regió de Nuruega is situated beside Suessia and Dasia, completely surrounded by mountains, and here we read: 'This region of Norway is very rugged, very cold, mountainous, wild and covered with forests. Its inhabitants eat more fish and meat than bread; there is no abundance of barley because of the reigning cold. There are also many beasts, like deer, white bears, and gyrfalcons.'

FRA MAURO | In Venice in the mid-1400s, monk Fra Mauro is in conversation with a captain who was once shipwrecked on the coast of Norway. In the early summer of 1431, Pietro Querini set sail from Crete for Bruges in modern Belgium, the three ships in his fleet loaded with wine and spices. But out on the Atlantic they encountered a violent storm that drove the ships far off course. In the lifeboats, the crew fought the storm, cold and hunger for several weeks, and just after the new year in 1432, the boat containing Querini and eleven other survivors ran ashore on an island at Røst in Lofoten, where the crew was cared for by the local population for three months. Once safely back home, Querini wrote a book entitled *In the First Circle of Paradise*, in which he couldn't praise the hospitality of the coastal inhabitants of northern Norway enough. He is now one of the experienced seamen – '*i marinari experti*' – who Fra Mauro is consulting as he works on a large world map.

Fra Mauro lives and works in the Monastery of St Michael, situated on one of Venice's many islands. He is a cartographer, and the monastery foots the bill for his materials and paints. He has previously mapped an area in modern Croatia, and created a *mappa mundi* in 1449. The new world map he is working on is a commission from the Venetian authorities.

As a God-fearing monk, Fra Mauro is well versed in the symbolic maps of the Middle Ages. But he also lives in a city where new information about the world is continually being brought into port, and discoveries of far-off countries cast doubt over the supposedly eternal and holy truths.

Nevertheless, Fra Mauro starts with a traditional circle on a large piece of vellum. Here, he outlines the three continents Africa, Asia and Europe, but in a far more detailed manner than on the *mappæ mundi*. He follows the coastlines as they are drawn on the new nautical charts and, possibly inspired by Arabic cartographers, he orients the map with the south at the top instead of the east.

Outside the map, Mauro includes diagrams that provide answers to cosmographical questions. At the top left he draws the heavens surrounding the Earth, where the Sun, Moon, five planets and stars are located. In the top right we see the Moon's orbit around the Earth. At the bottom right is a round map, illustrating the five climatic zones, and at the bottom left is the Garden of Eden.

The question of where to place paradise became increasingly problematic for cartographers as the Far East became better known – not least after the *Travels of Marco Polo* was published around the year 1300. Some started to draw Eden in southern Africa, which was still largely unknown, but Fra Mauro locates it beyond the map. In the accompanying text he calls it '*paradiso terrestro*' – the earthly paradise – and cites Augustine of Hippo, who like Isidore of Seville believed that the Garden of Eden was located down on Earth. Fra Mauro, however, refuses to situate the Garden of Eden in a location he knows to be inaccurate, thereby combining the cartographic expulsion of paradise with an orthodox text in order to link the new geography to the old truths.

Fra Mauro comes up against a similar problem when deciding where to place Jerusalem. Again, new knowledge about the Far East is the issue here – it is so far away that Jerusalem has been revealed as being situated west of the centre of the world. Fra Mauro's solution is to explain that Jerusalem is not at the centre of the world in terms of longitude. But if we look at the population, he argues, because Europe is more densely populated than Asia, Jerusalem lies at the centre of all people.

The Holy Land takes up less space in Asia than it did on earlier maps: 'Those who are knowledgeable would put here Idumea, Palestine and Galilee, things which I have not shown, such as the river Jordan, the sea of Tiberias, the Dead Sea and other places, because there was not enough room', Fra Mauro writes on the map.

Fra Mauro gives geography precedence every time it contradicts the old truths. He believes the Tanais can no longer be the border between Europe and Asia, since it also runs through large areas of Europe, and states that 'I have this from very worthy persons who have seen with their own eyes'. The same applies to the question of strange beings living at the fringes of the world. Fra Mauro states that 'many cosmographers and very learned men write that in Africa [...] there are many monstrous men and animals', but that he himself has found 'not one person who could give me knowledge of what I have found written,' and therefore leaves the issue to be settled by others.

Fra Mauro's world map reflects the geographical confusion of its age – a confusion due not only to Marco Polo, but also to the fact that the Europeans of the early 1400s finally had access to Ptolemy's *Geography* in Latin translation. '*Andrea Biancho de Veneciis me fecit, mcccc xxxvi*' ('Andrea Biancho of Venice made me, 1436') is written on the outside of a folder containing three maps: the first is based on Ptolemy's coordinates; the second a *mappa mundi* decorated with Adam and Eve, people with dog heads and kings; and the third is a nautical chart that stretches from the Canary Islands in the west to the Black Sea in the east, and from the Nile in the south to Norway in the north. Biancho, a seaman and captain, has written nothing about the maps, but the fact that he has placed them side by side neatly illustrates the great cartographic question of the 1400s – how should the world be mapped? Fra Mauro's solution is to combine Ptolemy, *mappæ mundi* and nautical charts in a single map. He laments that some will probably complain that he hasn't followed Ptolemy to a greater extent in terms of form or the calculation of latitudes and longitudes, but adds that even Ptolemy believed he was unable to say anything certain about the parts of the world that were seldom visited.

But by this time the Europeans are travelling east towards Asia, west across the Atlantic and south towards Africa in search of goods; new countries and coastlines are being mapped, and even the northern regions are starting to be represented with more accurate contours. These are easily recognisable on Fra Mauro's map – Datia has worked loose from the continent to become an island, but retained its shape, and Norvegia and Svetia are a peninsula that stretches from south to north. 'In this province of Norway came ashore Piero Querini, as is well known,' he writes next to the Norwegian coast.

Fra Mauro changes his mind several times over the years in which he works on the map – many of its over 200 texts are entered on labels he has affixed over something else. Perhaps he wrote the labels when the map was finally finished, after receiving new information from an increasing number of travellers from distant regions – or perhaps the map was never finished, as it was dated 1460, the year after his death. But Fra Mauro did write a final greeting to all those who would study his map:

> This work [. . .] has not achieved all it should, for truly it is not possible for the human intellect without divine assistance to verify everything on this cosmographia or mappamundi, the information on which is more like a taste than the complete satisfaction of one's desire.

Fra Mauro's map could never be finished because he was working in an outdated format – it was almost bursting at the seams. The new discoveries in both the east and west meant that the land mass no longer fitted within a round map without minimising the old world. Almost 2,000 years after the Greek philosopher Democritus criticised round world maps, the Europeans once again began to understand that they should be oval. And just thirty-three years after Fra Mauro, even more countries would be discovered – this time far off in the west.

TRADITION | The medieval period is often presented as breaking with antiquity, but cartographic history shows that during the Middle Ages, scholars often both conveyed knowledge from antiquity and built upon it. The church fathers took up Augustine of Hippo's challenge to 'plunder the Egyptians' and use the knowledge obtained by the Greeks and Romans, and used this to draw the maps they needed – images of the world with all that is holy at their centre. These maps contained huge volumes of geographical, theological, historical and ethnographic information, but were almost useless for navigation. Christian geography combined time and space in a way that would have been incomprehensible to the Greeks and Romans – their religions involved no fall from grace, damnation or salvation; nor did they imagine a time at which world history would come to an end. If Greek maps had been scientific and theoretical, and Roman maps practical, medieval European maps were for the most part theological, didactic and narrative in nature. Later, practical needs led to the development of nautical charts – a genre begun by travelling Italian merchants and continued by the Portuguese, Spanish and Dutch when new ships and the desire for wealth triggered a period in which the Europeans set out across the high seas.

Nieu poort
Oostende
Blan kenberg
Oudenborg
Dixmuyden
Brugge
Sluys
Mypn
Dame
Ardenborg
Oostburg
oußelare
Bulscamp velt
R IA
Ingel munster
Tielt
Eeckloo
Middelburg
Bierulict
WAL CHEREN
Middelborn
LELANDIAE INSVLAE
Gorre
Scon hauen
WEN Zierk zee
Beiele voorn
Grinu sande
Delft
Vlaer dingen
Schiedam
Roxer
arlebeeck
Machelen
Leye fl.
Clyfe
Axele
D I A
Hulst
Goes
VITBE FLAE
DIVE LANT
OOL
Gor
Steyen
Yssl mont
Ostreghthec
Serdiet
okeren
Oudenarde
Geral
N I
VAN
Saftin gen
Steebergen
Rosendal
Oudenbosche
Dor drecht
Poadsberch bosch
Botelaere
Sottegem
Boudelo
WAES
Beweren
Bergen op zoom
7 Bergen
Loenhout
Geer truy en berge
Woreum
Gor
Geertsberge
Aelst
S. Niclaes
BR
ABAN
Bre da
DE LAN GE STRAET
Baerlen
Engien
Aesche
Londerseel
Ruppelmonde
Der monde
Antwerpen
Hoochstraete
Oosterwijck
Herto
Halle
Bruessel
Senne fl.
Vilvoorden
Machelen
Duffele
Liere
DE KE
TIA.
Turnhout
Oirschot
Bo
Signy
oeulx
Brane
Breyne
Soenien bosch
Vueren
Dyele fl.
Dromel fl.
Louen
Herentals
Aerel
Postel
Eersel
Dommele fl.
S. O. rot
Niuelle
Wauere
Bouterfen
Diest
Loenvel
Coursel
Gestel
Eyndhoue
Fontaines
Fleru
Reues
Gemblours
Touloign
Tienen
Siche nen
Beeringen
Meer
Helmont
Cranendonck
S

THE FIRST ATLAS

Antwerp, Belgium
51° 13′ 6″ N
4° 23′ 53″ E

With her brush, Anne Ortel carefully applies light-green paint to an area of woodland, then uses pale and darker brown to indicate the lowlands of Brabantia, Flandria, Hannoia and Hollandia. Two shades of blue denote the water: light for the vast ocean, and dark for the rivers, lakes and navigable waterways along the coast. She paints the ships brown and dark yellow, then dips her brush in red to colour the cities, one by one: Brueßel, Utrecht, Louen and Oosterwijck; Amsterdam, Delft, Eyndhouen and Antwerpen – her home town. In 1570, Antwerp is the richest city in the world thanks to the trade that takes place along the River Schelde. The significance of this waterway is clear, as a five-metre-long map of it was created in 1486. In Antwerp, the Spanish and Portuguese purchase copper and silver mined in southern Germany, before transporting it to India and Africa where they exchange it for spices, ivory and slaves. English cloth, Flemish embroidery and German leather goods are traded here, and the city itself exports luxury products such as glass, gems and wallpapers.

The Antwerp of Ortel's time is a cosmopolitan city. If you take a walk beside the port, where over 2,500 ships dock each year, you might hear merchants speaking Dutch, English, French, Italian, Yiddish, Portuguese,

---

Detail of a map of the Duchy of Brabant, which comprised parts of today's Belgium and the Netherlands, including Antwerp, Abraham Ortelius's home town. Printed in the 1570 edition of the *Theatrum orbis terrarum*.

Spanish and German, in addition to African and East Asian languages. Traffic to the city is so great, and the new, modern cranes so numerous, that Antwerp even has its own crane operators' guild. A network of canals spreads from the port to the city's many warehouses, and then further out into the Brabantian countryside. Like Alexandria 1,500 years earlier, Antwerp is a trading hub with a significant interest in geography and the wider world. Antwerp has no major library or renowned educational institution, but makes up for this with its many printing houses, booksellers and publishers – since German printer Johannes Gutenberg began producing books in the 1450s, the book market has developed at such a pace that the need for libraries has reduced. Dutch humanist Erasmus praised a printer friend by asserting that he was 'building up a library which has no other limits than the world itself,' and Antwerp's printing houses act as libraries, booksellers, publishers, workshops and meeting places for scholars of all kinds. Most of them are located in Kammenstraat, including Europe's biggest and most important printing house at this time, De Gulden Passer (The Golden Compasses), where business has increased to such an extent that the premises now span seven buildings located side by side.

Anne Ortel was named after her mother, who taught her how to colour maps. Her grandfather moved to Antwerp from the German city of Ausberg after hearing about the opportunities Antwerp had to offer, and did well for himself – the Ortel family were highly regarded in the city. Anne's father, Leonard, became an antiques dealer, and inherited his father's propensity for religious reflection. Like the rest of the city, which at this time was controlled by the Spanish crown, Anne's parents officially professed to follow the Catholic faith, but like many other Antwerpians held Protestant sympathies. In 1535, Leonard was forced to flee the city due to his involvement in the printing of reformist Myles Coverdale's English translation of the Bible.

Charles V, ruler of both the Spanish and Holy Roman empires, had little time for Protestantism, and the Inquisition burned both books and heretics with zeal. When Leonard fled Antwerp, he left behind his wife and children – including Anne's older brother, Abram, who was just eight years old. The Inquisition stormed the house, looking for forbidden, heretical books, but found none.

Anne's father died just four years later, leaving her mother to diligently and successfully continue the antiques business and instruct Anne, Abram and their younger sister Elizabeth in the art of colouring maps. Maps had always been part of their father's collections, and young Abram showed a keen interest in geography. There was a large market for maps in the Netherlands at the time, which expanded alongside the country's international trading activities – even outdated maps were desirable, and many of the period's artists painted everyone from the bourgeoisie to humble shoemakers in settings featuring maps on the walls. Maps were bought and sold at all price levels – and in the Netherlands, coloured maps were particularly in demand.

Abram and his sisters purchased black-and-white maps, which they glued onto linen canvases before stretching them over wooden frames to be coloured. They sold the coloured maps to private individuals, publishers and booksellers – a coloured map usually cost around a third more than an uncoloured one. Each map's appearance was dictated by the client – if someone wanted their home town coloured a bright shade of pink, well, their wish was granted. But colours could also be used to convey information. As early as the year 1500, German cartographer Erhard Etzlaub recommended the use of different colours to indicate where different languages were spoken. Later in life, however, Abram would disclose a preference for uncoloured maps. In a letter to his nephew, Jacob, dated 1595, he wrote: 'You ask for a coloured copy; but in my opinion an uncoloured copy is better; decide for yourself.'

Abram never gained an education – presumably because he had to work. Perhaps Leonard had hoped for his son to go to university – he had at least done his best to educate him in Latin and Greek – but according to a friend who referred to him in a letter after his death, Abram was 'hampered by circumstances, having a widowed mother and two young sisters to support.' The University of Leuven, around sixty kilometres away and one of just two universities in Europe offering cartography as a discipline, must have seemed almost within reach and yet a distant dream. Another friend wrote that Abram 'studied and practised [mathematics] without an instructor or teacher, attaining only by his own pains and industry, to the great admiration of others, even to the understanding of the great and deepest mysteries of the same.'

What books might Abram have read? The professor teaching cartography at Leuven in Abram's time was Gemma Frisius. Crippled and orphaned as a young boy, Frisius grew up under the care of his poor stepmother before being offered a place at the university reserved for talented students of limited means. He made the most of the opportunity, and became an astronomer, mathematician, doctor and instrument maker, creating a globe and publishing *De principiis astronomiae et cosmographiae* (*Of the Principles of Astronomy and Cosmography*) as a supplement to it in 1530, in addition to a small volume on surveying three years later. Both books were printed in Antwerp – the most important city in Europe for geographical publications and maps – and it is not improbable that the young Abram Ortel read both of them from cover to cover.

Abram also read travelogues and historical works: Herodotus, Strabo, works about Marco Polo and Ptolemy's *Geography* – probably in the editions published by Sebastian Münster in 1540, 1542 and 1545, the most recent of many versions published since the first translation into Latin over 100 years earlier.

PTOLEMY RETURNS | The European Renaissance began in 1397, when Greek scholar Manuel Chrysoloras arrived in Florence to teach Greek to the Florentine monks. Greek had been studied little by European scholars over the previous 700 years, and the monk Jacopo d'Angelo invited Chrysoloras to Italy after meeting him in Constantinople while he was there to study Greek. D'Angelo returned to Florence with a number of Greek manuscripts, including a copy of Ptolemy's *Geography*, and a certain anticipation spread through the city's humanist circles when Chrysoloras began to translate it – so far scholars had heard only rumours about the work, and been able to read only fragments from it. Jacopo d'Angelo took it upon himself to complete the translation when Chrysoloras moved on to other cities.

In the introduction to the translation of the *Geography*, d'Angelo wrote that Ptolemy showed us how the world looks ('*orbis situm ... exhibuit*'). He also emphasised that the Greek scholar offered something that was lacking in the Latin cartographic tradition – methods for transferring the geography of a sphere onto a flat piece of paper. But d'Angelo lacked the mathematical skills necessary to translate Ptolemy's somewhat complex instructions about how such projections should be created, and consequently the methods were poorly understood by Renaissance readers.

D'Angelo changed the title of the work from the *Geography*, or *Geographia* in Latin, to the *Cosmographia*. In the Middle Ages, the Europeans had no separate term for geography, and a definition of the word therefore had to be given every time it appeared in a translation – usually as 'that having to do with describing the world'. '*Cosmographia*', used by some Roman authors, often served as a synonym, although cosmography describes both the Earth and the heavens. Readers must not forget, d'Angelo reasoned, that the book was primarily concerned with the celestial bodies, since Ptolemy's longitudes and latitudes are based on observations of the Sun, Moon, stars and planets, and therefore show how these bodies influence the Earth. He thereby incorporated the *Geography* into a tradition where astrology and astronomy were two sides of the same coin, and this is how we must understand Ptolemy as being read by early-Renaissance readers: the *Geography* did not suddenly provide the Europeans with a new world view, nor a method of drawing maps that was more scientific than the ones they already had. Instead, they used Ptolemy in the same way they used other maps and astronomical observations – to adjust their existing ideas of the world based on the works of Pliny and the travelogues of the Middle Ages.

We don't know exactly when Florentine scholars started drawing maps based on Ptolemy's list of coordinates, but an undated letter from the early 1400s states that a Francesco di Lapacino was among the first individuals to produce one: 'He did it in Greek, with the names in Greek, and in Latin, with the names in Latin, which had not been done before

---

Next pages | The first known map of the Nordic region, drawn by Danish cartographer Claudius Clavus and published by the French cardinal Guillaume Fillastre in his version of Ptolemy's *Geography* in 1427. For reasons unknown, Claudius believed that the Nordic region had an east–west orientation, rather than north–south. At the bottom is the British Isles, with Scotland buckling towards the east. Iceland is a half-moon-shaped land mass out at sea, and Greenland extends from the west and out above the Nordic region in the north.

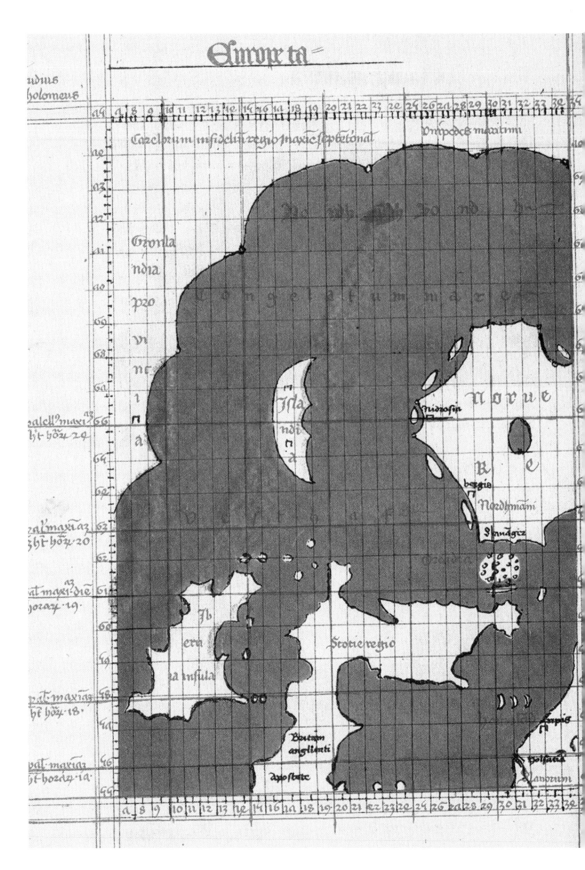

Claudius Clauus

Pigmei maritimi

Griffonum regio vastissima

Wildhlappelandi

Cronelandum mare

Grunnelandi

Dalmij

Berzelandi

Colozby

Staberg

Vermelandi

Gotha

fridhlappi

Douezfyeldh

Suetia Regio

Fio

Stokholm

findland

Damorum Regio

Vesgoti

Oslo

Valandi

Staung

Obezp

Jutones

Elefoni

greato Insidiahns

Domiaia

Perversa prutenou

nago ut nocio

Trez et ulmi patell maxi die hz hou 29

Triz patell maxiaz die ht hou 20

Tro ual maxiaz die ht horazu 19

Tig pat maxiaz die ht horaz 18

C 18 pat maxiaz die ht horazu 1a

Triq pat maxiaz die ht hou 1a et 30 a

Tio pat maxiaz die ht horazu 16

in this way'. In 1423, a Poggio Bracciolini purchased 'some maps from Ptolemy's *Geography*' from a Florentine statesman.

Ptolemy was rediscovered at a time when the southern Europeans were starting to venture out into the world. The Portuguese embarked on expeditions along the African coast to find gold, supplementing their old, heavier ships with caravels – light, manoeuvrable vessels that could also sail up rivers and in shallow waters. In 1418, two Portuguese ships were blown ashore on the island of Madeira in the Atlantic Ocean; they reached the Azores in 1427 and sailed past Cape Bojador on the coast of Western Sahara – known for its fog and inclement weather – in 1434. The Portuguese had long believed that nobody lived any further south than this, but when they reached the Gambia River, south of the Sahara, they had sailed the full length of the Arab trade routes that cut through the desert, and gold and slaves could be transported directly to European ports.

The Europeans now found themselves in the part of the world that classical sources claimed was uninhabitable due to the intense heat. After a church meeting in Florence in 1439, at which the Ethiopian delegates were asked a long list of questions about how far south their country was, the Italian Flavio Biondo wrote that 'Ptolemy, who only knew the smallest initial part of Ethiopia – that contained within Egypt – could not but be ignorant of the regions and kingdoms that lie beyond.'

To the north, Ptolemy's world map stretched no further than the mystical island of Thule at a latitude of 63 degrees north. In 1427, after the *Geography* had reached scholarly circles in Paris, Cardinal Guillaume Fillastre published an edition that included the northern regions. Of the map, Fillastre wrote:

> Beyond that which Ptolemy put here, there are Norway, Sweden, Russia and the Baltic Sea dividing Germany from Norway and Sweden. This same sea, further to the north, is frozen for a third part of the year. Beyond this sea is Greenland and the island of Thule, more to the east. And this fills all the northern region as far as the unknown lands. Ptolemy made no mention of these places, and it is believed that he had no knowledge of them. So that this eighth map might be more complete, a certain Claudius Cymbricus outlined the northern

regions and made a map of them which is joined to the other maps of Europe, and thus there are eleven maps (instead of ten).

This map expanded the Ptolemaic world view to include the countries up to a latitude of 74 degrees north.

THE NORTHERN REGIONS | The map was created by Claudius Claussøn Swart from Denmark – also known by the names Claudius Clavus and Cymbricus – who became familiar with Ptolemy's map while in Rome in 1424. Here, he may also have met Fillastre, who was responsible for maintaining contact with the Christian communities in the north, and together they may have agreed on the need for a map of the northern regions.

Claudius's map shows a Scandinavian peninsula that stretches from east to west, instead of from south to north. To the far west is Nidrosia, and in the east a road runs from Stockholm to Vadstena Abbey, marking the two most important places of pilgrimage in the Nordic countries. The north coast of Scotland is situated directly south of Stavanger, Norway, and the Orkney Islands in the waters between the two, while Iceland is a half-moon-shaped island out to sea. Furthest west is Greenland – the earliest representation of the country on a map. But in line with the beliefs of the time, Greenland is not an island, but part of a North Pole continent that stretches eastwards, north of the Nordic countries, before curving south to meet Russia, around where Novaya Zemlya sits like a potential and often ice-covered bridge between the land masses.

Claudius's influence is evident on the first printed map of the Nordic countries, which was included in a *Geography* printed by Nicolaus Germanus in the German city of Ulm in 1482. On this map, however, Greenland (Engronelant) has been moved to just north of the Nordic countries – it is connected to Russia by a spit of land named Pilappelanth, which in turn is connected to the northern part of Suetia by a spit of land named Gottia orientalis. The name Engronelant crops up again on the northern part of Norway, named Norbegia, further south.

Greenland is again located above Norway on the oldest surviving European globe, created by the German mariner Martin Behaim in 1492. Behaim wrote that the globe was created in accordance with Ptolemy's

Geography, but that 'the far-off places towards midnight or *Tramontana*, beyond Ptolemy's description, such as Iceland, Norway and Russia, are likewise now known to us, and are visited annually by ships, wherefore let none doubt the simple arrangement of the world, and that every part may be reached in ships, as is here to be seen.'

Looking at the globe, it also seems that Asia can be easily reached by ship from Europe, because Behaim underestimated the size of the Earth and placed Japan around where Mexico is located. From the island of Antilia, supposed to be situated out in the sea to the far west and populated by Portuguese who had fled there several hundred years earlier, it is only 50 degrees of longitude to the coast of Japan.

Christopher Columbus used Behaim's globe when he set out to look for the sea route to Asia, travelling westwards later that same year. When his ship was far out to sea, far further west than the old world, he looked towards where Antilia was supposed to be located at 28 degrees north. In his log, Columbus wrote that the island could not be seen, but at two o'clock in the morning on 12 October, as the Moon illuminated a beach some kilometres away, seaman Rodrigo de Triana called out that he had spotted land.

AMERICA | Fifteen years later, German cartographer Martin Waldseemüller began to create a new *Geography*. His original plan included no enlargement of the Ptolemaic view of the world, but he had just obtained a new nautical chart from the Genoan cartographer Nicolò Caveri, which featured large, recently discovered areas in the far west, and a book by Florentine explorer Amerigo Vespucci titled *Mundus novus* (*The New World*) – the biggest bestseller of the age.

Vespucci's book describes a voyage to the east coast of South America, where 'we discovered many lands and almost countless islands (inhabited as a general rule), of which our forefathers make absolutely no mention.' The book was the first to assert that the countries in the west were a separate continent, and not, as Columbus believed throughout his life, the east coast of Asia.

Caveri's map and Vespucci's book gave Waldseemüller new ambitions – he now wanted to do more than simply touch up Ptolemy's earlier work. Instead, he wanted to create a world map that combined Ptolemy's findings with new discoveries, a globe presenting the same, and a book explaining why it was necessary to create something other than yet another version of the *Geography*.

In the spring of 1507, Waldseemüller published the *Cosmographiae Introductio*. In Chapter 7, a fair way into what is a rather dry and theoretical section about the principles of geometry, astronomy and geography, is a passage that would change world geography for ever: 'the fourth part of the earth, which, because Amerigo discovered it, we may call Amerige, the land of Amerigo, so to speak, or America.' In Chapter 9, after describing Europe, Africa and Asia, Waldseemüller elaborates as follows:

> . . . a fourth part has been discovered by Amerigo Vespucci. Inasmuch as both Europe and Asia received their names from women, I see no reason why anyone should object to calling this part Amerige, i.e., the land of Amerigo, or America, after Amerigo, its discoverer, a man of great ability [. . .]. Thus the earth is now known to be divided into four parts. The first three parts are continents, while the fourth is an island, inasmuch as it is found to be surrounded on all sides by the ocean.

The text is remarkably prophetic. In 1507, nobody had yet discovered that America was surrounded by water – it would be another six years before the first European, Spanish explorer Vasco Núñez de Balboa, would cross the continent at Panama to set eyes on the Pacific Ocean, and another thirteen years before Portuguese explorer Ferdinand Magellan sailed around the continent's southern tip.

Waldseemüller's world map was published later the same year. It was large, measuring 240 by 120 centimetres, and divided across twelve sheets – an ambitious example of just how advanced geography had become through the combination of the classical and the modern. This combination of knowledge is expressed at the top of the map – where hundreds of years earlier an image of Jesus watching over the world would have been included, two human representatives of their respective ages with their scientific instruments, a quadrant and a compass, now look down over their respective parts of the world: Ptolemy above the old *oikoumene* – Africa, Asia and Europe – and Vespucci above the new world. The map's full name is '*Univer-*

salis cosmographia secundum Ptholomaei traditionem et Americi Vespucii aliorumque lustrationes' (*The Universal Cosmography According to the Tradition of Ptolemy and the Discoveries of Amerigo Vespucci and others*).

Much of Ptolemy remains in the map, including an over-dimensioned Taprobane (Sri Lanka) out in the Indian Ocean, while elements from the Middle Ages are also included in the form of African cannibals. The way in which the northern regions are represented is recognisable from the work of Nicolaus Germanus: Nidrosia is situated furthest west; Engronelant is north of Norbegia; Thule is south of Bergen with the Orkney Islands to the west; and Finland doesn't exist at all.

The map breaks with Ptolemy's work in the reproduction of the fourth part of the world over in the west. Not only is this the first map to present America as a separate continent – it is also the first on which the name 'America' is used. The representation of the southern part of the continent is so strikingly correct that it makes one wonder whether Waldseemüller had access to sources other than Vespucci's travelogues and the logs of Spanish and Portuguese ships, but if he did, he never mentions them. Along the coast, several rivers and place names are marked, but no names are to be found in the interior – the western areas are a *'Terra ultra incognita'.* At 10 degrees north, the southern part of the continent relinquishes its grip on the northern – America is presented as two large islands. We can see what looks like the Gulf of Mexico and Florida stretching down towards the island of Isabella (Cuba), and here, too, several places along the coast are named, but the western part of the land mass is once again an unknown area. In the north, the continent ends with a straight line and beyond this yet another *'Terra ultra incognita'.*

Other cartographers copied the map and adopted the name America, including Peter Apian (1520) and Sebastian Münster (1532), but after a time Waldseemüller began to have doubts about both the continent and its name. When his world map for inclusion in the *Geography* was completed in 1513, he was content to call America *'Terra incognita',* and on a nautical chart from 1516 went one step further, giving the southern part of America the names *'Terra papagallis'* ('Land of Parrots') and *'Terra nova'* ('New Land'), and naming the northern part *'Terra de Cuba. Asie partis'* ('Land of Cuba, Part of Asia').

Here – as on so many other occasions both before and since – the events of history are steeped in a dark irony. Amerigo Vespucci died in 1512, without ever knowing that an entire continent had been named after him, while the person responsible for this died in 1520 – after changing his mind about both the continent's name, and whether there was actually a continent there at all.

OLAUS MAGNUS | In the summer of 1527, however, history suddenly brightened once more when Swedish archbishop Olaus Magnus travelled to Antwerp and saw Waldseemüller's nautical chart. Although Waldseemüller was wrong when he made America a part of Asia, the nautical chart is far more modest than the speculative world map that had described all 360 degrees of longitude – even though a third of the area was unknown; and all the areas up to 90 degrees north – even though most of what lay above 70 degrees north was likewise unknown. Waldseemüller's nautical chart from 1516 made do with reproducing 232 degrees of longitude – most of America and what we now call the Pacific Ocean was not included. And up in the north, Waldseemüller added a text admitting that he didn't have a very good overview of the northern areas due to the many contradictory accounts from this part of the world.

Olaus Magnus had little choice but to accept this apology – on Waldseemüller's map, the northern regions are little more than a shapeless lump decorated with a four-legged walrus-like creature. Olaus began creating his own map of his part of the world that same year.

For a man of his time, Olaus was extremely well travelled. He made his first voyage abroad as a teenager, if only as far as Oslo, Norway, and studied in Germany from 1510 to 1517. In the spring of 1518, when he was an appointed canon in Uppsala, Sweden, he received a mission from the Pope – to travel northwards selling indulgences to raise money for the building of St Peter's Basilica. Olaus rode up the east coast of Sweden to Ångermanland, then west to Jämtland, and over the mountains to Trondheim in Norway, where it is not unthinkable that he may have met Erik Valkendorf, the geographically skilled archbishop of Nidaros, who two years later wrote a description of Finnmark to provide the Catholic Church with a glimpse of life in the north.

From here, it is difficult to say with certainty where Olaus travelled to next. Did he spend the winter in Nordland, Troms and Finnmark while travelling along the Norwegian coast, or did he only hear about these areas from Valkendorf? Is it true that he was particularly interested in observing the fishing activities around Lofoten and just outside Bergen? Did he see the Moskstraumen tidal eddies and whirlpools with his own eyes? Or did he simply sit in a warm nook by the fire as the archbishop described them? What we do know is that he travelled home via Jämt-land, and one midsummer evening in 1519 found himself in Torneå on the border between Sweden and Finland, where Belarusians, Karelians, Sami, Finns, Bjarmians, Swedes and Norwegians met and traded goods. We don't know how far north Olaus travelled, but he probably visited the chapel at Särkilax, the northernmost outpost in Uppsala Diocese, and from here may have travelled on to Pello, north of the Arctic Circle, where permanent settlements ended. We also know that in 1519 Olaus travelled to Stockholm.

Sweden was experiencing turbulent times. Christian 11, king of Denmark-Norway, took control of the country in 1520 with the support of the Swedish archbishop, but was overthrown in 1523 by Gustav Vasa, who worked to bring about the Reformation. Despite the fact that Olaus re-mained faithful to the Catholic Church, Vasa asked him to participate in negotiations with the merchants in Lübeck and the Netherlands regard-ing access to Swedish ports, probably because the king knew Olaus had a good overview of the Swedish coastline and so would be able to defend the country's interests. Olaus therefore arrived in Antwerp in the summer of 1527, where Abram Ortel had been born on 14 April that same year, and from there journeyed on to Gdansk, where he started work on the map that would give the continent a more accurate idea of the northern regions.

In Poland, Olaus met his old friend the cartographer Bernard Wapowski, and made the acquaintance of Nicolaus Copernicus, who sixteen years later would write *De revolutionibus orbium coelestium* (*On the Revolu-tions of the Celestial Spheres*), in which he proved it is the Earth that moves around the Sun, and not vice versa. Gdansk was buzzing with seafarers and merchants who were familiar with the Baltic Sea, and Wapowski had obtained a map that showed all the trade routes between the Baltic region,

Finland and Sweden. In a letter to a friend, he also expressed his thanks for a map of Denmark, Sweden and Norway he'd been permitted to borrow. In Gdansk, Olaus sat down to combine all this information with the experience he'd gained from his travels – and began to draw.

In 1537, Olaus left Poland for Italy, and in Venice two years later borrowed 440 ducats to finance the printing of his map. But the *Carta marina et descriptio septentrionalium terrarum* (*Marine Map and Description of the Northern Lands*) is more than just a map – in the tradition of the medieval *mappæ mundi*, it also acts as a kind of illustrated encyclopedia, providing information about the Nordic countries' peoples, kings, fauna, religion and natural resources. In 1555, the map was followed by a large work about the history of the Nordic peoples, which explained many of the map's illustrations. 'Here you may see a woman, her hair loose, aiming arrows,' wrote Olaus to explain an image of a couple hunting in Finmarchia, 'nor is it any wonder, because those who live under the celestial Pole find in the huge compass of their forests such rich abundance of game that the men alone would not suffice to hunt them down if their womenfolk did not race to their sides. Therefore the women join the chase with the same swiftness as the men, perhaps even with greater.' In Helgeland, people are described as burning fish on their fires: '*Horum pisciu capitibus utitur loco lignorum*' ('These fish heads are used instead of wood'), wrote Olaus, explaining that fish was so abundant that the heads could be used for firewood.

On Olaus's map, parts of the Baltic Sea are covered by ice – including the Gulf of Finland, where we see two armies, one from 'Moscovie pars', about to enter into combat. This is a reference to a battle that occurred in 1495, when the Muscovites attempted to conquer Viborg by riding over the ice.

Next pages | The first printed map of the Nordic region was included in a *Geography* printed by German cartographer Nicolaus Germanus in 1482. Ptolemy's Scandinavian islands have grown larger and are attached to the mainland, if at a rather imaginative location; Finland is not included, but Norway features the cities of Nodrosia, Bergensis and Stavangerensis. The mythical island of Thule has moved south-west of the Norwegian coast, and Engronelant (Greenland) north of the Nordic region. '*Mare congelatum*' means 'The frozen sea'. The map has been drawn on a slope to simulate the spherical globe.

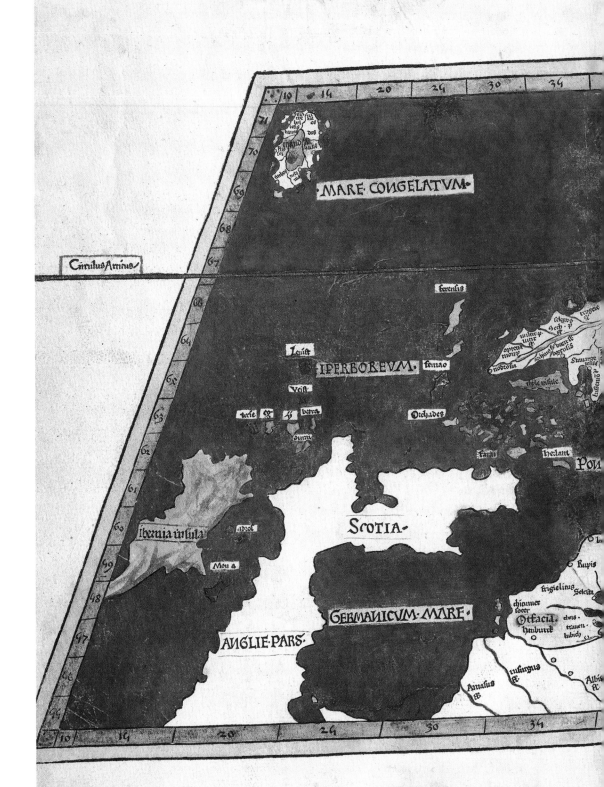

MARE·CONGELATVM·

Circulus Arcticus

IPERBOREVM·

ferenis

feriao

Iquis

Veist

trie· · · betra

dum

Orchades

thile insule

farni

heslant

Pon

Ibernia insula

idrol.

SCOTIA·

Rupis

l.

Mou a

frigielius Selcin

GERMANICVM·MARE·

thiemuer soter

Otfacia

hamburk

ebrs·

trauen·

lubich·

ANGLIE·PARS·

iusingus

ft·

Albis

ft·

Amalus

ft·

Continue quando videlicet sol fuerit in medietate tauri
usque ad medietatem leonis hoc est a principio mensis maij
uz medietate inlij. Et noctem similiter trium mensium
quido sol fuerit insignis: z mensibus 6 oppositis.

Vigesimus nonus paralellus h'us diem maiore duoru mensiu

continue quido videlig. sol siut circa pncipiu gemini usque
ad sine tauri hoc est a medietate mensis maij usque me
dietatem mensis iulij fere

Vigesimus octauº paralellus h'us diem maiorē cōntinue

unius mensis quido videlicet sol siut circa medietate gemi
quoti usque medietatem Cancri hoc est a pncipio uuij
usq; ad finem eiusdem.

Vigesimus septimus par. h'us diem maiore hōz z g. qui videlig.
Sol siut cōa finem geminorū

26. par differt ab equinociali hōz ii hus diem maic in hōz 24

Vigesimus quintus par. differt ab equinociali hōz io
hus diem maiorem horarum 22.

Vigesimus quartus par. differt ab equinociali hōz 9.
hus diem maiore horaru 21.

Vigesimus tercius par. p'hilē. differt ab equnoci
ali hōz 9. hus diem maiore hōz 20.

Vigesimus secundus par. differt ab equinociali
hōz 7½. h'us die maiore hōz 19½.

Vigesimus p'mus par. differt ab equnoci
ali hōz 7. hus die maiore hōz 19.

Vigesimus par. differt ab equnocia
li hōz 6½. hus diem maiore hōz 18½.

19. par. y catur circto ciuij
differt ab equnociali hōz
6. hus diem maiore hōz

18. par. differt ab equ
ali hōz 4½. h'us dy
maiore hōz 17

17. par. differt
ab equnociali hōz
hus die maiore
hōz 17

16. par. di
ab equnociali
hōz 4. hus dyē
maiore hōz

Congelatum

ladi p'mo
na p'mo

Engronelant·

Pilappelanth

Gottia orientalis

Venthelant·

Vermelant·

finlappelant

Suetrique et
gottia
occidentalis

Einlant

liuo
nia

tuderin

staure
na

Aujla

GOTTICVM MARE·

nordvegia·

limapia

bahus
hallaudia

Gottia m·

Scania et Dacia

Bernholn

stlanth

SABVLOSVS·PONTVS·

Sarmacie curope pars·

Selandia

falster

falster

lalant

prīmū
Prussie litus

ura
insula

stetin

danthg

allu
stha

marie pars·

Out in the Norwegian Sea, Olaus has included some digs at the Reformation. On the southern tip of the Faroe Islands, a safe harbour is shown behind a cliff shaped like a monk; swimming just to the west of this is a threatening sea monster with a wild boar's head, sharp tusks, dragon feet and eyes on its flank – the Protestant sea swine. According to Olaus, this creature was observed in 1537 – the year in which the Reformation was completed in Denmark-Norway. Olaus had obtained information about the sea swine from the Italian pamphlet *Monstrum in Oceano*, which stated that the creatures had been observed off the coast of Germany, 'along which shore there also roam very many monsters which have devised for themselves new laws of the Christian faith and religion.'

The kings at various locations around the map have each been allocated a quote from the Bible, and a similar pattern is evident here: the Catholic kings have been given quotes that are full of praise; the Protestant kings quotes filled with condemnation. But Norway is an exception – partly because Norway had no king at the time. The quote allocated to the Norwegian king – '*Nemo accipiat coronam tuam*' ('No one may seize your crown') – must reflect the fact that Olaus viewed Norway as an independent country.

In 1539, the *Carta Marina* was without a doubt the best available map of the Nordic region. Five years earlier, German humanist Jacob Ziegler had published a map that was a clear improvement on its predecessors; he placed the Nordic region in the correct north–south orientation, provided fairly accurate distances, with Vvardhus and Asloia at around 70 and 60 degrees north and included Finland as a separate country, rather than an appendage of Sweden. The representation of Finland was not particularly accurate, however; Denmark extended towards Stafanger and Bergis, Funen and Zealand were dissolved into small islands, Copenhagen was not included, Iceland extended from north to south, and Greenland was attached to northern Norway. Compared to that created by Olaus, Ziegler's map appears rather primitive.

The *Carta Marina* has Denmark snugly positioned between Norway in the north and Sweden in the east; the islands in the Baltic Sea are fairly accurately represented, as is Finland. In the north the Scandinavian peninsula bends off towards the west without linking up with Greenland, showing that it is possible to sail there, and Iceland has its correct east–west shape. But Olaus's original map enjoyed only a short lifetime – probably because it was printed in such low numbers. And perhaps demand for such a gigantic map of the remote Nordic region – as large as 170 by 125 centimetres – wasn't so great. A smaller version, published by the Italian Antonio Lafreri in 1572, was more popular, and it was Lafreri's version that most people became familiar with. Olaus's scaled-down folio edition of his history book also received more widespread attention than his original map – the book was a huge success, and translated into and published in many languages, including Dutch in Antwerp. Here, the folio map would be studied by a renowned cartographer, who to the best of his ability would draw a map of the northern regions for inclusion in what would become the world's first modern atlas.

ORTELIUS | Abram Ortel was twelve years old when the *Carta Marina* was published; this was also the year his father died. Surviving accounts from those who knew him portray him as an earnest young man who took his studies seriously, and everyone seems to have agreed that Abram remained calm, friendly and thoughtful throughout his life – the only thing that disturbed his mild temperament was being interrupted while reading, perhaps because the time he wasn't forced to spend working and earning money was so precious. At some point during his youth – we don't know exactly when – he became an apprentice to an engraver who made maps.

Antwerp's first printing house opened in 1481, and by the time young Abram had started his apprenticeship the city had sixty-eight printing houses, forty-seven booksellers and 224 typographers and publishers.

At this time, the printing houses were replacing their woodblocks with copper plates. Copper made it possible to reproduce far greater detail and was a more durable material, although more expensive and labour-intensive – the drypoint technique used to engrave the pattern on to the copper plates required a skilled hand. In 1547, Abram became a member of the Sint-Lucasgilde, the Guild of Saint Luke, a city guild for artists, engravers and printers – but not as an engraver. He joined the guild as a map colourist – *afsetter van carten*. He never engraved maps himself.

As a member of the guild, Abram Ortel was not only permitted to Latinise his name to Abraham Ortelius; he could also run his own business. Following in his father's footsteps, he founded a shop where he bought and sold antiques, books, coins, art, prints and curiosities. He specialised in maps and items relating to geography and history, as these were the subjects he was most passionate about.

Twice every year, a book fair was held in Frankfurt, attracting people from all across Europe – from Basel, London, Prague and Rome – including printers and booksellers, authors looking for a publisher, publishers looking for authors, and anyone who was interested in obtaining the most up-to-date maps based on the latest information from travellers returning from distant lands. Swarms of people descended on the part of the city between the St Leonhard church and the river, particularly on Buchgasse – Book Street – with its tightly packed rows of stalls occupied by booksellers and purveyors of maps. Abraham Ortelius also came here, both to buy new items and to sell his wares.

MERCATOR | It was in Frankfurt, in 1554, that Abraham Ortelius struck up a friendship with the greatest cartographer of the age – Gerardus Mercator. Ortelius looked up to Mercator even before their meeting – Ortelius was twenty-eight years old and not yet particularly well known, while the 43-year-old Mercator was a celebrated academic, globe maker and cartographer who was read across Europe whenever he published a new work. According to Ortelius, Mercator was 'the Ptolemy of our times.' Their meeting in Frankfurt signalled the start of a long friendship, and the pair exchanged letters and shared geographical information with one another for the rest of their lives.

Mercator was born slightly further down the River Scheldt, in the small town of Rupelmonde, twenty kilometres south of Antwerp. When he met Ortelius, he was dividing his time between Duisburg, the German city to which he had moved after being imprisoned in the Netherlands for religious reasons, and Leuven, where he worked at the university. His father had been a poor shoemaker who died young; his mother had passed away shortly after. Mercator was actually born Gerard Kremer, but was given the name Mercator upon admission to the university under the same scheme for poor students that had enabled Gemma Frisius to attend. Frisius became Mercator's tutor when Mercator began to study mathematics, astronomy and cosmography, and in 1536 the pair collaborated to make a globe commissioned by the king of Spain.

As far back as antiquity, Strabo had believed that the best way to replicate the Earth was on a globe – the Earth is of course round, and any attempt to replicate it on a flat surface necessitates the sacrificing of certain geographical truths. But a globe provides little space for details of the kind you need to navigate a coastline or to find the route from one city to another. Globes are also much more expensive to produce than flat maps on paper.

Over the years, globes had been made out of metal, wood and paper, with the image drawn or engraved directly onto the sphere. In the 1500s, the first sphere to be created from papier mâché was made – this was then covered with a layer of plaster and varnished. Paper strips featuring a drawing of the world were then glued on top of the dried varnish as carefully and accurately as possible.

The paper strips were the most difficult part of this process – the technique required the printing of twelve concave strips that would fit together and form a complete image after being glued to the globe's surface. As mountain ranges, coastlines, rivers and borders often crossed several strips, there was a significant risk of distortions in the final product, and engravers knew that names should be placed on individual strips wherever possible. Painstaking care then had to be taken when gluing the strips into place to avoid wrinkles, misalignment and gaps.

Before starting work on their globe, Mercator and Frisius consulted all the latest maps. Olaus Magnus's map would not be published until the following year, so they used Ziegler's when drawing the northern regions – which at least meant that Finland was included on a globe for the first time in history.

Scholars had also recently begun to understand that the Mediterranean took up a smaller portion of the Earth's surface than the more than 60 degrees of longitude allocated to it by Ptolemy. But reducing the size of the Mediterranean would also result in Spain becoming smaller. This was not something the king of Spain was likely to look upon with favour – Charles v had high hopes that this globe would show the Spanish Empire in all its glory. From a safe distance away in Paris another cartographer, Oronce Finé, had already reduced Spain to half its Ptolemaic size on his

1531 world map, but Frisius and Mercator chose to play it safe and follow Ptolemy's dimensions.

As always, Asia was a work in progress – the eastern areas of the continent were being redrawn almost every year. In 1522, the survivors of Ferdinand Magellan's expedition had returned home to Spain, and the crew's accounts had resulted in the world's largest island, Taprobane – which according to travelogues from the time of Alexander the Great was situated where the small island of Sri Lanka is today – being moved far to the west, as nobody had seen any trace of it in the location it was said to occupy.

South America had stabilised as a kind of triangular-shaped continent, with its tip at the Strait of Magellan in the south; but slightly north of the equator, around today's Central America, was where cartographers' problems began. About what lay north of this, little was certain – and this applied to both the size of the land mass and the question of whether or not it was part of Asia. On his map, Finé had written 'Asia' over a North America and Asia that were joined together, but on their globe, Frisius and Mercator chose to make America a separate continent. Regarding its size, however, they were reserved, making the continent a meagre 30 degrees of longitude across – 83 degrees of longitude too narrow.

Like Ortelius, Mercator had studied the art of engraving, and in doing so had become convinced that Latin characters were far easier to read than the gothic characters that were the norm in northern Europe at the time. Frisius's globe is both the first Dutch map to feature Latin characters, and the first to bear Mercator's signature: 'Gerardus Mercator Rupelmundanus'.

BIBLICAL MAPS | The first map Mercator created was made on commission for a reformer and map collector who wanted a large map of the Holy Land – *Terrae sanctae* – to hang on his wall; a map that would shine with the clarity, precision and beauty that only modern copper-plate printing could provide.

A map of the Holy Land included in a book published by Lucas Brandis in the German city of Lübeck in 1475 is the world's first modern, printed map. The map is modern in the sense that it is based on eyewitness accounts, rather than purely classical and biblical sources

– Brandis drew the map while reading *Descriptio terrae sanctae* by the monk Burchard of Mount Sion, a pilgrim who travelled around the area between 1274 and 1284.

In Mercator's time, Dutch readers were familiar with a map included in the Lutheran Bibles published in Antwerp from the year 1526. The map was drawn by Lucas Cranach, a friend of Martin Luther; its main motif was the journey of the Israelites from Egypt to the Holy Land. The map broke with traditional Catholic imagery, which only illustrated certain scenes from the text. The reformers liked the map because the Israelites' journey symbolised the movement from slavery into freedom; from ignorance to knowledge of God. For them, Egypt represented the corrupt papacy from which they were trying to break free.

A version of this map was used in Myles Coverdale's English Bible – the Bible Ortelius's father Leonard had been involved in printing, and which had resulted in him having to flee Antwerp in order to avoid the Inquisition.

Mercator had grown up with Cranach's map. He also consulted a map of the area drawn by Jacob Ziegler. 'We have drawn this map of Palestine,' Mercator wrote, 'and the Hebrews' route into it from Egypt through the stony regions of Arabia, from Ziegler, the most faithful cartographer of these things.' Although Mercator was unsure how satisfied he was with his map's final result, it was at least an improvement on that drawn by Ziegler, who had never completely finished his version.

In 1538, Mercator announced on a world map what his life's work would consist of – 'a division of the world along broad lines', followed by 'individual maps of particular regions'. The message was brief, but clear – his world map provided an overview of the world, but the next maps would provide detail. Mercator, now twenty-six years old, had decided that he wanted to

Next pages | In 2001, Martin Waldseemüller's large world map from 1507 was acquired by the American Library of Congress for the sum of $10 million because it was regarded as America's birth certificate: the map is the first to apply the name 'America' to the newly discovered lands in the west. But debate about whether these lands constituted a separate continent or were simply the eastern part of Asia continued for some years after Waldseemüller had drawn his map.

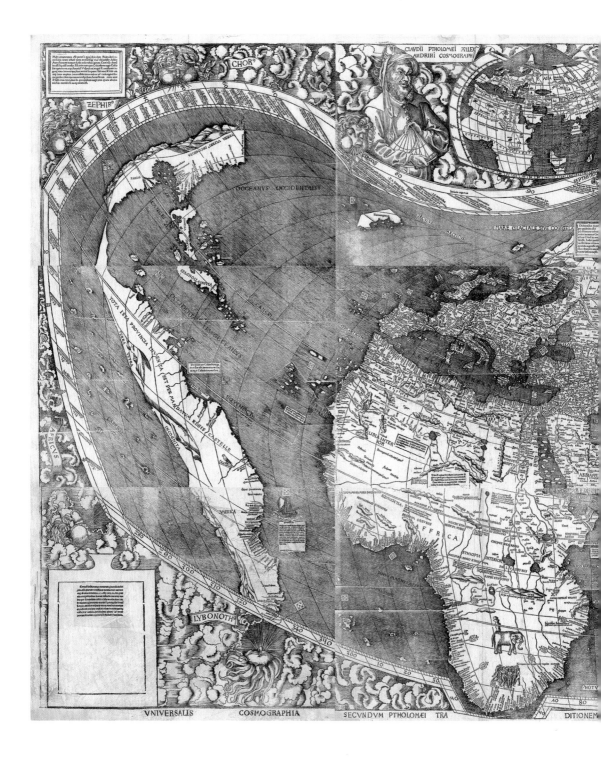

spend his life describing and exploring the world through maps. He hadn't yet seen the sea or mountains – and nor would he, as the great geographer would never travel further from his birthplace than the city of Frankfurt, 400 kilometres away. His world was Flanders, with its fields, canals and church spires, and this was the very first place he wished to map.

The area was in full revolt. In 1537, Ghent, the capital of Flanders, re-fused to make a financial contribution to the king of Spain's war against France. While some citizens fled the city, others took up their weapons and barricaded the city gates, while others fled the city, and a huge festi-val was planned to celebrate the city's illustrious past. Pierre van der Beke created a map of Flanders with clear nationalistic undertones for the oc-casion; this was necessary, he wrote, because 'until now no description has been accurately made, appropriate to the situation of the said country.' The map emphasised Flanders' strategic location between Brussels and the sea, the land cut through with sailable canals, and was richly decorat-ed with caravels and galleys bearing the colours of all the countries that traded goods in the area. After the festival, Charles V sent two messen-gers from Spain to spread the word that he intended to pay the city a visit.

Charles V was highly interested in maps, and may well have seen that created by van der Beke. But Pierre de Keyzere, the man who had print-ed the map, was taking no chances, figuring that both his business and his life would be safer if he published a map re-establishing Flanders as a loyal province as soon as possible. Mercator agreed, as did several merchants and other cartographers, along with the authorities in Brussels. Mercator worked quickly, removing the waving flags and instead decorating the map's upper and lower borders with portraits of the rulers of Flanders up to and including Charles V. The map also featured an extravagant dedication to the king.

We don't know whether the king ever saw Mercator's map, but he was displeased nonetheless. He marched into Ghent with an entourage that took no more than five minutes to break through the barricaded city gates. Thirteen rebel leaders were beheaded, and judges, mayors, six represent-atives from each guild and fifty citizens, dressed in black and with halters around their necks, were forced to walk barefoot from the courthouse to the castle, where they were made to fall to their knees and beg for forgiveness. The city lost all political rights, and an entire district was razed to the ground to make way for a new fortress. Finally, the king took the large city clock away with him. The glorious city of van der Beke's map lay in ruins.

Mercator continued to work on mapping all the world's regions. Never before had anyone published modern, regional maps of the world, which was now known to be much larger than Ptolemy had been aware of, and the project would take time. Unfortunately, time was something that Mercator was lacking – he was continually forced to take on commissions to care for his growing family. Barbara, his wife, had already given birth to two daughters and two sons; another child arrived in 1541, and before long the couple had a total of seven children. Mercator worked every waking moment – whenever high-ranking officials asked him for a new globe, or a printer wanted him to write a book about cartographic typography, he always said yes, and postponed his work on the regional maps. In 1543 he was charged with dabbling in Protestantism and jailed for seven months; the Inquisition ransacked his home, but found nothing. In 1552 Mercator moved to the other side of the Rhine, to the small German town of Duisburg, and it was here that he was finally able to complete the map of Europe he'd been working on for fourteen years.

As he was drawing northern Europe, Mercator took one last look at Ziegler's map before combining it with Olaus Magnus's *Carta Marina* and Dutch nautical charts, which he believed represented the Norwegian coast better than the *Carta Marina* did. The map of Europe 'attracted more praise from scholars everywhere than any similar geographical work which has ever been brought out,' wrote a humanist at the time, and Mercator understood that he had finally published something that would earn him good money.

In good spirits, Mercator travelled up the river to the book fair in Frankfurt, where for the first time he met the 28-year-old map colourist from Antwerp – grey-eyed, golden-haired, and with an idea of how the whole world could be made to fit between the covers of a book.

A ROUGH ATLAS | In 1554, Jan Rademacher, a friend of Ortelius, started working for Gillis Hooftman – 'the well-known merchant of Antwerp' – whose ship traded goods from near and far. Hooftman purchased all the maps he could get his hands on, as this not only helped him to calculate the distances from one place to the next and to understand the dangers that might await his crew should they choose one route over another, but also to keep up to date on the European wars. 'And as the period was rich in disturbing events, he would buy maps of all the parts of the world that existed,' wrote Rademacher in a letter late in life.

Time and again, the enterprising Hooftman – who wasn't one to waste time and would therefore fold out his maps while eating or discussing where it was worth going with others – found that the maps were produced in a format more suited to a wall than to a table full of food and drink. Rademacher suggested that it might be a good idea to gather a number of smaller maps together to make a book, and Hooftman agreed. He therefore tasked Rademacher with finding as many small maps as possible, and Rademacher passed the assignment on to Ortelius. The result was a small book of thirty-eight maps that proved to be extremely practical – Hooftman could now leaf through the maps while sitting at his dining table or in bed. Ortelius had created a rough version of what would become his life's work – the world's first modern atlas.

CHRISTOPHER PLANTIN | Four years later, 31-year-old Ortelius walked into De gulden passer – the Golden Compasses – the printing house and bookshop of Christopher Plantin. Plantin was French, and originally a bookbinder, but became a printer and publisher after a drunken man attacked him with a sword, delivering such a blow to his arm that the injury left him unable to bind books. After Ortelius left, he noted: 'Le 13 Janvier 1558. A Abraham paintre des cartes 1 Virgilius Latin rel. en parchemin' ('13 January 1558. For Abraham who colours maps 1 Virgilius in Latin, bound in parchment').

Like Mercator, Plantin became one of Ortelius's lifelong friends, and not long after their first meeting hired Ortelius to colour thirty-six copies of a map of the landscape of northern France. From the 1560s, Plantin also acquired the original maps that Ortelius had begun to make.

The oldest known map signed by Ortelius is from 1564, a large world map measuring 148 by 87 centimetres, printed across eight sheets, and modelled on the maps of German Caspar Vopel and Italian Giacomo Gastaldi from

1545 and 1561. Ortelius also consulted Marco Polo's travelogues, classical sources including Ptolemy, and Spanish and Portuguese maps, spending much time studying what other cartographers had done and scrutinising everything in the greatest possible detail. The result was a map that reproduced all the latest and most reliable information Ortelius could lay his hands on.

Ortelius's first map had little impact on other maps; nor did the next two maps he completed, one of Egypt and one of the Holy Land, attract much attention. But in 1567, when Ortelius showed Plantin a wall map of Asia, Plantin sensed that significant sales were ahead and purchased 100 copies for one guilder each. This was the success that made Ortelius's name among the cartographers of the age.

In a text addressed to those who viewed the map, Ortelius noted that Giacomo Gastaldi, a worthy geographer, had recently published a map of Asia based on a version by Arab cosmographer Ismael Abulfeda, and had not included the original creator's name. Ortelius never tried to hide the fact that his map was based on Gastaldi's version – through a friend, he had learned that Gastaldi had failed to credit his source, Abulfeda, and criticised Gastaldi for the omission. Ortelius would not make the same mistake when gathering maps he could use in the book he was planning – an expanded and more thorough version of the simple collection of maps he had created in 1554. He carefully noted down the name of the creator of every map he wished to include.

THE WORLD BY LETTER | 'I therefore send you my map of Wales, not completed in all its details, but faithfully drawn,' wrote Welsh cartographer Humphrey Lhuyd to Ortelius in 1568. Ortelius had sent Lhuyd a copy of his map of Asia, simultaneously asking for permission to use

Next pages | Abraham Ortelius's map of the northern regions from 1570. '*Septentrionalium*' was the Latin name for the north, because the Romans called the group of stars known as the Plough '*Septentriones*' – the seven oxen. Because this constellation is always visible in the north, *Septentriones* also became the Roman name for this cardinal direction. Note that Greenland is drawn as an island – this is something Ortelius could not possibly have known at the time, since no Europeans had travelled so far north.

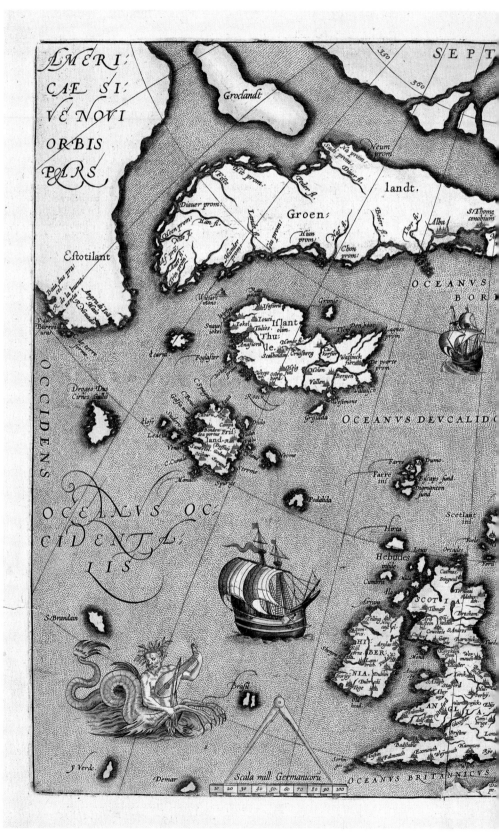

RIO

Parall: 80. gradus lat:

60

50

40

Pigmei hic habitant.

Colgoieue   Pechora

Permia

MARE CON: GELATVM
Petzorke vulgo

Morzouitz

Parall: 70. gradus lat:

Tcutick
Cametick
Stanuvische
Aymu
Canlensche
Stanckwische
C.S. Ioäis

Condora

Mezens

Mezen fl.

Slowoda

Lampas

Morzouitz

C. bone fortune.
P. Penticost.
Zolotitia.
Faßnos.
Polda.

Kouloai

Nicolai

Corpus Christi

Poulogue

S. Michel.

Pin ego,

Santi Rustenes

Motka prom.

Semes saxum & prom: naucis formidabile.

Warahus

Caienska semla

Berge

Scarsigur

Pele.

Olsbi

Lacus Albus

Tetreut
Diauen fl.

Norden borg

Varzina fl.

Colmogro.

S. Nicolas.

Owna

Saloski

Pingo fl.

Biarmia

Serickfinnia

Onega fl.

RVSSIA.

ORIENS.

Warahus

Carleborg

Parall: 60. grad: latitud:

BOD.

DIA.

FIN:

LANTS
VERMO

Nouogrod

Lodoga

Kexholm

Onegaborg

Iegobor

Egropt

Lapauesi

Ecclesia noua

Corela

Pskoue

Narua fl.

Ceutzko

Derbt

Wildmar

Marienborch

Liuoniæ pars.

SVEDIA.

Baddicus

Finmar

N.OR.

GOTIA

NIA.

DA.

Oostsee

Bornholn

Prussiæ pars.

Pomeraniæ pars.

maniae pars.

GER.

DI.

G

Cum priuilegio.

Curouia

Nobil

Dune borg

Candau

Liba

Memmel

Ragnet

Coningsberg

Dantzg   Marien: werd:
Gaudentz.

Stolpin

Coslin

Camin

Stetin

Vistula fl.

SEP TEN TRI ONA LIVM RE GIONVM DESCRIP.

Lhuyd's map of Wales in his forthcoming book as he knew it was the best available map of the region. Lhuyd continued: 'You will also receive a map of England with its ancient and modern names, and another map of England tolerably accurate.'

Ortelius had a large network of cartographers and geographers he could contact to obtain the best possible maps. Historian Johannes Pannonius sent him a map of Transylvania, English explorer and diplomat Anthony Jenkins gave him a map of Russia and so on and so forth, until Ortelius had a large pile of maps to work from.

Ortelius redrew all the maps he received in the format of his new book, editing and improving them wherever possible. This process, which no one had ever attempted before, gave the maps a standardised appearance. The Italians had a tradition of creating books of maps by gathering individual maps together and binding them, but these maps were all of different sizes and featured varying typography, symbols and colours – Ortelius's atlas is known as the first of its kind because he aimed to create a standardised depiction of the world between the covers of a book. It was a huge undertaking, and took its toll – in July 1568 Ortelius wrote a letter to a doctor friend describing the heart palpitations he'd been experiencing.

After Ortelius had drawn the maps he passed them to his good friend Frans Hogenberg, one of the best engravers of his time, who incised them onto copper plates. In determining the order in which the maps should be presented, Ortelius followed 'Ptolemy, prince of geography', who recommended opening with a world map before presenting the countries from the north-west to the south-east. In September 1569, Ortelius purchased forty-seven rolls of paper from Plantin. He paid for the publication himself.

At this time, however, Plantin was occupied with printing a multilingual version of the Bible in eight volumes, which is probably why he didn't have time to print the first edition of his friend's atlas. Ortelius therefore approached Gillis Coppens van Dienst, a master printer with over thirty years' experience with maps and cosmographic works, and it was van Dienst who noted down the day on which the *Theatrum orbis terrarum* was published – 20 May 1570.

THE EYE OF HISTORY | 'Abrahamus Ortelius of Antwerp to the benevolent reader,' begins Ortelius's preface. 'Seeing, that as I think, there is no man, Gentle Reader, but knoweth what, and how great profit the knowledge of histories, doth bring to those which are serious students therein, I do verily believe and persuade myself, that there is almost no man [...] that is ignorant how necessary, for the understanding of them aright, the knowledge of Geography is, which in that respect therefore which is of some, and not without just cause, called the eye of history.'

To make this connection between history and geography was not unusual. In the Middle Ages, certain church fathers emphasised that knowledge of the Holy Land's geography resulted in a greater understanding of holy scripture. During the Renaissance, the connection followed the scientific reproductions of a world that had become much larger and much more accurately described than previously – reproductions that meant people could now 'see things that were done, and where they were done, as if they happened in the present,' as Ortelius put it – almost like watching events unfold in a theatre.

For the first time, those who could afford it were now able to purchase the whole world, bound within a book. The cover of the *Theatrum* presents four and a half continents represented by female figures. At the top, Europe sits on a throne, wearing a crown, two globes placed to her left and right. Directly beside her is a third globe, which she's holding with the help of a cross, as she's responsible for bringing Christianity to the world.

Asia is also clad in noble robes, but has a tiara rather than a crown, and is subordinate to the European queen, as is Africa – more sparsely clad and wearing a halo inspired by the Sun to emphasise the heat where she lives. At the very bottom is their American sister, but little about her is reminiscent of the advanced civilisations – the Incas, Mayans and Aztecs – encountered there by the Spanish. This is primitive, cannibalistic America, holding a European man's head in her hand – naked and armed, she is a femme fatale who both seduces and devours European men. Beside her is a bust that represents the as yet only partly discovered continent furthest south: '*Terra australis nondum cognita*' – 'The southern land not yet known'.

AUSTRALIA | The ancient Greeks had long ago imagined that there must be large, unknown land masses south of the equator. 'There must be a region bearing the same relation to the southern pole as the place we live in bears to our pole,' wrote Aristotle in his *Meteorology*. In around the year AD 400, Roman philosopher Macrobius drew a map featuring a large, cold continent far to the south: '*Frigida Australis*'. Magellan believed that he had the southern continent on his port side when in 1520 he sailed through the strait between the islands of Tierra del Fuego and the American mainland.

'Some call this southern continent "Magellanicam" after its finder,' Ortelius has written on *Terra australis*, and on the part of the continent located below South America he uses the name Magellan gave the region: '*Terra del Fuego*'. Further away, below Africa, he has written '*Psitacorum regio*' – 'Region of Parrots'. The name is Portuguese, and has resulted in speculation about whether the Portuguese had already mapped parts of Australia at this time in connection with their trading activities with the Spice Islands slightly further north, and whether Ortelius had access to these maps. This suspicion is strengthened by the fact that Ortelius has drawn in a strait between New Guinea and *Terra australis* – a strait that was not officially discovered by the Europeans until Spanish explorer Luís Vaz de Torres sailed through it in the year 1606.

That same year, Dutch navigator Willem Janszoon became the first European we know of to map parts of the northern coast of Australia and go ashore there. It would then be another thirty-six years before another Dutchman, Abel Tasman, embarked on a long voyage south to find a place on *Terra australis* rumoured to be full of gold. While he didn't find what he was looking for, he did discover the island of Tasmania south of Australia, and was the also first European to reach New Zealand and subsequently map parts of these two islands. In 1644, Tasman travelled to the north and north-west coasts of Australia, thoroughly mapping this region and dubbing it '*Niew Holland*'. A world map from two years later is the first to feature New Zealand.

But since the Dutch found neither spices nor gold, nor anything else of value in these areas, they soon lost interest, and the rest of the region remained unknown until the British captain James Cook mapped

New Zealand in 1769 and the east coast of Australia in the following year. But the question of whether or not the south coast was linked to a large continent at the south pole remained open. Only when British navigator Matthew Flinders sailed around the entire continent and published the 'General chart of *Terra Australis* or Australia: Showing the parts explored between 1798 and 1803 by M. Flinders Commr. of H.M.S. Investigator' was Australia no longer a '*nondum cognita*'.

A SUCCESS | The first edition of *Theatrum orbis terrarum* contained sixty-nine maps. To create these, Ortelius built upon the work of eighty-nine cartographers, and named each and every one of them – the list is a kind of *Who's Who* in European cartography at the end of the 1500s. Mercator, of course, features here, represented by '*Palæstinæ, siue Terræ Sanctæ*' and '*Item Flandriæ*', together with Humfredus Lhuyd ('*Angliæ Regni Tabulam*'), Antonius Ienkinsonus ('*Rußiam*') and Olaus Magnus Gothus ('*Regionum Septentrionalium Tabulam*').

On the world map – '*Typus orbis terrarum*' – is a quotation from the Roman politician and lawyer Cicero, which provides a glimpse of the deeper meaning Ortelius saw in cartography: '*Quid ei potest videri magnum in rebus humanis, cui aeternitas omnis, totiusque mundi nota sit magnitudo*' ('For what human affairs can seem important to a man who keeps all eternity before his eyes and knows the vastness of the universe?').

After the world map come the maps of the continents: '*Americae Sive Novi Orbis, Nova Descriptio*'; '*Asiae Nova Descriptio*'; '*Africae Tabula Nova*' and '*Europae*'. England, Scotland and Ireland have the honour of being the first countries to have individual maps included, since Ortelius had no maps of the westernmost, American countries to include in the first edition. The order in which the maps are presented is as classical as Ptolemy, and as modern as that which can still be found in atlases today.

In his preface, Ortelius apologises that many readers will search the atlas for a map of their homeland in vain. He assures these readers that the missing maps have not been consciously omitted, overlooked or left out because he didn't wish to spend money on them, but rather because he was unable to find maps of a high enough quality for inclusion. Ortelius therefore encourages readers who either have or know of maps he might use in the next editions of the atlas to send them to him, so that 'hereafter they may be inserted into this our book.'

This was a relatively common strategy among cartographers at the time – on his map of Europe, Mercator had appealed to the 'benevolent reader' to supply him with cartographic sketches and astronomical coordinates for use in his next project. Such requests formed the basis for a productive collaboration between cartographers and the public – a friend sent Ortelius a map of Moravia, and one day he received a letter and enclosed map of Sina from an Italian, who encouraged Ortelius to use the map in his next edition of *Theatrum*, 'which, I believe, will soon be necessary.'

The atlas sold well – the first printing of 325 copies was followed by a second just three months later, and the Dutch translation, *Theatre oft Toonneel des Aerdtbodems*, was published the following year. The French and German editions were published in 1572: *Théâtre de l'univers* and *Theatrum oder Schawbüch des Erdtkreijs*. 'All extol your *Theatrum* to the skies and wish you well for it,' wrote one enthusiastic reader, and in a letter to Ortelius dated in 1570, Mercator wrote: 'I have examined your *Theatrum* and compliment you on the care and elegance with which you have embellished the labours of the authors, and the faithfulness with which you have preserved the production of each individual, which is essential in order to bring out the geographical truth, which is so corrupted by map-makers.'

Most of the individuals who purchased the *Theatrum* were academics and wealthy citizens. The atlas was uncoloured, but those who wanted a coloured copy could pay Anne Ortel or another colourist to colour it for them. In May 1571, Plantin noted that Mynken Liefrinck, one of his employees, had received six guilders and fifteen stuivers for colouring an entire atlas – around the same price as that paid for the book. Some years later, Liefrinck was handsomely rewarded for a magnificent edition for the Spanish court, painted in in silver and gold: '*Afgeset een Theatrum in Spaens met gout ende silver tot 36 fl.*' – thirty-six guilders.

Less affluent readers could buy the entire atlas unbound, as a sheaf of separate sheets, or purchase individual map sheets of the areas they were interested in – these cost two stuivers each, or five if they were coloured.

The *Theatrum orbis terrarum* was continually improved and expanded as Ortelius both added new maps and replaced outdated ones. The

1573 edition includes sixty maps – seventeen more than the first edition – and in 1579, when Plantin finally had capacity to print the atlas, the book featured ninety-three maps. Ortelius continued to maintain contact with the world's most prominent cartographers, including Mercator, who in 1580 wrote to Ortelius to inform him that he had heard of someone creating a wonderful new map of France, and that he himself had received a new world map, on which the Far East was depicted particularly well. Ortelius enthusiastically replied that English sea captain Francis Drake had embarked on a new expedition, while Mercator responded that captain Arthur Pitt had set out to explore Asia's northern regions, and that he would probably return home across the north side of the American continent. In this way, they kept each other informed about the world while *Theatrum* continued to grow, and in 1591 the atlas reached its largest format, containing a total of 151 maps.

In December three years later, Ortelius received a letter: 'Gerardus Mercator died on the 2nd inst. about midday sitting in a chair as if about to take a nap before the fire.'

In January 1598, Ortelius wrote to a nephew: 'Farewell, I write no more for I am dying from day to day.' In July, one of Ortelius's friends wrote to the same nephew: 'I therefore inform you that the pious Abraham Ortelius died and rested in the Lord on June 28 and was very decently buried in the Church of St Michael, mourned by many good people who still wished him to live; but his course was to end [...]. He is at rest, we still moving.' Anne outlived her brother by two years.

Ortelius died unmarried and childless, but sold 7,500 copies of *Theatrum orbis terrarum*. Plantin's children and grandchildren took responsibility for the last editions of the atlas, right up until the year 1612.

EPIGRAPH | In 1630, one of Plantin's grandsons wrote that he did not wish to publish a new edition of Ortelius's atlas – that it was better to allow Ortelius to remain the Ptolemy of his time. Perhaps the old geographer would have shed a tear of joy to hear the comparison – which he had once used to complement Mercator – applied to himself.

With his life's work, Ortelius had rendered Ptolemy redundant, and now it was he who had become a monument to time past. Ptolemy remained a source for almost 1,500 years – mostly because the time around him had seemed to stand still. But Ortelius was set aside just thirty years after his death, although this is probably as he would have wished – being so indefatigably critical of maps and discarding those that were unfit for purpose or outdated, including his own. Ortelius understood that maps are not set in stone. On the copper plates, the engravers polished out incorrect city names to engrave new ones; hammered out mountain ranges that had been located too far north; and added new information brought home on the merchants' ships. The world was in a state of constant change. Ortelius raised the curtain on the theatre of the world – but others played on. The atlas quickly became established as a standard of the cartographic tradition for which there was great demand.

THE BUSINESS | The maps of the Renaissance were a continuation of the late-medieval nautical charts – generally created with practical purposes in mind, rather than religious ones, and influenced by the Europeans' increasing voyages out into the world. The translation of the works of Ptolemy into Latin in the early 1400s resulted in a gradual change in direction to a more scientific and experience-based attitude to map-making, and a more professional one – individuals like Abraham Ortelius and Gerardus Mercator were among the first to make a living from their maps as an enterprise. The art of printing enabled a distribution of maps that would have been impossible when every single copy had to be drawn by hand; rich merchants, diplomats, professors, aristocrats and others had the necessary funds to finance increasingly accurate and up-to-date maps. In the Middle Ages, a schematic map from the year AD 800 might appear in a book published 400 years later, but in the Renaissance maps had a much shorter lifetime.

In 1533, Dutch cartographer Gemma Frisius published a small book about land surveying. This drawing shows how he constructed a network of triangles starting in Antwerp, and used simple geometry to calculate the distances to the neighbouring cities of Bruxel (Brussels), Mittelburgum (Middelburg), Louamum (Leuven) and others. His method was used all the way up until the invention of positioning using satellites.

Dese figure bewijst dat eerste Capittele
datment metter ooghen mercken mach.

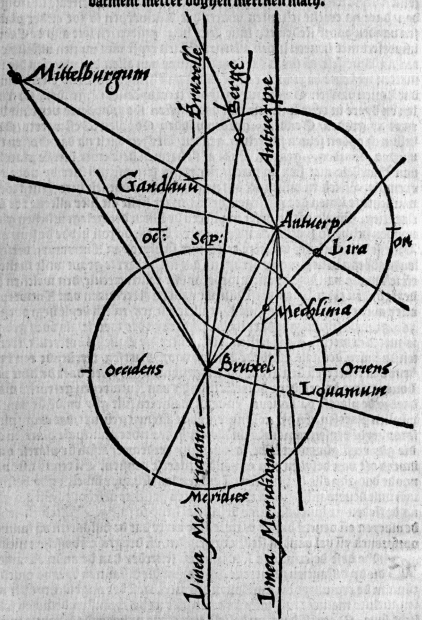

Middelburch . 30. graden van twesten na tnoozden/ Bergen opden zoom 20. graden vanden Noozden Westwaerts. En dese plaetsen selen v ghe- noech zijn voor een exemple. Dit nu hebbende/so stelle ick een punct inde middelt van eenigen planen dinghe/ dwelck Antwerpen beteeckent/ ende ick make van dyen puncte eenē circule/ den welcken ick in. 4. deelen deyle

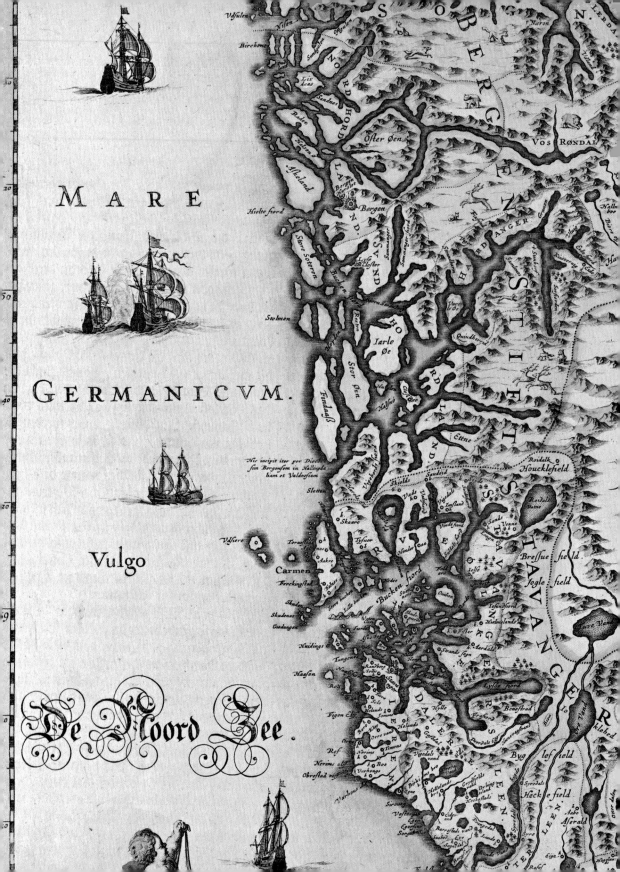

Venturing Out

Hardangerfjord, Norway
59° 36′ 18″ N
5° 12′ 41″ E

This is where the journey through the Diocese of Bergen to Hallingdal and Valdres starts. The bishop of Stavanger, Laurids Clausen Scavenius, sails into the Hardangerfjord between Ryvarden and Bømlo in western Norway, past the old abbey on the island of Halsnøy, to visit the most remote areas of his diocese. At the innermost end of the fjord, at the village of Eidfjord, a crew is waiting to transport him over the Hardanger mountains to the long valleys in the east. Scavenius takes notes along the way, with the intention of drawing a map.

Scavenius is responsible for a geographically challenging and divided diocese. Since the year 1125, the cathedral in Stavanger has been responsible for the inland areas of Hallingdal and Valdres, but since they border on Trondheim to the north, Bergen to the west and Oslo to the south, Scavenius is forced to travel through the Diocese of Bergen in order to visit them. Scavenius grew up in Copenhagen and studied in northern Germany, and so at the time of his consecration on Whit Sunday in 1605 had never before seen a fjord or a mountain. As he sails into Eidfjord, Mount Oksen and the peak of Toraldsnuten shoot straight up from the water, rising 1,240 metres into the sky on either side of him. As he makes

Excerpt from the 1644 edition of Johannes Janssonius's map of the Diocese of Stavanger from 1636. The map states that the bishop of Stavanger's journey through the Diocese of Bergen starts south-west of the island of Findaass (Bømlo).

his way over the mountains he can see the Hardangerjøkulen glacier when the weather clears.

Scavenius notes down distances and the names of bridges, rivers, mountains, villages and lakes: Vatnedal, Lia bro, Brommen, Biordals Vand, Fielde field and Marrete Stuen. He had already familiarised himself with the Diocese of Stavanger, entering a list of the incomes of each parish and deanery in his land register, *Gràgàs*. After returning from his journey to Hallingdal and Valdres, back home in his episcopal palace, he uses his notes to complete an area of the map he is working on.

Scavenius's original map has unfortunately not survived, but we know of its existence because some years later a Danish historian wrote that the map was created in 1618, and because Dutch cartographers Joan and Cornelius Blaeu printed the map *Dioecesis Stavangriensis & partes aliquot vicinæ, opera L. Scavenii, S. S (Diocese of Stavanger and Some Adjacent Regions, prepared by L. Scavenii, S. S)* in 1638.

Nor do we have any papers from the episcopal archives, or Scavenius himself, that give any indication of how the map was created. But what we do know is that Peder Claussøn Friis, a parish priest in Undal and provost of the Deanery of Lister, and author of the book *Norriges og omliggende Øers sandfærdige Bescriffuelse (A Truthful Description of Norway and the Surrounding Islands)*, also wrote *Stavanger Stifts Bescriffuelse (A Description of the Diocese of Stavanger)*, and gave this to Scavenius some time around the year 1608. Friis was primarily familiar with the southern part of the diocese – about Hallingdal and Valdres he knew little more than that the mountains 'between Setesdal and Hallingdal are called Halnefield' and 'between Hallingdal and Hardanger is Hardangersfield'.

Scavenius's source for the coast to the north of his diocese – the part of the Diocese of Bergen he had to sail through to reach Eidfjord – was a map of western Norway drawn by the bishop of Bergen, the Dane Anders Foss, some years earlier. This map has survived, and is the oldest surviving map of a part of Norway to be drawn by someone who lived there.

The map presents the region of Vestlandet (western Norway) from the Trondheimsfjord to just south of Stavanger, and although the map is only a sketch, it is far more accurate than the Dutch nautical charts that best represented Norwegian waters at this time, and clearly the result of much hard work. All the fjords and islands within the diocese are accurately located, and an entire 700 place names and 120 churches are marked. To the north and south of the Diocese of Bergen, however (i.e. north of the Stad peninsula and south of the municipality of Karmøy), the representations are fairly approximate, which emphasises the fact that this is a diocese map.

The Diocese of Bergen included Nordfjord in the region of Fjordane, a county given to the Danish astronomer Tycho Brahe by the king. Brahe obtained most of the income required to run his large Danish observatory from here – the fjord's farmers paid him taxes in the form of dried fish, animal skins, tar, butter, cheese and small amounts of money. Brahe's income from the county amounted to around 1,000 daler (the Scandinavian currency at the time) per year.

Anders Foss was a friend of Brahe's, who often made visits to the astronomer's observatory and gave him his map of western Norway in 1595. Brahe wrote the words '*Descriptiones littorum Noruagiae & quedem alia*' ('Descriptions of Norway's coasts and some other areas') on the map, packed it up, and took it with him when leaving Denmark after losing his royal support some years later. The map then remained lost for 300 years, until it was rediscovered among Brahe's posthumous papers.

It was therefore via Scavenius's copy that Foss's map became a part of the geography of the 1600s. The bishop of Stavanger, who most likely discussed geography with the bishop of Bergen whenever they visited one another, must have drawn the stretch of coastline from Bømlo and down to Karmøy on his map – the part of the Diocese of Bergen through which the bishops of Stavanger must travel. Scavenius noted this at the mouth of the Hardangerfjord: '*Hic incipit iter per Diocesim Bergensem in Hallingdaliam et Valdresiam*' ('Here starts the journey through the Diocese of Bergen to Hallingdal and Valdres').

BLUE WILLEM | Brothers Joan and Cornelius Blaeu retained this text when they redrew the map before printing it in 1638. But from what source did they obtain Scavenius's map? We simply don't know. All we know for sure is that maps, in the pockets of travelling traders, seamen and military personnel, often moved throughout the landscapes they described – and sometimes even beyond them.

Joan and Cornelius made up the second generation of the map dynasty founded by their father Willem, who was born Willem Janszoon in 1572. As an adult, Janszoon took his grandfather's nickname *'Blaeu Willem'* – 'Blue Willem' – as his surname. The Janszoons were a merchant family, but Willem had a passion for mathematics, and so ended up at Tycho Brahe's observatory in the year 1595 – the same year that Bishop Foss visited Brahe and gave him the map of western Norway. If Blaeu had taken a copy of the map with him upon returning home, perhaps Foss's map might have been included in one of Blaeu's many atlases long before 1638.

In 1605, Blaeu established himself as one of Amsterdam's many booksellers and printers. The city had taken up the position Antwerp had lost twenty years earlier, when the Spanish had given Antwerp's Protestant population four years in which to leave. The Republic of the Seven United Netherlands, which had earned itself a hard-won kind of independence in 1579, benefited greatly from all the talented individuals fleeing Spanish rule and making their way north. Blaeu acquired premises in the district of Op het water ('By the water'). Not only was the area teeming with ships and seamen, it was also the heart of publishing in the city, and a central location for booksellers. Blaeu hung a sign featuring a golden sundial and opened his shop, *De vergulde sonnewijser.*

The Dutch East India Company had been founded in Amsterdam just three years before Blaeu arrived in the city, and was the Dutch answer to the Spanish and Portuguese spice trade with the Indonesian islands. Although the Dutch lacked the resources and crews of the Iberians, they had printers, engravers and cartographers who could disseminate the latest geographical information via maps, globes and atlases. Ortelius, Mercator, Waldseemüller and others proved that it was possible to make a living from producing maps, and in 1590s Amsterdam a large number of cartographers competed to offer the trading companies the best maps available. The Spanish and Portuguese stuck to hand-drawn maps in a futile attempt to keep the information about their trade routes secret.

During the 1500s, the production and sale of nautical charts, pilot books and maritime atlases developed into an independent branch of cartography, and as the waters of northern Europe started to equal trade regions such as the Mediterranean in importance, these areas were also more thoroughly mapped. The first pilot books were handwritten texts combining descriptions of navigable waterways, ports and the tides with simple maps and drawings of landmarks along the coasts, and were created by experienced seamen, rather than cartographers.

The first printed pilot book, *De kaert vader zee* (*Nautical Chart*), was published by Jan Seuerszoon in 1532, and provided detailed descriptions of the North Sea coast, France, Spain and the south coast of England, as well as information about how to sail to Norway, Gdansk, Gotland, Riga and Tallinn.

Lucas Janszoon Waghenaer set a new standard when he published his *Spieghel der zeevaerdt* (*Mariner's Mirror*) in 1584. This was a two-volume work in the same format as Ortelius's *Theatrum*, also printed by Christopher Plantin in Antwerp, and a clear indication that the Dutch were setting sail for ever more distant horizons. In the preface, Waghenaer explains that he himself sailed from the Spanish city of Cádiz to the western coast of Norway. One route map covers the area from the North Cape to the Canary Islands, and from Iceland to the Gulf of Finland, and in Waghenaer's subsequent publication, *Thresoor der Zeevaert* (*Treasure of Navigation*), the maps also covered the Norwegian coast along the entire county of Finnmark all the way to Arkhangelsk. A notable feature of the maps of Norway created by the Dutch was the denoting of so many lumber mills – '*zaghe*' and '*zaghen*'. For the Dutch, Norway was first and foremost a place to purchase timber for shipbuilding, and the reason they called the Oslofjord '*Zoenwater*' – the town of Son in Akershus was an important port of export for timber.

Not wanting to miss out, Willem Blaeu jumped on the pilot book bandwagon and published his *Het licht der zeevaert* (*The Light of Navigation*) in 1608 – the work that represented his breakthrough as a cartographer. The book followed the same template as that used by Waghenaer – a rectangular format featuring a number of chapters of text along with outline drawings of the coastlines. The book was innovative in that Blaeu used the astronomy he had learned from Brahe to make the navigation more accurate, but it also shamelessly copied Waghenaer's content. This didn't stop Blaeu from protesting loudly when he himself became the victim of plagiarism, however – or from requesting that the authorities protect him from the vultures who made pirated copies of his maps as soon as the pilot book was published. He could provide for his family honestly and by the grace of God, he claimed – if only certain people would stop copying his maps before the ink had even dried.

Blaeu was not the only cartographer to complain – plagiarism flourished in the 1500s and 1600s, and a cartographer might easily accuse another of stealing a valuable detail he had recently received from a sailor who had just returned home. Some even went as far as intentionally including minor geographical errors – a non-existent city or lake – in order to find out whether their maps were being copied by others. Cartographers might collaborate, only to later get into a heated disagreement where insults and court cases flew thick and fast, before agreeing to collaborate on new projects once again. Cartographers are human too, after all.

In 1618, cartographer Johannes Janssonius moved into the property next door to Blaeu. The two were already acquainted, having fallen out in 1611 when Janssonius published a world map suspiciously similar to one Blaeu had created three years earlier, and ending up as neighbours only intensified what would become a long and active hostility towards one another. Just two years later, when the copyright on *The Light of Navigation* expired, Janssonius printed his own version, under the same title and using the same title page, not even bothering to remove Blaeu's name. Blaeu responded by publishing a new and better book: *Zeespiegel* (*Sea Mirror*).

Janssonius was married to Elisabeth, the daughter of Jodocus Hondius, a Flemish cartographer who had fled Flanders in 1584 to escape the religious conflicts. Hondius had established himself in Amsterdam in 1593, where four years later he would draw a map of the Nordic region that would come to play an important role in Danish-Norwegian history.

VOYAGE TO THE NORTH | One day in 1597, King Christian IV of Denmark was given Hondius's map by his advisors, and saw that Hondius had drawn Sweden as extending all the way to the Varanger Peninsula with access to the sea in the north. Northern Norway was cut in two –

Vardøhus and its environs were isolated from the rest of the kingdom of Denmark-Norway.

The map made the king see the seriousness of the situation: Swedish and Russian expansion posed a threat to the old hereditary areas. As one of the king's advisors wrote: 'Not so long ago, Kola belonged to Norway, but due to the oversights of the Danish and Norwegian commanders, the Russians have been able to take possession of the area.' The English, Dutch, Scots and French also sailed through Danish-Norwegian waters – 'per fretum nostrum Norvagicum' ('our Norwegian straits') – to undertake trading activities on the Kola peninsula, and most failed to pay the toll demanded by the king in Vardø.

Christian IV started investigations into what his 'evil neighbour' – Sweden – was doing to gain access to the sea and then decided to personally inspire his subjects. In April 1599, the royal ship set sail from Copenhagen along with seven others, all setting their course for the far north. Flying his colours to show his supremacy, the king sailed all the way to Kola – the voyage a demonstration of power affirming Denmark-Norway's right to the northern regions.

The Swedes, however, did not surrender so easily. For King Charles IX of Sweden, the mapping of Finnmark was of primary interest, and so in 1603 he tasked civil servant Andreas Bureus with drawing a map of the Nordic countries. Nine years later, Bureus submitted to King Gustav II Adolph of Sweden his *Lapponia* map – a prelude to his large map of the Nordic region that was yet to be finished. Bureus took measurements and made observations as he travelled around on public business, gathering information about the other Nordic countries – and here Scavenius pops up again. At some point, Bureus obtained a copy of Scavenius's map of the Diocese of Stavanger. Where Bureus obtained the

Next pages | Mercator's famous map of the world is actually a nautical chart intended to make it easier to navigate between the continents. Note the map of the North Pole at the bottom left. Mercator added to this because he knew that his projection contorted the geography of the polar region beyond comprehension. Various versions of his projection continue to be used today.

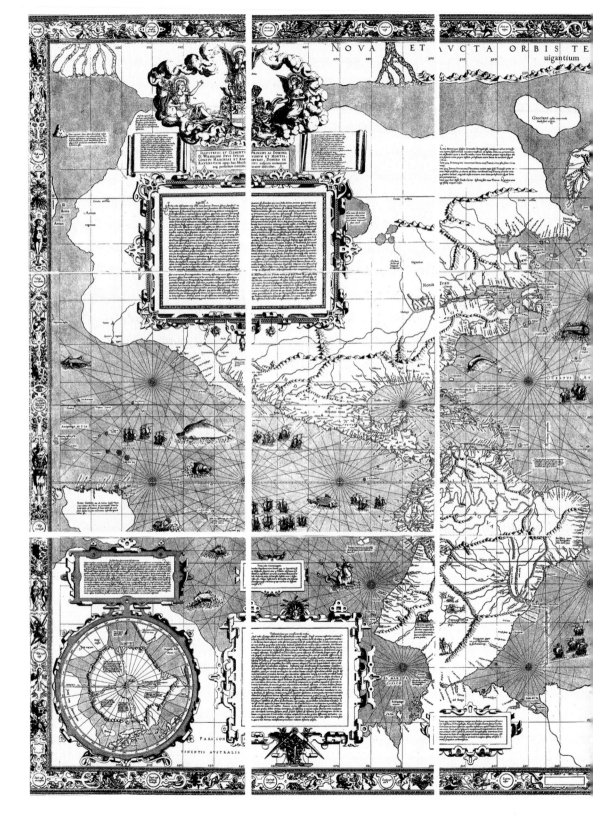

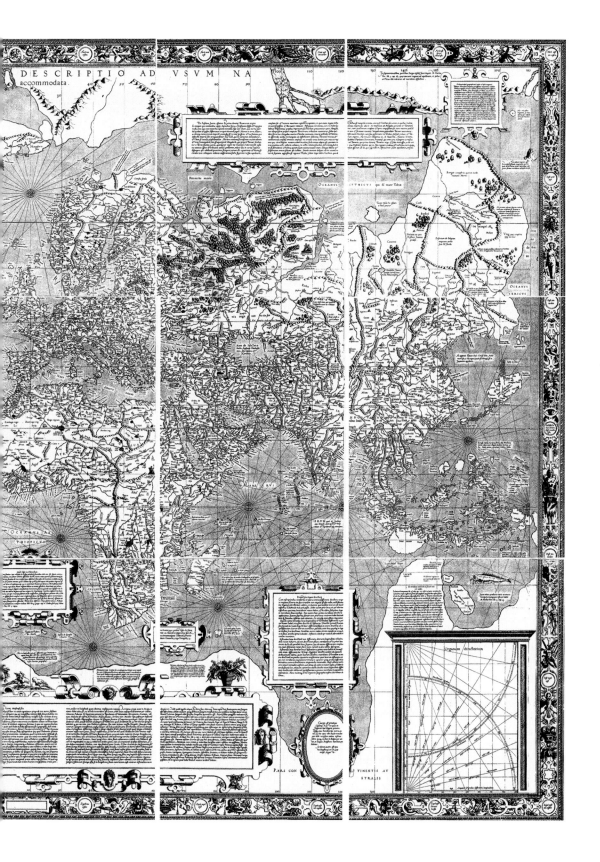

map is unclear, but like Scavenius, Johannes Rudbeckius, the bishop of Västerås in Sweden, drew a map of his diocese, and may have received a map from his Norwegian colleague, which he then allowed Bureus to copy. Regardless, the reproduction of the Diocese of Stavanger on Bureus's map completed in 1626 – *Orbis arctoi nova et accurata delineatio* (*New and Accurate Section of the Northern World*) – is clearly based on Scavenius's map.

The king of Sweden was extremely pleased with the map, which allocated Sweden far larger areas in the north than the country actually possessed. He decided that the map should be printed and sent to all the regents of Europe, and Bureus's map thereby became the template for the cartographic representation of the Nordic region throughout the 1600s. Jodocus Hondius the Younger, brother-in-law to Johannes Janssonius, got hold of a copy in the year it was published, and his map of Europe from 1632 shows that Sweden had increasing access to northern waters.

Like the Blaeu brothers, Jodocus Hondius the Younger was, as his name suggests, the second generation in the cartographic dynasty founded by his father. The Hondius family dominated the Dutch market for atlases – the foundations for this had been laid back in 1604, when Hondius the Elder paid 'a significant sum' for Mercator's copper plates at auction. Just two years later he had published a new, updated collection of Mercator's maps, supplementing the book with a drawing of himself and Mercator working on a pair of globes – despite the fact that by this time Mercator had been dead for over a decade.

ATLAS | Mercator's life's work had been to create maps of all the countries of the world, but Mercator had never managed to complete the task he'd set for himself. In the years subsequent to his meeting Ortelius in 1554, he had missed out on a professorship, completed a rigorous land survey of Lorraine that had almost killed him, engraved maps for others and started planning a work about the history of the entire world. But in order to provide a good overview of this history, Mercator also had to give a good overview of the world, and therefore sat down to draw a new world map. In 1569 he published his *Nova et aucta orbis terrae descrip-*

tio ad usum navigantium emendate accommodata (*New and More Complete Representation of the Terrestrial Globe Properly Adapted for Use in Navigation*) – a world map drawn using Mercator's groundbreaking projection, which has continued to shape the west's view of itself right up to the present day.

As its name suggests, the map was primarily created to simplify navigation. Mariners were struggling to follow a straight course across the seas using nautical charts that featured lines of latitude and longitude that twisted and turned to simulate the spherical shape of the Earth, and Mercator's solution was to straighten them out. Instead of adding the lines of longitude curving from pole to pole, he inserted them as straight lines beside each other, and made all the lines of latitude equal in length instead of increasingly shorter circles towards the poles. This meant that the directions of north–south and west–east became straight lines that were much easier to navigate by – even sailors wishing to travel diagonally, to the north-west or south-east, could use a ruler to find the course from port to port.

The projection, however, had an inherent error – it resulted in the areas along the equator being represented correctly, while the areas to the north and south expanded as the lines of longitude, which should meet at the poles, were kept apart. This prevented the poles from ever meeting, and caused the lines of longitude to extend into infinity.

To compensate for this, Mercator's map is the first map of the world to feature a separate map with the North Pole at its centre down in the bottom left corner, beside which Mercator wrote: 'As our chart cannot be extended as far as the pole, for the degrees of latitude would finally attain infinity, and as we yet have a considerable portion at the pole itself to represent, we have deemed it necessary to repeat here the extremes of our representation and to join thereto the parts remaining to be represented as far as the pole.'

Mercator's polar map has a fanciful geography, in which the North Pole is symmetrically surrounded by four large islands. In a letter, Mercator wrote that his depiction of the area was based on the eye-witness account of an English monk who visited the northern regions in the year 1360. The book the monk wrote about his travels, *Inventio fortunata* (*The Discovery of Fortunata*), was given to the king of England as a gift, but has since been lost. Mercator learned of the book from another book, *Itinerarium* by Jacobus Cnoyen, in which the monk's tale is retold by a priest from the northern regions who visited King Magnus in Bergen in 1364. Mercator wrote:

> The priest [...] related to the King of Norway that in 1360 AD, there came to these Northern Islands an English Minorite from Oxford who was a good astronomer, etc. Leaving the rest of the party who had come to the Islands, he journeyed further through the whole of the North, etc., and he put into writing all the wonders of those islands, and he gave to the King of England a book which he called in Latin *Inventio Fortunatae*. This book began at the last climate, that is to say in Latitude 54°N; and it continued all the way to the North Pole.

Inventio fortunata provided a somewhat motley description of the northern regions. According to the monk, northern Norway bordered on a mountain range on four islands comprising a ring around the North Pole at 78 degrees north. Between the islands, broad rivers flowed into a polar sea towards an enormous maelstrom. At the Pole itself was a huge, black mountain of magnetic stone. The island closest to Europe, which bordered on Norway, was inhabited by people no more than four feet tall. Mercator wrote that the monk had clearly only been able to complete such a journey with the help of magic.

Today, most historians agree that even if the monk did not travel all the way to the North Pole, it is fairly certain that he made it to the area around southern and western Greenland, and travelled on to Canada, since he described a heavily forested landscape. The description of all the islands and the strong tidal currents is an accurate description of what is today known as Baffin Bay. The Magnetic North Pole is also situated in this area. The priest who met the monk and then travelled on to meet King Magnus was probably Ivar Bårdsson, religious leader at the bishop's palace at Gardar, Greenland, for several years. We know that he visited Bergen in the year 1364.

Mercator, who was otherwise scientifically inclined, used Cnoyen's presentation of Bårdsson's account of what the English monk had seen 200 years earlier to create a map of the northern regions. The map follows the description closely, with a few exceptions. Mercator did not connect Norway to one of the North Pole's islands because he knew that it was possible to sail past Vardøhus and on to Russia – this is already evident on his map of Europe from 1554.

In the midst of all this erroneous polar geography, however, is a mystery: the depiction of Greenland is strikingly correct. When creating a world map thirty years earlier, Mercator had followed the tradition stemming from Claudius Clausson Swart, and presented Greenland as a peninsula linking to a large North Pole continent. But on his map from 1569, Greenland is a separate island – something Mercator simply couldn't have known, because then – as now – the northern part of the country was packed in ice. Nor had any seamen at this time sailed far enough north to find themselves in the immediate vicinity. In 1924, the Danish polar explorer Lauge Koch wrote that up until 1852, 78 degrees and 20 minutes north marked the limit of the Europeans' geographical knowledge of Greenland. But there is no denying that Mercator's map represents Greenland more accurately than later maps from the 1800s.

Mercator never stated the source of his information, which may explain why later cartographers ignored it. Perhaps they thought that it was simply impossible for him to have produced an accurate map of Greenland, and that what he had drawn was a product of his imagination.

Most cartographers therefore continued to draw Greenland as part of the northern mainland. As late as 1865, August Petermann, one of the leading geographers of his time, claimed that Greenland was attached to Siberia. Only in 1891, when American polar explorer Robert Peary and Norwegian Eivind Astrup set out on an expedition to once and for all discover whether Greenland was an island or a peninsula, and from Navy Cliff saw the Independence Fjord stretching out into the Wandel Sea, was it established that Greenland is in fact an island. Mercator's Greenland from 1569 remains one of cartography's unsolved mysteries.

Mercator's new world map was not an immediate success – at least not at sea, possibly because it was over two metres wide. It was therefore not until 1599 that anyone used Mercator's projection to create a new map, and another fifty years would pass before anyone used it to produce a nautical atlas. The map was simply too unusual for most seamen, and they didn't like the enlarged land masses – but they eventually realised that this was the price that had to be paid for a map that more easily set them on the right course.

As a 26-year-old, Mercator had vowed to create maps of all the world's countries and regions, but forty years later had only managed to create maps of Flanders and Europe. In 1578, he wrote that the project – which he now looked forward to getting fully under way – demanded 100 maps. Time was running out – the 66-year-old noted that his eyes were no longer as sharp as they had once been.

In the autumn of 1585, Mercator arrived at the book fair in Frankfurt with fifty-one maps of France, the Netherlands, Switzerland and Germany. Expectations were high – everyone was looking forward to seeing the start of Mercator's masterpiece – but unfortunately the disappointment was equally great. For a public who were used to maps adorned with sailing ships, compass roses, extravagant cartouches, colour, mythical creatures and painstakingly crafted frames, Mercator's were grey and boring, featuring few or none of the usual embellishments. Mercator was ahead of his time. The new maps were influenced by his idea for a '*nieuwe geographie*' – a new geography characterised by simplicity, objectivity and sober-mindedness – an idea much more common today than it was 400 years ago.

But Mercator made no concessions to his audience at the next opportunity. His maps of the Balkans, Greece and Italy, published four years later, featured even fewer decorations – only one monster and two ships across a total of twenty-one maps.

Mercator also wrote a preface to his great work, stating 'I have set this man Atlas, so notable for his erudition, humaneness, and wisdom as a model for my imitation.' Atlas was a Greek god who, after fighting for the Titans in the war waged and won by the Olympians, was condemned to hold up the sky on his shoulders at the western edge of the world. Both the Atlas Mountains in Morocco and the Atlantic Ocean are named after him. In later narratives, Atlas became a wise king of Mauretania, someone who knew all there was to know about the night sky, and it was to honour 'Atlas, King of Mauritania, a learned philosopher, mathematician, and astronomer' that Mercator titled his work *Atlas, sive cosmographicæ meditationes de fabrica mundi et fabricati figura* (*Atlas, or Cosmographical Meditations Upon the Creation of the Universe, and the Universe as Created*). The title page features Atlas, bearded and clad in flowing robes, studying two globes – one representing the Earth, and one representing the night sky.

After drawing the central and southern parts of Europe except Spain and Portugal, Mercator started on the northern regions. Iceland had been fairly inaccurately represented on his map of Europe from 1554, but Mercator had now obtained a map from 1585, probably drawn by an Icelandic bishop, and the result was a dramatic map featuring an erupting Hekla Volcano. There's even a monster splashing in the sea to the north of the island. Norway and Sweden had to make do with sharing one map between them, while Denmark was given an entire map to itself as Mercator had been supplied with information by a Danish viceroy.

Not long after completing the maps of the northern regions, Mercator suffered a heart attack that left the entire left side of his body paralysed. He was greatly frustrated at not being able to work, but Mercator, who was now seventy-eight years old, knew that he would need another lifetime to complete everything he'd started. A text about the creation of the world was the last work he managed to complete before his death towards the end of 1594.

One of Mercator's sons and three of his grandchildren pulled together his posthumous works, and just four months after Mercator died, his *Atlas* was published, giving the world the name of a new genre of books. Ortelius had been the first, but Mercator was more greatly respected as a geographer, and perhaps this is why we say 'atlas' today, rather than 'theatre of the world'. Sales of the book, however, were disappointing. Compared with *Theatrum*, Mercator's *Atlas* was incomplete. It lacked maps of both Spain and Portugal, and only three maps – drawn not by Mercator but by his son and grandchildren – covered the world beyond Europe.

Disappointed by the book's failure, and in desperate need of money after Mercator's last son died, leaving his wife and children with no income, the family sold the copper plates to Jodocus Hondius the Elder – who knew how to turn them into a moneymaking machine.

RIVALRY | Hondius the Elder understood that people didn't buy maps to find out the exact location of Venice or Puerto Rico – far more important was that the maps were attractive to look at and contained more information than the purely geographical. He therefore supplemented Mercator's copper plates with extravagant, baroque illustrations of people in national costume, small city maps, more ships and larger cartouches. Mercator would probably have turned in his grave to see the result – but the *Atlas* sold. After its first printing in 1606, twenty-nine editions of the Mercator–Hondius *Atlas* were printed in Latin, Dutch, French, German and English.

Jodocus Hondius the Elder died in 1612. His two sons, Jodocus the Younger and Henricus, took over the running of the firm, but disagreements caused them to part ways. Henricus joined forces with his brother-in-law Johannes Janssonius – Blaeu's neighbour and copyist – while Jodocus started to produce maps for a new atlas. Jodocus, however, died suddenly at the age of just thirty-six before ever publishing a single copy of his work. And who ended up purchasing his posthumous copper plates? None other than Willem Blaeu – arch-rival of Johannes and Henricus.

Blaeu was ecstatic. He would now be able to compete in the market for atlases, and just one year later published the *Appendix Theatri A. Ortelii et Atlantis G. Mercatoris* (*Appendix to A. Ortelius's Theatre and G. Mercator's Atlas*). Of the sixty included maps, an entire thirty-seven were the work of Hondius the Younger, but Blaeu simply replaced Jodocus's name with his own, writing nothing of the deceased young man in his preface. Although the atlas appendix was inconsistent in terms of both the quality of the printing and its geographical scope, it was a hit among wealthy citizens looking to buy an atlas that had not been created by Henricus. Henricus and Johannes hit back almost immediately with a new appendix to their own atlas. Three years later, they published an expanded, French edition of the Mercator–Hondius *Atlas*, in which they attacked Blaeu, calling his atlas a 'concoction of old maps'. This was the start of an atlas rivalry, in which each side constantly tried to surpass the other with increasingly larger and more painstakingly crafted editions.

Blaeu gained a significant competitive advantage when he was appointed the East India Company's official cartographer in 1632. Not only did the position give him the opportunity to earn significant amounts of money, it was also his job to stay up to date with all the new geographical information brought home by the company's ships.

In February 1634, Blaeu placed an ad in an Amsterdam newspaper: 'At Amsterdam is now being printed by Willem Jansz Blaeu a large book of maps, an *Atlas*, in four languages: Latin, French, German and Dutch. The one in German will appear about Easter, the ones in Dutch and French in the month of May, or early June at the latest, and the one in Latin shortly thereafter. All editions on very fine paper, completely renewed with newly engraved copper plates and new, comprehensive descriptions.' The new atlases were slightly delayed, and not finished until the following year, but ultimately contained a total of 207 maps divided between two volumes.

Blaeu's map of the Nordic region from 1635 bears clear signs of having been based on Andreas Bureus's simplified representation of the Diocese of Stavanger, and it must therefore be the case that Scavenius's map arrived in Amsterdam by some unknown means just after this version of Blaeu's atlas was published. The following year, the *Nova et accurata tabula episcopatum Stavangriensis, Bergensis et Asloiensis vicinarumque aliquot territorium* was printed by Janssonius and Hondius for the first time – without crediting Scavenius.

On the other hand, in 1638 Joan and Cornelius Blaeu called the map *Dioecesis Stavangriensis & partes aliquot vicinæ, opera L. Scavenii, S. S*, giving Scavenius the credit he deserved. The map was decorated with what the Dutch believed to be a typical Norwegian, equipped with an

---

Next pages | Joan and Cornelius Blaeu's map *Dioecesis Stavangriensis & partes aliquot vicinæ, opera L. Scavenii, S. S. (Diocese of Stavanger and some adjacent regions, prepared by L. Scavenii, S. S.)*. Telemark is a large, blank space as the Dutch had little knowledge of the area. '*Mare Germanicum Vulgo De Noord Zee*' means that 'North Sea' is the usual name for these waters.

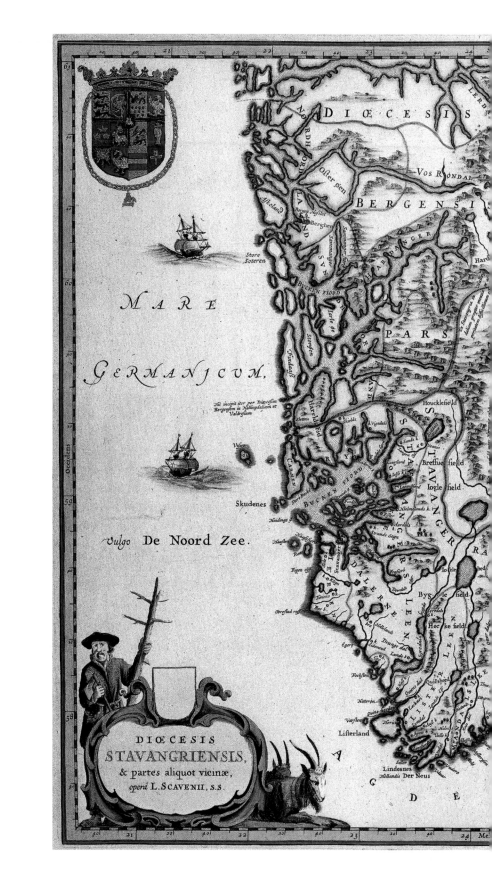

MARE

GERMANICUM.

Hic incipit iter per Diœcesim Bergensem in Hallingdaliam et Valdrosiam

Vulgo De Noord Zee.

DIŒCESIS
STAVANGRIENSIS,
& partes aliquot vicinæ,
operâ L. SCAVENII, S.S.

DIŒCESIS

BERGENSI

PARS

Skudenes

Listerland

Lindesnes
Hollandis Der Neus

field.

WALDERS
VR·DAL

Slire k.
Vangs

TAVANGER STIFT.

Thems dal
Offuenal
Adt

 Sperdillen Vand

LLING

Brommen

DAL

Krefarn

OSSO

LLE

RCK.

Aggers Hufler
Opslo vulgo
Aslo

Nofund

Kopt
Raupt

Sifers
Tanberg

VIGSIDEN

STIFT.

LAG
Conpdal
k.
Duth k.
Wifhiel
Schaerforst
Ooke
Lagefland

Oghiel

Beffum
offu
Refham

Herfum ef Jalen

Haumen ef Jalen

Sandaram

Harmans hoffued

Patornafter

Marfrand

Iutiæ pars

Shau

Milliaria Germanica communia.

1 2 3 4 5 6

Apud Ioh. et Cornel. Blaeu.

Oriens

25 20 30 26 20 40 27 30 50 28 20 40

61

60

59

58

axe and logs to supply them with timber for shipbuilding, and flanked by typical Norwegian animals – two mountain goats.

Willem passed away the same year, and the Blaeu brothers inherited both Europe's largest printworks with nine printing presses, of which six only printed maps, and the position of official cartographer with the East India Company, which Joan assumed. At the same time, Henricus Hondius withdrew from the map-making profession, and it became Blaeu vs Janssonius once again.

BATTLE OF THE TITANS | In 1640, the Dutch merchant shipping fleet had a total of 2,000 ships – far more than any other country. The East India Company alone employed an entire 30,000 seamen, and the West India Company sailed to South Africa, west Africa and America, where in 1614 the Dutch founded New Amsterdam on an island the Native Americans called 'Mannahata'. The income generated from the trading of pepper, ginger and nutmeg – goods highly valued in a Europe that had developed a taste for spices – was huge.

All the ships needed maps to navigate by, and the captains and mates tasked with travelling to the Spice Islands were usually given a set of nine maps. The first showed the route from the Dutch island of Texel to the Cape of Good Hope; the second showed the Indian Ocean from Africa to the Sunda Strait between Java and Sumatra; the next three presented the Indonesian archipelago, and the last four were individual maps of Sumatra, the straits, Java and Jakarta.

All these maps were created by Joan Blaeu and his assistants. A cartographer's salary wasn't much – just 500 guilders a year – but Blaeu was also able to sell new maps to the company, which in 1668 resulted in him earning an astronomical 21,135 guilders. These earnings, combined with the access to information brought home by maritime personnel, put Blaeu in the privileged position of being able to continually publish new atlases in an increasing number of volumes – but the competitive pressure applied by Janssonius was intense. Both parties were locked in a battle to create the greatest atlas of the age. They doubled and redoubled their efforts, printing increasingly larger, more ambitious and more costly atlases over the 1640s and 1650s. The results of this competition read almost like football scores, the number of volumes published like the number of goals:

1640: Blaeu 3 – Janssonius 3
1645: Blaeu 4 – Janssonius 3
1646: Blaeu 4 – Janssonius 4
1650: Blaeu 4 – Janssonius 5
1654: Blaeu 5 – Janssonius 5
1655: Blaeu 6 – Janssonius 5
1658: Blaeu 6 – Janssonius 6

It was neck and neck. Blaeu set out to create an atlas that would surpass his rival once and for all – a magnificent work giving complete descriptions of the land mass, the seas and the heavens: *Atlas maior, sive cosmographia Blaviana, qua solum, salum, coelum, accuratissime describuntur* (*Grand Atlas or Blaeu's Cosmography, in Which are Most Accurately Described Earth, Sea, and Heaven*). Blaeu dedicated all his resources to completing the work, holding a closing-down sale at his bookshop in 1662 because he wanted to do nothing other than work on the atlas. When the atlas was finally published later that year, it became clear why Blaeu had needed both time and money. The *Atlas Maior* was gigantic – nobody had ever printed anything like it before. The eleven volumes comprising 4,608 pages and 594 maps made all previous atlases pale into insignificance. The price was congruous with its product: 430 guilders for a coloured edition, almost as much as Blaeu's annual salary and the equivalent of around £25,000 today. In other words, the book was not something for the general public, but rather for aristocrats, diplomats and merchants.

The *Atlas Maior* can easily be said to be the world's most beautiful and most impressive atlas. But it was also a statue with feet of clay; a dinosaur. Blaeu and Janssonius prioritised quantity over quality, and extravagance over accuracy – their strategy was to spew out as many maps as possible. Some of the maps in the *Atlas Maior* were thirty years old, and this lack of innovation on Blaeu's part may have been due to commercial reasons – he had invested so much money in the project that he didn't want to risk introducing new, unfamiliar maps. Perhaps he had also learned from Mercator's failure upon presenting his new, accurate and markedly unspectacular maps eighty years earlier. In any case, Blaeu's work was no failure: the *Atlas Maior* sold well, and has remained popular as a deluxe edition – the greatest cartographic publication of the extravagant Baroque era.

MILITARY MAPS | While Blaeu and Janssonius were caught up in their own private battle, the Dutch had been fighting a much bigger war – and the conflicts with Spain continued even after the Netherlands had informally declared its independence in 1579. While private cartographers were most concerned with atlases, globes, world maps and city maps, the military required strategic maps of border areas and fortifications. In 1600, Leiden University started offering a programme of study within mathematics, engineering and land surveying, and textbooks such as *Practijck des lantmetens* (*Land Surveyor Practice*) were published the same year. The Dutch engineers soon gained a reputation for their innovative practices – including beating the Spanish troops by destroying strategically constructed dams to flood the enemy – and many were offered appointments abroad. One of them even managed to get lost on his journey northwards to a Danish province.

Isaac van Geelkerck, a cartographer's son, drew his first map when he was around sixteen years old, and was therefore highly experienced by the time he was employed as a cartographer and military engineer by the Danish-Norwegian Army in 1644 at the age of twenty-nine. Two years later, he drew a map of Bergen featuring suggestions for new fortifications – the oldest surviving map of the city. Later, van Geelkerck also drew maps of the border areas, the seaward approach to Gothenburg, the Diocese of Trondheim and the city of Fredrikstad. In 1650, he was recalled from leave to complete a map of Norway he had started work on. This map was probably never finished, but just a few years later a map of Denmark and Norway – *Daniæ et Norvægie tabula* – was created, partly 'ex Is. Geelkerckij' – 'by Isaac van Geelkerck'. His work on the map must have already been well under way when he left Norway in 1657.

On one of van Geelkerck's maps of the border areas, *Abris der Smaa Lehnen* (Østfold), *Båhuslen* is shown as a part of Norway – a part that was transferred to Sweden the year after van Geelkerck had left the country. At the same time, a treaty regarding the demarcation and setting of the new international border was signed.

The border between Norway and Sweden had always been fluid. Not even in 1645, when Norway had to admit that 'regarding Jemptelandh and Herredalen, to a certain extent Herredalen is situated on the Swedish side of the mountains,' was an accurate border line drawn. But in the summer and autumn of 1661, the border from Iddefjord to Hisøya/Hisön in Nordre Kornsjø was determined and entered on an official map, and the 'Riksrøys 1' border stone can still be seen here today. But the border further north would not be finally settled until seventy-seven years later.

THE BORDER | The border disputes at Finnmark continued after Christian IV of Denmark's voyage around the Cap of the North to show his power. In 1709, when Denmark-Norway went to war with Sweden yet again, the disputes were mentioned in the declaration of war. Only when the two countries were back on truly amicable terms in 1734 was a treaty signed, which stated that the countries must settle disputes 'in all the places where any dispute regarding the Norwegian border may arise.' But settling border disputes was not the same as establishing an international border, and in an official communication Christian VI wrote that the aim should be to 'compose a complete map and drawing of the boundary line and area between Norway and Sweden on both sides.' The commissaries asked whether the border area should be 'approached *geometrically*, with all lines, angles and curvatures stated in their net length and breadth,' or simply '*geographically*', based on the statements of local

Next pages | The middle section of the tripartite *Norlandia Map*, which shows the shipping routes from Troms to Trøndelag, and more specifically from Andsnes to Leka and Gutvik, using a dotted line. This part of the map shows a small boat between Kielsøe (Tjeldøya), Hindøen (Hinnøya) and Hameröe (Hamarøy), a large ship flying the Danish flag in the Westfiorden, another out by Røst and two small boats sailing along the dotted line past Engelvær and Brixvær (Bliksvær), respectively. The map is neither signed nor dated, but is thought to be from around the year 1750. It measures 215 x 38 cm. The border, featuring a decorative gold pattern, is possibly made from wallpaper.

people. The king ordered the first method – a decision indicative of the accuracy he was striving to achieve.

The boundary survey began at Hisøya on 1 August 1738. When surveying of the first area was completed – an area at a boundary marker where the Norwegian municipalities of Aremark and Marker butt up against Sweden – the Norwegian land surveyors created a map on which they clearly marked where Norway believed the border line to be. The border line according to Sweden was marked on the map with a fainter line, and the area between the two lines marked with a separate colour. The disputes here related to what had long been regarded as completely insignificant areas. But when the land surveyors reached the village of Indre, east of Elverum, they arrived in the regions occupied by Sweden almost 100 years earlier. In earlier times, the border of Indre Parish towards Rendalen had passed through the lake at Femunden from south to north, and based on this the Swedes submitted a map on which the international border followed the same path. Norway would have liked to reclaim part of Indre, but even more important was to ensure that the copper mill at Røros, a significant consumer of timber for its smelting works, had access to large areas of forest. Denmark-Norway therefore proposed a compromise. In exchange for Denmark-Norway not requesting the return of all of Indre Parish, the international border would be set twenty to twenty-five kilometres east of Femunden, and the country enlisted the help of Major Peter Schnitler to submit this request.

Schnitler was both a military officer and a jurist. After having submitted his 'Deduction of the Nordenfields border line between Norway and Sweden', and having had a certain level of success with this – today the border runs over ten kilometres east of Femunden – he was tasked with travelling up the entire border from Røros to Varanger to perform surveys and hold court sessions to ask the local population where they believed the border to be. During his travels, Schnitler proved to be a capable cartographer. In October 1742, he was 'held up by the weather' at Inderøy, and used the time to create 'an approximate map, with the border drawn as explained by witnesses', of the areas he had visited so far: Inderøy, Namdal, Helgeland and Salten. He later also produced maps of the rest of Nordland, Senja, Tromsø and Finnmark. In early 1746 he wrote in his journal: 'From 16 January to 16 February, created preparatory geographical maps of Nordland's Lappmark, to the extent it belongs to the bailiwick of Senjen and Tromsø, and sent them to the royal officials at the same location.'

Schnitler sent all his maps and journals on to the Norwegian military engineers, who worked in his tracks. They accurately measured what Schnitler had drawn only by eye, used the information he had obtained from the locals in the negotiations with Sweden, and added all the border markers he had witnessed to their completed maps. It is difficult to overemphasise the importance of Schnitler's role in locating the northern border between Norway and Sweden where it remains today.

On 2 October 1751, the treaty regarding the longest border between two countries in Europe was signed, regulating the approximately 2,200-kilometre-long border from Hisøya to Golmmešoaivi, south of the Varangerfjord, where the areas common to both Norway and Russia began. The border was marked with border markers and surveyed by land surveyors from both countries over the next fifteen years.

During the work on the border with Sweden, Norway had gained its first college to educate land surveyors, but the timing of this was co-incidental. There was dissatisfaction among the ranks of the Danish-Norwegian Army because officers were not required to possess any form of education, and consequently promotions were generally given to those who were of noble birth, or had connections or the money to buy themselves a title. These individuals, it was said, contributed little 'strength or competence' to the profession. Someone noticed that a German citizen in Trondheim, Georg Michael Döderlein, was offering to teach 'officers or officers' children in the mathematical sciences', and that several of his students had become good engineers. The king was asked whether it would be possible to make better use of Döderlein to rid the army of its 'ignorance', and in December 1750 Döderlein was appointed the first leader of Den frie matematiske Skole (the Free Mathematical School) in Oslo. Here, students could learn 'the spherical trigonometry and land surveying' – for the first time, Norway had an educational institution at which one could learn to make maps. This was the start of both the Norwegian Military Academy and the Norwegian Mapping and Cadastre Authority.

A NORWEGIAN MAP OF NORWAY | In 1756, Norwegian officer Ove Andreas Wangensteen mobilised his troops to the Danish city of Rendsburg on the German border. War had broken out in Europe yet again, but for once Denmark-Norway had managed to keep out of the fray, and Wangensteen was therefore able to commit to surveying activities. His *Charta over Kongeriget Norge, aftegnet i Rendsborg, Aar 1759 af O. A. Wangensteen* (*Map of the Kingdom of Norway, Drawn in Rendsburg in the Year 1759 by O. A. Wangensteen*) was a draft version of a larger map that Wangensteen completed two years later: *Kongeriget Norge afdelet i sine füre Stifter, nemlig Aggershuus, Christiansand, Bergenhuus og Tronhjem, samt underliggende Provstier. Med Kongelig Allernaadigst Tilladelse og Bevilling forfærdiget Aar 1761 af O. A. Wangensteen Capitain ved det Norske ArtillerieCorps* (*The Kingdom of Norway, Divided into its Four Dioceses, namely Akershus, Kristiansand, Bergenhus and Trondheim, and underlying Deaneries. Completed under the most gracious permission and licence of His Majesty the King in the year 1761 by O. A. Wangensteen, Captain of the Norwegian Artillery Corps*).

With its anything but round or rectangular shape, Norway has always been a difficult country to represent on a single sheet of paper. In 1680, Dutch cartographer Frederik de Wit had been the first person to solve this problem by dividing the country in two and presenting the northern and southern regions side by side. Wangensteen followed this model, which resulted in the region of '*Nordland og Finmarken under Tronhiems Stift*' ('Nordland and Finnmark under the Diocese of Trondheim') being somewhat unfairly reproduced to a much smaller scale. But the map provides a good overview of Norwegian trade and industry at the time, with its fishermen, hunters, loggers and shipping sector. *Kiøb-Stæder* (trading hubs), *Sølvværck og Gruber* (silver mines), *Kaabberværck* (copper works) and *Iernværck* (ironworks) are marked using dedicated symbols, and in Hurdal and Eidsvoll a *Glaspusterie* (glass-blower) and *Guldmine* (gold mine) are marked.

Wangensteen clearly saw that there was a German market for maps. In the cartouche of his map he wrote in German: 'The German nation should note that in the names where a V is used, this shall be read as a W; likewise a double aa shall not be pronounced as a long a, but almost like an o. Therefore Vaage in Nordland shall not be read as "Faage", but rather as "Woge"; likewise Vaaler in Solöer shall not be read as "Faler", but as "Woler", etc.'

Wangensteen's map was the first map of Norway to be both drawn and published by a Norwegian cartographer. It was also clearly more accurate than any of those produced abroad – two years after the map was published, Norwegian historian Gerhard Schøning described how 'up until now, we have lacked correct and comprehensive geographical descriptions of the Kingdom of Norway [...]. Everything produced by foreigners and outsiders in this context has been quite deficient, and serves more to confuse than to inform, so that from their maps one may learn only as much about Norway's correct division, extent, location and place names as ordinary maps may teach us of the true nature of the Great Tartary and those countries that lay deep within Africa and America.'

But the first edition of Wangensteen's map featured a grave error. The border between Norway and Sweden passed straight through Femunden, where the Swedes had originally set it – Wangensteen had failed to keep up to date with the latest border negotiations. He drew a new, correct border on the second coloured edition of his map, but never quite managed to erase the old borderline – it remains on his map to this day.

FORESTRY MAPS | During his work, Wangensteen searched in vain for some maps he knew had been created by the *Generalforstamtet* – the forestry commission – twenty years earlier. The maps were part of the first attempt to regulate both public and private forestry in Norway, as in the 1600s and 1700s fear of deforestation was great. In 1688, half of all the timber mills in southern and eastern Norway were closed because 'the forests in many places have been destroyed.'

The silver mine at Kongsberg was one of the largest forest owners, and German brothers Johann Georg and Franz Philip von Langen travelled to the area in 1737 to map not only the silver mine's forests, but all the forests in the country, whether belonging to the king or others.

The task of drawing maps of the outer coastal areas – 'in so far as for-ests may be found on the coastal mainland' – was allocated to seaman and cartographer Andreas Heitmann. Having been granted a boat and the funds to hire a sailor, Heitmann set out to chart the coast north of Trondheim in the spring of 1743. Due to headwinds and some remaining survey work between Karmøy and Bergen, he didn't arrive in Trondheim until August, and by then it was too late to start work on the regions to the north. But the next summer, Heitmann worked his way up towards the municipality of Træna, and by the time he was finished had mapped the coast all the way up to *Andnæs* (Andsnes) on the border to the coun-ty of Finnmark.

An anonymous offshoot of Heitmann's map was created a couple of years later. The *Norlandia Map* is an amateurish but colourful and part-ly improved reproduction of Heitmann's original, drawn with a specific purpose in mind: to reproduce in detail the *Nordfahrleden* – 'the sail-ing route' – through the straits and between islands and reefs. From the strait between Leka and Gutvik in the south, a dotted line follows a small boat as it sails along the coast until it reaches Andsnes in 'Pars Finmarchiæ' in the north.

The forestry commission never managed to map the entire country. Christian VI had wished that 'across this Kingdom, started maps shall be completed of the entire country', but this was an unpopular measure among forest owners and timber merchants, who didn't like the idea of any restrictions being placed on their activities, and when the king died in 1746, the mapping of the forests was stopped.

The forestry maps were shrouded in secrecy from the very start. In 1743, a diocese governor wrote to the forestry commission requesting a copy of the map of the Diocese of Kristiansand, but was told that no copy could be supplied without permission from the king. After the commis-sion was dissolved, the maps were immediately stashed away in a cup-board in Copenhagen, and it was not until 1772, when the Swedes could be heard rattling their sabres, that General Heinrich Wilhelm von Huth took the maps with him when he was sent to Norway to ready the troops. Here, they would become part of the foundations for the first modern, scientific surveying of the country.

NEW BRANCHES | The story of Scavenius's map shows how in the 1500s and 1600s, maps of Europe travelled the continent and were used by those in need of the latest and most accurate data. Cartographers became rivals, vying to be the first to get hold of the latest information – geographical information could be converted into jangling coins in one's pocket. But at the same time, various types of maps became increasingly differentiated from each other. Maps influenced by religion – a legacy of the Middle Ages taking a partly new form in Protestant areas – were still important; traders required greater numbers of maps in connection with their activities; and the state and military needed maps they could use for purposes of administration, management and warfare – a trend that would grow stronger with the mapping of Denmark, France, Great Britain, Germany and Norway over the coming years.

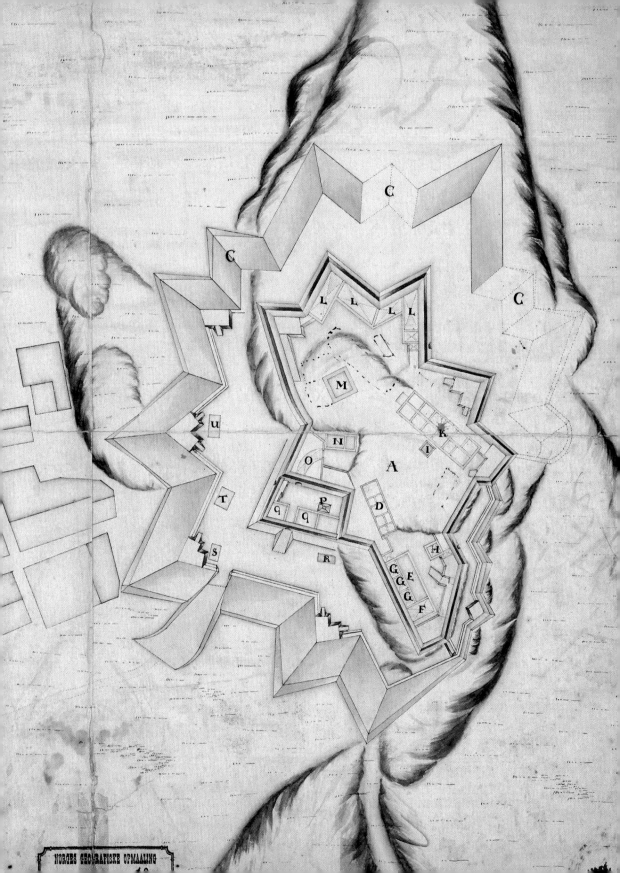

THE GREAT SURVEYS

Kongsvinger Fortress, Norway
60° 11′ 57″ N
12° 00′ 40″ E

The story of the modern mapping of Norway starts with two lieutenants standing on two separate hills to the north of Kongsvinger and sending smoke signals to one another. The year is 1779 – one of the lieutenants stands at Brattberget, the other at Esperberget, and using fire and gunpowder they attempt to find out the distance between the two hills. The aim is to measure a baseline they can use in the work to map this strategically important area close to the Swedish border, but the method encounters problems due to all the burning of foliage and waste also being carried out in the area.

So the lieutenants try again – and again. Both have a pendulum clock set as accurately as possible in accordance with the Sun's movements. One of the lieutenants fires off a shot when his clock shows the time at which the Sun is at its highest at his location, the other when his clock shows the same slightly later, and the time difference between the two clocks – around one minute and seventeen seconds – provides a rough distance between the two hilltops.

The lieutenants combine the figures from the four days on which they have achieved the best measurements with astronomical observations,

Detail from the *Cituations Cart af Kongs Wingers Festning* (*Situational map of Kongsvinger Fortress*) from 1750 by an unknown cartographer. The map was drawn during the construction of new ramparts: '*CCC endnu ikke ferdig*' means 'CCC not yet finished'. The flagstaff where Norway's prime meridian was established in 1779 is unfortunately not marked.

and the results provide a distance of 62,322 Danish feet, or 19,555 modern metres, between the two hills. The margin of error, however, is around 100 metres. In February of the following year, they therefore take along four pine rods, each measuring four metres in length, to take a control measurement on the flattest surface that exists in Norway's bumpy landscape – a frozen body of water. They make their way to Storsjøen lake, a few miles north-west of Kongsvinger, and use the rods to measure yet another baseline. They then connect this to the first using surveying instruments. Finally, they have calculated a distance between Brattberget and Esperberget that they are satisfied with: 62,139 feet. A significant distance in Norway has been measured using scientific methods for the very first time. The modern mapping of the country had begun.

THE SURVEY | The initiative to survey the country had been taken seven years earlier, when King Gustav III of Sweden staged a *coup d'état* to obtain greater power. Denmark-Norway reacted by preparing for a possible attack. Head of the Danish-Norwegian Engineer Corps, General Heinrich Wilhelm von Huth, reacted by strengthening Denmark-Norway's border defences. Fortresses were reinforced, the artillery was improved and, on 14 December 1773, the country's first surveying institution was founded: Norges Grændsers Opmaaling (the Border Survey of Norway). The organisation's first priority was to create military maps of the areas where the war with Sweden usually played out – along the stretch of the country between Halden and Trondheim. Von Huth wrote: 'These maps will now mainly represent the terrain that lies between Glomma and the border. The work has been started at Ingedahlen, and aims to continue on to Stene bastion at Trondheim.'

By 'Ingedahlen', von Huth probably meant the contentious border area of Enningdalen south-east of Halden – as a German, von Huth was not always completely reliable when it came to recounting Norwegian place names.

The Border Survey of Norway was allocated premises in the same building as Den frie mathematiske Skole (the Free Mathematical School), and the new institution's first task was to gather all available information from previous maps – including maps of bailiwicks, nautical charts,

Wangensteen and von Langen's maps, and whatever else they could find – to put together a single, large map, measuring around three metres wide and four metres high in two parts, and thereby establish what was already known. The surveyors then went out into the terrain to check the accuracy of the map, noting down discrepancies where the old maps were incorrect, and started to draw new maps.

These new maps were mostly produced in a square-mile format, each covering 1x1 Norwegian mile. In 1773, a Norwegian mile was not the same as it is today, but 18,000 *alen*, equivalent to 11.295 kilometres. Details such as churches and parishes were added to the maps, along with bailiwicks, roads, rivers, farms, smallholdings and military depots. The military need for information about the negotiability of roads and quartering opportunities for the troops along the way were the most important considerations.

The Border Survey of Norway was granted a budget of 1,500 *riksdaler* per year – a modest sum that enabled no more than two to four cartographers to be sent away on assignments lasting six months at a time. The cartographers started in the southernmost regions of the county of Østfold, at Halden and Enningdalen, and worked their way north between the Oslofjord and the border with Sweden. The most common method of surveying used in Norway at this time involved the use of an instrument known as a plane table – a square plate mounted on a tripod. The drawing paper was attached to this plate, usually using clips, along with a ruler and telescopic sight. Using the sight, the surveyors would locate a point with a known position, such as a church spire or a mountain, and then start to enter details on the map using this as a starting point.

But the surveyors had failed to establish a common starting point – a prime meridian – before beginning their work, and minor errors could therefore be magnified from one map to the next. Sometimes, as much as two or three kilometres might be transferred from one map to another, and by the year 1777 the surveyors had moved so far off course that something would have to be done. One of the professors at the Free Mathematical School recommended that the officers be trained in newer, more accurate surveying methods, but due to his tight budget von Huth felt unable to offer such training to his staff – despite admitting that it was highly desirable.

As the cartographers moved north into increasingly difficult, wooded regions and less populated areas, the disadvantages of using the cheapest method became more and more apparent – the cartographers were forced to both perform measurements and redraw their maps again and again. At the same time, the actions of the king of Sweden seemed to indicate that the threat of war was no longer imminent. In 1778, General von Huth contacted Thomas Bugge in Copenhagen to request a modern survey plan.

DENMARK | Thomas Bugge was a professor of astronomy and director of the observatory in Copenhagen's *Rundetaarn*, or Round Tower. In the summer of 1763, at the age of twenty-three, he had been one of the first two surveyors to be sent out into the field after the Royal Danish Academy of Sciences and Letters passed a resolution to survey Denmark. Royal decree prohibited any obstruction of the land surveyors' work, or the removal of any of the markers they established. Statutory provisions also stated that from 1 May until the end of September, 'or longer if weather conditions so permit', the surveyors had the right to requisition 'four to six farmers and farmhands, of which the latter must not be too old, but rather young boys, although not below the age of sixteen years; among these shall be an aging person who is familiar with the surrounding places, including the borders between counties, rural municipalities and parishes, etc'.

But despite this, the surveyors still encountered problems. One complained about acts of theft and 'the mean farmers' reluctance and repentance in all they are asked to do [...] several such uncomfortable circumstances have, if not confused me, then at least prevented activities from moving forward, and in addition to this: that, for the most part, the surveying situation has been extremely complex and arduous.'

The Danish mapping project was extensive, thorough and ambitious, and meant that tiny Denmark soon became one of the leading European nations within land surveying. The island of Zealand was divided into

A trigonometric map of Zealand, Denmark, by Thomas Bugge from 1779. All the triangles the surveyors have measured and used to map the island are clearly shown. The '*Kiöben-havns Observatorii Meridian*', one from north to south and another from east to west, cross at the observatory in the Round Tower in central Copenhagen.

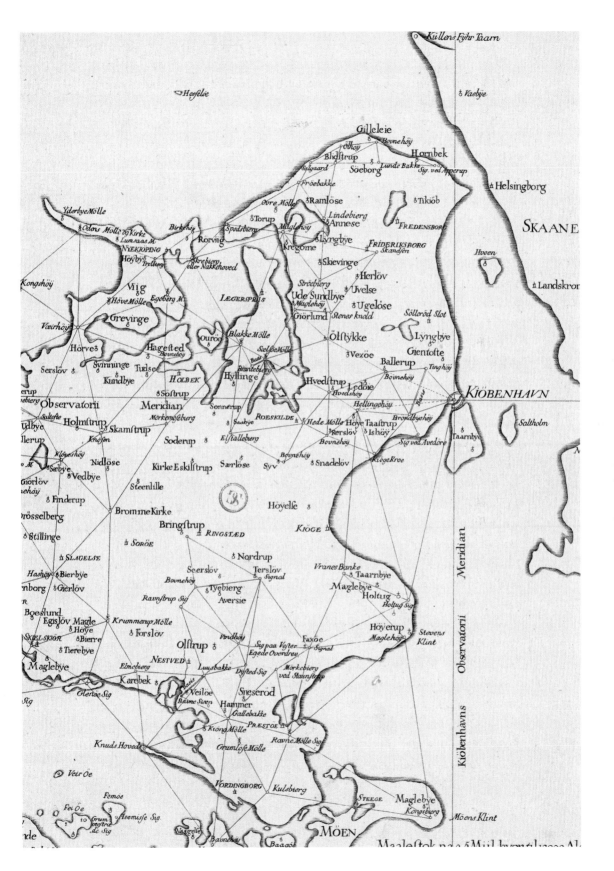

Kullens Fyhr Taarn

Vasbye

Hæsseløe

Gilleleie
Ollhöy   Bovnehöy
Blidstrup   Hornbek
Salgaard   Lunde Bakke
Söeborg   Sig: ved Apperup
Fröebakke

Helsingborg

Övre Mölle   Ramlöse
Lindebierg   Tikiöb
Torup   Annese
Maglehöy   FREDENSBORG

SKAANE

Yderbye Mölle
Odens Mölle og Kirke   Birkhöy   Slyngbye   FRIDERIKSBORG
Lumsaas M.   Rörvig   Kregome   Skandsen
NYEKIÖPING   Spodsbierg
Höybye   Trollsig   Ströebierg   Hveen
Höybye   Skrebierg   Skievinge
eller Nakkehoved   Herlöv   Landskron
Kongshöy   Viig   Ströebierg   Uvelse
Höve Mölle   Maglehöy   Ugelöse
Egeberg M.   Ude Sundbye   Sölleröd Slot
Grevinge   LÆGERSPRIS   Görlund   Stenes knold   Lyngbye
Væirhöy   Ouroe   Blakke Mölle   Ölstykke   Gientofte
Horve   Hagested   Selse Mölle   Vexöe   Ballerup
Serslöv   Bovnehøy   Brantebierg   Bovnehoy   Ting höy
Svinninge   Tudse   Hyllinge   Hvedstrup   Ledöie
Kundbye   HOLBEK   Sostrup   Hvedshoy   KIOBENHAVN
Observatorii   Meridian   Sonnerup   Hellingehöy   Brøndbyehöy
Holmstrup   Saltofte   Mørkempseburg   Saabye   ROESKILDE   Hede Mölle Hove   Taastrup
Udbye   Skamstrup   Knebøn   Elstalleberg   Serslöv   Ishöy   Taarnbye
ellerup   Soderup   Bovnehøy   Saltholm
Klöveshöy   Bovnehøy   Kiöge Kroe
Giörlöv   Sæbye   Vedbye   Kirke Eskilstrup   Særlöse   Syv   Snadelov
nehøy   Finderup   Steenlille   Höyelse
rösselberg   Bromme Kirke   Kiöge
Stillinge   Bringstrup   RINGSTÆD

Meridian

Nordrup
SLAGELSE   Soröe   Seerslöv   Terslöv
Hashøy   Bierbye   Bovnehøy   Signal   Vranes Banke   Taarnbye
nborg   Gierlöv   Tyebierg   Aversie   Maglebye   Holtug
Ravnstrup Sig   Holtug Sig
Boeslund   Egislöv Magle   Krummerup Mölle   Vndhöy   Höyerup
Höye   Forslöv   Faxöe   Maglehoy   Stevens
SKELSKÖR   Bierre   Olstrup   Sig paa Vester   Klint
Tierebye   NESTVED   Egede Overdrev   Signal
Maglebye   Elmebierg   Luusbakke   Dysted Sig   Mörkebierg
Karebek   Veilöe   Sneseröd   ved Staunstrup
Glenoe Sig   Baune Skien   Hammer
Sig   Knuds Hoved   Gallebakke
Kiong Mölle   PRÆSTOE
Grumlese Mölle   Ravne Mölle Sig

Meridian

Observatorii

Kiöbenhavns

Veir Öe   VORDINGBORG   Kulsbierg   STEEGE   Maglebye
Femoe   Kongsbierg
Fei Öe   Asemisse Sig   Möens Klint
Grum imestrue   de Sig
Vaagelse   Baineshøy   MÖEN
Baagöe

Maalestok paa 5 Miil bruun til vasa Al

fifteen principal lines from north to south, with a distance of 10,000 *alen* between them. This was achieved by stretching out a fifty-foot surveyor's chain over and over again; or, to put it another way: the surveyors walked up and down the length of Zealand fifteen times, measuring as they went. They then did the same from east to west. Using the grid they had created in this way, they were able to accurately locate villages, castles, country estates, churches, individual farms and houses, as well as all the lakes, marshes, forests, rivers and country roads within the area, in addition to the borders of rural municipalities and counties.

In the autumn of 1778, General von Huth sent two lieutenants, Johan Jacob Rick and Ditlev Wibe, to Thomas Bugge in Copenhagen, where they would learn about the modern mapping method Denmark had been one of the first countries in Europe to adopt – trigonometric triangulation.

TRIANGULATION | The ancient Egyptians and Sumerians had used triangulation many years earlier when measuring their lands and drawing maps. But the problem with the old method of triangulation was its unsuitability for surveying larger areas – as the mapping of the border regions had shown. Dutch mathematician Gemma Frisius founded the modern method of triangulation when, in a small book published in 1553, he explained how a network of triangles enables us to measure areas of any size. Frisius took his instruments up to the top of Antwerp's high church tower, and from there was able to see the towers in the neighbouring cities of Bergen op Zoom, Brussels, Ghent, Leuven, Lier and Mechelen, which he entered on a geometric map. It was then possible, he wrote, to observe the same cities from a tower in Brussels and, knowing the distance from Antwerp to Brussels, calculate the distances between the other towers. In order to prevent inaccuracies, Frisius recommended that the selected control points, such as the towers in Antwerp and Belgium, first be located using astronomical calculations.

Danish astronomer Tycho Brahe was among the first individuals to use this epoch-making method. In 1597, from the observatory on the island of Ven in Øresund, he completed the measurement of angles and distances across the water to Copenhagen, Malmö, Lund, Landskrona, Helsingborg, Helsingør and Kronborg. He used astronomical observations of Ven's location and a baseline of 1,287.90 metres from the observatory to the eastern tower of St Ib's church as his starting point, and based on his measurements was able to draw a map of the island – one of the first in the world to be based on trigonometric triangulation.

Brahe's measurements were the first stage of a plan to publish an improved map of Denmark and Norway – King Frederick II was aware of and supported the plan, as in a letter dated 1585 he asked his librarian to provide Brahe with all the castle's maps of the two countries. Brahe's large-scale mapping project would never be completed, however – probably because a friend of his had similar plans.

Brahe left Ven in 1597. Christian IV, who had ascended the throne the year before, had no desire to use his funds on Brahe's observatory, and so in 1600 Brahe left Denmark-Norway to become the official imperial astronomer to Rudolph II in Prague.

In Prague, Brahe was visited by the Dutch mathematician Willebrord Snel van Royen, known to the English-speaking world as Snell. Snell was also interested in triangulation, and just a few years later, in 1616, also put Gemma Frisius's method into practice. Using a surveyor's chain – a completely new invention designed to ensure more accurate survey measurements – Snell first created a baseline from north to south measuring 327.80 metres (from A to B). Using triangulation, he then measured the distance between two points to the east and west of this (C and D) – 1,229 metres. He then stood at point C, and from here measured the angles to the tower of Leiden town hall and the church tower in Zoeterwoude, before doing the same from point D, creating two triangles. Using these, he was then able to calculate the distance between Leiden and Zoeterwoude: 4,118 metres.

And so on and so forth. Using his first, short baseline, Snell was able to measure increasingly greater distances, until using thirty-three triangles he had found the distance between the cities of Alkmaar and Bergen op Zoom – situated 130 kilometres apart.

For Snell, the objective of this triangulation process was to repeat the experiment performed by Greek mathematician Eratosthenes over 1,850 years earlier – to measure the Earth's circumference. Like his predecessor, Snell started with the distance between two places located on roughly the same longitude, using Alkmaar and Bergen op Zoom where Eratosthenes had used Alexandria and Syene (Aswan). Snell also had the advantage of being able to measure the distance between his two locations with much greater accuracy than his predecessor, who had calculated the distance between Alexandria and Aswan based on how long it took to ride between the two cities by camel. In his *Eratosthenes Batavus* (*The Dutch Eratosthenes*), he explained both his method and his result: 38,639 kilometres. He was incorrect by a margin of less than 4 per cent.

CARTE DE FRANCE | France was the first country in the world to use these modern triangulation methods on a large scale. Here, the method was refined by Italian astronomer Giovanni Cassini, who arrived at the court of Louis XIV – the Sun King – in 1668. Cassini, a professor at the University of Bologna, had agreed to take part in the construction of a new observatory just outside Paris, and the Pope, for whom Cassini worked, had granted Cassini permission to travel. Both the Pope and Cassini himself believed the stay in France would be a short one, and so at first Cassini made no great effort to learn French. But Louis XIV offered a good salary, and Cassini eventually became so involved in the newly established Académie des sciences – the French Academy of Sciences – that he changed his mind. Three years later he became known as Jean-Dominique Cassini, and had taken on the role of leading the academy.

Here, Cassini worked alongside Jean Picard – priest, astronomer and surveyor – who used Snell's method when measuring the distance between the towns of Malvoisine and Sourdon – also with the intention of finding the Earth's circumference. Picard later built upon this triangulation method when he created a map of Paris and the surrounding areas – the *Carte particulière des environs de Paris* set the standard for the large-scale mapping of France, which was just around the corner.

The reasons for the establishment of the French Academy of Sciences were largely characterised by utilitarianism. Even before the academy was founded, the French Minister of Finance had ordered the creation of an updated map of the entire country, in order to obtain an overview of France's resources and where they were located, and whether particular regions were best suited 'to agriculture, to commerce or manufacture – and also of the state of roads and waterways, the rivers in particular, and of possible improvements to them.'

At the same time, the academy was characterised by fairly free research – not unlike the position enjoyed by the library in Alexandria in its time. The researchers' guaranteed and generous income signalled that they were part of the governmental apparatus at the highest level. The academy was a place where information was collated, research was conducted and results were disseminated – and attracted international expertise.

In 1679, King Louis XIV ordered the academy to produce the most accurate map of France possible, and Jean Picard was chosen to lead the first stage of the process – the mapping of France's coastline. Earlier maps of France had been based on a prime meridian that passed through the Canary Islands – a prime meridian inherited from the Greeks, who had used the outermost point of their known world. But the distance from the French coast to the Canary Islands had never been accurately measured. When over the course of three years Picard and an assistant measured latitude and longitude values from Flanders in the north to Provence in the south-east, Picard used the prime meridian that he himself had established, which passed through the observatory in Paris.

In 1682, the corrected map of France – the *Carte de France corrigée* – was met with astonishment from both the academy and the king. Picard had presented the results of his survey on what had until then been the official map of France, using thick lines to highlight the differences. Suddenly, everyone was able to see that France covered an area 20 per cent smaller than previously believed. The Atlantic coast was pulled eastwards, the Mediterranean coast northwards, and it was revealed that important seaports such as Marseilles and Cherbourg had on earlier maps been situated far out to sea. 'France has lost more territory to the Academy of Sciences than to all our enemies combined,' Louis XIV is said to have exclaimed upon studying the map. Picard was probably well aware that his map would not necessarily prove popular – he took care to enter text on his new map that clarified it was *'corrigée par ordre du Roy'* – corrected by order of the king.

Picard's new map showed that the academy had good reason to tear all its old maps to pieces, and plans were made for the thorough surveying of France based on Picard's triangulations and Cassini's new method of finding a location's longitude by observing Jupiter's moons.

Cassini's method was made possible by the latest telescopes, which gave astronomers a clear view of Jupiter's moons. By noting the times at which one of the moons came into view, disappeared behind Jupiter and then re-emerged, and comparing these times with those noted at another location, the difference in longitude between the two locations could be determined. The method was also a result of the fact that more accurate clocks with which to tell the time were now available. But the great map-making project was set aside when Jean Picard died in 1682, and France went to war with the Spanish Netherlands the following year.

Instead, work continued to extend the Paris meridian from north to south through the entire country in order to answer one of the greatest questions of the 1600s – what was the Earth's definitive size and shape? The theory of gravitation proposed by English scientist Isaac Newton indicated that the Earth was slightly squashed in appearance, because gravity seemed to vary at the equator and the poles. But the academy disagreed, adhering instead to French philosopher René Descartes' theory that the Earth was shaped like an egg. The answer to this question eventually became a matter of national honour on both sides of the English Channel.

The academy asked the king for support for expeditions to the northern regions and the equator in order to measure the distance between the lines of latitude there. If the distance between the lines of latitude was shorter in the north than in the south, then the Earth was shaped like an egg; if the distance was longer, then Newton was right.

The first expedition set out for Peru in South America in 1735; in the following year, a second journeyed to Sápmi in the border areas between Sweden and Finland. The expedition to Peru was catastrophic – the ship came ashore at a location so rife with mosquitoes that many of the crew contracted malaria. They rode on mules through jungle, forced to cut their way through the vegetation using machetes, slept in cabins on stilts when rainstorms raged, climbed mountains and slept in freezing caves at night and, finally, two years after they had at last started to take their measurements, realised they had made a mistake and had to start all over again. It was a decade before the first expedition member returned home.

Luckily, the journey to Sápmi went more smoothly. The expedition used the frozen River Torne to calculate a 14.3-kilometre-long baseline from the spire of Torne Church to Mount Kittisvaara, but the results presented to the academy in November 1737 came as a shock. The degrees of latitude had been found to be slightly longer in the northern regions, which meant that the Earth was a slightly squeezed sphere and that – perhaps worst of all – Newton and the British had been right. The French Academy of Sciences' method had disproved the academy's own theory – but this defeat was soon turned into a victory when the academy emphasised the excellence of its method. It was neutral, verifiable and scientific, provided an objective view of the world, and could be used by anyone, no matter their beliefs or ideology.

By 1730, France had returned to its regular cartographic activities – Philibert Orry, the country's new controller-general of finances, had little time for philosophical discussions about the size and shape of the Earth. Orry was more concerned with the fact that the Department of Public Works lacked accurate maps that could be used in the upgrading of the country's infrastructure, and in 1733 he asked Jacques Cassini – son of Giovanni Cassini, the man who had led the academy's map-making project – to start the triangulation of the entire country.

Orry also took it upon himself to implement the governmental education of engineers and surveyors, with the aim of creating standardised maps that would help the navy to navigate more easily and the army to build fortresses along international borders. Later, he also asked the surveyors to prepare standardised road plans for the entire kingdom. The purpose of maps – and the words used to describe them – was starting to change. The role of the state, public benefits and standardisation

---

Next pages | A map of Marseilles and its environs from César-François Cassini's huge *Carte de France* project, started in 1748, taken over by Cassini's son Jean-Dominique in 1784 and transferred to the Dépôt de la Guerre in 1793 in the wake of the French Revolution. The project was a great success, although technically never completed.

120000 M.

Batterie du Cap d'Arone
Batterie
les Neuves Infirmeries

St Just
St Barbe
St Barnabe
Olier

MARSEILLE
Poste
Port St Jean
le Fanal
Entree du Port

Batterie de Tête de More
les Vielles Infirmeries

N. D. de la Garde

Bec de Tiboulen

I. de Ratoneau

Batterie

le Canonnier Bc

Cap de Daume

Cap Gros
Plage de Daume

I. de Pomegue

Batterie

le Sourdara
Danger

Chan d If

I. de Daume

Plage
de
Veaune

N. D. de Bonne Voyge

Matargues

N. D. de Montredon

Batterie du Cap Se

Port de la Rose

I. de Tiboulen

les Goudes

Cap de la Pounen

I. de le Maure

Creux
Calalongue

OUEST

I et Tour du Planier

I de Jaros

I de Calaseraigne

Cap de Morgiou

I de Riou

120000 M.

120000 M.

325000 P.

M   E   R   M   E   D   I

500

1   2   3   4

Eche

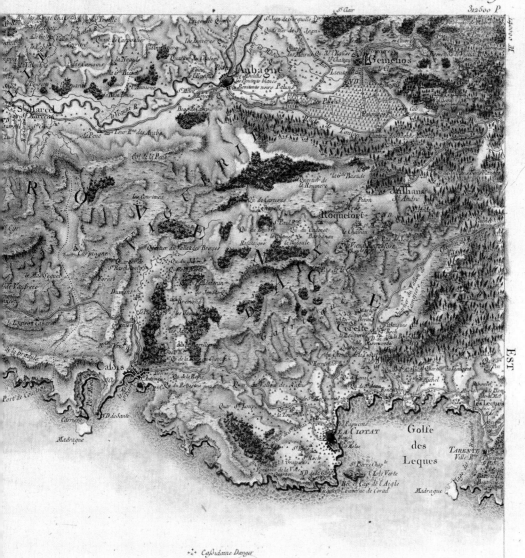

EST

ERRANÉE

Cassidaine Danger

Toifes

6   7   8   9   10000 T

were becoming increasingly more important than royal favour, merchant benefits and scientific contemplation. Geographers were in the process of becoming civil servants.

The surveyors had to venture out into unknown and rugged terrain. So far, triangulation had for the most part been undertaken in the Netherlands, Denmark and northern France, in areas where the terrain was relatively unchallenging, but now the surveyors were setting out for the eastern and southern mountains. Encounters with the locals were not always friendly – in the Vosges Mountains, in the border regions with Germany and Switzerland, the surveyors, with their suspicious behaviour and strange instruments pointing here, there and everywhere, were accused of being political agitators. One was even beaten to death because he was believed to be using his instruments to put a curse on the fields. Their equipment was constantly stolen, they were denied transport and nobody was willing to show them around, preferring instead to pelt them with stones.

But in 1744 the work was finally completed, the surveyors having measured 800 triangles and nineteen baselines. The *Nouvelle carte qui comprend les principaux triangles qui servent de fondement à la description géométrique de la France* (*New Map Including the Principal Triangles that Form the Basis for the Geometric Description of France*) was published as a collection of eighteen sheets that same year, but the work was incomplete. Large areas, such as the Pyrenees, Jura Mountains and the Alps, were only outlined, and the map said little about the country's topography, being only a network of triangles – a geometric skeleton – featuring a broad range of points that followed the country's coastlines, rivers and roads. But the map fulfilled the controller-general of finance's wish for an overview that could be used in planning activities.

During the survey, a third generation Cassini – César-François Cassini de Thury – had taken over responsibility for the work and felt it was now complete, although he admitted that the surveyors had not visited every farm nor measured the course of every river. But public or private institutions could now fill in the details on regional maps.

But history would not turn out as Cassini had planned – France went to war with Austria before the map was finished, and in 1746 battles with the Austrian Netherlands raged. Cassini was sent away to help the military engineers to map the battlegrounds. After France had won the war, Louis xv visited the engineers and Cassini, comparing Cassini's map with the terrain. He was impressed: 'I want the map of my kingdom to be done in the same way, and I charge you [Cassini] with doing it.'

Both the king and Cassini knew that mapping France in detail would be an enormous project, and although Cassini had his doubts about what it would be possible to achieve, the opportunity to undertake an even greater survey, this time including every river, village, mountaintop and copse of trees, was an offer he couldn't possibly refuse. He estimated that it would take him eighteen years and 180 maps to cover the entire country – placed side by side, they would create a map of France measuring twelve by eleven metres. Ten maps would be produced each year, each of them with a budget of 4,000 livres to cover equipment, triangulation and printing costs. The first print run would comprise 2,500 copies, with maps each costing four livres – significantly more than other maps at the time. If all the maps sold, they would bring in a total of 1,800,000 livres for the national treasury, which had been seriously depleted by the latest war. The controller-general thought the project sounded like an excellent idea.

But the project's execution proved more difficult than expected. Cassini was an exceptionally thorough person, obsessed by details and accuracy. He inspected and controlled all aspects of the work, from the survey itself to the printing of the maps, checking and double-checking every last detail. Local residents were also consulted to a greater extent now that every little stream and place name had to be included. The skeletal map from 1744 was fleshed out; given muscles, arteries and skin. It would become the body of Marianne, goddess of liberty – the symbol of the French Republic.

After eight of Cassini's estimated eighteen years had passed, only two maps had been completed. In the summer of 1756, when Cassini was granted an audience with the king to show him the second map, Louis xv dropped a bombshell: 'My poor Cassini,' said the king, 'I am terribly sorry, I have bad news for you: my controller-general doesn't want me to go on with the map. There's no more money for it.' And the king had a point – the map wouldn't be finished before the next century if work on it continued at the present pace. Undeterred, Cassini responded: 'The map will be made.'

Cassini changed tactics. With the king's approval, he established the Société de la carte de France, its fifty members requested to contribute 1,600 livres per year. This doubled Cassini's budget, meaning that the project would be able to be completed within ten years. In return, the society's members would receive a share of the profits, in addition to two copies of each map. It was a brilliant move – the shares sold like hot cakes, and leading members of the nobility, eminent politicians and even the king's mistress, Madame de Pompadour, purchased subscriptions. Cassini acquired more money than he needed, and was able to employ more surveyors, cartographers and engravers.

Over the next three years, Cassini published as many as thirty-nine maps, each in a print run of 500 copies. The maps sold well, and in 1760 a total of 8,000 copies of the first forty-five maps had been sold. Maps were circulated as never before and, for many, Cassini's map production became a symbol of the French nation. Farmers with large holdings and members of the bourgeoisie were also interested in purchasing shares to invest in a little piece of France. Cassini set up a public subscription, which could be purchased for a third of the *Société* price.

Much of the project's success and popularity was a result of what had previously threatened to derail it – Cassini's pedantic nature. It was obvious to anyone who viewed them that these maps were more beautiful and more detailed than any of those previously published. They were printed using the best inks on the best paper, and characterised by simplicity, clarity and a great number of details reproduced using modern typography and standardised symbols for everything from monasteries to mines.

But at the same time, what was actually deemed to constitute the French nation was becoming a politically charged question. France was characterised by regional autonomy and the fact that the country's inhabitants spoke a broad range of languages from Italian and German to Breton and Catalan, but Cassini mapped all the regions in the same way and used the same Parisian French to write the various place names, contributing to the standardisation and uniting of the entire nation. The project collapsed in a wave of democratisation at the end of the 1700s, with an increasing number of individuals arguing that it was the nation itself, and not the monarchy and nobility, who should hold political power.

After the bitterly cold winter of 1788–9, and the subsequent drought that sent food prices through the roof, the old regime was overthrown through the French Revolution.

Cassini III had passed away three years previously, and it was the fourth-generation Cassini, Jean-Dominique, who was now close to completing the project. The survey was finished; all that remained was to publish the last fifteen maps. But the revolutionaries had other ideas – the new French Republic was under threat from neighbouring countries, and the need for maps was great. The head of the French Army's engineering corps was also afraid that Cassini's maps might result in sensitive information falling into enemy hands: 'His map may be good or bad. If it is good, it will have to be banned, and if bad, it would hardly deserve favour.' The National Convention decided to confiscate the map and hand it over to the Dépôt de la Guerre. Cassini was heartbroken. 'They took it away from me,' he wrote in his memoirs, 'before it was entirely finished and before I had added the final touches to it.' In 1794, Cassini was thrown in prison, only just managing to avoid losing his head to the guillotine before being released a few months later.

Technically, the map was never completed. The Dépôt de la Guerre allowed the project to lie fallow right up until 1804, when Napoleon Bonaparte, at this time at war with practically all of Europe, wrote to his military chief of staff: 'If we had stuck to making maps on Cassini's scale, we should already have the whole Rhine frontier. [...] All I asked was that the Cassini map be completed.' The Dépôt de la Guerre appointed twelve engravers to update the old copper plates and print new editions, and the last maps of Brittany were finally published in 1815. But by then, sixty-seven years after it was started, the map was out of date, and Cassini's map was archived – not because a new king ordered that this be done, nor because the map failed to correspond to the ideology of a new republic, but because of what a modern nation quite rightly needs: an updated survey.

THE ORDNANCE SURVEY | The Napoleonic Wars also influenced the production of maps on the other side of the Channel. The British had established their mapping agency, the Ordnance Survey, in 1791, and began publishing maps from 1801. But in 1810, when Great Britain had been at war with France for almost twenty years, the publication of maps was deemed too great a threat to national security. Public maps were withdrawn from the market the following year, and would not become available again until Napoleon was well and truly defeated at the Battle of Waterloo in 1815.

Just thirty years earlier, the triangulation of Great Britain had been started as a result of a French invitation – in typical French fashion, this was made both as an insult to and in recognition of the British. In 1783, Cassini de Thury wrote to Joseph Banks, president of the Royal Society, stating that it would be interesting to know the exact difference in longitudes and latitudes between Europe's most renowned observatories – Paris and Greenwich. Although the latitudes and longitudes were regarded as well-known, Thury wrote, it was still the case that the English and French calculations were not concurrent to a worrying degree. Particularly doubtful, Thury believed, was Greenwich's position – and the solution was to perform a joint British–French triangulation across the Channel.

The British had started discussing the triangulation of their territory not long after the French had started to triangulate theirs. With support from the Royal Society, cartographer John Adams had measured a baseline in 1681, but just seven years later was complaining about the lack of support to continue the work, and all later mapping had been carried out using the old methods, with significant inaccuracies as a result.

Nevertheless, many members of the Royal Society were irritated by Thury's invitation. How dare the French imply that the British were unsure about where their own observatory was located! Nevil Maskelyne, British Astronomer Royal at Greenwich, didn't bother to dignify Thury's suggestion with a response, but an old notebook shows that he cared enough to initiate his own secret experiment to calculate the distance between the two observatories.

Banks, on the other hand, was not so easily offended, and took the request to William Roy, an officer who had been on many military surveys, and who saw in the letter a golden opportunity to remedy the British mapping situation and finally get started with triangulation. That same summer, Roy had measured a baseline on his own initiative – the plan being to start the triangulation of London and the surrounding areas on his own.

Two thousand freshly minted pounds from George III enabled Roy to start a new and accurate triangulation of the area where Heathrow Airport is situated today – Hounslow Heath. But the summer of 1784 proved to be an exceptionally wet one – the wooden measuring rods shrank and expanded so much in the rain that they eventually became useless. A friend of Roy's suggested that they might be able to obtain new glass measuring rods, and on 2 August, two months after they had started work with the wooden rods, they started over again. At the end of the month, the result was clear: 27,404.7 feet. 'There never has been so great a proportion of the surface of the Earth measured with so much care & accuracy,' Roy declared.

In September 1784, Cassini de Thury's death resulted in his son, Jean-Dominique, taking over the French side of the project, but this would not be started until three years later, as it took the British this long to create the world's most sophisticated theodolite.

In July 1787 the British started triangulating from Roy's baseline on Hounslow Heath, sighting Banstead Church, Windsor Castle, Hanger Hill Tower and St Ann's Hill in Chertsey, Hundred Acres, Norwood, Greenwich and Severndroog Castle. Eventually, they had created a network of triangles across Sussex and Kent to Botley Hill and Wrotham Hill, but the work progressed slowly. 'General Roy is at some distance from London ... but from what I hear, he has not reached very far yet,' wrote a Briton to the French, and it was decided that both sides would head straight to the coast to start the collaboration.

Cassini and Roy met in Dover in September, and agreed that 'white lights [with] extraordinary brilliance' should be attached to the surveying flagstaffs to illuminate them through the thick fog that often hung over the Channel. Over the next three weeks, the French and British alternately lit signals and conducted observations that criss-crossed the Channel, between Dover Castle and the windmill at Fairlight Head on England's south coast, and the Montlambert hilltop, Cap Blanc Nez, Dunkirk tower and the Notre-Dame church in Calais, all on the northern coast of France.

By the middle of October the measurements were completed, and Britain and France had been trigonometrically bonded. But what about Greenwich's position? Maskelyne's secret experiment to measure the distance between the two observatories had reached a longitudinal distance of 9 minutes and 20 seconds – Roy calculated the difference to 9 minutes and 19 seconds, and this largely agreed with the results of the French astronomers.

Some view the establishment of the Ordnance Survey in 1791 as being due to the British fear of France after the revolution – the need for good maps with which to defend the nation. 'But the truth is not quite so simple,' writes Rachel Hewitt in *Map of a Nation: A Biography of the Ordnance Survey*. Hewitt believes that 'the Paris–Greenwich triangulation had laid the groundwork' at a time when the Anglo-French relationship was more benign, and that George III 'was an enthusiastic sponsor of Enlightenment and nationalistic endeavours [. . .] and the mapping project pricked his interest.' The Ordnance Survey was also indebted to the Society of Arts' attempt 'to make accurate Maps of Districts, till the whole Island is regularly surveyed' and the many map-makers' widespread acceptance of triangulation as the most accurate technique for large areas.

THE FLAGSTAFF | The town of Kongsvinger is situated along one of the few easily accessible roads between Norway and Sweden – that which runs from Oslo to Magnor and Eda, and from there into the gently rolling landscape of Värmland. Construction of the fortifications here was started in 1673 to secure the ferry landing on the River Glomma and the surrounding areas against Swedish troops. In the summer of 1779, the two lieutenants Johan Jacob Rick and Ditlev Wibe arrive in Kongsvinger to put the town on the map. 'The survey shall hereafter be supported by astronomically determined points [. . .]. Lieutenants Rick and Wibe have therefore been trained by Professor Bugge in Copenhagen and shall take over this work,' wrote General von Huth.

Using the cutting-edge new instruments they have brought with them from Copenhagen – two surveyor's transits used to measure the angle from one point to another, two pendulum clocks and two seven-foot-long telescopes – the lieutenants perform the necessary astronomical calculations to find out the exact latitude and longitude of their current position. The fortress's flagstaff will have the honour of marking Norway's prime meridian. The light summer nights make celestial observations difficult, but they manage to calculate a latitude for the flagstaff of around 60 degrees, 12 minutes and 11 seconds north based on observations of the clearest stars and the movements of the Sun. On 14 June, they observe the time of a solar eclipse in order to determine the longitude. Throughout the autumn, however, they struggle with bad weather, which prevents them from observing a single lunar eclipse of the stars or eclipse of Jupiter's moons, and they therefore never obtain a good enough basis on which to establish an astronomically calculated prime meridian. Their observations and the baseline they established through the use of smoke signals and by taking measurements across the ice do, however, provide them with enough information to undertake further observations across the country. And now they must move northwards.

Equipped with a large officers' tent, two smaller tents for assistants, four canteens, four metal pots with lids, four saddlebags containing provisions and a pass that entitles them to free transport with the local farmers, the lieutenants set out on their journey north. From 1779 to 1784, during the summer months, Rick and Wibe measure the latitudes and longitudes of a broad range of mountaintops and church spires as they construct an increasing network of triangles along the border, erecting small observatories where no appropriate premises in which to set up their instruments can be found.

During the winters, they make observations at Halden, Oslo, Kristiansand and Copenhagen to find the latitude and longitude values at each of these locations, and establish new baselines on frozen lakes to avoid minor errors becoming magnified as they work. In January 1781, they measure a six-kilometre-long line across the Osensjøen lake, in March the same year a seven-kilometre-long line across Mjøsa, the following year a seven-kilometre-long line at Femunden and in 1785 a final line at Jonsvatnet, south-east of Trondheim. Their assignment was complete – a strategic area of Norway had been mapped using the most accurate and most scientific method of the age.

Danish cartographer Christian Jochum Pontoppidan was the first person to use this new information when he published a new map of southern Norway in the same year that Rick and Wibe completed their work. In the introduction to his *Geographisk Oplysning til Cartet over det sydlige Norge i trende Afdeelinger* (*Geographical Information to Accompany the Map of Southern Norway in Three Sections*), he writes that 'the survey, which was undertaken by Captain Rick and Lieutenant Wiibe in the years 1780, 81, 82, 83 and 84 using trigonometric operations, and which stretched from Kongsvinger to Egge church in the bailiwick of Inderøen,' has been one of the 'most distinguished aids' he has ever used. He also used von Langen's forest survey and the border survey from 1752 to 1759. The result is an effective and accurate map, which would become the new template for maps of southern Norway. Andreas Bureus's map from 1626, and its presentation of Norway as envisaged by someone outside the country, had finally been superseded.

THE TRANSIT OF VENUS | Rick and Wibe suggest to Professor Bugge that the next stage of their project should be the mapping of the Norwegian coast from Trondheim towards the south, and in 1785 a royal decree determines 'that the Norwegian coast and all islands and rocks beyond the same from Haltenø – the outermost point of the northern reaches of Trondheim – and to Fredrikshald shall be surveyed, since good sea charts are so sorely lacking.' The Danish-Norwegian shipping industry has boomed due to the country's neutrality during the American War of Independence, in which France, the Netherlands, Spain and German states have participated – so the need for good nautical charts is great.

Bugge prepares a detailed set of instructions for the surveyors: 'When Trondheim's meridian becomes the prime meridian in the surveying of the entire Norwegian coast, to which all the longitudes of stations along the coast shall refer, it will be of the utmost importance to accurately establish Trondheim's longitude, which as yet remains unknown.'

Bugge is well aware of the problem. He visited Trondheim twenty-four years earlier to observe a transit of Venus – a phenomenon in which

Venus is seen passing across the surface of the Sun. As early as the year 1716, British astronomer Edmond Halley had calculated that transits of Venus would take place in 1761 and 1769, and then not occur again until over 100 years later. At this time, knowledge of the distances between the Earth and the Sun and Venus respectively, and therefore the size of the solar system, comprised little more than vague assumptions, and so Halley recommended that the transit of Venus should be observed from many different locations around the world. The various times at which the planet crept across the face of the Sun would provide the figures necessary for calculating the distances, and they would also be able to be used to work out longitude values. On the day before the first transit, 6 June, 200 astronomers from various countries had travelled to the edges of the world, including Siberia, Madagascar and Saint Helena, taking their instruments with them. The transit of Venus that took place in 1761 was the world's first collaborative scientific project.

But Venus behaved strangely; the planet did not simply move across the Sun's surface as anticipated. The observers noticed that it became oval in shape, before becoming round again when it had moved a good way towards the centre of the solar disc. It was also difficult to know when the transit had actually started, and this is evident in the results from Trondheim. Bugge obtained results that differed from those of another observer stationed in the same place to undertake the same task – their recorded times at which Venus was first visible against the Sun's surface differed by two whole minutes. At the time, many believed the phenomenon offered proof that Venus had an atmosphere, but today scientists believe that this was due to disturbances in the atmosphere of the Earth.

Next pages | Ten years after Carl Joachim Pontoppidan published the map *Det Sydlige Norge* (southern Norway), he also published the map *Det Nordlige Norge* (northern Norway). In his *Geographical Explanation of the Map of Northern Norway in Two Parts*, published in 1795, he wrote: 'The mainland of the county of Nordland consists of a narrow stretch, where the distance between the border and the coast varies, from 6, 8, 12 to 16 geographical *mil*. Finnmark's greatest distance from the border in the north to the sound between Jelmsøen and the mainland is 35 *mil*.'

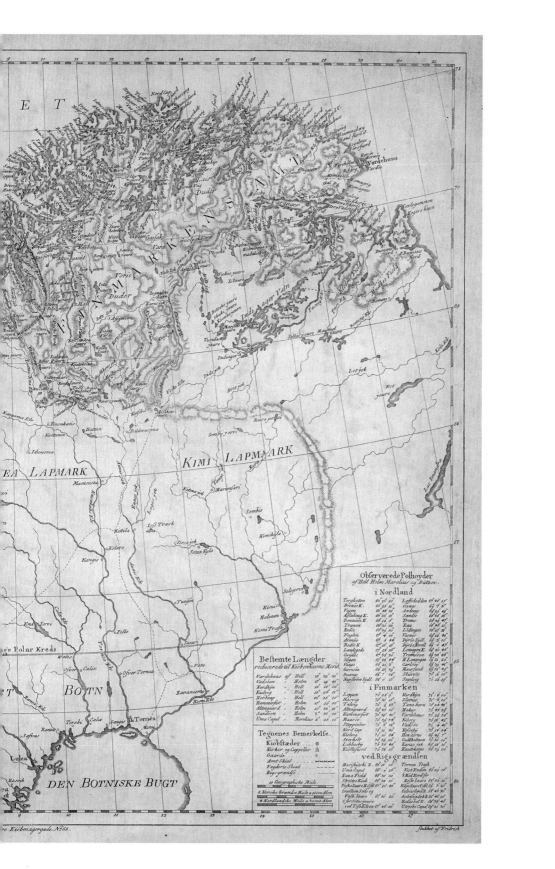

The next transit of Venus was estimated to take place eight years later, on 3 June 1769, and Copenhagen seized the opportunity to attract the most distinguished experts to the city. A letter was dispatched to Hungarian priest Maximilian Hell, the royal imperial astronomer in Vienna, inviting him to travel to Vardø and observe the transit of Venus from there. As a Jesuit, Hell would not usually be permitted to enter Denmark-Norway, but given the prestigious nature of the project, the law was set aside on this occasion. King Christian VII would pay all Hell's expenses.

Hell and a colleague set out from Vienna on 28 April 1768, and arrived in Vardø seven months later. Once there, they set up an observatory as an extension of the bailiff's house. Luck was with them on the day – the skies cleared just before Venus entered the Sun's disc, before clouding over for the next six hours, and then clearing once again just in time for Hell to observe and record Venus's exit.

Hell compared his results with those the British captain James Cook had obtained in Tahiti in the Pacific, as well as the measurements taken at Hudson Bay in Canada by British mathematician William Wales, and calculated the Earth's distance from the Sun to be 151.7 million kilometres – not far off the true distance of 149.6 million kilometres.

Back home in Vienna, Hell drew four maps: one of southern Norway, one of the northern counties, one of the county of Finnmark and one of the municipality of Vardø. The map of Vardø was printed and published, but only test prints were made of the maps of southern Norway and Finnmark – the map of the northern counties was never even engraved, because the copper engraver Hell worked with died. When he received the test prints for review, Gerhard Schøning created a list of place names that had been spelled incorrectly, but believed that the map of southern Norway, based on Wangensteen's map, represented a significant step foward, and that the map of Finnmark was also a clear improvement on previous maps. 'That the locations of many places are more correctly described here than previously, all the places to which P: Hell himself has been, is clearly evident,' wrote Schøning. Today, we know nothing about either of the test prints – only the map of Vardø has survived, and so it is difficult to say whether Hell's maps helped to improve any later maps of Norway.

MAPPING THE COAST | Rick and Wibe settle down in Trondheim to calculate the city's longitude value, converting a building just south of the city's cathedral into an astronomical observatory. In the summer of 1785 they are provided with a transit instrument – a large telescope specially created for observing the transits of stars – and mount it on a pine column inside the observatory. But despite the column being driven two metres into the ground, the winter's bitterly cold temperatures cause the column to move, and the observers have to accept the telescope's position when it finally stabilises slightly to one side of the meridian through the cathedral they are currently working to establish.

Surveying of the coast gets under way, with Rick and Wibe triangulating their way across the Trondheimsfjord until they reach Kristiansund in early autumn. Wibe's brother, Nils Andreas, follows in their wake, taking measurements at sea. He draws maps on which he marks lights, stakes and other sea markers, measures the tides and currents, and describes ports and notes 'with which wind one may come in and out.'

In 1786, Rick has married and moved to Oslo; Wibe continues on towards Molde, triangulating the area alone, and General von Huth is once again worried about his budget. Von Huth would rather survey the stretch of the country between Kongsvinger and Trondheim in detail than map the coast, and so in 1787 the work started by Rick and Wibe is stopped. The following year, however, the Admiralty finds funds to continue the project. The Wibe brothers triangulate their way down the coast, while Danish lieutenant Carl Frederik Grove takes over responsibility for the measurements at sea from Molde towards the south.

In 1791, the Wibe brothers establish a new prime meridian in Bergen, which they use right up until they reach Kristiansand four years later.

Next pages | Two maps of Norway in 'square mile' format, of Enningdalen in Østfold (1775) and Øyeren in Akershus (1802). All the white areas on the map of Enningdalen belong to Sweden – the red and yellow line is the international border. This is the first map of its kind to be drawn out of a total of 210. The series covers most of Østfold, and parts of Akershus and Hedmark all the way up to Sør-Trøndelag. Reling Öen, Elver Sand, Qvae Holmen and Raas Holmen in northern Øyeren look rather different today, since the area is a continually changing delta.

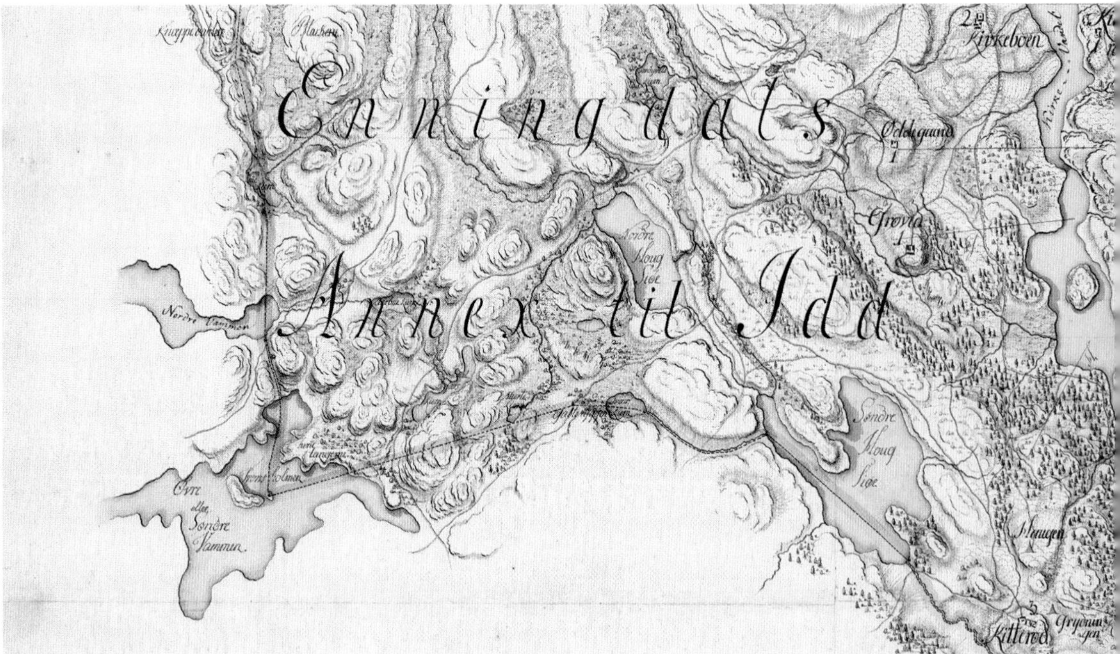
Enningdals
Annex til Idd
Kirkeboen
Grovia
Sondre Sloug Sioe
Sondre Sloug Sioe
Nordre Vammen
Ovre eller Sondre Vammen
Kittrød
Haugen

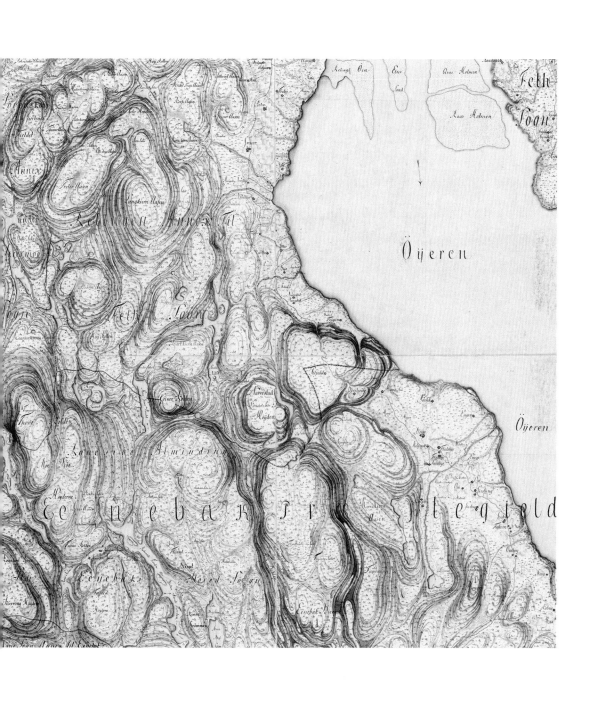

Here, they build an observatory and measure yet another meridian in their work up towards Agder, Telemark, Vestfold and Oslo, and down through Østfold to the Iddefjord and the Swedish border. Once the triangulation project and nautical survey have been completed Grove starts to draw maps, completing the first in 1791: *Trondheims Leed med Ud-øerne og Skiærene udenfor Leedet fra Haltens Øe og til Christiansund* (*Trondheim's Waters with the Outermost Islands and Reefs Beyond from Halten to Kristiansund*). A total of seven maps, engraved on copper and printed in Denmark, were published between 1791 and 1803, and are today known as '*De groveske drafter*' ('Grove's drafts'). The king expressed his 'utmost pleasure' upon viewing the maps.

1814 | In 1805, a resolution to undertake a combined military and economic survey is passed – much to von Huth's despair. Von Huth fears that the military will be deprioritised – the Rentekammeret, the Ministry of Finance, is taking over responsibility for the project, despite the fact that the survey will be performed using the same methods as previously. The agency changes its name to Den combinerede militaire og oekonomiske Opmaaling (the Combined Military and Economic Survey). The economic part of the project will involve the marking of all borders between properties, fields and pastures, along with area calculations for each property. But not everyone wants to be surveyed. A collective of farmers from Hedmark send a request to the National Assembly, at work on preparing Norway's constitution, in 1814: 'Our farms, which we have rightly and legally inherited from our forefathers, we most humbly request should not be surveyed; when another has the right to survey my property, then my rights to the property cease.' The farmers feared that the maps would be used to increase their taxes – but the economic survey was cancelled that same year due to insufficient funding.

In parallel with the coastal survey, the surveyors also follow in Rick and Wibe's footsteps along the Swedish border in order to enter further details on the trigonometric network. In addition to drawing maps, they note where there are opportunities to cultivate new fields; whether the locals practise arable farming, breed livestock, produce timber or fish; the condition of the roads; and whether any metal ores are present in the bedrock.

The surveyors also triangulate the areas stretching from Kongsvinger and southwards down to Enningdalen, and the network from Kongsvinger is connected to the coastal survey through triangulation in the areas of outer Østfold and Romerike. They then continue with the areas west of the Glomma River: from Eidsvoll to Oslo, Hadeland, Ringerike, Modum and Eiker, across the Mjøsa lake to Ringsaker, Vardal and Toten in 1806, down the west side of the Mjøsa and back to Eidsvoll, and finally Gudbrandsdalen, Valdres, Jarlsberg and Larvik in 1807. But then a new war with Sweden not only puts a stop to the work but sends the survey into a state of chaos – officers take original maps out into the field, where they are destroyed or lost, key persons are killed, and the military requisitions the project's drawing room to provide premises for a garrison school. When the war is over, not a single person possesses a complete overview of the project's activities.

After the peace treaty was signed in 1814, and Denmark ceded Norway to Sweden, all Danish maps of Norway were also transferred to Sweden. King Carl Johan also requested a joint, general map of the two countries, and in 1818 two surveyors each worked on their side of the border to link together the Norwegian and Swedish networks of triangles.

At this time, plans were also under way to create a coastal map of the northernmost regions of the country. This would not only prove useful for the shipping industry; it was also desirable to establish the position of the Norwegian–Russian border – but due to budgetary constraints Parliament was unable to grant funds for this purpose before 1824. Four years later, the surveyors of the northern counties are equipped with three small boats, all in a 'most mediocre condition', of which two were previously used as postal boats. They start at the outermost end of the Trondheimsfjord, triangulating their way up to the Namsenfjord before winter arrives. They reach the Arctic Circle and the island of Hestmannen the following year, and then Nesna, Gildeskål, Engelvær, Lødingen, Vesterålen, Senja and Loppa. They round the North Cape in 1837, and finally – ten years after setting out on their voyage – they reach the Russian border.

The maps of northern Norway highlight the fact that 'Grove's drafts' from 1803 no longer satisfied the requirements of an expanding shipping industry and the cartographers of the age. In 1847, it was decided that the coast between Trondheim and Oslo would be mapped once again, and four years later, the Sømandsforeningen (Seaman's Association) in Porsgrunn demanded that a more detailed map of the Oslofjord also be created.

THE OBSERVATORY | The modern mapping of Norway continues with increasing accuracy – the surveyors fine-tune the calculations of their predecessors, uncover errors and inaccuracies, remeasure and retriangulate, add more and more details – and even, on rare occasions, find funding to purchase more advanced instruments. The combination of the country's rather lean public treasury and demanding topography is a constant challenge, in contrast to Denmark, which with its relative wealth and easily navigable landscape had been able to be mapped by the surveyors simply taking a stroll through the countryside. The Norwegian solution was to turn the country's disadvantages into benefits. A map showing all the triangulation points from 1779 to 1887 shows that most were located on mountaintops, and from Gaustatoppen – which on a clear day offers a view of one-sixth of Norway's land mass – as many as twenty-three baselines radiate out in all directions.

The increasing accuracy of the mapping project was also due to professor of mathematics Christopher Hansteen being made director of the project in 1817, and thereby responsible for the civil and scientific side of the survey. He was a driving force in ensuring both the provision of more detailed instructions to the surveyors and the procurement of new instruments, his dream being to establish a state-of-the-art observatory. Since 1815, the survey project had made use of a small, octangular observatory just south of Akershus Fortress, but as this was really little more than a shack, Hansteen often chose to make his observations at home, from his garden.

In 1830, the Norwegian Parliament grants funding for the construction of an observatory on a small plot at Solli, just outside the capital – its cornerstone features the inscription 'Et nos petimus astra' ('Also we are seeking the stars'), and Hansteen made good use of the stars when he sought to put Norway on the map by finding the observatory's accurate latitude and longitude values. In 1848, after completing thousands of celestial observations, Hansteen is satisfied with his result of 59 degrees 54 minutes 43.7 seconds north.

The Round Tower in Copenhagen became the basis for comparison when attempting to determine the observatory's longitude and, in the summer of 1847, twenty-one precision clocks are sent back and forth between Oslo and Copenhagen by steamer in order to measure the variations in time between the astronomical observations. The results of 119 comparisons show that Hansteen's observatory is situated seven minutes and twenty-five seconds west of the Round Tower. This prime meridian then formed the basis from which all longitude values on Norwegian maps were ascertained, right up until the international prime meridian was established at Greenwich in 1884.

SCHOOLS AND TOURISM | In 1832, Hansteen becomes the first director of Norges geografiske Opmaaling (the Geographical Survey of Norway) not to have come from a military background – change is afoot in terms of both the function and distribution of maps. No longer are maps the sole preserve of the state, military, traders and maritime personnel – they are increasingly becoming a part of everyday life for more and more members of society. This is connected to the gradual changes being made to the school system – and a slight increase in wealth that enables an increasing number of people to go on holiday.

The world's first travel agency, the British company Cox & Kings, was established in 1758 and, two years later, J. H. Schneider published the first atlas for children: *Atlas des enfants* consists of simple maps, with many accompanied by question-and-answer-style texts to teach children about each of the various countries' climate, system of government, religion, clothing, cities and more.

In Norway, geography became a part of children's schooling when Ludvig Platou published the school atlas *Udtog af Geographien for Begyndere* (*Excerpts from Geography for Beginners*) in 1810, Carl Bonaparte Roosen drew his *Kart over Norge til Brug ved Skoleunderviisning* (*Map of Norway for Use in School Teaching*) in 1824, and Georg Prahl published the *Kart over den sydlige Deel af Kongeriget Norge, udarbeidet til Platou's*

Lære og Haandbog i Geographien (*Map of the Southern Part of the King-dom of Norway, Prepared for Platou's Handbook for the Study and Teach-ing of Geography*) in 1836. The subject was formalised through the new Education Act of 1860, which stated that the objective of schooling was not only to give students the Christian education necessary for confirma-tion, but also to provide them with 'the knowledge and skills that should be possessed by every member of society.' Chapter 2, paragraph 5 of the act stated that students should understand 'selected sections of the text-book, and primarily those relating to the description of the Earth, the nat-ural sciences and history.'

In 1863, Peter Andreas Jensen, a priest and author from Bergen, published the *Læsebog for Folkeskolen og Folkehjemmet* (*Textbook for Elementary School and Home*), which contains the following passage about the Earth:

> If we were able to see the entire Earth at once, we would find that it is round like a ball, and not flat like a baking stone, as many may still be-lieve. The reason the Earth looks flat to us is because we are only able to see a very small part of its surface. [...] In order to see the Earth's shape and its entire surface at once, we can draw its land and water on a ball, which is then called a globe. If you cut this down the middle, from the North Pole to the South Pole, this forms hemispheres – the eastern hemisphere and the western hemisphere. These hemispheres can also be drawn on a flat sheet of paper, to create a *planiglobium* or a world map. Such a map can be found in every well-equipped school, and on it your teacher will show you the large areas of land and sea that you will now hear more about.

The section ends with a footnote: 'The following sections should not be studied in school without the teacher allowing the children to follow along on the wall map.' The children may then read about the difference between the mainland, peninsulas and islands, and the old world and the new. The most important countries to learn about are listed as Sverige (Sweden), Danmark (Denmark), De britiske Lande (Britain), Holland og Belgien (Holland and Belgium), Frankrige (France), Spanien og Portugal (Spain and Portugal), Italien (Italy), Schweiz (Switzerland), Tysk-land (Germany), Det preussiske Rige (the Kingdom of Prussia), Østerrige (Austria), Tyrkiet (Turkey), Grækenland (Greece) and Rusland (Russia). Asia, Africa, America and Australia are then each represented with their own chapter. About Ny-York (New York), the book states: 'Many of our countrymen also arrive here, seeking a new home in this part of the world.'

New methods of transport mean that people move around more than they used to, but the unavailability of good maps results in a market for travel handbooks that provide the distances between various places and the locations of coaching inns. As early as 1774, Danish writer Hans Holck published his *Norsk Veyviser for Reysende* (*Travellers' Guide to Norway*), a fairly inaccurate overview of the distances and travel fares charged along the main roads between the cities of Bergen, Oslo, Stavanger and Trondheim.

The situation improved when Jacob Lehmann published the *Landev-eiene mellem Norges Stæder* (*Country Roads Between Places in Norway*) in 1816, and a survey to measure the lengths of the roads started the same year. But the farmers protested at this – and for good reason – because the survey resulted in the roads being listed with shorter distances, there-by reducing the fares the farmers were able to charge for a lift. Many re-sponded by scribbling out the distances given in local handbooks. 'Long have we lacked a reliable road map of Norway,' lamented *Hermoder* magazine in 1822 – but seven years later the magazine's prayers were answered when Lieutenant C. H. P. Lund published his *Veikart over Norge* (*Road Map of Norway*) – even if this only covered the southern part of the country. The *Lomme-Reiseroute* (*Pocket Travel Route Guide*), published anonymously in 1840, describes the travel routes from Oslo to Trondheim via Gudbrandsdalen and Østerdalen. Here, the reader learns that the landlord at Kongsvoll coaching inn has two 'comely daughters';

Next pages | Ivar Refsdal's world map from the *Atlas for skole og hjem* (*Atlas for School and Home*) published in 1910 bears witness to the age of colonialism. Indonesia is '*Sundaöerne (Ned.)*', Bangladesh, India and Pakistan are '*For-Indien (Br.)*', Namibia is '*Tysk S.V.A.*', Bot-swana, Lesotho, Swaziland, South Africa, Zambia and Zimbabwe are somewhat errone-ously labelled '*Rhodesia (Br.)*' and Finland is a part of Russia. Norway and Sweden are the same colour, but divided by a border.

2

Planiglober
i flatetro projektion.

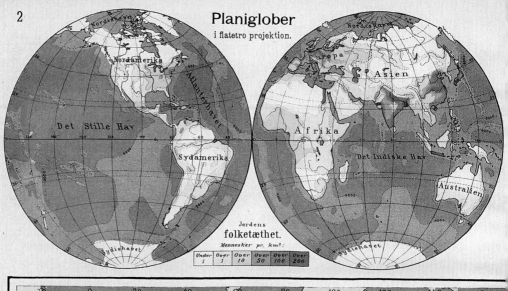

Jordens
folketæthet.
Mennesker pr. km²:

Under 1	Over 1	Over 10	Over 50	Over 100	Over 200

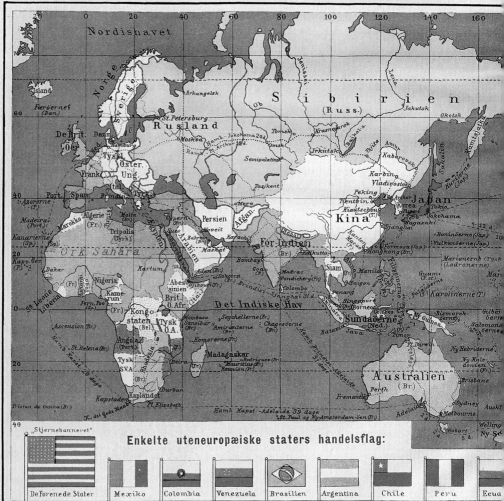

Enkelte uteneuropæiske staters handelsflag:

"Stjernebanneret"

| De Forenede Stater | Mexiko | Colombia | Venezuela | Brasilien | Argentina | Chile | Peru | Ecua |

the second edition includes routes to the western and southern parts of the country.

Throughout the summers of 1842 and 1843, historian and cartographer Peter Andreas Munch hikes through the mountains of southern Norway. He's on a study tour in a mostly uncharted area to find the places and roads he's read about in the *Sagas* and other works from the Middle Ages. For a handwritten book about his journey through the mountains, he draws a *Kart over Fjældstrakten mellem Hardanger, Voss, Hallingdal, Numedal, Thelemarken og Ryfylke* (*Map of the Mountains Between Hardanger, Voss, Hallingdal, Numedal, Telemark and Ryfylke*) – the first to properly depict the mountains. In his introduction, he criticises Pontoppidan's map from 1785 – 'the best and most complete to have existed of Norway until now' – for only having covered 'the more accessible and inhabited areas [...] The mountains he has not added nor specified, but rather only hinted at,' and one area even seems to be 'imaginary'. In a letter to a friend, Munch described how useful it had been for him to draw the map. 'Only upon undertaking my map works has it become clear to me how important, yes, how immensely important, the study of topography is for our history.'

Much followed his first map with a *Kart over det sydlige Norge* (*Map of Southern Norway*) in 1847, and a *Kart over det nordlige Norge* (*Map of Northern Norway*) in 1852. The map of southern Norway features almost 40,000 place names. Since the country had for many years been mapped by Danes and Norwegians writing Danish, most previous maps of Norway were full of place names such as *Walöer* for Hvaler, *Quievogh* for Kvivaag, *Steinbergdalen* for Stemberdalen and so on. An important part of Munch's project was therefore to enter as many Norwegianised name forms as possible on the map. His map of southern Norway became so popular that it had to be reprinted four times and, in the English book *Norway and Its Scenery* by Thomas Forester published in 1853, was presented as indispensable for anyone planning to visit the country.

Den Norske Turistforening (the Norwegian Trekking Association) was founded in 1868, and became an enthusiastic proponent of the improved mapping of areas popular with tourists. The association also had members who drew their own maps and published them in the association's yearbooks, including a *Kart over Haukelid-Fjeld* (*Map of Hauke-lifjell*) from 1868, a *Kart over Galdhøpiggen* (*Map of Galdhøpiggen*) from 1873, a *Kart over Jotunfjeldene med omgivelser* (*Map of the Jotunfjell Mountains and the Surrounding Areas*) created through a collaboration with the Kontoret for private opmaalinger og kartarbeider (Office for Private Surveys and Map-makers), and a *Kart over Jostedalsbræen* (*Map of the Jostedal Glacier*) from 1890. The association also issued a standing request to its members: 'Since it is of great importance that the Geographical Survey of Norway obtain all serviceable information for the revision of older maps, any tourists who during their travels encounter inaccuracies in the published maps are encouraged to report the necessary details to the survey, either directly or through the association's secretary.'

The errors in the maps of the mountainous regions may be due to any number of problems the surveyors were forced to reckon with – the following diary entry from Jotunheimen, dated 1873, provides an insight:

4th.   Arrived at Gjendin. Fog in the Jotun mountains.

6th.   Intense flurries of snow; tent snowed under. No work done.

9th.   Climbed Semmetind; ascent extremely strenuous due to the amount of fresh snow. Worked by the cairn and sighted a few locations, but at 3 p.m. the snowstorm returned as intensely as before, and so no more could be done.

10th. Bad weather with driving snow and full storm, impossible to endure any more as blankets and walking clothes are wet. Decamped to the tourist hut down at Gjedin.

The country's infrastructure was in a state of flux, with the horse and cart being replaced by more mechanical means of transport. Munch drew a road map, published posthumously in 1867, which shows the planned railway lines. Eighteen years later, on the second printing, the map featured 200 railway stations across eight lines. According to the *Fedraheimen* newspaper, Albert Cammermeyer's travel map from 1881, drawn by Per Nissen, includes 'the names of all coaching inns, docks, telegraph offices and railway stations; all roads are clearly represented, including main roads, country roads and the most important mountain passes,' according to the *Fedraheimen* newspaper. The reviewers also liked Cammermeyer's *Lomme-Reisekart over Norge* (*Pocket Travel Map of Norway*): 'All tourists and mountain climbers can be pleased about this map, which contains an overview of most of Jotunheimen. Considering what little I know about the mountains, I like the map; all the roads are visible, and everything is clearly presented. The blue water stands out against the brown-coloured rock, and the snowy mountains all seem to rise up with their white tops.'

The *Kart over Nordmarken og Sörkedalen for Skilöbere og Turister* (*Map of Nordmarken and Sörkedalen for Skiers and Tourists*) was published by engineer Ernst Bjerknes in the year 1890 – and is the world's first ski map. Bjerknes has marked both 'generally trafficked ski trails and winter roads' and 'steep slopes or sharp turns,' and notes that 'at the farms, whose names are underlined in red, food and lodgings can be obtained.'

People also started to cycle – and in 1894 Nicolay C. Ræder created the *Hjulturistkart over det sydlige Norge* (*Bicycle Touring Map of Southern Norway*) for the *Norsk Hjulturist-Forening* (Norwegian 'Wheel-tourist' Association), which was supplemented with details of the incline of the roads. A handbook providing information about what can be seen along the thirty-one routes accompanied the map.

The bicycle touring map gradually became a map for motorists, and in 1908, with 100 cars and fifty motorcycles in Norway, a brief 'List of points to remember for motorists' is added to the handbook – a useful supplement to the traffic rules, which were still yet to be written. Nine years later, the Kongelig Norsk Automobilklub (Royal Norwegian Automobile Club) published the first *Automobil Kart over det sydlige Norge* (*Automobile Map of Southern Norway*).

THE WORLD OF YESTERDAY | Students of the academic year 1902/1903 became the first in Norway to peruse an atlas that would constitute many Norwegian schoolchildren's first encounter with the wider world for several generations to come: the *Atlas for skole og hjem* (*Atlas for School and Home*) by Ivar Refsdal. Continually reprinted, it became a permanent fixture of classrooms until well into the 1960s, and when geography became a separate subject through the new Education Act of 1889, Refsdal wrote that the discipline was not given particularly high standing, and that 'most teachers must be content with a minimum of teaching materials, and the little that exists is often so poor, that it is almost equal to having none'. Refsdal drew his own maps, which were simple, clear and pedagogical, and was highly praised by teachers and geography experts alike. He also drew wall maps for use in Norwegian classrooms.

On the 1910 edition of Refsdal's map, Asia and Africa are characterised by colonies; Poland is not a country in its own right, but is split between Germany and Russia; Finland is part of Russia; Ireland belongs to Great Britain; and the Czech Republic, Slovakia, Slovenia, Croatia, Romania, Moldova and Bulgaria all form part of 'Austria-Hungary', which dominates the southern part of central Europe. 'I was born in 1881 in the great and mighty empire of the Habsburg Monarchy, but you would look for it in vain on the map today; it has vanished without trace', wrote Austrian author Stefan Zweig in his memoir *The World of Yesterday* from 1942.

Above Refsdal's world map is a small, extra map, which symbolises one of the newly independent Norway's sources of pride – the western Arctic. It is titled *Nordamerikas arktiske öer* (*North America's Arctic Islands*), and states that 'the lands discovered by Sverdrup are coloured red'. This is the height of Norwegian Arctic Ocean imperialism, with Fridtjof Nansen crossing Greenland on skis, the *Fram* crossing Arctic waters, Roald Amundsen reaching the South Pole, and expeditions to Svalbard, Jan Mayen, Bear Island and Bouvet Island. Norway put itself on the map by putting other countries on the map.

KART
over
Dr. FRIDTJOF NANSEN'S

POLAREXPEDITION
1893-1896

"Frams" Rute fra 14. Marts 1895.

Dr. Nansen's Polareise.

ALASKA

Mackenzie Flod

Wrangel L^d

Berings St.

Ost Cap

Nordvestl. Grænse til 1869.

Jeannettes Drift i Den 1881.

Ny Sibiriske Øer

Onmulog B.

Jeannette O — C. Camenni
Henrietta O — Ny Sibirien
Jeannettes Undergang — C. Wyssoki
Faddejew O
Emma — De Long Øer — Bennett O — Bere schnich C. — Figurin O — Amisgie C.

Nahe O
Lille O — Liachow Øer
Kessol O — Stolbovoi O
Bjelkow O — Barkin
Sannikou L^d — Sugastyr

Seljat
Borchaja B.

Siklach
Balun Tatjanskoje

Fram' i Isen — NORDENSKJØLD
22. Sept. 1893 — SØ — Sept.

Bolkolak

Chalanga R.

Østl. Taimyr Halvø

C. Tscheljuskin

Taddæsh

Nansen og Johansen forlader "Fram" 14. Marts 1895.

Taimyr

Vestl. Taimyr Halvø

POLAR

86° 14'
7. April 1895

POL
85° 86° 87° 88° 89°

REGION

Dickson Hav

Markham 1876

Smith Sund

C. Washington

Petermann L^d — Franz — Wilscek L^d
Kong Oscar Ld Joseph — Salm O
Overvintring 1895-96 — Mac C. Clintock O
Alexandra L^d — Northbrook O — C. Nassau
Clarke L^d — C. Hallen Broken

C. Mauritius

KARISKE HAV

Peary og Astrup

Independance Bai

BAFFIN-BAI

GRØN-

Peary 1827

Syv Øerne

80 Mosse B.
SPIDS — Nordost L^d
Dan — BERGEN

BARENTS HAV

Samojed Halvø

Kara Bus

Parry 1827

set Land 1772

GRØN-

C. Bismarck

Peary og Maigaard

Shannon O

Bären O

Kuløujew O

Kola Halvø

Kenia

LAND

INDLANDS

Nansen 1888

Sound

Cap Dan

Jan Mayen

Nordkap
Hammerfest
Tromsø

Vardø

St. Petersburg

ISLAND

nordl. Polarkirkel

Greenwich Meridian

Badø

Trondhjem

Stockholm

Fær' Øer

Stadt

Shetlands Øer — Bergen

Kristiania

SCOTLAND — Kristiansand

| | Skovland |
| | Høifjeld og Heder |

→ kolde Strømme

→ varme D°

Tegnet af Knud Bergslien.

Forlagt af Cammermeyer's Boghandel, Kristiania

Ny revideret Udgave

Kristiania Litografiske Aktiebolag 1896.

WHITE SPACES IN THE NORTH

Isachsen, Canada
78° 46′ 59″ N
103° 29′ 59″ W

One September morning in 1896, a few days after the *Fram* had arrived home from its first expedition to the Arctic Ocean, Captain Otto Sverdrup was unloading the ship in Lysaker Bay when Fridtjof Nansen came aboard. He wanted to hear about whether Sverdrup was interested in heading north once again – both Consul Axel Heiberg and the owners of the Ringnes brewery, brothers Amund and Ellef Ringnes, were willing to provide the necessary funds to equip a new polar expedition.

'I cannot say otherwise than that I was pleased at this flattering offer. There were still many white spaces on the map which I was glad of an opportunity of colouring with the Norwegian colours, and thus the expedition was decided on,' wrote Sverdrup in his travelogue *New Land* seven years later. The first *Fram* expedition had proved that there was no mainland at the North Pole – at least, not in the eastern parts of the region through which the expedition had sailed. But there was still much uncertainty surrounding the areas further west. On a map from 1896, which shows the route the *Fram* followed across the Arctic Ocean, parts of northern Greenland and the area to the west of this – and from here all the way around the polar region to the Ny Sibirske Øer (New Siberian

A map of the route taken by the first *Fram* expedition, which took place from 1893 to 1896. The map was drawn by Knud Bergslien in 1896 to mark the expedition's achievements. Fridtjof Nansen was somewhat surprised not to find any new land in the waters through which they sailed. The first *Fram* expedition is described on pages 281–282.

Islands) – are completely blank. Only parts of the east coast of Ellesmere Island had so far been explored, and Sverdrup believed Norway could lay claim to the areas he and his crew mapped.

The expedition set sail on 24 June 1898, the original aim being to map the northern and unknown parts of Greenland. The *Fram* would first sail up Greenland's west coast, as this was as far north as the crew would be able to travel before being forced to harbour for the winter and undertake sledding expeditions to go further north and east – but due to challenging ice conditions this plan was abandoned in favour of exploring the Arctic islands of northern Canada. Spending the next four years in these waters, the crew explored and mapped an area the size of southern Norway – more than any expedition before them had ever achieved within the Arctic region.

The expedition's cartographer was Gunnar Isachsen, of whom Sverdrup wrote: 'Gunerius Ingvald Isachsen, the cartographer of the expedition, was a first lieutenant in the cavalry. He was born at Drobak, in 1868, and has been in the army since 1891. Subsequently to the latter date he had passed through the Central School of Gymnastics.' Isachsen's first task was to find the location at which the *Fram* would harbour for the winter, Hayes Sound at Ellesmere, and he determined both the longitude and latitude values through observations of the Sun and Moon. The expedition possessed three theodolites, three sextants, a compass, a telescope, three large chronometers and six pocket chronometers. They created a surveyor's table onboard, and set markers out in the landscape when performing triangulations. The sleds were also equipped with odometers – small wheeled devices that measured the distances they covered.

On Wednesday 14 September 1888, at 4.30 a.m., Isachsen set out on his first mapping expedition, together with Sverdrup and jack of all trades Ivar Fosheim. Sverdrup was eager to find out whether Hayes Sound really was a sound, or simply a large fjord.

The journey was hard, and progress through the steep, unstable terrain was slow. None of the team were experienced in dog sledding, and when the dogs pulled like crazy and set off down the slopes at a furious pace, Sverdrup 'quite expected them to do for themselves and for us too.' Neither Isachsen nor Fosheim had ever slept in a tent before: 'Tent-life was something quite new to Isachsen and Fosheim, and they were very keen to experience it.' Fosheim felt as if he was suffocating with his head inside his sleeping bag. 'On no account would Fosheim keep his head inside; he said he felt as if he was being suffocated, and thrust it out again, but not for long,' recounted Sverdrup – the temperature was around 30 degrees below freezing.

Mapping the polar regions at this time posed a highly specific set of challenges – not only did one have to contend with freezing ears, fingers and toes, but strong winds, huge volumes of snow and thick fog also made it difficult to perform any surveying activities at all. 'In such circumstances one has time to fret one's self almost distraught,' wrote Sverdrup after attempting to take measurements on a day with particularly bad weather. If the crew found themselves on a glacier, it was almost impossible to take measurements because it was difficult to see the horizon, and since the Magnetic North Pole is in a different location to the geographic North Pole, they were unable to rely on their compass. It was also often necessary to turn back to the ship before the work was completed because provisions were running low.

On this first excursion, Sverdrup's desire to settle the question of whether the water formed a fjord or a sound would have to wait. 'We ought, of course, to have investigated this,' wrote Sverdrup after Isachsen had been high up into the mountains and seen a fjord that penetrated into the land further north, 'but the dogs' food had given out, and we were compelled to return to the ship.'

A few days later, however, the company returned with eleven men, sixty dogs and extensive provisions, and set up camp to explore the area in greater detail. 'The work first on our hands was to find a base[line] for the mapping operations,' wrote Sverdrup. Isachsen had brought along a 20-metre-long steel tape for this purpose, and used it to measure a 1,100-metre-long baseline for the triangulation activities. The following spring, they measured a new baseline 1,500 metres in length slightly further north, and – to be completely sure that their results were correct – two more baselines further east along Hayes Sound, which was renamed the Hayes*fjord* following their investigations. The fjord split in two at its innermost point, and the names they gave to the southernmost arm and the place where it ends –

Beitstadfjorden and Stenkjær – testify to Sverdrup's longing for home: these were the names of places he had lived as a young man.

During the expedition's first autumn and winter, the crew mapped their immediate surroundings. On Tuesday 23 May 1899, when the brief Arctic summer had scarcely started, Isachsen and Ove Braskerud, the ship's stoker and general handyman from Solør, set out on a long trip to explore the western parts of Ellesmere Island. In his report, Isachsen wrote: 'The orders I received were agreeably brief; they were: with one man as a companion, two six-dog teams, and victuals for thirty days to traverse the inland ice of Ellesmere Land. I was to choose the direction myself, and I chose westward and endeavoured to reach the west coast, afterwards proceeding as far south as I could.'

Isachsen and Braskerud made their way up onto a glacier, and from there travelled in a south-westerly direction. The dogs had 'plenty of time for rest during our reconnaissances, which were frequent, and often of long duration.' At midnight on 2 June they spotted a fjord on the west coast, but decided not to make their way down to it – Isachsen wished to stay as high up as possible, ascending the mountaintops in order to obtain as good an overview of the landscape as possible. 'From a good point of vantage we observed that the chain of mountains stretched as far as we could see to the south-east, and that they were free of snow; while at the same time they shut in the view to the west and south-west.' On other days it was impossible to carry out their planned tasks: 'Unfortunately accurate measurement of [the mountain's] height was in the circumstances impossible.' Snowstorms and fog meant that they returned to the ship ten days late: 'We were very sorry that our supply of tobacco had given out, though Braskerud's waistcoat pocket, which had once had tobacco in it, did service in our pipes for three whole days.'

But the crew of the *Fram* were not alone in the ice fields – their first winter harbour was right at the centre of Inuit hunting terrain. Sverdrup, full of awe and admiration, believed that polar researchers must 'take lessons from the two races of native peoples' who were best able to cope in these harsh surroundings – 'Finnen og Eskimoen' – the Sami and the Inuit. That spring, the *Fram* received its first visit from an Inuit man who Sverdrup described as looking 'very intelligent for a so-called "savage".'

They allowed him to look through polar researcher Eivind Astrup's book *Blandt Nordpolens Naboer* (*Among North Pole Neighbours*), published in 1895, and it turned out that the man had been Astrup's companion. 'By the help of a map, with which he seemed as much at home as a professor of geography [...] we got out of him that he was from the island of Kama, in Inglefield Gulf.'

VIKINGS | Naturally enough, the exploration of the northern regions started with the first people to travel north and settle there – the Inuit, who live in Greenland, northern Canada and Alaska, are the descendants of people who crossed the Bering Strait from Siberia some time around the year AD 1000. But the Inuit also tell legends about a people they drove away when they arrived, and archaeological excavations have confirmed that the Tunit or Sivullirmiut, which means 'the first inhabitants', lived in the Arctic region over 2,500 years ago, and that other people also inhabited the area before them, 5,000 years ago.

The Sami have lived in Scandinavia for at least 2,000 years, and a broad range of other native peoples live across Siberia – but unlike the first Norwegians, these people left behind no written sources we can study. The *Sagas* are the earliest sources to provide us with first-hand information.

When Icelander Eirik Raude, known in the English-speaking world as Erik the Red, raided Greenland in the year AD 982, he found traces of settlements, boats and stone artefacts on both the east and west coasts, 'from which it was evident that the same kind of people had lived there as inhabited Vinland and whom the Greenlanders called "Skraelings",' wrote Are Frode in his *Islendingabók* (*The Book of the Icelanders*) from AD 1130. 'Skraelings' was the Norse people's name for the Americans.

Erik the Red's son, Leif Eriksson, has had the honour of being named the Norse discoverer of Vinland – America – despite the fact that the *Saga of the Greenlanders* states that a man named Bjarni Herjolfsson was the first to set eyes on the country after becoming lost on one of his voyages – although he never went ashore there.

The Vikings sailed across great distances, from Norway, Sweden and Denmark to Iceland, Greenland, America, the Faroe Islands, Ireland, Scotland, England, Russia, France, Italy and Turkey. Sigurd the Crusader travelled all the way to Jerusalem, and the *Landnámabók* (*Book of Settlements*) makes reference to a country that may be Svalbard. In light of this, it is astonishing that the Vikings never made a single map – not a single stretch of coastline or group of islands was ever reproduced by them. We can therefore only conclude that the Vikings managed perfectly well with verbal maps. Archaeologist and author Helge Ingstad imagines how this might have worked:

> Skippers, seamen and farmers would gather to discuss their experiences of many long voyages, sharing wise words about the winds, currents and ice, distant waters and far off coasts. Knowledge was added to knowledge, and a great many fixed routes were established – a tradition emerged.

The *Hauksbók* (*Book of Haukr*) from 1308 provides an example of such a verbal map:

> So say wise men that from Stadt in Norway it is seven days' sail to Horn on Iceland's east coast, but from Snøfellsnes it is four days' sail to Hvarf on Greenland. From Hernar in Norway one must sail quickly west to Hvarf on Greenland, sailing north of Shetland so that one may see the land in clear weather, but south of the Faroe Islands such that one only sees the mountains at half height, and so far south of Iceland that the country's seabirds and whales may be seen . . .

Close to land, it was possible to navigate by landmarks and to ask for directions, while at sea it was necessary to navigate by the Sun and the stars. For longer voyages, the Vikings would have a navigation expert aboard – a 'leidsagnarmadr' – who would '*deila ættir*', or establish the cardinal directions. *The Saga of the Greenlanders* also tells of how Leif and his crew took measurements of the Sun when they constructed houses in America and spent the winter there: 'There was more *jamndøgr* there than in Greenland or Iceland. The sun there had *eyktarstad* and *dagmálastad* on *skamdagen*.'

Jamndøgr is the equinox, when day and night are equal in length, and *skamdagen* is the shortest day of the year, the winter solstice, 21 December. *Eyktarstad* and *dagmålastad* are the positions of the sun at *eykt* and *dagmåla* – dinner and breakfast. In Vinland, unlike Scandinavia, the sun is up at both *eyktarstad* and *dagmålastad* at the winter solstice.

Based on this information, historian Gustav Storm and astronomer Hans Geelmuyden calculated Vinland's location as 49 degrees 55 minutes northern latitude – in northern Newfoundland. The fact that Ingstad also found ruins of houses dating back thousands of years in the area also confirms Storm and Geelmuyden's result.

An Icelandic map from 1590, known as the Skálholt Map, also features a 'Winlandiæ Promontorium' where Newfoundland is situated. Another map, drawn by Danish theologian Hans Poulson Resen in 1605, is similar to the Skálholt Map, but Resen wrote that it was based on a map that was only 100 years old (*'ex antiqua quadam mappa, rudi modo delineata, ante aliquot centenos annos ...'*). Ingstad believed that both the Skálholt Map and Resen's map were based on a common map dating from before the time of Columbus.

A third map, the Vinland Map, on which America is represented as an island – 'Vinlandia Insula' – was revealed to the public in 1965, after some of the world's most eminent map experts from Yale University and the British Museum concluded that the map was drawn at some time around the year 1440, fifty years before Columbus set out across the Atlantic. The map was therefore deemed the oldest known map of America – but others were less convinced. First, nobody knew of a single source from the year 1440 or later that referred to the map, and second, Greenland had been reproduced just a little too accurately. Leif Eriksson's name, mentioned in one of the map's texts, had also been Latinised to 'Erissonius' – a practice that only became common from the 1600s. Following much study, the map is today believed to be a forgery from more recent times.

Next pages | A map of the Arctic Ocean, based on the notes of Dutch explorer Willem Barentsz and made just before he died in Novaya Zemlya in 1597. The map depicts the sea and stretches of coastline in the north with impressive accuracy. The Barents Sea north of Norway was later named after Barentsz. *Het neuwe land* is Svalbard, and this is the first time the group of islands featured on a map.

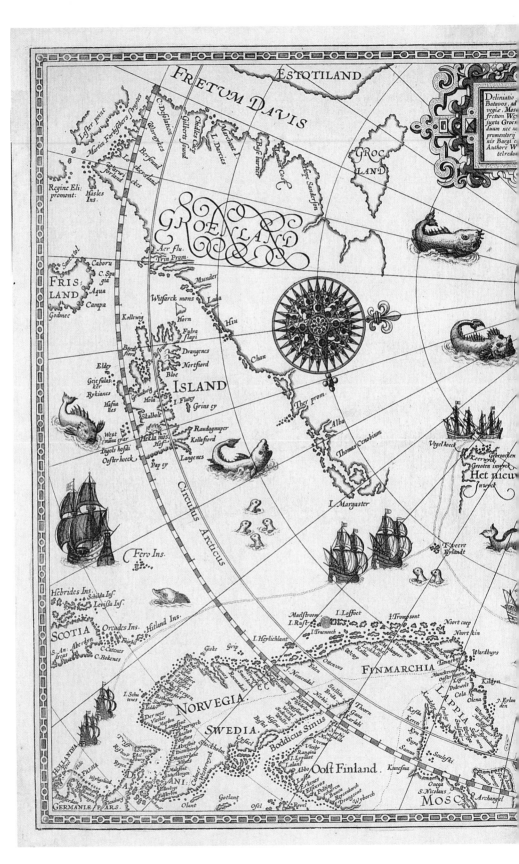

ESTOTILAND.

FRETUM DAVIS

Lester point

C. Defolacion

Martin Forbishers Freyets

Gilberts Sound

L. Darcies

Warwykes

Brisound

C. Aberland

Charles Cape

Marchant I.

Baß harnes

Hope Sandefon

Tyrwit forland

L. af Larwes rockes

Regine Eli: promont:

Haßles Ins.

GROC LAND

GROENLAND

Aer flu.

Trin Prom.

Santstol

Caboru

C. Spagia

FRIS: LAND

Aqua

Campa

Godnec

Kollewig

Witsarck mons

Munder

Lada

Horn

Fulva stapi

Hiu

Chan

Eldey

Gcie fulas ker

Rykianes

Hafna iles

Drangencs

Nortfiord

Bloc

ISLAND

Grundwig

Hola

Skalholt

I. Flatey

Grins ey

Raudagnuper

Kollafiord

Hekla mos

West emana eyar

Ingols hofdi

Oofter hoeck

Hof

Langens

Pap ey

Circulus Arcticus

Ther prom.

Alba

Thomas Cenobium

Vogel hoeck

Keerwyck

Gebrocken

Grooten inwyck

Het nieuw Inwyck

I. Margaster

Fero Ins.

Hebrides Ins.

Schilda Inf.

Levißa Inf.

Hitland Ins.

SCOTIA

Orcades Ins.

S. An: dreas

Aberdyn

Buthil

C. Catenes

C. Bokenes

Giske

Gryp

I. Heylichlant

Maelstroom

I. Ruft

I. Loffoet

I. Tracnoech

I. Tromsont

Noort caep

Noort kin

Wardhuys

FINMARCHIA

Tanet bay

Mancken voert

Oofter Haven

Leger

Podewolt

Cola

Olena

I. Erylan den

T. veere Bylandt

LAPPIA

NORVEGIA.

I. Schutenes

SWEDIA.

Stockholm

Boddicus Sinus

Thoorn

Gutus Caribli

Abbo

Oost Finland.

Kinesma

Lyplant

Lalant

Erckens

Elfynoo

Pelting

Onega

S. Nicolaus

Archangel

HOLLANDIA

FRISI

DANI

Scagen

Calmer

GERMANIÆ PARS.

Olant

Gotlant

Ofel

Revel

Wyborch

Drangcent

Rescuborch

MOSC

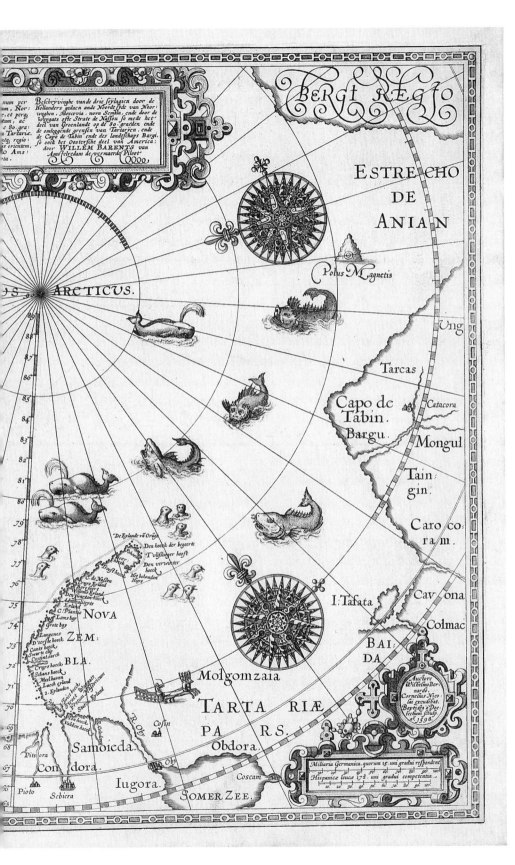

BERGI REGIO

ESTRECHO
DE
ANIAN

C. Polus Magnetis

ARCTICVS.

Ung

Tarcas

Capo de
Tabin.
Bargu.

Catacora

Mongul

Tain-
gin.

Caro co-
ra m.

I. Tasata

Cav ona

Colmac

BAI
DA

NOVA

ZEM:

BLA.

De Eylandē vā Oranj
Den hoeck der begeert:
T'vlissinger hooft
Den verwinter
hoeck
Het behouden
Huys

C. de Nassou
Orangi Eylandt
Maersser
Willem Eyland
Lamsvliet plis
Eylant
C. Plancio
Lems bay
Grote bay
Langenes
D'croes te hoeck
Cants hoeck
Swarte clip
Costintsarch
Crus hoeck
Schans hoeck
Meelhaven
Linck Eland
2. Eylanden

Molgomzaia

TARTA RIÆ
PA RS.
Obdora.

Samoieda.

Con dora.

R. Oby

Cossin

Iugora.

Pits ora

Pioto

Sebiera

Valdom hoeck

R. Colmac

Ob

Coscam

SOMER ZEE.

Auctore
Wilhelmo Ber-
nardo,
Cornelius Nico
lai excudebat.
Baptista à Doe-
techum sculp.
aͦ 1598.

Miliaria Germanica, quorum 15. uni gradui respondent
Hispanicæ leucæ 17½. uni gradui competentia.

Beschryvinghe van de drie seylagien door de
Hollanders gedaen ande Noorde syde van Noor-
weghen, Moscovia, nova Sembla, ende door de
Wergats ofte Strate de Nassou so mede het
deel van Groenlandt op de 80. graden ende
de omleggende grensen van Tartaryen, ende
de Capo de Tabin ende des landschaps Bargi,
so oock het Oostersche deel van America:
door WILLEM BARENTS van
Amstelredam de vermaerde Piloot.

But the idea that someone might have drawn such a map around the year 1440 is not an improbable one, because the voyages made to and from America, Greenland and Iceland continued. In the year 1075, in his *Account of the Diocese of Hamburg, the archbishop's activities and island kingdoms in the north*, Adam of Bremen wrote: 'The King of Denmark has also told me about yet another island, which many have observed in this ocean. It is called Vinland, [...] and this is not idle rumours nor fabrication, I have heard it from trustworthy Danish sources.' The *Icelandic Annals* from 1121 state that 'Erik, bishop of Greenland, set out to search for Vinland,' while those from 1347 state: 'A ship came from Greenland. [...] There were seventeen men onboard and they had sailed to Markland, but were driven here by a storm at sea.' Markland was the name Leif Eriksson gave to an area north of Vinland. A cosmography possibly originating from Abbot Nikolás of Munkatverå, who died in 1159, states: 'South of Greenland is Helluland. Then comes Markland, and then it is not far to Vinland the Good, which some believe goes out of Africa, and if so, the sea must flow between Vinland and Markland.' *Hauksbók* tells of Ari, who set out to sea and reached White Men's Land, also known as Great Ireland: 'It lies in the ocean to westward, near Vinland the Good, said to be a six-day sail west from Ireland.'

But how much of this Norse knowledge of the northern regions found its way to the continent's cartographers? Very little. On none of the most important medieval maps, such as the Hereford Mappa Mundi and Ebstorf Map, do we find any real attempt to represent that which lies north of Thule and the Arctic Circle. But there is one exception – the prayer book map from the mid-1200s, on which there are two islands to the north of Norway, Ipboria and Aramphe, which are named for two peoples – the Hyperboreans and the Arampheans – who the Greeks believed lived in the far north.

In the year AD 77, in his *Naturalis Historia*, Pliny the Elder wrote about the Amalehian Sea, 'a name that in the language of the natives means "frozen"'; in the vicinity of this sea were islands inhabited by people with hooves instead of feet, or ears so large they could cover their entire body with them. Adam of Bremen wrote that 'beyond Norway, which is the outermost country in the Nordic region, there are no human settlements, only the terrible and endless sea, which surrounds the whole world.' In 1410, Cardinal Pierre d'Ailly wrote in his *Tractatus de imagine mundi*: 'Beyond Thule, the last island of the Ocean, after one day's sail the sea is frozen and stiff. At the Poles there live great ghosts and ferocious beasts, the enemies of man.'

NORTHERN PASSAGES | The systematic mapping of the polar regions only began when the Europeans attempted to find a sea route to Asia that avoided sailing to the south of Africa or America – a Northwest Passage north of America, or a Northeast Passage north of Eurasia.

Once certain individuals had started to imagine that America might not be part of Asia, as Columbus had believed, they started to look for a way around or through this new continent in order to reach the riches of the East. In 1487, Italian explorer John Cabot kicked off the search for the Northwest Passage when attempting to sail north of the American continent – twenty-three years before Portuguese explorer Ferdinand Magellan sailed around the continent's southern tip. Cabot was therefore the first person to sail into the Arctic labyrinth that would be only gradually mapped over the next 400 years, until Norwegian polar explorer Roald Amundsen and his crew aboard the *Gjøa* finally reached the Pacific Ocean in 1906. Cabot was far from achieving his goal when he came up against land and ice, having only made it as far as Newfoundland. On his second expedition in 1498, Cabot and four of his ships disappeared without trace – an ominous omen of what awaited any explorer who dared to venture into these waters.

Cabot's maps have unfortunately not survived, but from looking at Spanish cartographer Juan de la Cosa's map of the east coast of America from 1500 it is clear that they were circulated. Here, at 52 degrees north, de la Cosas has drawn five English maritime flags, and written: *'Mar descubierta ynglesie in'* ('Sea discovered by the English'). The Portuguese also made attempts to find a route eastward via the west – explorer Gaspar Corte-Real reached Greenland, Labrador and Newfoundland in 1500 and 1501, and on an anonymous map from 1502, these areas are littered with Portuguese maritime flags. A text beside Greenland states that the area 'was discovered on behalf of Dom Manuel, King of Portugal, they believe this is outermost Asia.' Corte-Real also disappeared without trace.

But the British didn't give up hope of finding their way through the northern regions, and in 1541 Roger Barlow, a merchant from Bristol, presented his *Brief Summe of Geographie* to Henry VIII. Here, he wrote that since the Spanish and Portuguese had established their overseas empires in the east, south and west, there was only one direction left in which to discover anything, and this was 'the northe'. In 1553, a British expedition set out along the Norwegian coast in an attempt to find the Northeast Passage along Russia's as yet unmapped northern coast – they were able to do this because Olaus Magnus's *Carta Marina* from 1539 had shown that to the north of Scandinavia was open sea. As they rounded the northern tip of Norway, one of the captains named the cliffs at Knyskanes the North Cape – and the name continues to be used today. But just a short time later, the expedition was shipwrecked. Sixty-three men aboard two of the ships died of starvation and disease while overwintering on the Kola Peninsula.

The cartographers of the age disagreed on whether any northern passage to Asia existed, whether to the east or west. Many believed that America and Asia were one and the same continent, meaning that no passage was necessary – you would simply return to the Atlantic if you sailed along the north side of the continent towards the west. On the Portuguese map from 1502, the easternmost coast of Asia continues east off the map, perhaps indicating that it connects to America somewhere beyond the parchment, and the same is true of two Italian world maps produced a few years later.

In 1507, Johannes Ruysch, a Dutchman who may have been a member of Cabot's first expedition, created a world map on which Greenland is clearly connected to the eastern part of an Asian-American continent. Ruysch also connected Norway with a spit of land named Ventelant, which is in turn connected to Filapelat and Pilapelant, which extends northwards towards an island all the way up at the North Pole named Hyperborei Europe.

On a globe dating from around 1505, North America is broken up into a number of small islands that pose no obstacle whatsoever to anyone wishing to reach Asia in the east. These same islands are also included on German geographer Johannes Schöner's globe from 1515, but on his later globes, from 1520, 1523 and 1533, the North American continent becomes larger and larger, until it eventually links up with Asia.

The lack of reliable information meant that the areas of the Atlantic above 55 degrees north not only posed a challenge to cartographers – they also offered them free rein. Not everyone was as conservative as the Italian cartographer Giacomo Gastaldi had been in 1556, when he drew a map on which the northern regions were completely blank – and nor did Gastaldi remain so himself. On a world map from 1562, he added an opening between America and Asia that he named the Streti di Anian – the Strait of Anian. He probably took the name from Marco Polo's travelogues, where Ania is the name given to one of China's provinces, but the strait was pure conjecture. It remains striking, however, that Gastaldi placed it exactly where in reality the Bering Strait divides the two continents.

The Strait of Anian enjoyed a long life on European maps – it appears again on a map included in the English chronicler George Best's book *True Discourse* from 1578. Best had been a member of Captain Martin Frobisher's expedition in search of the Northwest Passage two years earlier, equipped with Mercator's world map from 1569 and Ortelius's atlas from 1570. Both showed a navigable route to the Pacific via the north side of the American continent. When in late July they sailed into Frobisher Bay, a bay at the south-east corner of Baffin Island, Frobisher thought he had Asia to his right and America to his left, and that the Pacific was just on the other side. In reality, 4,390 kilometres remained before the expedition would reach Asia's easternmost point. Due to heavy snow and the loss of a lifeboat, Frobisher turned around, just thirty-two kilometres from the end of the bay, convinced that he had discovered the Northwest Passage. He named it Frobisher Strait to indicate its status as the Strait of Magellan's northern counterpart. On the map included in *True Discourse*, the area Frobisher's expedition had reached is represented as a kingdom of islands, where the large and open 'Frobussher's Straightes' runs all the way to the Pacific via the Strait of Anian. Once back home in London, Frobisher sent word of where he had been to both Mercator and Ortelius. Ortelius made the journey across to England to obtain firsthand information about the new discoveries.

Meanwhile, Dutch navigator Willem Barentsz was looking for the Northeast Passage, and in 1596 made a third attempt to sail past Novaya Zemlya and on to the east. On 4 June, his expedition sighted the North

Cape – but from here, an obstinate skipper set the expedition's course a good deal further to the west than Barentsz had instructed. The next day they encountered the sea ice, and crew member Gerrit de Veer wrote in his diary that this also drove them westwards: 'therefore we wound about south-west and by west until two glasses were run out, and after that three glasses more south south-west, and then south three glasses, to sail to the island that we saw, as also to shun the ice. The ninth of June we found the island, that lay under 74 degrees and 30 minutes, and (as we guessed) it was about 20 miles long.' They called the island Beyren Eylandt – Bear Island – after having fought a polar bear: 'we saw a white bear, which we rowed after with our boat, thinking to cast a rope about her neck; but when we were near her, she was so great that we dare not do it, but rowed back again to our ship to fetch more men and our arms, and so made to her again with muskets, rifles, halberds and hatchets,' de Veer wrote, describing how the crew fought the bear for two hours because their 'weapons could do her little hurt,' before the bear finally succumbed.

Ten days later, the crew spotted a number of jagged mountaintops at 80 degrees north, and Barentsz named the area Spitsbergen. Despite the fact that they sailed north of these mountains, and travelled on down the west side as they mapped the coast from north to south, turning eastwards again when they reached the southern tip, they believed the area to be a part of Greenland.

Barentsz and four members of his crew would never return home – they died at the northern tip of Novaya Zemlya, where they were forced to spend the winter when their ship became stuck in the pack ice. But during the winter, Barentsz completed a map of the northern regions, which was published posthumously in 1598 – the first map to show Bear Island and Svalbard, and the first of many on which islands were no longer drawn around the Pole, and which instead presented the open Arctic Ocean.

NORTHWEST | In 1610, English explorer Henry Hudson discovered what is today known as the Hudson Strait, and was therefore the first European to sail into the huge Hudson Bay in northern Canada. Considering the bay's size, it is little wonder that Hudson believed he had reached the

Pacific and would arrive in California if he simply followed the coast to the south-west. The expedition therefore came to an abrupt end in James Bay, with a highly unpopular overwintering that led to mutiny. Hudson and eight other members of his crew set out in a lifeboat, but were never heard from again.

The mutineers must have taken Hudson's logbook home with them – or at least it appears that way, since Dutch engraver Hessel Gerritsz seems to have used it as a source when drawing a map of the area for the book *Detectio Freti Hudsoni* (*Discovery of the Hudson Strait*) in 1612. The map shows a *Mare Magnum* – large sea – in the far west, which Hudson would have discovered if only he had stayed further north.

The British therefore returned to Hudson Bay to look for an opening further west. In 1615, navigator and cartographer William Baffin noticed that the strongest tide, which he believed to come from a north-westerly sea, flowed from the northern Davis Strait alongside Greenland, and not the westerly Hudson Strait. Baffin therefore set the expedition's course for the north, and he and his crew made it as far as Smith Sound at 78 degrees north – only half a degree from the sound where the *Fram* would harbour for the winter just 282 years later. Along the way, Baffin discovered several sea routes that stretched out towards the west, and on 12 July recorded in the ship's log that they were situated off 'another great Sound, lying in the latitude of 74° 20′ N, and we called it Sir James Lancaster's Sound.' Little did Baffin know that his ship was lazily bobbing off what in the 1800s would turn out to be the entrance to the Northwest Passage. Unaware of just how close he had come, Baffin wrote that his hope of finding a passage through the north was diminishing day by day due to the overwhelming masses of ice. Members of his crew were also suffering from scurvy and other diseases. Safely home in England, he concluded resignedly: 'There is no passage.'

But Baffin's pessimism did not sit particularly well with Samuel Purchas, the editor who published Baffin's travel writings and who was keen for Britain to take to the seas once again. Purchas therefore only published Baffin's log, and not his maps, and so these have been lost. This is a shame, as Baffin, perhaps the most eminent navigator of his time – he was a pioneer when it came to finding longitude values through observations of the Moon – probably put more work into the creation of his maps than the log. Instead, Purchas chose to use *The North Part of America* by mathematician Henry Briggs – on this map, the Pacific coast of America extends out to the north-east, towards a Hudson Bay described as 'a fair entrance to ye nearest and most temperate passage to Japan & China.' Purchas's desire to find a passage was so strong that he prioritised a speculative map drawn by an armchair geographer over a map drawn by someone who had actually been to the region in question.

In 1619, three years after Baffin, a Dano-Norwegian expedition led by Jens Munk sailed into Hudson Bay. King Christian IV, inspired by the Norse *Sagas* about the discovery of settlements, had dreams of recreating a kind of northern empire, and so dispatched a frigate, the *Enhiörningen*, and a yacht, the *Lamprenen*, with a total of sixty-five men on board. But the expedition ended in catastrophe – forced to spend the winter on the west coast of the bay, an entire sixty-two men lost their lives. The three survivors, with Munk among them, incredibly managed to sail the *Lamprenen* all the way back to Bergen – where they were thrown in jail for having destroyed one of the king's ships. They were eventually pardoned, however, and in 1624 Munk wrote his *Navigatio, septentrionalis. Det er: Relation Eller Bescriffuelse om Seiglads oc Reyse paa denne Nordvestiske Passagie, som nu kaldis Nova Dania* (*Navigatio, septentrionalis. Or: A Relation or Description of the Voyage to the Northwest Passage, which is now called Nova Dania*), which included three maps. Considering the expedition's terrible fate, and the fact that no permanent settlements were founded, it is surprising that the name Nova Dania stuck. It was featured on several future maps – and appeared in Dutch cartographer Tobias Conrad Lotter's pocket atlas as late as 1762.

In 1717, almost 100 years after Munk's expedition, British explorer James Knight arrived at the location where Munk had spent the winter to discover shallow graves and the remains of bones spread across the area – 'a revelation of that which awaits us if we do not lay in supplies before the winter sets in … I pray that the Lord may protect and preserve us.' Knight later disappeared without trace on another expedition further north.

NORTHEAST | The Russians explored and laid claim to the areas to the east and north of the Eurasian continent, and in 1648 an expedition led by Cossack explorer Semyon Dezhnev arrived in the northern part of the Pacific that, 128 years later, would be named the Bering Strait – the true Strait of Anian between Asia and America.

Vitus Bering was a high-ranking Danish captain in the Russian Navy. After having set out on an expedition to travel as far east as he could towards the end of the 1720s, all the way to the Kamchatka Peninsula and the northern Pacific, he was tasked with mapping the entire northern coast of Russia by Tsarina Anna Ivanovna. Three years later, four groups of men each began mapping their allocated sections – fighting against challenging ice conditions, freezing cold and inaccessible routes to complete the enormous project. A significant number of officers had to be demoted before the project was finally completed in 1741.

On 4 June the same year, Bering set out from Kamchatka with two ships in order to explore the waters to the east. The expedition crossed over to the north-west coast of America – a territory the Europeans were so unfamiliar with at this time that author Jonathan Swift, in his satirical travelogue *Gulliver's Travels* from 1726, could locate the enormous fictitious peninsula of Brobdingnag there without anyone questioning it. Bering and his expedition mapped the islands to the south and west of the Alaskan coast.

The Russian government decided that the results of Bering's expeditions should be kept secret – something they only partly achieved. When French cartographer Joseph-Nicolas Delisle, employed by the Academy of Sciences in St Petersburg, returned to France in 1747, he took maps and documents from Bering's expedition with him. He then shared the information with Philippe Buache, France's leading cartographer at the time,

Next pages | Jens Munk's map from the attempt to find the Northwest Passage in 1619. All the way to the right, which on this map is furthest west, is Munkenes Winterhaven, where sixty-two of the expedition's sixty-five members died while wintering over. In his diary, Munk wrote: 'On the fourth of June, which was Whit Sunday, I was the fourth person remaining alive. We lay helpless, unable to assist one another.' Munk and two other crew members finally returned home to Norway, where Munk wrote a travelogue and drew this map.

Cfarwel

Snecer

Fredim Roÿ

Münkenes

Frenim

Renfind

harfont

and the pair published a map of North America in 1752. But in creating the map, Delisle and Buache combined the information from Russia with the highly questionable 'discoveries' of Spanish explorer Bartolomé de Fuente from 1640. At 53 degrees north on the American west coast, de Fuente was said to have sailed into the continent along a river he called Los Reyes – travelling so far east that he finally encountered a ship from the east coast. Delisle and Buache were more interested in reproducing the non-existent system of lakes and rivers that led to Hudson Bay in the east than the Russian discoveries in the north; British newspapers praised the map because it showed 'a shortcut to East India'. But in reality, no European before Bering knew anything about the west coast of America above 43 degrees north.

In St Petersburg in 1758, Gerhard Friedrich Müller finally published an official map based on Behring's discoveries. Müller also wrote an open letter in which he criticised Delisle and Buache, snidely remarking that 'it is always much better to omit whatever is uncertain, and leave a void space, till future discoveries shall ascertain the affair in dispute'. On Müller's map, north-west America is almost completely blank.

James Cook, the English captain who had previously sailed across ocean where cartographers had drawn land, and found land where they had drawn ocean, was lured to the Northwest Passage by a map of the North Pacific that would in retrospect turn out to be rather theoretical. A 'Map of the new northern archipelago' by Jacob von Stählin from the academy in St Petersburg was said to be based on discoveries made by a lieutenant in the Russian Navy – but was this was decidedly false. On this new map, 'Alaschka' was no longer a peninsula but an island, and between it and the American continent was an open strait leading straight into the Arctic Ocean at 65 degrees north.

On their way towards this strait, Cook and the crew could only conclude that the coast did not lead directly northwards, as it did on Stählin's map, but that it curved around to the west. In a letter dated October 1778, Cook wrote: 'we were upon a Coast where every step was to be considered, where no information could be had from maps, either modern or ancient'. In his log, he described Stählin's map as 'a Map that the most illiterate of his illiterate Sea-faring men would have been ashamed to put his name to.' It was Cook who gave the Bering Strait its name when he and his crew arrived there – only to encounter a Russian officer who was equally perplexed by Stählin's map.

Cook and his crew did what they could to correct Stählin's errors – using chronometers, sextants and observations of the positions of the Moon, they were able to perform many calculations to determine latitude and longitude values along the coast. The maps that were published in 1784 were the first to depict north-west America reasonably accurately, but Cook never found the Northwest Passage. The expedition's ships were foiled by the ice at Icy Cape, to the north-east of the Bering Strait.

FAILURES | Meanwhile, the British had also been busy on the other side of the passage. In 1747, explorer Henry Ellis wrote: 'We may consider Hudson's-Bay as a kind of Labyrinth, into which we enter through Hudson's-Straits, and what we aim at, is to get out on the other side.' But French cartographer Jacques Nicolas Bellin made their blood run cold when he drew the *Carte Reduite des Parties Septentrionales du Globe* (*Reduced Map of the Northern Regions of the World*) in 1757. In the northwest corner of the map he wrote: 'The English are looking for a passage in these regions, but there is none to be found.'

The British put their expeditions on hold for the twenty years or so that they were at war with France, but three years after Napoleon was defeated at Waterloo new ships were dispatched to resume the search. Captains John Ross and W. E. Parry were instructed to search Baffin Bay for a route to the west, and on 21 August 1818 they sailed into Lancaster Sound – the entrance to the passage Baffin had seen but failed to investigate 200 years earlier.

The sentiments of the two expedition leaders were strikingly different – Ross was pessimistic, Parry enthusiastic; Ross was certain that Lancaster Sound was only a bay, while Parry felt sure they would discover the west coast of America. Unluckily enough, Ross was in command of the faster ship, and on the afternoon of 31 August, with Parry's ship out of sight somewhere behind him, Ross went out on deck to observe the view after the fog had cleared, and saw 'land round the bottom of the bay, forming a connected chain of mountains.' Ross ordered both ships to turn back – and once again, the British failed to discover the North-west Passage.

Many have since wondered why Ross claimed to have seen a chain of mountains where there was nothing but open water. Could it have been an Arctic mirage? And why didn't he consult the other officers? Parry was bewildered as to why they'd had to turn back.

Ross had to explain himself at a public hearing, and Parry was made responsible for arranging a new expedition. He prepared for the fact that they might have to overwinter in the ice and the consequent risk of scurvy, taking along supplies of lemon juice, malt extract, sauerkraut and vinegar in addition to canned meats and soups. Canned foods – which would later become a cruicial part of the polar diet – were so new in 1819 that the can opener had not yet been invented, and the cans therefore had to be opened using axes and knives.

On 28 July, Parry wrote in his log of the 'almost breathless anxiety' onboard as the ship sailed into Lancaster Sound. Would they see mountains after all? The masts were full of sailors keeping a lookout, but as they sailed slowly to the west they passed the point at which Parry had previously been forced to turn around without catching sight of so much as a rock. On 4 September they reached Melville Island at 110 degrees west, and twenty days later harboured for the winter, building an observatory. In the bitter cold, they placed a piece of cloth against the sights of their instruments to stop the skin being ripped from their faces – a technique they had developed from experience.

News of the expedition reached Europe via the whalers. On 14 October 1819, the Norwegian *Morgenbladet* newspaper reported that 'whalers recently returning from the Davis Strait give the greatest hope that the Northwest Passage will finally be discovered.' Parry was hugely optimistic – but it would later appear that 1819 had been a year with abnormally low levels of ice.

The summer of 1820 was so cold that the ships remained stuck in the ice until August – the waters to the west were so thick with it that the expedition made little progress, moving only sixty miles in seven weeks. They reached 113 degrees west, knowing that almost 130 miles remained before they would reach Icy Cape, where Cook had made his about-turn on his voyage east. Now Perry also made the decision to turn back – he and his crew couldn't face another winter.

The expedition was both a success and a complete fiasco. Nobody had ever sailed further west, but the amount of sea ice beyond Melville Island had been so overwhelming that Parry concluded finding the Northwest Passage was 'nearly as uncertain as it was two hundred years ago.'

Nevertheless, Parry set out on yet another expedition. After sailing around Hudson Bay in the summer of 1821 without finding any new openings to the west he met Iligliuk, an Inuit woman with an exceptional talent for drawing maps, when the ship had harboured for the winter. Parry gave Iligliuk a piece of paper, on which she drew an outline of the coast. Parry was particularly interested in how Iligliuk depicted the coast as curving to the west north of the Melville Peninsula, of which they were on the south side. Here, Parry thought, was the passage, and in July set out towards the north. Iligliuk's map was accurate – but the strait was once more filled with ice. Yet again, Parry and his crew were forced to return home with unfinished business.

In parallel with the expeditions at sea, a number of expeditions to map Canada's northern coastline had also been undertaken on foot, and open ocean had been spotted on several of these. The question, then, was how to get there by ship. In 1819 Parry had sailed down the Prince of Wales Strait, which runs in a southerly direction from Lancaster Sound, but turned back because he wanted to go west. Perhaps the way down to the coast was here?

In May of 1824, Parry set out on a final attempt. The Prince of Wales Strait was full of ice when they reached it, and so once again the crew harboured for the winter, constructed an observatory – and became the first to discover that the Magnetic North Pole is constantly moving. The distance between it and the true geographic North Pole had increased by 9 degrees since they were last in the same area five years earlier.

At the end of July 1825, Parry's crew had to saw the ships loose from the ice. They managed to sail a little further down the strait, but then encountered a violent storm – the ships were battered by huge pieces of ice and rocks blown down from the cliffs. One of the ships sustained extensive damage, and the crew gazed dejectedly down the strait at the open water they were unable to reach. '[...] A more promising step towards the accomplishment of a North-West Passage never presented itself to our view,' wrote one of the expedition's crew members – but this was wishful thinking. The Prince of Wales Strait is not part of the Northwest Passage.

CATASTROPHE | 'I perceive that certain people at the Admty are quite tired of Polar Philosophy,' wrote geographer James Rennell in the wake of Perry's last expedition. The maps of the explored areas also revealed a pervading sense of hopelessness – they were full of names such as Repulse Bay, Ne Ultra, Point Turnagain, Hopes Checked, Frozen Strait and so on and so forth.

But simply accepting defeat was no alternative for the British. In 1844, the First Lord of the Admiralty wrote that it would be senseless to stop the search 'after so much has been done, and so little now remains to be done.' The following year, Rear-Admiral John Franklin embarked on what would turn out to be the greatest and most terrible expedition of them all –and all due to an inaccurate map.

The HMS *Terror* and HMS *Erebus* were two wind- and steam-powered bomb vessels weighing 325 and 372 tonnes respectively. With their re-inforced bows and hulls strengthened with metal sheeting, these ships would break up the ice, sweep it aside, crush it – and conquer it.

The unexplored area remaining on the map was one the size of Great Britain, located south-west of the Prince of Wales Strait. Beyond the strait, on the left by Cape Walker, was an unexplored opening that stretched south-wards towards this area. The hope was that this would be the strait that led down to the ice-free waters that had been observed from the mainland coast, and on the morning of 19 May 1845, the two ships set sail with twenty-four officers and 110 sailors on board. At Greenland, five sailors were sent home for disciplinary reasons – Franklin refused to tolerate drunkenness and cursing. But these five sailors would be the expedition's sole survivors. The crew aboard a whaling ship in Baffin Bay were the last Europeans to see the Franklin expedition, and 150 years would pass before details of what happened to the men aboard the two ships would finally come to light.

By March of 1848 nobody had heard from Franklin or his crew, and so three rescue expeditions were dispatched. The first set sail for the Bering Strait, the second set out on foot along the mainland coast, and the third set out for where Franklin had last been seen. None of the expeditions found any trace of him, but all three mapped large, previously uncharted areas along the way.

Ironically, the Franklin expedition gave us more geographical knowledge through its tragic end than would have been the case if Franklin had managed to make it safely through the passage. The three rescue expeditions were only the first of many that searched the area looking for the two ships that had disappeared without trace. In 1850, eight new expeditions were sent out, and the first traces of Franklin – the remains of his 1846 winter encampment at Beechey Island in Lancaster Sound – were discovered that summer. But where had he gone from here? Towards the north? West? South? The rescue expeditions searched in all directions, across both the water and the ice on foot and by sled, all the while mapping increasingly larger areas and travelling further west and north than the British had ever gone before.

Surgeon John Rae concentrated on searching towards the south. In April 1854, he met an Inuit man who told him of thirty or forty white men who 'had died of starvation, a long distance to the west of where we then were, and beyond a large River.' Later, he met others who had seen a group of thin white men making their way south, pulling a boat and some sledges and hunting for seals at King William Island.

John Ross and his nephew James had been in these waters fifteen years earlier. For his *Narrative of a second voyage in search of a North-west passage* from 1835, he had drawn a map that claimed that it was not possible to sail east of King William Island – Ross's nephew had believed it to be a peninsula. They had even given names to several of the promontories within what they believed was a bay. But east of King William Island was exactly where Roald Amundsen would sail seventy-three years later. For the second time, John Ross erroneously believed a passage to be closed.

Next pages | *Orientation map of the second Norwegian Polar Expedition 1898–1902* by Gunnar Isachsen. The expedition discovered and mapped the entire eastern part of Ellesmere Island, Axel Heiberg Island, Amund Ringnes Island, Ellef Ringnes Island and King Christian Island. Hassels Sund, Hendriksen Sd, Fosheims Halvö, Scheis Ö, Svendsens Hö, Baumanns Fj, Bays Fj, Isachsens Ld and Kap Isachsen were named after the expedition's members.

Prins Gustav

Kronpring Gustavs Hav

Kap Isachsen

Hei-

-bergs

Pr. Patrick

Ö

Fitzwilliam Str.

Adolfs Hav

Isachsens Ld.

Ellef

Ringnæs'

Ld.

Amund

Ringnæs'

Ld.

Kap S.V.

Land

Storø

Melville

Hecla og Griper B.

Ö.K.Richards

Kong Christians

Land

Ö

Hassel Sd.

Ld.

Hendriksen Sd.

N. Cowall

Norske

Grahams

Ld.

Bj-

kap

bugt

Erskine Str.

Belcher Kanal

Heibergs Porten

Cardigans Sig.

V.kort. 00-01

V.kort 01-02

Ö

Bathurst

Ld.

Penny Str.

Grinnell

Ld.

Corn

wallis

Wellington K.

Jones

North

Melville Sd.

Mc Clintock Str.

Prins

Wales Land

Peel Sd.

North

Somerset

Barrow Str.

Prins Regent Str.

Lancast

Franklin Str.

70

Boothia

Cockburn Ö

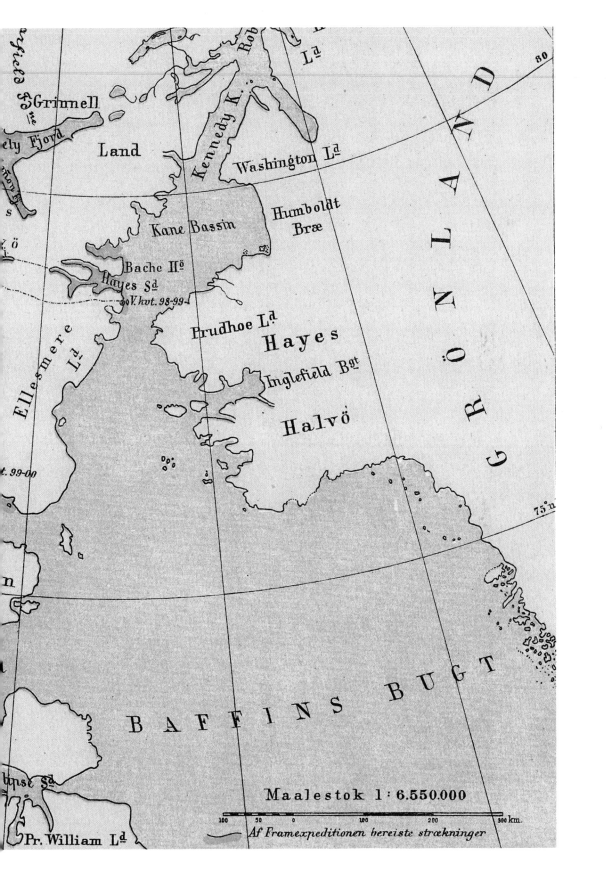

Grinnell

Land

Kennedy K.

Washington L^d

Humboldt Bræ

Kane Bassin

Bache H^ö

Hayes S^d

V. kvt. 98-99

Prudhoe L^d

Hayes

Inglefield B^gt

Halvö

Ellesmere L^d

G R Ö N L A N D

t. 99-00

75° n

B A F F I N S   B U G T

Pr. William L^d

Maalestok 1:6.550.000

100   50   0   100   200   300 km.

Af Framexpeditionen bereiste strækninger

Based on Ross's map, the Franklin expedition had set its course west of the island. Although the waters here are far wider than on the island's other side, ice is also continuously driven down from the north, and it was here that both ships froze fast. '25 April 1848. H.M. Ships Terror and Erebus were deserted on the 22nd April, 5 leagues NNW of this having been beset since 12th Septr 1846,' stated a message found on the island by one of the rescue expeditions in 1859. The message described how the remaining surviving members of the crew had set out towards the mainland to the south. All of them had either starved or frozen to death.

The fate of the Franklin expedition, along with the knowledge that the discovery of the Northwest Passage would be of little practical significance when the conditions were so difficult and unpredictable, changed the British view of the region. There would be no more expeditions to the north, and London ceded responsibility for the waters to the local Canadian authorities in 1880.

Francis McClintock, leader of the expedition that found the Franklin expedition's final message, reflected on the search after returning to his ship: 'More than 40,000 miles have been sledged, including 8,000 miles of coastline minutely examined [. . .] sledge parties travelled in every month excepting only the dark ones of December and January, in temperatures not unfrequently 40° below zero, and occasionally even 10° or 15° colder still.' In 1859, the British map of the area was quite different in appearance than it had been on the morning that Franklin set out fourteen years earlier. New islands to the north and south of the Lancaster Sound, Barrow Strait, Melville Strait and McClure Strait had been explored, and the British expeditions had reached as far west as Prince Patrick Island and Banks Island. But the maps still remained fairly blank above 78 degrees north.

NEW LAND | At the end of August 1898, the *Fram* had harboured for the winter at 79 degrees north. On 16 October Otto Sverdrup wrote:

What might not these four months' darkness bring us? Things so terrible have occurred up here in the polar night that they might well make anyone pause and think. Here came Franklin, with a hundred and thirty-eight men. The polar night stopped him; not one returned.

The following August, the expedition was forced to 'give up the journey round Greenland' due to the ice. Instead, Sverdrup and his crew turned to the south, towards 'Sir Eobert Inglis Peak, the farthest point reached by Inglefield in 1852' when searching for Franklin. On the south side of Ellesmere Island they harboured for yet another winter. Isachsen and mate Sverre Hassel used what remained of the autumn to map the stretch of coastline to the east and west of their position.

After several spring reconnaissance trips, they decided to set out on a longer expedition: 'Tuesday, March 20, was the great day of departure.' Sverdrup, Fosheim, Isachsen, Hassel and two others forged their way across a sound so difficult to traverse that they christened it Helvedesporten – Hell Gate. Further north, the journey was no easier: 'The ice [. . .] in some places was so bad that, to be honest, I began to doubt if there were any use in trying to go on,' wrote Sverdrup. At one point, 'three men, eighteen dogs, and three sledges with their loads' fell 'pell-mell' down a hole in the ice. But none of this could dampen their spirits: 'a way was now open to us where we might reasonably expect to make progress.'

Some days later, the company spotted a 'very large mountain' in the west, and set out across the ice 'in the belief that we were advancing towards a new land.' This was in fact an undiscovered island, and so was named Axel Heiberg Island after one of the expedition's sponsors. A few days later, the group set up camp below two mountaintops for which they found it difficult to agree on a name:

> Early in the morning a name more descriptive than tasteful had been suggested for them. Fosheim, who on several occasions had shown himself to be the most gifted advocate of modesty of the expedition, said nothing, but his face promised ill. He went on pondering all day, and when in the evening an allusion was made to the same name, he declared indignantly it would not do at all; it was too ugly. No, they should be called 'The Two Craters' ('De to Kratere'), and so they are to this day. Virtue has had its reward.

Around Easter, the crew gave the new places they discovered names such as Paaskelandet (Easter Island), Skjærtorsdagskappet (Cape Maundy

Thursday) and Langfredagsbugten (Good Friday Bay). They gradually made their way northwards and, as the land began to bend around towards the east, they made some observations to determine the westernmost point. 'When I got back I found Isachsen observing for longitude, and as he had already been lucky enough to get a meridian altitude we had thus determined both the longitude and latitude of the spot,' wrote Sverdrup.

One day, Sverdrup climbed up to a lookout point in order to 'get a view over the ice' and spotted 'something greyish-blue far away in the west. What could it be? It must be new land.' Isachsen and Hassel were sent west 'to pay the new land a visit.' There, they reached an island they named Amund Ringnes Island, but didn't stay long – they returned to explore the south and east coasts of Axel Heiberg Island, and the sound between this and Ellesmere Island.

In April of the following year, 1901, Isachsen and Hassel turned back, making their way south across Amund Ringnes Island towards a high mountain that turned out to be on a neighbouring island already named North Cornwall by the British, and so named the sound between the two islands Hassel Sound. Not long afterwards they discovered a neighbouring island, which they named after Amund's brother – Ellef Ringnes Island. From the southern tip of this island they spotted yet another island, which they named after the king of Denmark – King Christian Island – with Skagen as its northernmost point. The sound between the islands they named the Danish Sound. At the north-westernmost point they reached, Isachsen finally had a bleak, flat, scree-covered piece of land named after him: Isachsen Land, with Cape Isachsen as the final outpost.

The group set out on more excursions, and reached the expedition's northernmost point when Sverdrup and Per Schei, the expedition's geologist, travelled to Greely Fjord between Ellesmere Island and Axel Heiberg Island, and didn't stop until they had reached 81 degrees 40 minutes north. Isachsen set off back towards North Cornwall, south of Amund Ringnes Island, to map the island's northern coast. On 30 July 1902, the expedition began its journey back to Norway.

In April the next year, Sverdrup travelled to London to give a presentation to the Royal Geographical Society, who awarded him a gold medal for all he had achieved. After Sverdrup's speech, one of the event organisers said: 'We looked upon that part of the Arctic regions as so peculiarly our own that we spoke of it as if the Queen's writ was free to run through it to the North Pole. But we can no longer make that boast; Captain Sverdrup has been there, and he has discovered other lands farther north, so that we cannot look for any immediate increase to the British Empire in that direction.'

Sverdrup believed that Norway should have laid claim to the islands he and his crew had discovered. Canada had neither explored nor laid claim to the area, nor settled any of its citizens there, and so in accordance with the rules of the day had no right to it. But King Oscar II had little interest in barren lands in the Arctic, and so no claim to the area was made – to Sverdrup's great disappointment.

SVALBARDI | 'When we look at the map and think about what the Kingdom of Norway once was, we must recognise that over time our country has been woefully reduced, parts of it given away, pawned off and forgotten,' wrote Isachsen in an article about Arctic exploration. He was thinking of the Arctic islands – Bear Island, Greenland, Jan Mayen and Svalbard – that he believed had belonged to Norway in ancient times. And he wasn't alone – towards the end of the 1800s an increasing number of historians asserted that Norway had 'justified sovereignty and right of ownership of the Polar islands,' basing their claim on the Norse sea voyages and settlements, and Icelandic chronicles that described a new land, Svalbardi – 'the cold coasts' – discovered in 1194 and identical to the group of islands Willem Barentzs sailed around 400 years later – or so the historians believed. Isachsen agreed, concluding: 'All Norwegians would feel diminished to see the flag of a country other than Norway waving over Spitsbergen.'

After the *Fram* docked safely in Norway, Isachsen served for two years in the French Army. But when his desire to map more uncharted areas of the Arctic grew, he chose Spitsbergen – as the group of islands is still called to this day – and managed to equip two private expeditions to the area in 1906 and 1907.

Isachsen journeyed to north-west Spitsbergen, to Kapp Mitra, Kongsfjorden and Prins Karls Forland, where he and his crew pulled sledges containing 280 kilos of equipment across glaciers and up mountain-tops in order to map the land. The expedition explored an area of almost seven square kilometres during just two brief summer months, sprinkling forty-nine Norwegian names across the region as they went. The Norwegianisation of Spitsbergen had begun.

After the expeditions, Isachsen and Fridtjof Nansen attended a meeting of the Norwegian Ministry of Foreign Affairs to discuss the claiming of the islands by Norway. Everyone was rather constrained, but in 1909 Isachsen was given state support to undertake new expeditions, since Norway had interests in the north that included whaling, fishing, sealing, tourism and mining. The obtaining of accurate nautical charts and topographical and geological maps would make it possible to use the available natural resources more effectively, Isachsen believed, and the expeditions themselves would strengthen Norway's position in the area.

The Norwegianisation of the area continued with a map Isachsen created in 1910. The English *Geographical Journal* had agreed to print the map, but the fact that Isachsen had given new Nordic names to all the places that had previously been named by the English and Dutch infuriated the journal's editors. They printed the map with a note that many of the names differed from those on English maps. Others were also offended by the fact that Isachsen had named the sea between Norway, Iceland and Svalbard the Norwegian Sea, and so derisively referred to it as 'that which Isachsen and certain Norwegians have chosen to call the Norwegian Sea.'

The First World War called the European borders into question, and in the spring of 1919 Isachsen was asked to travel to Paris to assist the Norwegian delegation during the peace negotiations. Here, the Svalbard Treaty gave the islands to Norway in 1925, and one of the first things the country did was change the area's name from Spitsbergen to Svalbard in recognition of the theory that the islands were in fact the Svalbardi that had been discovered 731 years earlier. The Norwegianisation was complete – and the Dutch and William Barentsz dethroned.

This period of Norwegian history became known as one of Arctic Ocean imperialism. Expeditions were dispatched to the north and south to defend Norwegian interests – to Greenland, Franz Josef Land, Jan Mayen, Bear Island and Antarctica: 'On Norwegian expeditions to Antarctic and Subantarctic regions, possession has been taken of several stretches of land in the name of the King of Norway [...]. Bouvet Island was occupied on 1 December 1927 and taken under Norwegian sovereignty by royal decree on 23 January 1928, and Peter 1 Island, which was occupied on 2 February 1929, was taken under Norwegian sovereignty by royal proclamation on 1 May 1931,' wrote Isachsen in the book '*Norvegia*' *rundt sydpollandet. Norvegia-ekspedisjonen 1930–1931* ('*Norway*' *Around the South Pole. The Norway Expedition 1930–1931*). The expeditions had journeyed to these waters to undertake meteorological and oceanographic surveys to create maps for the whalers, and to look for Truls Island, the Nimrod Islands and Doghery Island – all of which were marked on maps but did not necessarily exist.

Norway had started whaling in the Southern Ocean in 1905. 'The difficulties for the whalers were however not only that there were so few maps, but also that the few that were available were deficient and inaccurate,' wrote Isachsen. After many accidents and shipwrecks, the Hvalfangernes Assuranceforening (Whalers' Assurance Association) began to publish maps of the South Shetland Islands, South Georgia, the South Orkney Islands, the South Sandwich Islands and the Ross Sea. Later, they also began to publish maps of the hunting grounds. 'To these maps, which show the entire ocean surrounding the South Pole, the whalers may add their experiences, currents, ice limits, banks and coasts. [...] When the whalers come home in the spring, their new information will be collated and used to create new maps, which the whalers will then be able to take with them when they return to the south in late summer,' wrote Isachsen.

EPILOGUE | At this time, the British disputed Norway's right to Jan Mayen, claiming that their countryman Henry Hudson had discovered the island long before anyone else. Shortly before his death, Sverdrup would see the Norwegian authorities arguing with the British, asserting that in that case, Norway was entitled to the Sverdrup Islands, as they were now known. In 1930, the British chose to acknowledge Norway's right to Jan Mayen – fourteen days after Norway acknowledged Canada's right to the Sverdrup Islands.

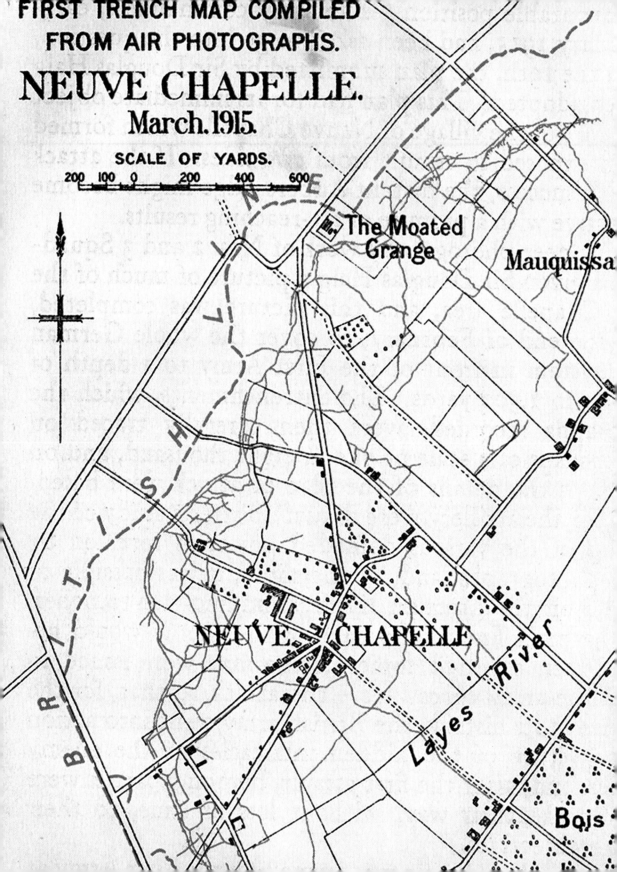

FIRST TRENCH MAP COMPILED
FROM AIR PHOTOGRAPHS.

NEUVE CHAPELLE.
March. 1915.

SCALE OF YARDS.

200 100 0 200 400 600

The Moated
Grange

Mauquissa

NEUVE CHAPELLE

Layes River

Bois

As seen from above

Neuve-Chapelle, France
50° 35′ 4″ N
2° 46′ 52″ E

When the battle was over, more than 20,000 soldiers were dead, injured, missing or taken prisoner from the battlefield, and the village of Neuve-Chapelle was just a name on a map. Wednesday 10 March 1915 dawned with a light snowfall that soon thickened into damp fog; nonetheless, British aircraft took to the air to fly over enemy positions, bombing railway lines and advancing reinforcements while the artillery aimed their guns at the German targets. At 7.30 a.m. the British launched the biggest artillery attack in history, pulverising the German trenches. In his diary, British officer Herbert Stewart wrote: 'The earth shook and the air was filled with the thunderous roar of the exploding shells. To the watching thousands the sight was a terrible one: amidst the clouds of smoke and dust they could see human bodies with earth and rock, portions of houses, and fragments of trench hurtling through the air.' In just thirty-five minutes, the artillery fired off more ammunition than that used by 500,000 British soldiers over the whole three-year duration of the Boer War fifteen years earlier.

A reconstruction of the world's first map based on photographs taken from a plane – a map prepared by the British military prior to the attack on the Germans in the French village of Neuve-Chapelle in 1915. The map was regarded as a great success – although the attack didn't go as planned, it laid the foundations for the use of aerial photographs in the creation of maps.

The First World War was not like previous wars. Industrialisation had given rise to a broad range of new, powerful weapons such as machine guns, grenades and poison gas, in addition to new vehicles including tanks, submarines – and planes. Prior to the battle, the Royal Flying Corps – the air arm of the British Army – had defied the weather to take a vast number of aerial photographs of the German positions. 'My table is covered with photographs taken from aeroplanes. We have just started this method of reconnaissance, which will I think develop into something very important,' wrote Brigadier General John Charteris a few days before the attack.

The photographs were placed side by side to create a mosaic of the landscape. The army – and the Royal Engineers in particular – then assisted the anti-aircraft artillery in creating a map based on the photographs, with red and blue lines denoting attack plans and artillery targets. This was the world's first map based on aerial photographs.

THE WRIGHT BROTHERS | On 17 December 1903 a cold, light breeze blew across the long, flat beaches of Kill Devil Hills in North Carolina, USA, where four men and a teenage boy stood observing a group of inventors attempting to make a spindly-looking plane take flight. The inventors succeeded – Orville Wright covered a stretch of thirty-seven metres in twelve seconds in history's first-ever powered flight.

Did Orville and Wilbur – the Wright brothers – consider this breakthrough the start of what would take human beings ever higher, until we would eventually crash through the atmosphere and travel out into space? Or were they simply two inventors with a good idea? Probably both. The plane that took flight that Thursday was the result of work the brothers had started as young boys in 1878, when they were given a toy by their father – a kind of helicopter made from paper, bamboo and cork, operated by an elastic band. After they played with it so much that it fell to pieces, they made their own.

The idea of humans learning to fly was in the air when the Wright brothers were growing up, and many inventors were experimenting with various devices. Hot air balloons were already well-established – the first successful hot air balloon flight had taken place as far back as the year 1783. Eleven years later, the French Army sent a man up in a balloon to obtain an overview of enemy positions, and in 1859 French officer Aimé Laussedat developed the first camera specifically created for mapping purposes. Clambering up and onto the church towers and roofs of Paris, he photographed easily identifiable locations at least twice and from various angles, and used the images to draw reasonably accurate maps. This work laid the foundations for photogrammetry – the science of ascertaining measurements from photographs. During the American Civil War, the northern states established the Union Army Balloon Corps, whose leader demonstrated photogrammetry techniques to President Abraham Lincoln in 1861 by floating 150 metres above the White House lawn. The United States Army Corps of Topographical Engineers used the view from hot air balloons to draw maps based on aerial observations.

Many people lost their lives during the first experiments with various aircraft. The Wright brothers concluded that an effective steering mechanism was the key to successful flight – Wilbur studied birds, and noticed that they changed the angle of their wingtips when turning to the left or right. The brothers believed that the same principle would work on aeroplanes, and after experimenting with gliders developed a system that enabled them to turn left and right, move up and down and roll from side to side – a system still in use today. The next step would be to attempt to take off in a motorised plane.

In 1908, the brothers travelled across the Atlantic – by boat – to demonstrate their invention to the sceptical Europeans. During a demonstration for the king of Italy, a film camera was attached to the aircraft for the first time and recorded a film clip, just under two minutes in length, of what almost nobody had ever seen before: the world – in this case an Italian village with cows, a man on horseback and the ruins of a Roman aqueduct – as seen from above.

The Italians were the first to use aircraft in warfare. After declaring war on the Ottoman Empire, they launched a reconnaissance mission beyond enemy lines in October 1911, and in the following November were the first country in the world to drop bombs from a plane. A year later, they took the first aerial reconnaissance photograph – the pilot was only able to take one image, since it was impossible for him to simultaneously operate the plane and change the glass plate (the medium used as film during this period).

The French were the first to develop an aircraft specifically for aerial photography. In 1913, the British magazine *Flight* reported from Paris Aero Salon that one of the planes in the exhibition was named the *Parasol*, because its wings were attached in a higher position than on other aircraft: 'This arrangement has, of course, the very great advantage that an excellent view of the country is obtained, as the planes [wings] are above the pilot's head, and he thus has an unrestricted view in a downward direction [...] behind the observer's seat is situated a special camera, which is pointed straight downward, so that photographs may be taken while the machine is in flight. The camera is operated from the observer's seat by means of a single string, which serves the double purpose of actuating the shutter and the plate-changing mechanism.'

AERIAL PHOTOGRAPHY | The First World War started with the Germans marching through Belgium and Luxembourg, before they defeated French attacks and moved quickly towards Paris, where they took up a position just seventy kilometres from the outskirts of the city. British and French aircraft noticed that the German forces had split in two and so attacked in the gap, forcing the Germans to retreat to north of the River Aisne where they dug trenches to hold their ground – establishing both the Western Front and trench warfare, with each side locked into positions stretching hundreds of kilometres from the North Sea and Belgium, through France to Switzerland.

Upon arriving in France in August 1914, the British forces possessed three maps based on surveys performed during the Napoleonic Wars 100 years earlier: two of Belgium and north-eastern France and one of France alone. They planned to update the maps using traditional methods: 'I hope none of you gentlemen is so foolish as to think that aeroplanes will be usefully employed for reconnaissance purposes in the air,' said a general with the cavalry.

Members of the cavalry were used to acting as the army's spies – venturing behind enemy lines and reporting on movements and reinforcements – but static warfare in the trenches provided no such freedom of movement. The plane therefore became the answer to the question of how to keep the enemy under surveillance.

Not that this was easy. The first British reconnaissance planes got lost because visibility was poor and the pilots poorly acquainted with the area. One pilot wondered whether it would be 'rather bad form to come down and ask people the way' – something he ended up having to do – while another flew over Brussels without recognising the city. Often, the only thing the pilots were able to report on with certainty was where the Germans were *not* to be found – or they might spend half the day attempting to find the enemy and the rest finding their way back – but aerial reconnaissance gradually assumed the cavalry's former role. In September 1914 a British general lauded the 'magnificent air report' that had exposed the movements of the German troops. Information gained by the aircraft was noted on the maps – as a French pilot wrote: 'I discovered the positions of twenty-four guns on the line to the west of Vitry. I marked them on the map at 1/80,000 and informed the corps concerned.'

Strategic aerial photography began rather incidentally – the first images were taken by pilots who photographed cities, landmarks and beautiful landscapes using their personal cameras to have something to show to their family and loved ones. But despite this, nobody had thought of using systematic aerial photography in map-making – when French captain Georges Bellenger established a dedicated aerial photography division and presented his superior with images he believed could be used to create maps, his superior informed him that he 'already had a map'. Nonetheless, Bellenger developed a technique for creating maps from photographs – this required a good understanding of the landscape and the ability to interpret black-and-white photographs taken from a vibrating plane by unsteady hands.

The winter of 1914–5 was characterised by a cold standstill in soaking-wet trenches, and the landscape was so heavily bombed that this alone made it difficult to advance. Behind the front lines, however, intensive work was under way to enable the aircraft – the only things able to move to any great extent – to take better pictures, and with the war's first spring came the first movements in the lines.

NEW MAPS | Neuve-Chapelle is situated in the French lowlands, close to the Belgian border. The town is neither large nor important, but as fate would have it Neuve-Chapelle became part of the northern Western Front, and therefore a strategic target. If the Allied forces could pass through the town and make it to the larger city of Lille, they would also be able to intercept the railway lines, roads and canals used as transport routes by the Germans.

British planes photographed the town and surrounding countryside in detail prior to the planned attack – the obtained images formed the basis for a map that was printed in 1,500 copies and distributed to the troops who would go into battle. The information was invaluable – the Allied forces could now study the battlefield and analyse where a German counter-attack was most likely to occur. For the first time in British military history, the army was able to stage an attack with a full overview of the enemy's defence lines, positions and hideouts.

'Our intelligence show was successful, in that we found the Germans exactly as we had located them, and their reinforcements arrived to the exact hour that we had predicted they would,' wrote Brigadier General Charteris afterwards. The fact that the attack was not a complete success, since a number of the German reinforcements managed to stop the advance, forcing the British to dig new trenches not so far from where they started, was of little consequence – the preparations were deemed a huge step forward. From this point onwards, maps based on aerial photographs became an integrated part of the Allied strategy, and a system was established in which the day's aerial photographs were submitted to the cartographers at 8.30 each evening – the cartographers then worked flat out through the night to prepare and print up 100 maps for the troops by 6 a.m. the next day.

Before the war, nobody had received training in how to take photographs from a plane, but as the need for images increased the armies scoured their ranks to find men who knew their way around a camera – who understood how to take a photograph and what an image could convey. One described the recruitment process as follows: 'I had had a camera as a boy, and had taken, developed and printed some very amateurish photographs. On the strength of this, I was appointed the squadron's official air photographer.' The British founded the School of Photography, Mapping and Reconnaissance to cover their forces' needs.

Aerial photography was demanding. Both the pilot and photographer occupied the plane's cold, wet, wind-battered cockpit, while the enemy attempted to kill them. The pilots had to fly steadily back and forth along straight lines at a constant altitude to enable the photographers to work as methodically as possible – this predictable course made the reconnaissance aircraft easy targets for those tasked with shooting them down from the ground. One pilot wrote: 'Photography again. I am getting thoroughly fed up with this job. It is the most difficult and dangerous job a pilot can get.' Another wrote simply: 'Photography is a good job when you don't get hurt.'

For their part, the photographers were tasked with operating a large camera in a confined space. They had to figure out when to take the photographs to achieve the desired overlapping pattern – most often by counting in their heads – and change the glass plate after each image with fingers stiffened by the cold. And then there was the turbulence to deal with. But one of the photographers described braving the harsh conditions and difficulties as worth it: 'It was something hugely satisfying, however, in both these pursuits ... To go over the lines and look vertically down on the enemy's most treasured and private property, and to know that you had it in your power to make sure they either got destroyed or conquered, was truly a work worth doing.'

On the ground were those who drew the maps based on the photographs. James Barnes, who held the unofficial title of 'aerial photograph interpreter', wrote in his biography:

Next pages | Pilot Viggo Widerøe participated in an expedition to the Antarctic in 1936–7 to map both the South Pole and the surrounding waters. Whaling and sealing in the area were significant economic interests for Norway, and the country claimed areas of land by mapping and naming them. Note how Norwegian names dominate – Kong Haakon VII hav, King Kaakon VII vidde and Ingrid Christensen Ld have since been given other names, while Lars Christensen Ld has become the Lars Christensen Coast.

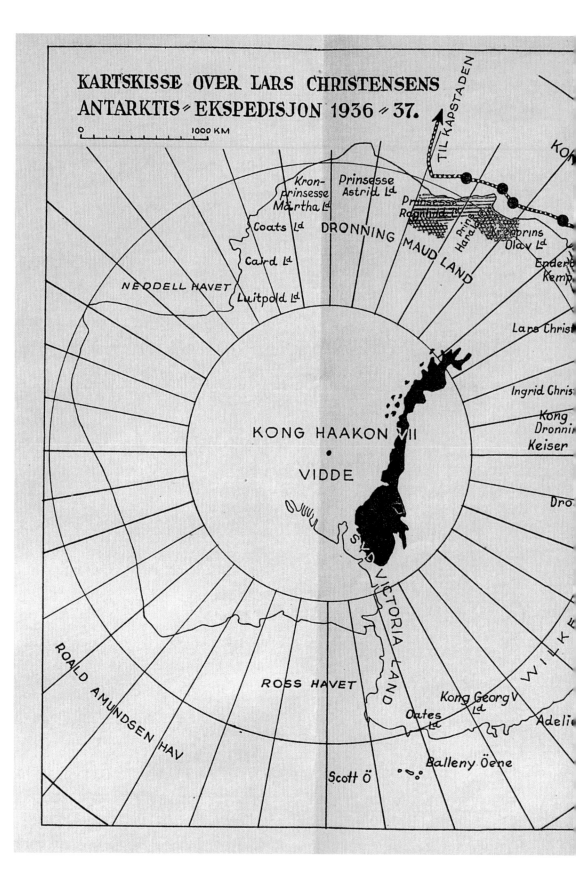

KARTSKISSE OVER LARS CHRISTENSENS
ANTARKTIS-EKSPEDISJON 1936-37.

0   1000 KM

TIL KAPSTADEN

KON

Kron-
prinsesse
Märtha Ld

Prinsesse
Astrid Ld

Prinsesse
Ragnhild Ld

Prins
Harald

Kronprins
Olav Ld

Coats Ld   DRONNING MAUD LAND

C>aird Ld   Enderb
                                                 Kemp

NEDDELL HAVET   Lars Christ

Luitpold Ld   Ingrid Chris

                                                 Kong
                                                 Dronni
                                                 Keiser

KONG HAAKON VII   Dro

·

VIDDE

SYD VICTORIA LAND

ROALD AMUNDSEN HAV

ROSS HAVET   Kong Georg V
                                                 Ld
                                        Oates   Adeli
                                        Ld

                                        Balleny Öene

Scott Ö

WILKE

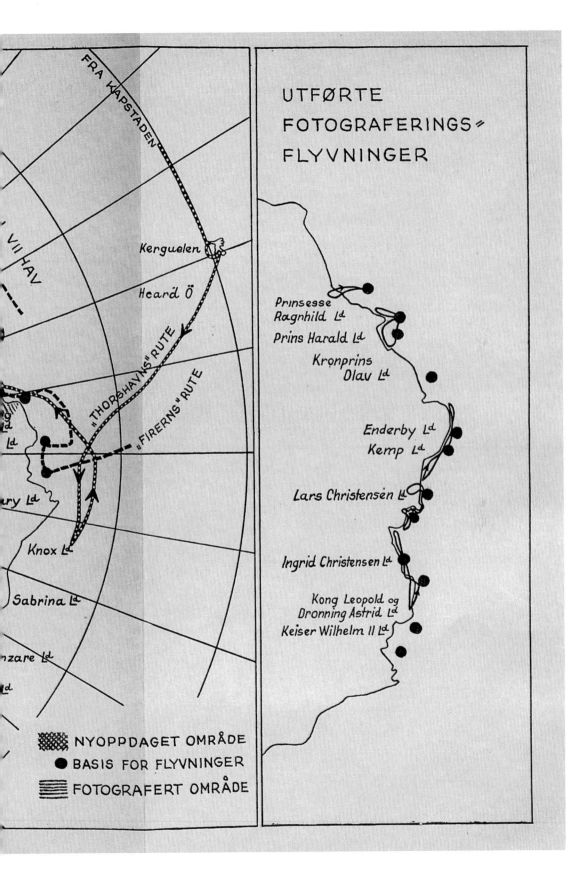

FRA KAPSTADEN

VII HAV

Kerguelen

Heard Ö

"THORSHAVNS" RUTE

"FIRERNS" RUTE

Knox Ld

Sabrina Ld

nzare ld

ld

ld

ry Ld

UTFØRTE
FOTOGRAFERINGS=
FLYVNINGER

Prinsesse
Ragnhild Ld
Prins Harald Ld
Kronprins
Olav Ld

Enderby Ld
Kemp Ld

Lars Christensen Ld

Ingrid Christensen Ld

Kong Leopold og
Dronning Astrid Ld
Keiser Wilhelm II Ld

NYOPPDAGET OMRÅDE
BASIS FOR FLYVNINGER
FOTOGRAFERT OMRÅDE

The reading and interpretation of airplane photographs demands a peculiar mind – the type of mind that would work out chess problems or, nowadays, crossword puzzles, perhaps. To the uninitiated a photograph of a line of entrenchments and myriad shell holes might mean very little, but to the puzzle solver, working over a clear photograph, with a magnifying glass, those shadows and lines and suggested slopes and rises mean much. They tell a story. Often his imagination is set on fire by some puzzling little, thing, the reason for which he cannot quite discover; and then, all at once, he has it! Those funny little dots are iron fence posts with strong wires strung along them. The men who went to that big shell hole left no trace of a path, for they reached their hidden machine-gun emplacement by walking along the lower wire as a sailor would use the foot rope on the yard of a sailing vessel. That well-traversed path some hundred yards away, leading to another rounded pit in lower ground is a deliberate deception; there are no guns there. The battle between the camera and camouflage was on. It was like a poker game with aces up the sleeve.

In the wastelands of the First World War a new kind of cartographer was born – one who occupied a dark room and used advanced optical instruments to interpret images, rather than going out into the world to view its physical geography.

The increasing need for aerial photographs forced the civil camera industry to produce increasingly better cameras, with ever-improving lenses that could be used for cartographic purposes. Of course, the higher the planes could fly while still obtaining a detailed image, the less the risk of being shot down, and cameras that could reproduce the ground in sharp detail from a height of 6,000 metres were soon developed. During 1918 – the last year of the war – aerial mapping was such an important part of the strategy that the Allied forces took more than ten million photographs. The maps of the Western Front were updated twice daily using new information obtained from the air. The Germans estimated that they had taken enough images to cover the country six times over.

'The First World War paved the way for aerial mapping – the creation of entirely modern, accurate maps with the addition of contour lines

– with the senseless loss of human life and unlimited consumption of funds possible only in war,' wrote topographer and captain Thorolf Ween in 1933. 'Developments steamed ahead at the pace the war demanded. And then came peace, and it became necessary to find a use for all these new inventions and branches of industry.'

NEUE SACHLICHKEIT | The interwar period was one in which the belief in planning and efficiency-improvement measures had a number of eloquent proponents. Scientific insight would be used to create more rational and improved ways of life, and social economists, architects, engineers and cartographers were among those who advocated a new objectivity based on knowledge and an overall perspective.

'We have flown above the country and seen such beauty, the land strewn with opportunities, and often thought that a certain responsibility must accompany all this we have been given to manage. But there is no one to take responsibility for the whole, and so, as often happens, the beauty may be trampled underfoot and the opportunities squandered,' wrote pioneering Norwegian aviator Helge Skappel of the interwar period. From the air, he described the conditions causing people to flee Norway's villages and rural areas, 'because there is no one to bring order to the villages' economic situation and help everyone to achieve liveable circumstances.' According to Skappel, it was impossible to 'build a society without the existence of maps and plans, on which everything appears in the correct form and dimensions. Mapping will thus be the foundation of healthy and rational social development.'

As a young man, Skappel had travelled to Berlin with the Widerøe brothers, Arild and Viggo – who would later go on to found the airline of the same name – to attend an aeronautical exhibition. 'The exhibition became a temple for us,' said Skappel. In a bedsit in Oslo, the three young men made lofty plans that would soon be shot down – upon starting out, the group had to make do with two motorised planes and a glider. After first earning an income through aerobatics performances at rallies and aerial advertising, they later offered passenger flights, flying lessons and aerial photography services. After two years of flying the three friends had collected 6,000 images from across

Norway – but had greater ambitions than the sale of attractive postcards.

'We wanted to photograph the country from the air, and through the presentation of economic maps obtain a basis for procuring a complete overview of the country's industry and business opportunities,' wrote Skappel. 'Photographs and maps should be laid out on the desks of scientists and scholars, and surveys and research projects initiated. The structure and development of our new society should then be planned through a collaboration between sociologists, social economists, geographers, agricultural experts, engineers and architects.' Skappel and the Widerøe brothers developed proposals for areas in which as many of the problems common to each specific part of the country as possible could be solved. In eastern Norway, they chose 'the rural areas of Ringsaker, Nes, Furnes and Vang, with the adjacent cities of Hamar and Lillehammer. [...] Within this area we will prepare a complete ground plan.'

The question of the creation of an economic map series of Norway had been raised at regular intervals since it was first proposed in 1814, but rejected each time due to budget constraints. 'Military conquests require military maps. Economic conquests require economic maps. To shed light on the situation, and to explore and obtain an overview of our country's amenities, an economic map series is just the thing that is needed,' wrote public official Jonas Endresen Mossige in 1910, but the project failed again and again due to the extensive funds that the creation of such a map series would require.

'Economic surveying has so far only been started by one county (Ringsaker), and in the current economic depression it is not possible to provide for new undertakings of this nature,' stated an official letter from the Ministry of Defence in 1931.

NO MAN'S LAND | The aerial mapping of Norway was therefore finally started due to the private occupation of Greenland. On 27 June 1931, the Norwegian flag was raised in Mosquito Bay, and hunter Hallvard Devold sent home a telegram declaring that 'the land between Carlsberg Fjord in the south and Bessel Fjord in the north [is] occupied in His Majesty King Haakon's name. We have named the land Erik the Red's Land.'

The basis for the occupation was the belief that historically, Greenland belonged to Norway. The old Norwegian states of Iceland, the Faroe

Islands and Greenland had not been regarded as part of Norway when the country was ceded to Sweden in 1814, and so remained part of the Kingdom of Denmark. The conflict came to a head in 1921, when Denmark claimed ownership of all of Greenland and its surrounding waters. Norway believed that this violated the rights of the Norwegian sealers and whalers who had operated out of east Greenland since the late 1800s, and so the Norwegian government supported the private occupation.

In the summer of 1932, an expedition set out from Ålesund, Norway, for east Greenland, equipped with a plane, maps, compasses, drawing materials, two cameras and 550 metres of film – enough to take 2,850 photographs. The aim was to supplement the survey Norway had already undertaken in the area over a period of three years. The plane was borrowed from consul and whaling shipowner Lars Christensen, who had whaling and sealing vessels in the area, while tobacco manufacturer J.L. Tiedemanns Tobaksfabrik sponsored the aerial photography activities with 2,000 Norwegian kroner. In just over a month, the expedition photographed an area covering 30,000 square kilometres – half of which was previously completely unknown territory. In other words, Norway did what most occupying powers and imperialists do after laying claim to a new piece of land – they mapped it to obtain strategic knowledge of the area's terrain and resources. But the occupation of Greenland would be short-lived. Norway lost the case in an international ruling in April of 1933.

On 21 June that same year, the Norwegian Navy's F 300 seaplane took off from the town of Horten. Due to poor weather inland, the pilot followed the coast around the south of the country, all the way to Bergen, where he landed just under four hours later. On the following day the crew flew north, arriving at Ramsund in Nordland after nine hours – including a stop to refuel and top up their oil in Brønnøysund. The aim was to map part of Norway from the air for the very first time. An area of around 100 square kilometres south of Harstad had not yet been surveyed in accordance with the latest standards, and had therefore been selected as a trial area. The previous year, land surveyors had triangulated the area, and marked a great number of points that could be seen from the air – one point per square kilometre.

On the first day, conditions were perfect. Topographer and captain Thorolf Ween was responsible for taking the photographs. 'All the equipment functioned perfectly and everything seemed to be going swimmingly – but suddenly, towards the end of our flight, I received a splash of oil to the face, and upon closer inspection noticed that the camera had been heavily sprayed with oil […].' Ween cleaned the camera and the crew completed the mapping exercise before returning to Harstad, where they developed the film. 'I was immediately aware that the entire shoot would have to be repeated,' said Ween – the photographs were covered in flecks of oil, and the plane needed repairs. 'Luckily – as a cartographer will say when he is forced to be inactive – the weather was terrible for these three days.' On the fourth day the necessary repairs had been completed and the weather was fine once again, with just a few small clouds scattered around the mountains at 1,500 metres, and so the mapping was started at 10.20 a.m. and completed around 12.55 p.m. 'Now the aerial mapping of the entire area is complete, and the results will be presented just like any other ordinary, original maps,' said Ween.

Unfortunately, however, things didn't quite work out this way – the images revealed that Norway's landscape is far too mountainous to be mapped from the air using a single camera. On the ordinary photographs taken from the air, the highest areas were represented at a smaller scale than the lowest due to being closer to the camera's lens. It was therefore necessary to use a stereoscopic surveying method, which works in the same way as a pair of eyes – two cameras placed beside each other take a photograph simultaneously; their slightly different perspectives make it easier to see the peaks and troughs in the landscape.

When the new method was tested in the municipality of Sør-Varanger, the Geographical Survey of Norway chose to collaborate with Widerøe, rather than the Norwegian Navy, who would of course always have to prioritise military considerations over civil ones.

NORTH AND SOUTH | In 1936, Arild Widerøe and Helge Skappel travelled to Sør-Varanger to photograph the area. 'The Finnmark coast was cold and bleak on our arrival, with low rainclouds spread across the countryside. We should have cut across and flown straight up to

Kirkenes, but instead were forced to take a route around the coast at the North Cape,' said Skappel. They landed at Svanvik, where the Paatsjoki River forms a great lake, and waited for clear weather: 'For those who love nature and to hike through forests, climb mountains and live the life of a free man, aerial mapping is easy work – especially in such virginal regions as Sør-Varanger.'

When the clear weather arrived, Widerøe and Skappel followed a carefully pre-prepared flight plan and a special map detailing the lines along which they would fly: 'We flew lines up and lines down, with the mapping equipment in operation. When our fuel ran out, or the weather clouded over, we went down, and waited for our next chance to take photographs.'

That same year, Viggo Widerøe received an assignment on the other side of the globe: to 'fly the unknown areas along the coast of the Antarctic continent from 80 degrees East to 10 degrees West. Aerial photographs would be taken along the stretch of coastline, and the images used to produce maps of the photographed areas.' Once again, Viggo Widerøe's employer was consul and whaling shipowner Lars Christensen.

'Many people are indifferent, or think it's a waste of time, to explore an area that lies so far from our country,' wrote Widerøe. But '[thanks to] Lars Christensen's research activities, Norway's position in the Antarctic is secured. Today, the Whaling Association's maps are used by all nations who undertake whaling activities, and the maps that have now been drawn based on our aerial photographs will lead the vessels safely towards the coast in the times ahead.'

Like Sør-Varanger, the South Pole is an area where it is often necessary to wait for clear weather. After several days of 'sleet and snow', 'rough, grey weather' and 'snow showers and brisk winds', Viggo Widerøe observed

a sunset that can only be experienced in the polar rains [...] But there was little time to make notes the next day, as the expedition was out from sunrise until long after the sun had set. My diary states only: Start 07.30, with full tanks ... Mapped the entire coastline eastwards to the Western Barrier ... Landing for refuelling ... Reconnaissance flight inland with Mrs Ingrid Christensen … Landing … Started again with full tanks and new roll of film … Mapped the entire coast westwards towards Thorshavn Bay, 800 km there and back [. . .]. This is what it's possible to achieve on the rare occasions there's good weather down here. We flew a total of 1,700 km that day, and photographed a stretch of coastline measuring 430 km long.

Viggo Widerøe's descriptions of the work provide a glimpse of how new land was claimed in these areas: 'Mrs Christensen accompanied me on the trip, and after we had been flying for just under an hour she pointed enthusiastically ahead. She had spotted a small, black hill peeking up from the white snow – it grew into a mountaintop, and we flew across land that nobody had ever seen before. Mrs Christensen threw down the Norwegian flag.' The area was later named the Prince Harald Coast, and on their final flight, Widerøe and Christensen mapped more unknown territory: 'Is it a mountain, or is it only clouds? [. . .] Ahead a mountain landscape rises up from the inland ice, peak after peak, as far as the eye can see. A mountainous land never before seen, a Rondane [mountainous national park in Norway] deep within the white surface of the Antarctic. In the fading light of the evening sun we fly along the mountains and let the camera do its work . . .'

The Widerøe company was given many more assignments – Røros Copper Works wanted to procure aerial photographs to help them in their search for new ore deposits, as did Orkla in the area around Løkken Verk. Lillehammer, Stavanger, Skien and Porsgrunn were photographed for the Geographical Survey of Norway, while the municipalities of Tønsberg, Nøtterøy, Tjøme, Asker, Bærum and Strinda wanted images they could use as the basis for zoning plans and road construction projects. In the spring of 1938, Widerøe procured equipment with which they could produce their own maps – and their first assignment was to create a tourist map of Stavanger and the surrounding areas, along with an economic map of the region.

But the industry failed to develop with the speed that Widerøe had hoped for. 'The importance of this new aid was obvious, and experts in all fields became our allies and pushed for us to be granted support for our mapping work. But the authorities held back [...] and we were forced to resort to finding work abroad,' wrote Skappel. The company submitted a tender for the topographical and economic mapping of El Salvador in Central America – a plan that unfortunately dissolved due to political complications – and worked to gain entry to Iran, who were interested in obtaining an overview of the country's oil and mineral deposits. But these plans also had to be abandoned when the political situation in Europe reached crisis point.

In the autumn of 1939, while out on an assignment in southern Sweden, Skappel flew across the sea just north of Poland, which had been recently attacked: 'Out on the horizon columns of smoke rose up from the sea. It was the warships. We suddenly felt that the war was very close to us.'

THE SECOND WORLD WAR | In 1938, Werner von Fritsch, general and commander-in-chief of the German Army, predicted that 'the military organisation with the best aerial reconnaissance will win the next war.' Many believed that Germany had both the most planes and the best cameras – the winners of the First World War had subsequently made no notable additional developments in aerial mapping techniques. 'After World War I, interest in photo intelligence diminished practically to the vanishing point. As a result, at the outbreak of World War II, the Armed Forces were caught with obsolete cameras and no organization, equipment, or trained personnel to exploit what was to become a major source of intelligence,' wrote the American *Infantry Journal* in 1949. The Royal Air Force was yet to obtain a single dedicated reconnaissance aircraft.

But the Royal Air Force did have a dedicated photograph interpretation unit – the Central Interpretation Unit – based at a stately home in the English countryside. To start with, the unit employed 114 officers and

Next pages | An imaginary map created by the Geographical Survey of Norway in 1959 in order to experiment with the use of symbols, colours and typography. The map is based on the area around the town of Sandnes, which has been named Storesand, while Jotunheimen, Lillesand, Rygge and Svelvik are in reality located elsewhere.

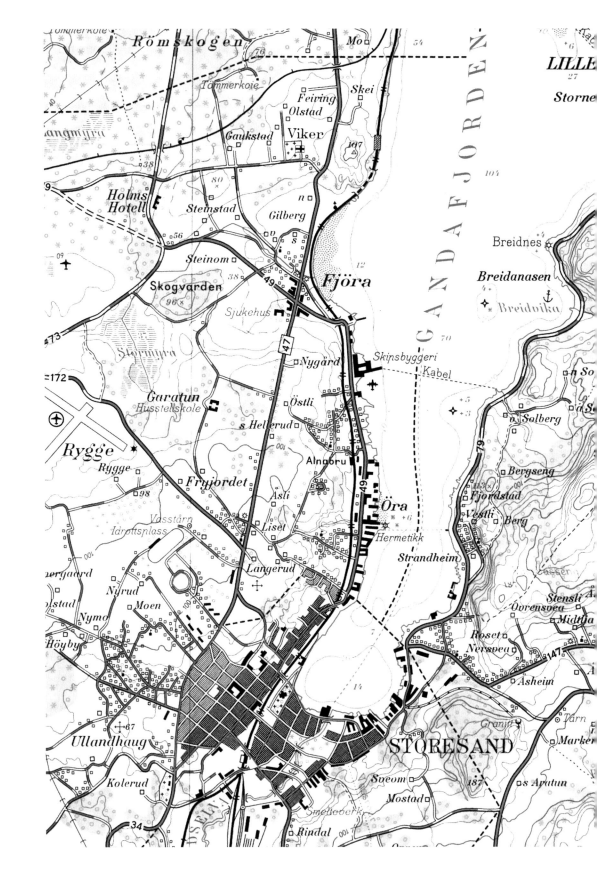

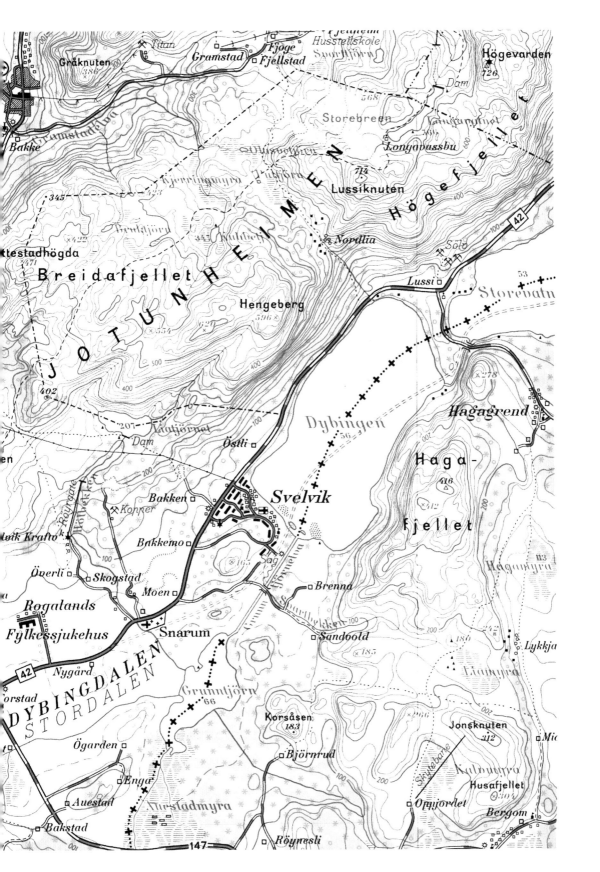

117 other members of staff, but by the end of the war these figures had increased to 550 officers and 3,000 other staff members, all working with the production of various types of maps – a happy mix of geographers, archaeologists, journalists, explorers, geologists and artists. Everyone based at the unit took a mandatory two-week course in photographic interpretation, through which they learned how to find out the scale of a photograph, make sense of what they were looking at – whether, for example, the image showed a road or a railway line, or a runway for fighter planes or bombers – and to differentiate between objects that were of military significance, and those which were not. Separate departments studied airports, camouflage, railways, roads, rivers, canals, industrial sites and military encampments.

The route flown by every single plane was marked on a map in order to establish what had been photographed, and – fairly often – what would need to be photographed again. Items of interest were marked on a main map, and three-dimensional model maps were created of the areas of greatest strategic importance. Carpenters, sculptors, artists and silversmiths were all appointed to work with these models, which were often large, measuring almost two metres across, and depicted landscapes with hills, trees, rivers, beaches, harbours, houses, locomotives, goods wagons, radars and military installations. Sometimes they were even lit to find out how the area would look on a moonlit night. Such models were constructed before the British bombed the Möhne and Sorpe dams – the pilots were instructed to 'look at these until your eyes stick out and you've got every detail photographed on your minds, then go away and draw them from memory, come back and check your drawings, correct them, then go away and draw them again till you're perfect.' The largest model construction assignment involved 97 three-dimensional maps of the beaches of Normandy, created as part of the preparations for D-Day and the landing operations of the Allied soldiers in France in June of 1944.

The Second World War – unlike the first – did not lead to any significant progress within aerial mapping. But if anything, it made the countries involved aware of how far behind they lagged in this area, and as soon as the war was over, the United States Air Force used its resources to map

Europe from the air before diplomatic considerations could complicate the issue.

NEW NEEDS | After the war and the occupation of Norway, one of Wideroe's first assignments was to photograph ninety cities and locations burned by the Germans during their retreat in Finnmark – new maps would be vital in planning the rebuilding activities.

Norway also became a member of NATO after the war, which introduced new requirements regarding military maps. The Norwegian Armed Forces submitted plans for a new, national map series at a scale of 1:50,000. Until this point, the country's main map series had been created at a scale of 1:100,000 – and still hadn't been completed. The requirements of the Armed Forces resulted in the Geographical Survey of Norway abandoning all plans to map the remaining areas of the country at 1:100,000 – instead, they began to survey the entire country again at 1:50,000. The intention was that the Americans would lend a hand, and in 1952 the Norwegian Army collaborated with the American Army Map Service to map the region of Øst-Troms. The formerly blank areas of the map of Norway were soon covered by thirty-three map sheets.

The success of this project led to the decision that the American Army Map Service would aerially photograph the entire region of southern Norway, and take responsibility for drawing two-thirds of the maps. But it soon became evident that the experience gained from the wide-open, sparse terrain of Øst-Troms did not easily transfer to the mapping of the rolling hills, densely populated areas and forest-covered regions in the south-west. The maps produced ultimately bore traces of the fact that the Americans' photographic survey methods were extremely different from those the Geographical Survey of Norway had developed for Norwegian conditions. In 1957, the two parties agreed to bring the collaboration to a close.

The Norwegian Army and the Geographical Survey of Norway continued the work to publish two map series, one military and one civil, with the names M711 and Norway 1:50,000 (N50). But not even this collaboration was without its problems. The Norwegian Armed Forces and the various public agencies had differing requirements when it came to the maps' content, but in a country with such limited resources creating different map series for different purposes was simply out of the question. 'As far as possible, our maps must be "all-purpose" maps,' wrote Kristian Gleditsch, director of the Geographical Survey of Norway after the war. All details included on the maps themselves were identical in both series, apart from the grid only included on the military series and the graticule only presented on the civil, while the accompanying texts were different.

Every update made to a map or map series entails changes in both the map's appearance and content that reflect changes in society at large – and the N50 map series was no exception. The outdated symbols for timber- and watermills were removed; a dedicated symbol was created for summer houses – and for the first time, roads were marked in red lines of varying thicknesses to denote the various types. The symbol for a farm was changed from a solid black square to an open one. 'We could discuss the farm symbol for all eternity,' wrote Gleditsch, adding that the former solid black square had proved too overbearing in appearance. 'I hope the open square will prove to be a good solution.'

In parallel with work on the main map series, debate continued regarding the economic map series for which Skappel and others had argued before the war. The time for such a map series had arrived – Norway was one of the few countries in western Europe not to have one. The costs involved had been one reason for this; the low population density and large areas that lay deserted another. Previously, an economic map series had primarily provided an overview of areas used in agriculture and forestry, and in Norway these areas made up only 25 per cent of the country's land mass, as opposed to 60 per cent in Sweden, 74 per cent in Finland and 83 per cent in Denmark. 'But the post-war period also brought many other requirements, in particular the increasingly urgent planning requirements for the districts that were being urbanised, often at a remarkable pace and without any real planning,' wrote Gleditsch. 'That which people found frightening when proposals for an economic map series were put forward was of course the involved costs. But a technological revolution had happened here in the period from around

1930 to 1950. Photographic survey methods made it possible to produce the maps far more cheaply than previously. [...] Towards the end of the 1950s, we were finally able to get all the governmental authorities to recognise what had happened.'

In 1964, the Norwegian Parliament published the *Landsplan for økonomisk kartverk* (*National plan for an economic map series*), which proposed that the entire productive area below the treeline – 135,000 square kilometres – should be mapped at a scale of 1:5,000; the remaining areas would be mapped at 1:10,000. The mapping would be completed over a period of fifteen years, and be a collaborative project between the Geographical Survey of Norway, the government, the county administrations, municipal authorities, landowners and private enterprises.

'Never before had a survey of such scope ever been undertaken – and we were starting almost from scratch in terms of knowledge and experience. The opportunities to make mistakes were legion at all stages,' wrote Torbjørn Paule in *Den økonomiske kartleggingens historie i Norge* (*The Story of the Economic Mapping of Norway*). 'The establishment of such a map series required a solid, all-out effort, with groundbreaking performance from many individuals and institutions. It is said that when the survey was presented to some Danish colleagues at the time, they exclaimed in shock: *Pffft, you Norwegians are crazy!*'

During the work, it became clear that the economic map series of Norway would have to be expanded; the original 135,000 square kilometres increased to 170,000 after the county administrations had obtained an overview of all the areas that should be included. There was also increasing awareness that the rapid pace at which areas were being planned and developed soon resulted in outdated maps. In 1975, it was estimated that a third of the produced maps were already so outdated that they would be of little use in connection with planning activities, and a conflict between the need for first-time surveys and updates consequently ensued. Only in the year 2002 was the first-time surveying of all identified areas finally completed – 185,000 square kilometres covered at a scale of 1:5,000.

DISPOSABLE MAPS | The role of maps changed in the consumerist so-
ciety of the post-war period. In 1969, Kristian Gleditsch, director of the
Geographical Survey of Norway, was asked whether he agreed that the
map had become an object of daily use in the public consciousness to a
greater extent than just a few years previously. He answered in the affirm-
ative: 'Yes, undoubtedly. In the time of our fathers, the map was a costly
jewel that was mounted, preserved and inherited – now maps have become a household item that is used, consumed and replaced. And this is
a gratifying development. But with the rapid developments in transport
and housing maps must be updated quite often, so it is good that they are
not used for long.'

Maps also became a part of public education and information. 'When
presenting plans and projects to politicians and the general public, the
provision of a thorough account using maps may help people to more easily engage with the plans, and their democratic influence may therefore
be more real,' stated a public report from 1975 titled *Om norsk kart-og oppmålingsvirksomhet* (*On Norwegian Mapping and Surveying Activities*):

> Today, there is a particular need for maps that can give ordinary peo-
> ple an improved overview of the current circumstances and proposed
> measures in many areas of society, such as:
>
> • The effect of acid rain on the natural environment over time (map
>   of Southern Norway).
> • An overview of the areas within a local municipality that are wor-
>   thy of protection.
> • Alternative plans for pedestrians, cyclists and motor traffic with-
>   in a school district.

The report also provides an overview of the areas in which maps may
be used, and by whom – as envisioned by the report's authors in 1975.
In a matter-of-fact and bureaucratic tone, the report leads us through
six areas of use, and the first, *Resource management*, reels off the need
for maps of the country's bedrock, plants and wildlife, water, air, land
ownership, settlements and public transport. The second is *Area plan-*

ning, the third the *Project planning* of homes, schools, industrial facilities, roads, bridges, airports, harbours, power stations, and facilities for energy transmission, telecommunications and water supply. The fourth area of use, *Operations*, is the largest, and includes agriculture, forestry (ownership), fishing (sea-floor conditions, navigation lines), mining (seismology), oil production, industry, water supply, power supply (grid, water resources), public transport on land (transport capacity, road quality), shipping, aviation (airports, aviation obstacles), telecommunications (network), trading, tourism (accommodation, capacity), the school system (development, capacity), health service (development, health of citizens), police, fire service (hydrants, supply network, water sources), defence and general administration. Then follows the fifth area, *Legal matters*, and the sixth, *Other areas of use*, which includes the collection and presentation of statistics, weather reporting, teaching, mass media, travel, outdoor recreation and orienteering.

Forty years earlier, Helge Skappel flew across the country thinking that it was impossible to build a society without maps and plans. Now, the official position of the authorities as expressed through the report was as follows: 'It is impossible to measure the significance of maps and survey data for society's economic activities. But this significance is undoubtedly great, since it is difficult to imagine a modern society being able to function without access to such tools.' And under almost every single area of use, where the report specifies what the maps are based on, the text reads: '*Flybilder*' ('Aerial photographs').

WAR AND PEACE | Aerial survey methods arose as a result of the technical innovations of the 1800s – through which photographic and aviation technologies developed almost simultaneously – and a war completely unlike previous wars, where the only things able to move to any significant extent were the planes and their cameras capable of fixing enemy positions in an instant. During peacetime, aerial mapping was used in civil operations, including everything from the search for metal ores and the mapping of marshland to municipal planning, the construction of roads and economic surveys. Eventually, aerial mapping became so cheap and effective that it became the standard – the Norwegian Mapping and

Cadastre Authority continues to map all locations in Norway from the air every seven years to keep its maps up to date.

The role of aircraft as the spies of the skies was reduced when the Soviet Union shot down the American U-2 spy plane in 1960. But in any case, three years earlier, an entirely new technology had taken the world by storm – when the first satellite was shot into space.

A map of a part of east Greenland from 1932. It was drawn during the two years in which Norway occupied the area, naming it Erik the Red's Land after the Icelander who established a settlement on Greenland in the 980s. The map is a highly detailed work, signed by both the Geographical Survey of Norway and Norges Svalbard- og Ishavsundersøkelser (Norway's Svalbard and Arctic Ocean Surveys), and shows how seriously the occupation was taken.

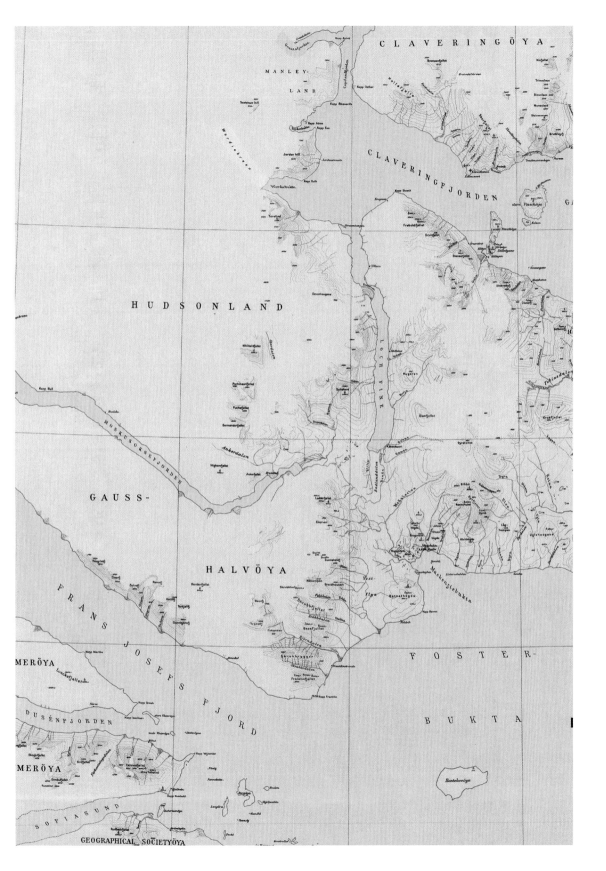

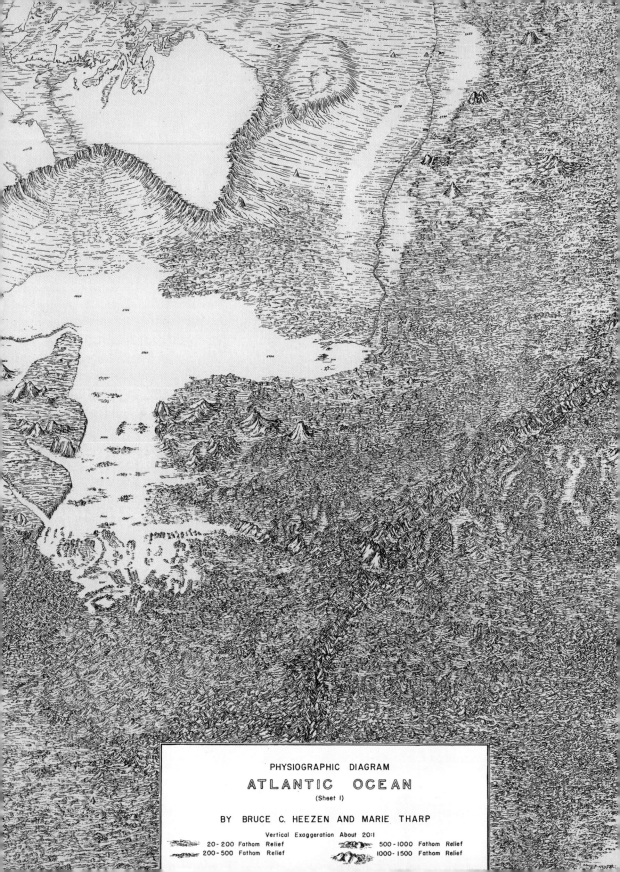

PHYSIOGRAPHIC DIAGRAM

ATLANTIC OCEAN

(Sheet 1)

BY BRUCE C. HEEZEN AND MARIE THARP

Vertical Exaggeration About 20:1

20-200 Fathom Relief
200-500 Fathom Relief
500-1000 Fathom Relief
1000-1500 Fathom Relief

Blue planet

Lamont Geological Observatory, usa
41° 00′ 14″ n
73° 54′ 25″ w

On 1 February 1957, the front page of the *New York Times* featured a map that troubled many of the newspaper's readers – a world map on which thick, black and unfamiliar lines divided up the oceans, some of them moving inland. 'A Huge Crack in the Floor of the Oceans Is Traced by Geologists', stated the headline; the accompanying article described how the Earth was 'ripping at the seams'. The Lamont Geological Observatory – the institution responsible for the findings – received letters from worried readers who feared the end of the world was nigh. In a response to one such letter, one of the observatory's geologists wrote: 'I do not believe that you have any immediate worry. The earth seems to have been "ripping at the seams" for a long time now (millions of years). Movements of inches a century are considered very fast. Thank you for your interest.'

The map featured on the newspaper's front page was a simplified version of a large nautical chart one of the observatory's researchers had been working on for the past four years. 'Miss Marie Tharp,' stated the *New York Times*, 'cartographer at the Lamont Observato-

---

The floor of the Atlantic Ocean, drawn as a physiographic diagram – a map drawn to have the appearance of an aerial photograph – and signed by geologists Marie Tharp and Bruce Heezen in 1956. At the time, nobody had ever seen such a map before. Parts of the northeast coast of America can be seen at the top left.

ry, had noticed that the locus of a great number of earthquakes in the North and South Atlantic in the past 40 years coincided exactly with the great trench there.' But the newspaper didn't credit Tharp as the map's creator – they had only interviewed two of her male colleagues, and it was not mentioned that it was Marie Tharp who had discovered the trench, shaken the discipline of geology to its foundations and made the most accurate map of the North Atlantic ocean floor ever to have been created.

Tharp had started work on the map one day in September 1952, when one of her colleagues, Bruce Heezen, set a huge pile of cardboard boxes on her desk. The boxes were full of rolls of paper. Tharp nudged a roll so that it opened to reveal a black line illustrating the varying depth of the ocean floor. 'Sonars,' Heezen said. 'What do you think?' His question was sincere – he wasn't giving Tharp the readings with instructions for what she should do. He was giving her them because he didn't know how to convert them into what he wanted – a topographical representation of what the Earth looked like under water.

The rolls contained the results of the sonar surveys the observatory had been conducting out in the Atlantic Ocean for many years – a total of 915 metres of paper. The observatory's oceanographers had sailed from America to Africa and Europe, marking their routes on maps and noting the latitude and longitude values of their positions, so that they would know where every single sounding had been taken. But the survey results were yet to be analysed in any detail. Tharp and Heezen decided to discover the complete pattern of the North Atlantic Ocean by converting the 915 metres of paper into a single drawing.

Tharp started by taping together enough sheets of paper to create a single sheet measuring over two metres across on which to enter all the details. She then drew in the routes sailed by the research vessels as six lines across the Atlantic – the northernmost from Martha's Vineyard to Gibraltar, the southernmost from Recife in Brazil to Freetown in Sierra Leone – and marked the depth of the ocean floor along these. Six weeks later, she had her first draft.

Oceanographers had long believed there to be a mountain range running from north to south below the Atlantic – the Mid-Atlantic Ridge, of which Iceland is a part. Tharp's map confirmed this – but also revealed much more. When she looked more closely, Tharp discovered a deep rift, over three miles wide, that split the mountain range in two.

'Girl talk,' said Heezen, when Tharp showed him the rift 'It cannot be. It looks too much like ...'

'Continental drift,' said Tharp.

Abraham Ortelius is the first person we know of who imagined that the continents might be moving. In the 1500s, like many who came after him, Ortelius noticed that the east coast of South America fits the shape of the west coast of Africa like a jigsaw puzzle, and wrote that it looked as if the two land masses had been ripped from each other. In his doctoral thesis *Strandlinje-studier* (*Shoreline studies*) from 1891, pioneering Norwegian geologist Andreas M. Hansen discussed ice ages and changes in the Earth's climate. Why had fossils of flowers that required a warmer climate than the island's current one been found in Greenland? Perhaps the continents had moved, Hansen suggested – thereby anticipating the theory Tharp would eventually confirm.

In 1915, German researcher Alfred Wegener published his book *Die Entstehung der Kontinente und Ozeane* (*The Origin of Continents and Oceans*), in which he posited the theory that the Earth's surface consists of continental plates in a constant state of motion. German books were not particularly popular in many other countries during the First World War, so the work would not be translated into other languages before 1922. But nor was the work especially popular upon its international publication. Geologists simply laughed at Wegener's theories, and his explanation of how the continents were moving was unfortunately not a particularly good one.

Heezen was therefore not in the least bit interested in hearing about continental drift. All geologists believed it to be impossible – to admit that continental drift might be true was to admit that things underfoot might be somewhat unstable. Heezen asked Tharp to check the details one more time. The results were the same, but Heezen refused to hear any more about it, and so the scientists agreed to disagree while sticking to their original plan: to draw a map of the ocean floor that everyone could understand. Tharp drew a physiographic diagram – a map that looks like an aerial photograph.

The method had been developed by Armin Lobeck, an American professor of geomorphology, when he had helped the various heads of state to establish the new European borders after the First World War. When he noticed that the men in power only stared blankly at his topographical maps, on which differences in height were marked with lines – Europe's leaders were 'unable to tell a mountain from a mole hill or a river from a valley or anything from a shoreline' – he developed the physiographic diagram, on which mountains actually look like mountains. Using Lobeck's method, Tharp believed, everyone could be made to understand the geography of the ocean floor – the seven-tenths of the Earth's surface that remained mostly a mystery.

IMMEASURABLE DEPTHS | Over the centuries, nautical charts have been created in an attempt to familiarise us with the parts of the ocean geography that surround us – islands, cliffs, sandbanks, reefs and rocks both above and under water. For many years, plumbing the depths was the only way to obtain information about that which was hidden below the surface – this is described in the Bible's New Testament, Acts xxvii, 27–29, when Paul is out at sea in a storm: 'It was the fourteenth night, and we were drifting through the Adriatic Sea, when about midnight the sailors suspected that land was near. After taking soundings, they found the depth to be twenty fathoms. A little later, they took soundings again and found it was fifteen fathoms. Fearing that we might run aground on the rocks, they dropped four anchors from the stern and began praying for daylight to come.'

In 1521, explorer Ferdinand Magellan attempted to find out the depth of the Pacific Ocean. When the line reached a depth of 750 metres, he declared the deepness of the water to be immeasurable, and we see something similar on Olaus Magnus's *Carta Marina* from 1539. On the Norwegian coast at Sogn og Fjordane is an image of a man with a plumb line; beside him is written '*Mos altissimus*' ('the greatest depth'). In the book that accompanied the map, Magnus wrote: 'A man who with a long rope and lead plumb attempts to measure the ocean depths. But he does not reach the bottom.'

Nor is measuring the depth of the ocean as simple as casting a plumb line overboard. In the open ocean the depths are so great that the weight of the line itself is enough to make it continue over the gunwale after the plumb has reached the bottom, and this can make it seem as if the ocean is deeper than it actually is. Another problem is that the drifting of the boat means the line rarely remains vertical. In the 1830s and 1840s, when mariners began sounding the ocean in their free time, unbelievable depths of over 15,000 metres were reported – quite erroneously.

In the wake of the mapping of the coast of northern Norway by the Geographical Survey, Lieutenant Henrik Hagerup, who had become familiar with the circumstances of the fishermen during his work on the survey from 1828 to 1832, suggested that the sea banks off the coast should be surveyed as this would provide a useful supplement to the nautical charts. Hagerup's suggestion was ignored until in 1840, Norwegian fishermen in East Finnmark complained that Russian fishing vessels were operating in their waters. The local governor submitted a proposal to perform soundings to create a map of the fishing grounds, but the Geographical Survey of Norway's land surveyors believed this to be a waste of time – since the fishermen reporting any illegal fishing activities would be unable to understand the map. The Norwegian Ministry of Finance disagreed, however – and found funding for the soundings under the budget item 'incidental expenses'. In 1841, the sea floor from Tanahorn to the Russian border was mapped, along with hazardous areas around the island of Karlsøy in Troms. The results were not particularly accurate, since the cartographer had only a rough idea of where and how the fishermen operated, but a report from 1843 stated that the

Next pages | *Oversigts-Kart over det af Nordhavsexpeditionen i 1878 bereiste Havströg* (*General map of the seas explored by the North Sea Expedition in 1878*), a map of the waters between Norway, Svalbard, Jan Mayen and Greenland, hand-drawn by oceanographer Georg O. Sars. The map shows 'Loddestimernes Træk' and 'Lofot-Torskens Sig' – the migration routes of Capelin and Cod from Lofoten – in addition to the 'Nordhavs-Barrieren' (North Sea barrier), 'Polar Ström' (Polar currents) and a 'Dyb Havdal indtil 2000 F' (Deep sea valley of up to 2,000 fathoms).

Grönland:

Norsk
Hav

Loddelinierne
Træk

Polar Ström

drivis

Polarstrømmens Grændse

vestligtræk

Drivis

Drivis

Polar-Strømmens Grændse

Jan Mayen

Atlanterhavs Ström

Syd Havdal indtil 20 ф. F.

Polar-Hav. — 22D / 79½

(Inquestedt mere end 300F.)

Spitsber-gen

Nordhavs-

Lofot=Torskens Sig

Polar

drivis

Strømmene Grændse

Lodde-Torskens Sig

Nordhavs

Hvirvelstr.

Loddedistrikt

Skreidistrikt

⊕ Stationer, hvor directe Undersøgelser over Fiskeriene er anstillet.

Oversigts-Kart over det af Nordhavsexpeditionen i 1878 bereiste Havstrøg.
G. O. Sars.

results 'will most likely lead to not insignificant expectations regarding the usefulness of a future accurate sounding.' Good maps would make the fishing grounds 'of greater importance due to their being able to be utilised during a greater period of the year.'

Norway became a leading country within the genre of fishing maps. 'Proper fishing maps such as ours have never before been published,' wrote *Skilling-Magazin* in a news report about the sounding vessel DS *Hansteen* in 1870. 'Finally, a steamship has been constructed and equipped exclusively for the sounding of the sea floor and the publication of fishing maps, which provide an accurate and clear overview of the conditions of the landscape inhabited by the fish.' The magazine provided readers with an insight into the work:

> As soon as the depth of the line is checked, the reel is started by a small steam engine, and the line pulled up at an average speed of 100 fathoms per minute. In the meantime, the necessary angles required for determining the current position are measured using a sextant, between the trigonometric points at the tops of the mountains wherever these can be seen, or other observations are made. Everything must be completed and the details noted before the line has been pulled up, as the ship must then make for the next sounding location at full speed. Calculations are then performed and the sounding is marked on the map, and after 5, 6 or 7 minutes the ship stops, and starts from the beginning again.

DS *Hansteen* started south of Færder in the south-east of Norway, working its way west around the coast to Mandal, Jæren, Stad and the Trøndelag and Nordland coasts, paying special attention to Hitra, Frøya, Lofoten, Vesterålen and Senja. Through the mapping project, the myths and legends about *Ut-Røst* and other unknown landforms out at sea, which were often used to provide an explanation for incomprehensible shipwrecks, were debunked once and for all. DS *Hansteen* discovered new fishing grounds and established where the border between Norway and Russia was located out at sea, and in 1875 the Geographical Survey of Norway was awarded a gold medal and diploma for its outstanding nautical charts at the International Geographical Congress in Paris.

ATLANTIS | Two differing views of the ocean floor dominated the thinking of the late 1800s. On one side were the dreamers, geologists and evolutionists who imagined the lost city of Atlantis or a sunken continent that might explain why the same types of rock and fossils were found on both sides of the ocean; on the other were those who were more conservative, and who believed that land masses were unable to rise and sink – that land was land and sea was sea, and had been since the Earth was created.

Both camps were represented among the researchers aboard the British ship HMS *Challenger*, which in December 1872 set out on a voyage across the world's oceans. The vessel crossed the Atlantic five times and the Indian Ocean and Pacific Ocean once each, and discovered the Mid-Atlantic Ridge and the deepest part of the world's oceans, the Mariana Trench between Japan and New Guinea. When making their way from Tristan da Cunha, a group of islands in the South Atlantic, to Ascension Island 30 degrees further north, they noticed that they often found themselves in shallow waters, but never took enough measurements to realise that they were sailing along the length of an underwater mountain range. The researchers therefore marked the area as a plateau.

Back home, the researchers' findings were first hailed as the discovery of a lost continent – and despite geological and biological samples taken from the ocean floor indicating otherwise, the idea lived on. The crew aboard HMS *Challenger* had travelled 125,000 kilometres, but taken no more than 492 soundings during their 713 days at sea, which meant that knowledge of the ocean floor remained so sketchy that it was perfectly possible to locate lost continents there.

THE NORTH SEA | The Norwegians were inspired by the British expedition. Two professors, meteorologist Henrik Mohn and oceanographer Georg Sars, pointed out that the waters between Norway, the Faroe Islands, Iceland, Jan Mayen and Svalbard were as good as unknown territory, and that the exploration of these waters was now 'more incumbent upon us Norwegians than on any other nation.' A scientific survey 'of the sea off the west coast of Norway is a task which, from the Norwegian perspective, should surely be able to be performed with the same fortune as the British expeditions of the same nature,' it was said. The Norwegians had also learned that 'the British Government will not let the *Challenger* take on this survey of our Arctic waters, which we have in mind.' The survey was named Den norske Nordhavs-Expedition – The Norwegian North Sea Expedition.

The professors felt that there were both scientific and practical reasons for setting out on the expedition. First, it would help to shed light on why Norway was blessed with a warm ocean current just off the coast, which made the country inhabitable and enabled agriculture. Second, the expedition would provide important information about fishing conditions – 'so that the many questions relating to our most important fisheries will hereby be answered. This is especially true for our highly important herring fisheries.' By surveying the sea's depths, floor and geological formations, they would become wiser about 'our migrating fish species' biological conditions.'

The steamship DS *Vøringen* set out from Bergen on the morning of 1 June 1876, and after mapping the bottom of the Sognefjord sailed west to survey 'the deep "Sloping Canyon" that runs alongside the coast towards the Arctic Ocean,' known today as the Norwegian Trench, before setting out on a long voyage from Kristiansund. The weather posed a significant challenge – storms raged from 1 July to 15 August, with howling winds of up to twenty metres per second and six-metre-high waves: 'The motion of the sea hindered our work on the depths.' A breaker did so much damage to the ship that the crew was forced to put into a port of refuge on the Faroe Islands, but after the necessary repairs had been made they forged out onto the waves again, measuring a depth of 1,215 fathoms north-east of the Faroe Islands between two storms, and seeking shelter by some islands off Iceland a few days later before resuming their work. 'Regardless of gale-force winds (wind speed of 10 to 16 metres per second) and rough seas,' they performed the soundings and surveys of the seabed with the calculated loss of equipment that had to be cut loose.

'After having endured eight storms in six weeks,' they finally docked at Namsos.

In the summer of 1877, the expedition performed soundings around the areas of Lofoten and Røst before undertaking a long crossing to the West Ice between Greenland and Jan Mayen to map depths and currents; the warm surface current from the Atlantic and 'the cold Polar current' in the Greenland Sea. Ashore at Jan Mayen, they 'determined the locations of the various visible peaks and glaciers using bearings and angular measurements using a sextant.' The result was a beautiful map of the island, on which glaciers, peaks and streams were named after the expedition's members.

In the expedition report from 1878, the name of the Arctic Ocean has been changed to the Norwegian Sea, because since 'time immemorial [it] has been traversed by our seamen.' In the final year of the expedition, DS *Vøringen* sailed to the far north, to Bear Island and Spitsbergen, where the crew collected fossils, surveyed the land and determined the heights of mountains.

The Norwegian North Sea Expedition gave rise to many scientific books and new maps. One of these books alone, *Nordhavets Dybder, Temperatur og Strømninger* (*North Sea Depths, Temperatures and Currents*), contains as many as twenty-seven maps illustrating subsurface temperature and pressure variations, winds and currents, and depths.

FRAM I | Henrik Mohn and Georg Sars wrote that 'the equipping of a true North Pole Expedition, with the aim of reaching the so-far unexplored Polar Region, is not our duty. We must entrust this to richer nations.' But fifteen years after DS *Vøringen* had completed its voyage, a government-funded expedition would set out for the North Pole in a specially constructed ship – the *Fram*. Sars and Mohn were both involved in the expedition planning, despite their earlier reservations.

In the autumn of 1884, Fridtjof Nansen had read in the *Morgenbladet* newspaper that the remains of a ship wrecked on the New Siberian Islands had drifted all the way to the coast of Greenland – several thousand kilometres further west. This gave him the idea for a sea voyage across the Arctic Ocean in a boat that drifted with the ice – perhaps the ocean currents would carry him across the promised pole. 'One of the scientific tasks of the expedition was to investigate the depth of the Polar Sea,' wrote Nansen in the book *Farthest North* thirteen years later. Before the expedition set out, the general consensus based on soundings performed in the Barents Sea and other adjacent waters was that the Arctic Ocean was shallow: 'I presupposed a shallow Polar Sea, the greatest depth known in these regions up till now being 80 fathoms,' wrote Nansen. Like many others, he presumed that 'the regions about the Pole had formerly been covered with an extensive tract of land, of which the existing islands are simply the remains.' He dismissed the idea that land might not also be discovered further north as 'ridiculous.'

But the first soundings gave surprising results. In March 1894, when the expedition was located at around 80 degrees north, the crew 'had out 2100 metres (over 1,100 fathoms) of line without reaching the bottom. [...] Unfortunately we were not prepared for such great depths, and had not brought any deep-sea sounding apparatus with us.' The solution was to unravel one of the ship's steel cables and tie the strands together to create a plumb line almost 5,000 metres long. They finally reached the bottom at 3,850 metres. 'I do not think we shall talk any more about the shallow Polar Sea, where land may be expected anywhere. We may very possibly drift out into the Atlantic Ocean without having seen a single mountain-top,' wrote Nansen in his log book. The discovery resulted in all theories of a North Pole continent having to be scrapped. Nevertheless, in 1895 the French newspaper *Le Figaro* reported that Nansen had planted the Norwegian flag 'in the mountains' at the North Pole.

Nansen wrote a pioneering work about the Arctic Ocean floor after the expedition, in which he posited a theory of changes to the Earth's crust. Based on the soundings he and his crew had completed in the shallow Barents Sea, and their surveys of the surrounding areas of land, Nansen believed that before the great ice ages the Barents Sea had been dry land, through which rivers spread outwards, cutting into the extensive plains – and later research would prove him right.

PING ... PING | When the seventh International Geographical Congress was held in Berlin in 1899, mapping of the ocean floor had reached a point where there was a need for common names that could be used on the maps. A commission was established to create a bathymetric map – a map of the ocean floor. Everyone agreed, however, that the first attempt – the *Carte générale bathymétrique des oceans* (*General Bathymetric Chart of the Oceans*) – was terrible. A significant technological leap was needed to enable the proper mapping of the ocean's depths – and this came after the *Titanic* collided with an iceberg in the year 1912 and 1,513 people consequently drowned. The need for an improved overview and increased safety led to the British taking out the first patent on a sonar system just one month after the *Titanic* sank.

The sonar system emitted a sound through the water, a so-called 'ping', and by measuring the time it took for the sound to return after hitting something below the water's surface, a single person could do in just a couple of seconds what had previously taken several individuals many hours. The principle was simple – but the challenge was to construct a device that was accurate enough. Sound moves through water four times faster than through air, which means that a half-second delay is equivalent to 1,000 feet. Harvey Hayes, a physicist in the United States Navy, was the first to invent an echo sounder that could be used in deep water. In the summer of 1922, he sailed from Newport to Gibraltar. Over just one week he performed 900 deep-water soundings – far more than HMS *Challenger* had performed during three and a half years. Hayes's invention finally made it possible to see the world's seas and oceans free from water.

From 1925 to 1927, the German vessel *Meteor* measured the depth of the Atlantic Ocean at an entire 67,388 positions using sonar. Had the crew been forced to lift and lower a plumb line manually, such a survey would have taken seven years with the crew working twenty-four hours a day, seven days a week. The researchers on board were interested in finding out whether it was possible to extract enough gold from the salt water to enable Germany to pay off the debt the country was left with after the First World War. Unfortunately, it wasn't.

While the German ship sailed up and down the Atlantic Ocean, one day in 1926 a six-year-old girl visited the south-east coast of the USA and saw the ocean for the very first time. Pascagoula, Mississippi, is a flat area where the land lies just a few centimetres above the ocean surface, slipping almost invisibly below it where the trees, grass, bushes and sand all come to an end. What did this six-year-old girl make of the apparently empty surface she saw before her? Did she imagine that the landscape continued somewhere out there below the water, where she was unable to see it? That there were mountains and valleys hidden somewhere out there, too?

The girl's father worked as a map-maker for the agricultural authorities, and so this period by the water was an exceptional time in her childhood – usually the family were based far inland, somewhere within the great farming states. She took off her shoes, allowing her feet to sink into the sand; feeling the waves wash back and forth across her toes. On the beach was a shipwreck, and the following day, when the tide was high, it was barely visible above the water. Far out at sea, the *Meteor* revealed that the Mid-Atlantic Ridge was a mountain range, not a plateau as the researchers aboard HMS *Challenger* had believed, and twenty-six years later this six-year-old on the beach – Marie Tharp – discovered this mountain range was being ripped apart because the Earth's continents are in a state of constant motion.

DOC | In 1930, American geologist Maurice 'Doc' Ewing became a professor at the age of twenty-four. He was an odd character – a large part of his teaching involved taking his students out into the field to blow things up using dynamite. This was illegal, of course – but the time it takes for a seismic pressure wave to return to the Earth's surface provides information about the types of geological structures present in the ground, and measuring this time delay is an excellent way for anyone wishing to make geological maps to obtain data. One day, Ewing was asked if he wished to study the American continental shelf. At this time, it was known that the ocean suddenly became deeper a couple of nautical miles from land – but nobody knew why. Doc had never worked out at sea before, but, he wrote in his autobiography, 'if they had asked me to put seismographs on the moon instead of the bottom of the ocean I'd have agreed, I was so desperate for a chance to do research.' He became the first person to use explosion seismology to map the ocean from the coastline to the end of the continental shelf.

Doc became obsessed with the ocean floor. Attempting to understand the Earth by investigating only the 30 per cent of it that exists above water was, he believed, 'like trying to describe a football after being given a look at a piece of lacing' – a thought that had never occurred to most other geologists. Nor did oceanographers at the time really understand what Doc was working on. Harald Ulrik Sverdrup, the Norwegian oceanographer who was head of the Scripps Institute of Oceanography from 1936 to 1948, wrote that the ocean floor was primarily only of interest by virtue of its being the place where the water ended, but Doc took a completely opposite view: 'The ocean is just a murky mist that keeps me from seeing the bottom. To be honest, I wish the whole thing'd just dry up.'

As early as the 1930s, Doc's surveys showed that the continental shelf mainly consisted of sediments – porous types of rock strewn across the bedrock, which often contained oil and gas. He asked Standard Oil whether they would be open to financing his research, but no – they were not interested in spending as much as five cents on looking for oil out in the ocean.

During the Second World War, the United States Navy contacted Doc – perhaps he could help them find German U-boats using sonar and the world's first underwater camera, in exchange for funding to develop his latest gizmos. 'During the war we used to talk about what fun we were going to have afterwards when we took all these instruments that were being developed and started doing science with them,' said Doc, and this was true – the period that followed the Second World War saw significant growth in oceanographic research. The Atlantic and Pacific Oceans were strategically important locations that separated the

Next pages | Maps of the Norwegian Continental Shelf from 1965 and 1971 respectively, which show areas assigned for exploratory drilling in the North Sea. The map from 1965, which has been coloured by hand, shows that twenty-two licences were awarded for seventy-eight areas in the first licensing round. The first major oil discovery was made four years later.

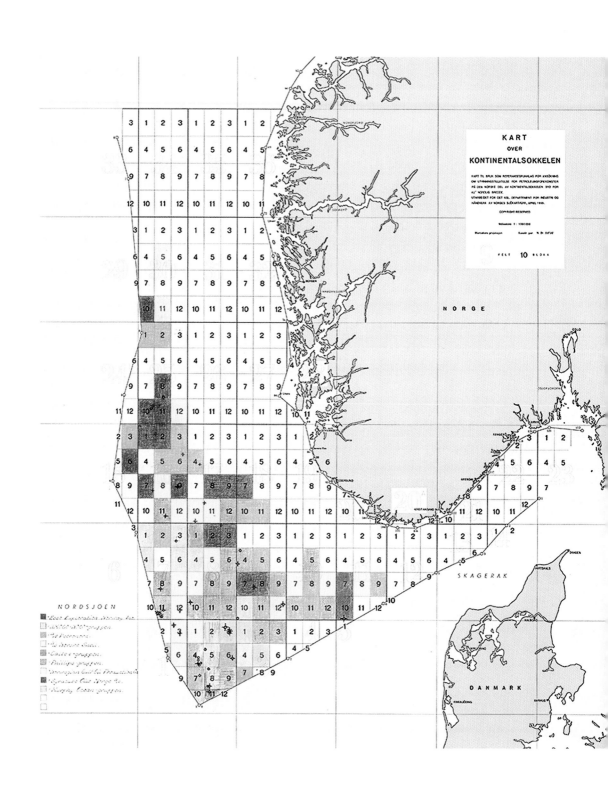

KART
OVER
KONTINENTALSOKKELEN

FELT 10 BLD 4

world's two superpowers. Doc became a professor at the recently established Institute of Geophysics at Columbia University in New York, and when a young woman with a prestigious geological education and experience visited him in 1948 to apply for a job, Doc asked her: 'Can you draft?'

THE PG GIRLS | The Second World War had given American women new opportunities. One day in 1942, as Marie Tharp was buzzing around the University of Ohio, unsure whether to continue studying philosophy, music, art, English, German, zoology or palaeobotanics, she saw a poster from the University of Michigan – geology students were guaranteed work in the oil industry after graduation. Tharp had studied a little geology already, as just one of three women out of a year group of seventy-three students. Her grades were nothing spectacular, but Tharp's lecturer thought she showed promise, and encouraged her to combine the subject with drafting so that she would at the very least be able to work with geology in an office. Taking women out into the field was not something male geologists were in the habit of doing.

Since most of the country's young men had been sent off to war, it was only natural that most of the geology students would be young women, who in Michigan became known as the 'PG girls' – the petroleum geology girls. Wearing jeans stuffed into tall hiking boots, they set out on excursions up to the Black Hills, where they studied rocks and drew maps of the terrain. At this time nobody was entirely sure about exactly how the area had been formed. Why were there mountains and valleys? Why was the Earth's crust not smooth, like a shell?

One of Tharp's textbooks admitted that 'the cause of crustal deformation is one of the great mysteries of science and can be discussed only in a speculative way. The lack of definite knowledge on the subject is emphasized by the great diversity and contradictory character of attempted explanations.' One lecturer at Harvard University had as many as nineteen different explanations as to how mountains were formed. Tharp studied the theory that suggested that the Earth shrank because it cooled after its fiery creation, which resulted in the geography being set in motion, and that of continental drift, through which entire continents changed places. Most geologists dismissed both theories. As for the other theories, the textbook informed her, there were simply too many to include. A significant part of being a geologist was about formulating more or less educated guesses.

As the Second World War was coming to an end, Tharp had completed the four semesters necessary to take a master's degree in geology, and took a fifth semester of physics, maths and chemistry because she felt she was lacking in these areas. All this cross-disciplinary curiosity unsettled her tutors, who were afraid Tharp would abandon geology. They therefore encouraged her to take a job in an oil company straight after graduation, for which she earned good money, but spent most of her day bored out of her wits – as a general rule women were given work for which they were overqualified. Tharp continued to study mathematics in her free time, and took spherical trigonometry, the science of how things relate to one another on a sphere; useful for anyone wishing to navigate larger distances across the oceans – or, as it would turn out, create a map of them.

Twenty years after she saw the sea for the first time, Tharp would see it again when she moved to New York seeking new challenges, which led her to Columbia University and the Institute for Geophysics. 'I'm looking for a job', she said to the institute's secretary. 'A job?' – 'Yes. I asked at the geology department upstairs and someone told me a Doctor ...' She checked the note in her hand. ' ... Maurice Ewing might be looking for people.' The secretary took her along to Doc, who, after hearing Tharp speak about her cartographer father, geology studies and the work she had performed for the oil company, asked her if she could draw.

AN UNEXPECTED RIFT | Marie Tharp's first geology tutor had been right – women with an interest in geology needed to learn to draw. Tharp informed Doc that she could, and so Doc gave her a job at the institute, where twenty-three people squeezed into three rooms attempted to understand the interactions between the ocean floor, dry land and the atmosphere. Tharp was the sixth woman to be employed at the institute:

Midge did the accounts; Jean, a mathematics and physics major, made coffee, typed things up on the typewriter and performed minor administrative tasks; Emily and Faye, both mathematics majors, worked as calculation assistants for one of the male staff; while Marie, with a graduate degree in geology, undergraduate degree in mathematics and additional qualifications in physics and chemistry, was employed to draw copies of maps and make table calculations.

Not long after Tharp was employed, the entire institute moved to new, larger premises beside the Hudson River, a gift from widow Florence Lamont, and changed its name to the Lamont Geological Observatory – a sign that the group was now studying more than geophysics alone.

But the move had no consequences for Tharp's work and, after four years, she'd had enough. She left for her father's farm in Ohio, and didn't return until she received a telegram: 'Consider this an extended vacation. Doc.' At the observatory it was decided that Bruce Heezen, a geologist who was both younger and less qualified than Tharp, would be responsible for her work. Their first meeting was described by a German society magazine many years later as follows: '. . . small waist, swinging long skirt, graceful line. She looked very charming. As he came over to her, she felt his warm manhood, the scent of his skin, and his voice was deep when he said: "Marie, we will be cartographers of the whole globe, its topography under the sea. Science will have to accept that." In this night they became a loving couple that stuck together for the coming lifetime.' We can only guess at what Tharp might have had to say about the veracity of this account.

What we do know, however, is that Tharp and Heezen collaborated closely until Heezen died of a heart attack in a submarine off Iceland in 1977, and that their work together started when Heezen set the cardboard boxes on Tharp's desk and asked her whether she could turn their contents into a map.

Tharp started the map by drawing coastlines, lines of latitude and longitude, and then the areas closest to land where centuries of soundings had provided a certain overview. She then drew the subsea landscape along the six routes that the observatory's oceanographers had explored using sonar.

The result was solid – the best representation of the Atlantic Ocean floor to have been produced to date – but Tharp wasn't satisfied. She hadn't discovered anything new. At the same time, however, there was something that gave her pause – the apparent rift in the Mid-Atlantic Ridge. And after Tharp and Heezen's first argument, which ended with them agreeing to disagree about whether the results suggested continental drift, something curious happened at one of the observatory's light tables.

At this time, Heezen and a colleague were working with a map on assignment from Bell Laboratories, owned by Western Electric, who made telephone cables, and American Telephone & Telegraph, who used them. The companies were now planning a transatlantic telephone cable. But where would it be best protected against earthquakes? Where was the flattest underwater landscape, so they could use as little cable as possible? In short, where should they lay the cable? The observatory staff were therefore in the process of creating a map that documented where in the Atlantic earthquakes occurred. One day, this map and Tharp's map – without either Heezen or Tharp being able to remember why – ended up being laid over each other on a light table, and clearly showed that earthquakes had a striking tendency to start exactly where Tharp believed the rift in the Earth's crust to be located.

Tharp used this new knowledge to make some educated guesses. On a new map, she drew a mountain range that stretched from Greenland in the north, down the southern Atlantic Ocean, around the southern tip of Africa, north-west into the Indian Ocean, where HMS *Challenger* had found shallow waters between Madagascar and India, and from here west into the mainland to the East African Rift – an area in which the Earth's crust is moving. She then compared the East African Rift with the subsea rift. They looked the same.

Next pages | The *World Ocean Floor Panorama* by Marie Tharp, Bruce Heezen and Heinrich Berann, completed in 1977. The map forced the world's geologists and oceanographers to look at the ocean floor from a completely new perspective. Tharp and Heezen had previously created maps of individual oceans, such as the Atlantic Ocean and Indian Ocean, but this was the first map to show how all the subsea mountain ranges link together.

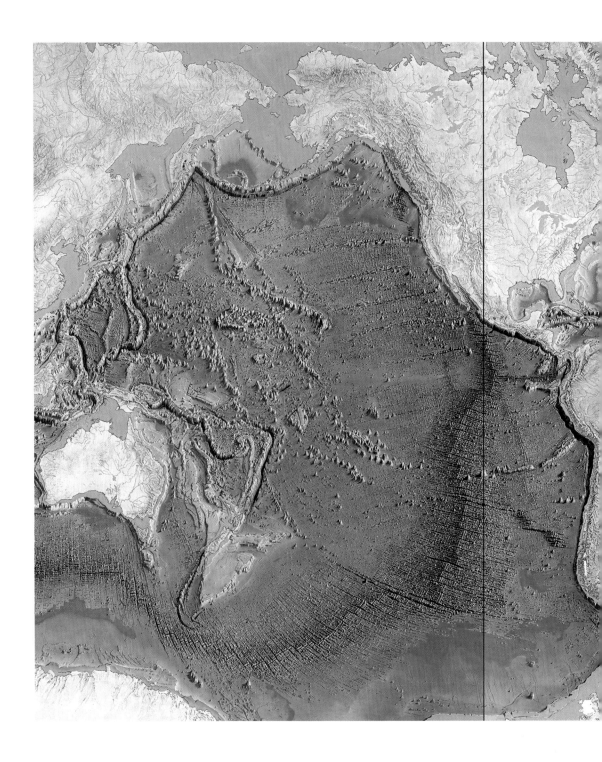

Eight months after Tharp had started to interpret the sonar readings, she was able to outline an almost continual rift that stretched all the
way around the Earth – a 6,500-mile-long underwater formation, probably the largest geological structure in the world. Now even Heezen was
convinced of continental drift.

THE EARTH CRACKS | But Tharp and Heezen didn't dare release the
news immediately – only four years later, in 1956, did Heezen and Doc
finally compose an article – full of reservations and caveats – about
an 'apparent' rift. That same year, Tharp redrew the map of the North
Atlantic ocean floor. But it was impossible to impose the reservations
made in the article on the map – on the map, the rift was clear. 'And like
the cartographers of old, we put a large legend in the space where we had
no data. I also wanted to include mermaids and shipwrecks, but Bruce
would have none of it,' Tharp wrote later. The article and the map formed
the basis for the *New York Times*'s story about the Earth ripping apart
at the seams.

Most geologists refused to believe what they saw on Tharp's map.
'They not only said it wasn't fair, they said it was a bunch of lies,' she said.
Her peers were insistent when the first International Oceanographic
Congress was held in New York in the autumn of 1959. 'Some 800 sci-
entists from East and West were told here today that they seemed to be
drifting apart – not politically, but geographically,' wrote the *New York
Times*. While Heezen was giving a presentation, one geologist called out:
'Impossible!'

The star of the conference was the French underwater photographer
and film-maker Jacques Cousteau. Heezen had met him the previous
year, and given him a copy of the map of the North Atlantic. Cousteau
had hung the map on the wall aboard his ship so that he could study it,
and when it was time to cross the Atlantic to participate in the conference, he decided to prove Tharp and Heezen wrong. He filmed the area
where the rift was supposed to be.

'Gentlemen,' Cousteau began one evening, addressing the handsome
tables set for a dinner party for the conference participants, 'I did not believe that the map of the North Atlantic recently published by Lamont

could possibly be right. I did not believe that the Mid-Atlantic Rift pictured on it could possibly be right. Too complete a story, I thought, from too little information. But it is there. It is true.'

The lights were dimmed; the projector hummed to life ... 3–2–1 ... and there was the ocean floor, sand, starfish and, further away, a dark area that, when the camera moved closer, was revealed to be a mountain range. The camera continued to film the mountainside, right until it reached the peak. And there, down below, was the rift – visible for as far as the camera cast its light. Tharp was finally able to see that which for the past seven years she had only been able to imagine.

Tharp used the next four years to draw a map of the southern part of the Atlantic, which was printed and published by the Geological Society of America, and in 1972 travelled with Heezen to Iceland to study the part of the Mid-Atlantic Ridge – and the rift – that can be walked across in the area. Aboard a plane flying above the island, Tharp drew sketches of the rift's formations.

BLACK GOLD | That same year, French planes took to the skies in Operation North Sea – a project to find out whether there were opportunities to find more oil and gas in the area than the Dutch had discovered along the coast three years previously. The aircraft explored the magnetism of the rock types below the surface. The sediments – the porous rocks in which oil and gas are generally found – are not magnetic, while the bedrock is. By combining magnetic soundings with ordinary ones, it is therefore possible to determine the thickness of the sedimentary layers.

Few were convinced that oil and gas would be found off the Norwegian coast – in 1958, geologists had submitted a letter to the Norwegian Ministry of Foreign Affairs, in which they presumed the continental shelf consisted of the same rock types as those found onshore. The Ice Age was thought to have scraped away the sediments. 'One may discount the possibility that coal, oil or sulphur may be found on the continental shelf along the Norwegian coast,' they wrote. But in the following year, Maurice 'Doc' Ewing from Lamont published a report on the Norwegian waters, in which he described indisputable findings of sedimentary rock types in the sea west of Trondheim. But his report never made it into the right hands.

In Denmark, exploratory drilling had been undertaken on Jutland for twenty-five years without oil being discovered, and so it was not the search for black gold that motivated geophysicist Markvard Sellevold to start exploring Skagerrak in 1962. He was more interested in mapping the geological border between Denmark and Norway – the place where the Norwegian bedrock gave way to the Danish sediments. Sellevold and his team set up seismic field stations along the coasts. They put 100 grams of dynamite and a lit detonator in a blown-up paper bag, then threw this overboard, repeating the process again and again in order to analyse the seismic sound waves. The Norwegian Geological Survey also measured magnetism in the area from the air, and to everyone's great surprise the results showed that the sediments stretched all the way to the pebbles on Norway's south coast – and that just twenty kilometres offshore was a sedimentary layer 5,000 metres thick.

In the application made to the Ministry of Foreign Affairs regarding further exploration of the continental shelf, emphasis was placed on the fact that 'these sediments are potential carriers of deposits of oil, natural gas, coal, iron ore, etc . . .'. In 1963, the Norwegian Geological Survey performed ten aerial expeditions to survey the conditions between Stad and Lofoten. The map showed that the magnetic patterns clearly changed in the transition from land to sea, and the results were so promising that a further twenty aerial expeditions were carried out between Loftoen and Senja the following year. The flights were followed by detailed surveys. On a 'Bathymetric Chart of the Norwegian Sea and Adjacent Areas', an anonymous bureaucrat has placed an 'A' off the coast at Vardø and another off the coast of Florø, and written in ballpoint pen on the mainland: 'A-A Contact basement sediments'. In other words: possible oil and gas deposits along the entire coastline. And of course the oil companies were interested now, too. An increasing number of foreign vessels on mapping assignments docked at the quay in central Stavanger, their holds full of explosives for use in seismic surveys.

The Norwegian authorities now understood that the North Sea was a potential gold mine, and on 31 May 1963 the Norwegian government declared the seabed and subsoil in the areas off the Norwegian coast subject to Norwegian sovereignty.

Just 200 years after Norway and Sweden had finally agreed upon the border between the two countries, and 140 years after the latest agreements with the Russians in the far north, Norway was forced to enter into negotiations with the British and the Danes regarding how far out to sea the country's boundaries extended. The border with Sweden had taken almost 100 years to establish, but the negotiations with the UK and Denmark were settled much more quickly. In 1965, all parties agreed to use the centre-line principle – to draw a line that split the waters between the countries equally. Norway was then able to seek applications from oil companies wishing to undertake exploration activities, and a single-column entry in the *Norsk Lysingblad*, a state publication for public announcements, kicked the whole thing off: 'Applications shall reference the field and block numbers specified in this announcement, based on the map deposited at the Royal Norwegian Ministry for Trade and Industry.'

The *Map of the continental shelf* shows Norwegian waters south of 62 degrees north. Across the south-western area a patchwork of red, yellow, green and other colours indicates which oil companies have been licensed to perform exploratory drilling in the various fields. The Norwegian oil age had begun.

OCEAN PANORAMA | At around the same time, a young girl from Austria sent a letter to *National Geographic*. She had seen the magazine's maps, she wrote, and believed that her father was able to draw much better ones. According to Tharp, the magazine had a weakness for letters from children; in any case, they sent their head cartographer to Austria to investigate – the girl's father, Heinrich Berann, had drawn many maps of the Alps – and so began Berann's long collaboration with *National Geographic*. In 1966, he was put in touch with Tharp and Heezen because the magazine wished to give its readers a map of the Indian Ocean – a large map that could be hung on the wall.

Berann had developed his technique based on the physiographic diagrams Tharp had started with in order to make her maps easier to understand, but while Tharp drew her maps using inks and pens, Berann was a painter, who used brushes and an abundance of colour. His aim was to paint as photographically and realistically as possible. Using light green for the shallow waters and continental shelves, a medium blue for the plateaus, a dark grey-purple for the smaller mountains closer to the surface and an even darker colour for the deepest trenches, Berann enabled everyone to see the peaks and troughs that lay hidden beneath the ocean.

The map was a hit among both geographers and readers, and *National Geographic* followed its success with a double map. On one side was 'the visible face of the Atlantic and the lands around it', on the other the same map, minus the water. The maps were distributed to six million American families.

Berann, Tharp and Heezen created two more maps for *National Geographic*: one of the Pacific Ocean and one of the waters around Antarctica. Tharp and Heezen then suggested that they create a panorama that illustrated how all the subsea mountain ranges were linked together, and how all the seas and oceans are actually interconnected to create a single great world ocean. The magazine wasn't interested – but the U.S. Office of Naval Research was, and in 1974 Tharp and Heezen began what would be their last project.

Berann created a large, specially designed board for the panorama. He outlined the land masses, applied a blue background colour to the ocean areas, and started to add in details from Tharp's drawings. Tharp updated the areas in which new information had become available since she first drew her maps, while assistants did the groundwork of collecting data from the large seafaring nations. Tharp's home looked like a cartographic production line, with people creating overviews of rifts, mountains and trenches before others created sketches based on these – and still others combined the sketches with sounding data, and so on. Tharp then created drawings for the map, which for the first time would show the 70 per cent of the Earth's surface that lies underwater.

In May 1977, Tharp and Heezen moved in with Berann to complete the enormous project. We can imagine them leaning over the map in Berann's study, with its smell of paint, solvents and coffee. The map measures almost two metres across, the blue, black and purple ocean floor presented in cool contrast to the yellow-green and brown land masses. Berann has made between thirty and seventy changes to the map every day since the two geologists arrived. Tharp studies the Bering Strait, the Kamchatka Peninsula and the Aleutian Islands, and says: 'I think . . .'

'Please, Mary, please, no more changes,' says Berann in his broken English.

Tharp slumps down into a chair. 'I was just going to say that I think everything looks good.'

One month later, Heezen would travel to Iceland to study the rift valley of the Mid-Atlantic Ridge at close quarters from a submarine. He suffered a heart attack and died there in the depths, aged just fifty-three.

Heezen saw just one of the panorama test prints before he passed away; after his death Tharp was left responsible for ensuring that the printing process provided the right results. 'I realized that color was not my forte,' she wrote after noticing that something was wrong with the test print but being unable to determine exactly what. A photographer friend pointed out that the printers had failed to add the colour red. This was the first delay of many, but just under a year later, at 7 p.m. on 17 May 1978 following several adjustments to both the colours and typography, the first copies of the *World Ocean Floor Panorama* began to roll off the press.

SATELLITES | The panorama is not an accurate map. Despite the immense amount of work behind it, it was based on the geologists' more and less educated guesses, and much of the panorama has been corrected and updated since it was made – as maps always are. Despite the fact that Tharp and Heezen possessed more knowledge of the ocean floor than anyone before them, given the vastness of the ocean, they knew ridiculously little. Tharp had, for example, just one set of sonar data that provided information about a 640-mile-long mountain range between Australia and the Antarctic, and this was therefore 'of necessity sketched

THEATER OF THE WORLD

in a very stylized manner,' she wrote. All the formations are also high-ly exaggerated, which is necessary – otherwise even a mountain with a height of 8,000 metres would be invisible on a map of the panorama's scale.

It is therefore not possible to use the map to find a specific mountain beneath the ocean's surface, as there is no guarantee that the mountain was included. In 1984, a team of oceanographers used the map when exploring the rift in the southern Atlantic Ocean – the rift was found twenty-four miles from where the map indicated it should be.

Oceanographers like to point out that the Moon has been more ac-curately mapped than our own planet. Even Venus – which at its closest is forty million kilometres away and covered by thick, poisonous gases – was mapped more accurately than the Earth when the Magellan satellite and its radar passed above the planet in 1992. This was able to map for-mations on the planet's surface larger than 300 metres – a level of detail oceanographers can only dream of.

The problem with radar is that it can't penetrate water, and so sonar remains the most accurate method of mapping the ocean floor. But boats are small and slow, while the ocean is vast – so immensely vast. Only be-tween 5 and 15 per cent of the ocean floor has therefore been mapped using sonar, depending on how one defines *mapped.*

But satellites have also been used to map the ocean. In 1985, the United States Navy sent up the GEOSAT satellite to measure the height of the ocean's surface. Even calm waters are never actually flat; they feature hills and valleys with differences in height of several hundred feet, but these are so gradual that ships are unable to detect them. Some of these variations occur where oceanic currents collide, such as where the cold part of the Atlantic meets the warmth of the Gulf Stream, but the biggest differences in height are the result of the Earth's gravity, which is strong-er in some places than in others. The GEOSAT map therefore shows both the height of the ocean surface and the distribution of gravity across the planet.

The GEOSAT map looked familiar to geographers – it looked like a map of the ocean floor. The reason for this is that gravity increases where there is significant mass, such as a mountain range, but decreases in flat areas and at significant depths. The ocean surface is an echo of the ocean floor.

David Sandwell and Walter Smith, American geophysicists and oceanographers, compared the measurements taken by GEOSAT and the European satellite ERS-1 with true soundings in order to establish the accuracy of the satellites' measurements. In 1997, they published a map that showed much of the ocean floor terrain that was previously unknown. 'This map is going to focus our attention on some places where we had not usually gone with ships, because they're in remote areas in the Southern Ocean, they're far from ports, and the weather down there is uncomfortable,' said Smith.

Sandwell and Smith continued to work with improving the original map, and in 2014 launched a map based on data from the European satellite CryoSat-2 and American satellite Jason-1. The map was two to four times more accurate than the previous one, and registered formations on the ocean floor measuring five kilometres or greater – but this is still far less accurate than the Magellan satellite's mapping of our neighbouring planet.

INTO THE DEEP | The mapping of the ocean floor has been – and continues to be – a tedious and difficult task. Technological developments have progressed from ever-longer plumb lines to sonar and satellites, but there is still a fair way to go to obtain a complete and accurate map of the entire ocean floor. But perhaps such a map isn't truly necessary. One of Bruce Heezen's former students, oceanographer Bill Ryan, who has developed various tools for mapping the ocean floor, believes the creation of a complete map to be a waste of time and money. 'The fact is we can learn how this planet works by seeing five percent of its surface. The next 95 percent looks like the first five percent,' says Ryan, who would rather prioritise the mapping of the various regions that form the marine opposites of the Alps, tundra, desert and so on. Tharp and Heezen's map featured only around ten different types of landscape – Ryan believes closer to 200 are required in order to accurately represent the ocean floor. But we need only explore one of each thoroughly, Ryan believes – because once you've seen one, you've seen them all.

Ryan may well be right. But it is hard to imagine that humankind will stop before the ocean floor has been mapped down to the tiniest detail. Information will be collated, and scientific expeditions to Atlantic, Indian, Arctic, Pacific and Southern waters – the world's five oceans – will continue to contribute pieces of the puzzle until, one day, the map of the ocean floor will finally be complete.

Global Marine Gravity, Version 23.1 from 2 October 2014. The map was made by geophysicists David Sandwell and Walter Smith using satellite images that show where gravitation is strongest. Where gravity is strongest mountains are probably present; it lessens in flat areas and at significant depths. Gravity is therefore able to provide us with information about the appearance of the ocean floor.

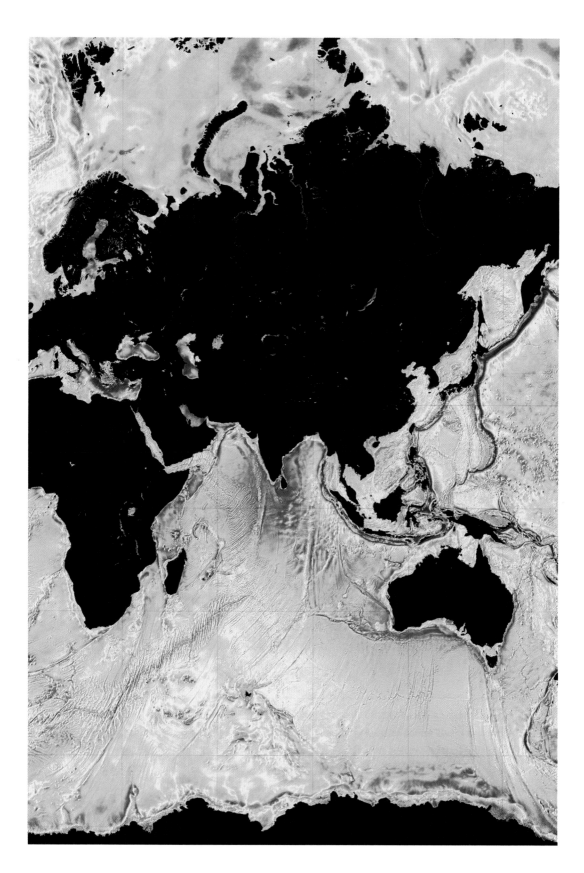

THE DIGITAL WORLD

Baikonur, Kazakhstan
45° 57′ 54″ N
63° 18′ 18″ E

It was visible, high up in the sky, after the Sun had set: a tiny moon moving faster than any other celestial body. Across the world, people took out their binoculars and set up their telescopes on roofs and in parks to observe the technological marvel of the age – using an amateur radio, it was also possible to hear the *beep-beep-beep* of the radio transmitters it carried. 'Until two days ago, that sound had never been heard on this earth. Suddenly it has become as much a part of twentieth-century life as the whir of your vacuum cleaner,' said a reporter's voice from the television set. On these autumn evenings in 1957, *Sputnik* – the world's first artificial satellite – ushered in the space age as humankind looked on, astonished.

Sputnik was launched from the Soviet Cosmodrome in Baikonur, Kazakhstan, and orbited the earth in just 96 minutes and 12 seconds at a speed of 29,000 kilometres an hour. It was only 58 centimetres in diameter and at its highest point travelled 940 kilometres above the ground, but was still visible due to its polished surface designed to reflect the Sun's rays. *Sputnik*'s engineers wanted the world to be able to follow the tiny metal ball's progress – a victorious feat of propaganda in a world

When the astronauts aboard the International Space Station pass above Kazakhstan, they can trace the path of the Syr Darya River to find the location from which they launched: the Baikonur Cosmodrome, where *Sputnik* – the world's first satellite – also started its journey in 1957. This image was taken on 10 April 2016.

characterised by the rivalry between two superpowers. During its second day, the satellite passed over Berlin thirteen times, New York seven times and Washington six times – where the Americans were forced to bitterly admit that their arch-rival had reached space before them.

On Monday morning, after *Sputnik* had dominated the news since Friday evening, physicists William H. Guier and George C. Weiffenbach were eating lunch in the cafeteria of the Applied Physics Laboratory (APL) in Baltimore, USA. They thought it was strange that nobody had studied the radio signals emitted by the satellite, and in the laboratory found a receiver and a small cable they used as an antenna. Late in the afternoon they heard *Sputnik*'s signals – *beep-beep-beep* – and started to record and analyse them, with no particular intention other than to save the data for posterity.

After a while, Guier and Weiffenbach discovered something interesting – the signals they heard when *Sputnik* first appeared on the horizon changed as the satellite came closer, only to change again as it passed over them and journeyed onwards – similar to the way the sound of a bell changes as you travel past it on a train at night. Using the changes in sound, the scientists were able to predict *Sputnik*'s trajectory and ascertain the satellite's position at any given time.

One day, Guier and Weiffenbach were asked to come into their boss's office and close the door behind them. He wondered whether it was possible to turn the finding on its head: using a satellite, was it possible to determine one's position on Earth?

GPS | Today, we are often a part of our maps in the form of a tiny, moving dot – whether we've asked our car to find the fastest route to the local amusement park or are looking for a bakery in an unfamiliar city, we can use our GPS, tablet or mobile to view where we are and understand the direction in which we are moving. Geography is digitised – above us, satellites constantly send out signals indicating their positions; our receiver obtains information from four of these to work out where we are. One satellite provides us with the latitude, another with the longitude and a third the altitude – while the fourth satellite performs the calculations that enable the GPS to provide us with an accurate position.

The maps we use are also often based on images taken by satellites. We use satellites to map the weather, air quality, ice conditions, desertification, urbanisation and deforestation. One of the benefits of using satellites is that they orbit the Earth in fixed trajectories and therefore take photographs of the same areas over and over again, making it easy to observe changes even in deserted and isolated areas. A satellite can photograph the entire Earth in just sixteen days. 'Man must rise above the Earth – to the top of the atmosphere and beyond – for only thus will he fully understand the world in which he lives,' said the Greek philosopher Socrates, and at the time of writing around 1,100 satellites are currently orbiting above us. They survey the Earth in such detail – from 800 kilometres above the Earth, they are capable of photographing two dogs playing in a garden in Houston, Texas – that we are now able to update our maps faster than ever before in history.

The first person to imagine a man-made satellite orbiting the Earth was British scientist Isaac Newton. In his *Philosophiæ Naturalis Principia Mathematica* (*Mathematical Principles of Natural Philosophy*), published in 1687, he described an experiment in which a cannon shoots a ball from the top of a high mountain. If the ball travels at a low velocity, it will fall to Earth, but if it travels at a high velocity, it will continue out into space. And if the velocity of the cannonball is just right, the Earth's gravity will pull it into orbit.

In 1865, French author Jules Verne wrote a book based on Newton's theory, *From the Earth to the Moon*, in which people travel around the Moon in a projectile shot from a cannon. In 1903, Russian rocket scientist Konstantin Tsiolkovsky enjoyed calculating how long Verne's cannon would have to be, and the pressures the people in the projectile would be forced to withstand. Not unsurprisingly, Tsiolkovsky's conclusion was that a cannon would be useless for sending people into space. Instead, he developed the principle of multistage rockets, in which the fuel tanks are disconnected as they are emptied. At the final stage, enough fuel remains to puff a small projectile into orbit. This was the principle that, fifty-four years later, gave us the first satellite as part of the space race between the two superpowers of the USA and the Soviet Union.

V-2 | The race between the Americans and the Soviets started towards the end of the Second World War as a race to acquire German missile technology. During the last phase of the war, the Nazis introduced a new weapon that sent shockwaves through the Allied forces – the V-2 rockets.

The missiles were first launched from the occupied Netherlands on a September morning in 1944 – people on the English side of the Channel saw three ribbons of smoke disappearing into the stratosphere. The missiles travelled eighty kilometres above the ground at supersonic speed – meaning that they crashed down in Paris and London just five minutes later, killing three people. The V-2 was the world's first space rocket.

In the 1920s, the lead architect behind the V-2 programme, Wernher von Braun, was one of several amateur rocket enthusiasts based at a disused warehouse just outside Berlin – a location known locally as Raketenflugplatz. After a time, the group had made so much progress that the German Army began to take an interest in their work, and in 1932 – the year before the Nazis came to power – the amateur rocket scientists became part of the army's development programme, with von Braun in the role of technical director. In 1942, the group managed to launch a rocket to such an altitude that it left the atmosphere, before landing 200 kilometres away. 'We have invaded space with our rocket and for the first time – mark this well – have used space as a bridge between two points on Earth,' an excited German general wrote in his report.

The V-2 rockets never achieved great military significance, and more people died as a result of the forced labour used to create them – 20,000 prisoners from the Nazi concentration camps – than from being hit. But both the Americans and the Soviets understood that this was the weapon of the future, and each side established specialist groups to gain access to German rocket engineers and drawings.

In February 1945, von Braun heard the Red Army's artillery advancing towards the rocket laboratory. He and several hundred other employees gathered up everything they could carry and set out south-west towards the U.S. Army – believing, quite rightly, that with the knowledge they possessed they were simply too valuable to be imprisoned. In early May, the Americans made their way to the V-2 factory, which in accordance with Allied agreements would be deemed to be on Soviet territory from

June onwards. Several tonnes of rocket parts were transported to Antwerp by rail convoy, and then on to the USA by sea. Von Braun and his colleagues also made the journey.

KOROLEV VS VON BRAUN | The Americans had won the first round – leaving little behind for the Soviets at the V-2 laboratory and factory – and so the Soviets decided to release Sergei Korolev, a brilliant rocket researcher who before the war had been imprisoned on the basis of false accusations and sent to Siberia. In August 1945, after a period of convalescence, Korolev was sent to Germany to discover how a V-2 rocket was constructed. 'You must understand,' a commissioner said to him, 'the Americans won't be resting. After the nuclear bombs of Hiroshima and Nagasaki, they will continue their work with nuclear arms. And now they have only one enemy – us.' The Soviets didn't like the idea of the Americans enjoying sole possession of both nuclear weapons *and* missiles – and Korolev was therefore assigned to make up some of the ground lost to von Braun's head start.

Due to the Cold War, the space race and arms race became two sides of the same coin, leaving both Korolev and von Braun frustrated at having to prioritise work on rockets intended for use in missile attacks rather than those that would put satellites into orbit. To varying degrees, both men were moon-sick dreamers who had far more desire to send people into space than to design ways to kill them. In an article, von Braun described how the Earth would look from above, echoing Socrates' description from over 2,000 years earlier: 'an enormous ball, most of it bulking pale black against the deeper black of space but with a wide crescent of day light where the sun strikes it. Within the crescent, the continents enjoying summer stand out as vast green terrain maps surrounded by the

Next pages | A satellite image map of San Francisco and the surrounding areas, photographed by *Landsat 5* in 1985. The satellite phototographed both visible and infrared light, so the red areas are forests, woodlands, grassy areas and marshes, while the dull regions represent dry vegetation, mountains or earth in the uplands. The green areas indicate where salt is extracted from the seawater or other areas with high evaporation.

Imagery Not Shown

P A C I F I C   *O C E A N*

SAN FRANCISCO
FARALLONES
DALY CITY
SAN FRANCISCO BAY
SAN FRANCISCO
PACIFICA
SAN BRUNO
BURLINGAME
SAN MATEO
SAN CARLOS
REDWOOD CITY
MENLO PARK
PALO ALTO
LOS ALTOS
RICHMOND
BERKELEY
OAKLAND
SAN LEANDRO
CASTRO VALLEY
LORENZO
HAYWARD
FREMONT

brilliant blue of the oceans. Patches of white cloud obscure some of the detail; white blobs are snow and ice on mountain ranges and polar areas'.

Both von Braun and Korolev attempted to convince their respective countries' governments and militaries that satellites could be used to map the enemy – and in 1946 the Americans' first V-2 rocket launches hinted at this. The space usually used to hold the explosives was instead used for the installation of scientific instruments and a camera, resulting in the first images of the Earth taken from space – a collage covering an area stretching from Mexico to Nebraska.

Korolev argued that satellites would act as the perfect spies for the Soviet military – capable of orbiting the Earth like a photographic eye, they would be able to observe even the tiniest details. He was told, however, that the Soviet Army was interested in obtaining weapons – not toys. Von Braun used the same arguments before the American military when he claimed that satellites would be able to lift any iron curtain, wherever it may fall.

In 1955, the American military published a report recommending the use of reconnaissance satellites – but first, they reasoned, it would be wise to send up a civil satellite and thereby establish the freedom to pass through space above any country. President Dwight Eisenhower announced that the USA planned to launch a satellite – 'a new moon' – in 1957.

Eisenhower's speech sent a tremor through the Soviets. They had already been panicked three years earlier, when the Americans changed Pacific geography by blasting the Eniwetok Atoll off the map with the detonation of the world's first hydrogen bomb – a bomb many times more powerful than the atomic bomb. After the Soviets detonated their hydrogen bomb in 1954 and decided to develop something even more terrible, Korolev was tasked with developing a rocket capable of carrying a warhead weighing five tonnes. Korolev immediately understood that such a rocket would easily have the power to put a satellite into orbit, and when he presented his proposed satellite to General Secretary Nikita Khrushchev in February 1956, his idea was approved at the highest level – Khrushchev liked the idea of celebrating the fortieth anniversary of the Russian revolution with the world's first satellite.

COMPUTING | Performing the calculations necessary to put a satellite into orbit might be routine today, but doing it for the first ever man-made satellite was anything but, and required the Soviets' most powerful computing technology. The Strela computer at Moscow University filled a 400-square-metre room, and was capable of performing up to 3,000 calculations per second. The machine would now be responsible for ensuring that a colossal rocket would nudge a tiny satellite out into space with just the right amount of force. Everything needed to be exact – and many test launches resulted in complete disaster.

The use of computers had increased during the Second World War as a means of both creating coded messages and cracking them. The computers were huge – there was a reason that the Allied forces' best code-cracking machine was named 'Colossus' – but developments in the field were rapid. In 1948, American electrical engineer Claude Shannon described how all information could be transferred digitally. 'If the base 2 is used,' he wrote, 'the resulting units may be called binary digits, or more briefly *bits*.' With this, Shannon described the age of digital information, which would later give us both maps created using computers and online maps. Today, all computerised data is encoded using two digits, 0 and 1, and data capacity is measured in bits.

The transistor – a device that enabled electrical impulses to travel with unprecedented speed – was invented a year before Shannon presented his theory. In 1957, the year in which *Sputnik* was launched, American electrical engineer Jack Kilby had the idea of linking a number of transistors in an integrated circuit to form the microchip, thereby laying the foundations for all personal computers, smartphones and tablets.

But in the 1950s, computers were reserved for universities, laboratories, government agencies, large companies and the military. Strela was the first computer used by the Soviets in data programming, and Korolev and his team watched *Sputnik*'s launch with pounding hearts, anxious to see whether the machine's calculations would prove correct. Late in the evening on Friday 4 October, white-gloved technicians placed the diminutive *Sputnik* atop a gigantic launch vehicle, and an hour and a half before midnight the ground shook as the engines lifted the rocket from a sea of flames up into the night sky. On the ground, observers nervously watched what appeared to be the perfect launch – until it suddenly seemed as if the rocket was returning to Earth. 'It's falling, it's falling!' several people exclaimed, before they realised that due to the satellite the rocket had been programmed to follow a different course to that of the test rockets. The engines shut down and sent *Sputnik* into orbit at 230 kilometres above the ground. Korolev smoked frantically while he and his team waited for the satellite to complete its first full orbit. When they finally received its signal – *beep-beep-beep* – Korolev asked everyone to listen: 'This is music no one has heard before.'

TRANSIT | On the following Monday, Guier and Weiffenbach sat in their laboratory in Baltimore listening to *Sputnik*'s signals, and two weeks after the launch, when *Sputnik*'s batteries were depleted and the radio signals silenced, started to analyse the information using a computer. The results confirmed that it was possible to determine a satellite's location by listening to the signals it emitted.

Head of the laboratory, Frank McClure, asked Guier and Weiffenbach whether they could turn this finding on its head, as he was assisting the marines with a project to equip submarines with atomic missiles. The idea was that the enemy would never know just how close they were to a nuclear attack, unaware as they were of the submarines' locations – but the problem was that the submarines themselves were also often unsure of exactly where they were. This was vital information if the missiles were to hit the desired targets – and ideally, the submarines would like to be able to determine their location without having to resurface to check the stars. McClure asked Guier and Weiffenbach how accurately they could calculate a position using satellites – they estimated that it should be possible with a margin of error of around 160 metres.

The Applied Physics Laboratory (APL) was thereby established, and work began on the Transit navigation programme – the forerunner of today's GPS. But first, the Americans had to prove that they too were capable of launching a satellite.

On the evening of *Sputnik*'s launch, Wernher von Braun had arranged a party for the new Secretary of Defense. A tense silence settled over the gathering when someone came in with news of the Soviet triumph – von

Braun, rather ungraciously, is said to have muttered: 'I could have done this a year ago.' After Eisenhower announced the USA's intention to launch a satellite, the U.S. Army, Navy and Air Force competed for the contract. Von Braun worked for the army, but despite the fact that he had the best solution some thought it problematic to allow the first American satellite to be created by Germans – particularly Germans with a Nazi background – and the contract was awarded to the navy. It was somewhat paradoxical that the American authorities had originally taken control of von Braun's experiments to prevent him launching a satellite for anyone else.

Sputnik made the entire world look to the skies, and Khrushchev claimed the historic event was proof of communism's superiority to capitalism. *Time* magazine called it a 'red triumph', and many feared that the Soviets were now capable of using atomic missiles against the USA. The Americans felt under pressure – which only increased when, two months later, *Sputnik 2* was launched with Laika the dog on board – the first living being ever to enter space.

This mounting pressure caused the Americans to declare that they would launch their satellite on 6 December. Millions watched the events unfolding live on television as the engines started, spewing out flames and billowing smoke, before the rocket rose exactly 1.2 metres into the air and tipped over onto its side, exploding on the launch pad. The tiny satellite lay on the ground beside the wreckage, mournfully sending out its signals.

The next morning, von Braun – with a touch of *Schadenfreude* – read newspapers filled with headlines such as 'Kaputnik', 'Flopnik', 'Goofnik' and 'Oopsnik'. The navy's failure gave him an opportunity – and on 31 January 1958, von Braun and his team put the first American satellite – *Explorer 1* – into orbit.

The navy and APL launched the *Transit* satellite from Cape Canaveral, Florida, the following year, and the satellite passed over the Atlantic Ocean for twenty-five minutes before it dropped into the sea just off the coast of Ireland. The rocket's third stage had failed to ignite, but despite this the mood was positive – during its short flight, the satellite had emitted its signals exactly as planned.

Many test satellites had to be launched before the *Transit* navigation programme could finally be put into operation. The project's engineers discovered one thing after another that disturbed both the satellites' signals and their trajectories, including the Earth's irregular shape, which results in variations in gravity as the satellites pass above it. The satellites jumped around without the engineers understanding why, until they discovered that the Earth was more uneven than first thought, in addition to being slightly more pointed in shape in the north than in the south. The engineers had to combine technology with geodesy – the study of the Earth's shape and size – and studied the work of Marie Tharp and Bruce Heezen, which showed how the Earth's surface is in constant motion due to continental drift, and how this affects gravity, which in turn affects the satellites. All irregularities had to be mapped and programmed.

Right from the experimental stage the scientists realised that localisation using satellites was more accurate than old-fashioned triangulation – discovering, for example, that ordinary maps put the islands of Hawaii several kilometres away from their true location.

With the successful launch of *Transit 5c1* in June 1964, the system was complete – three satellites orbiting the Earth, sending out signals that were received by the navy's ships and submarines. Three years later, *Transit* was made available for both public and commercial use, and Norway was one of the system's early adopters. During the first year in which the country had access to the system, *Transit* was used to determine positions on the mainland; in 1971 the Norwegian Polar Institute was able to determine positions on Svalbard, and measurements taken of Jan Mayen in 1979 showed that the island was situated 350 metres closer to Norway than previously believed. The Continental Shelf Office used the system to precisely calculate the dividing line between Norway and Scotland out in the North Sea, and to determine the exact positions of oil platforms. Even leisure boats installed the Transit system when receivers became smaller and more affordable. The system had a margin of error of just twenty-five metres.

SPY MAPS | In the shadow of the space race, the American military developed spy satellites. Although they had equipped their U-2 aircraft with cameras in 1954 – cameras that could photograph objects measuring just a metre across from altitudes of over 21,000 metres – they knew it was only a matter of time before the Soviets would manage to shoot the aircraft down. The Soviets detected and shot down a U-2 in 1960, but that same summer the Americans were also able to recover a roll of film containing images taken by a satellite.

The images taken by digital cameras at the time were nowhere near detailed enough for reconnaissance purposes, and so the spy satellites had to use rolls of film. At 9,600 metres in length these were somewhat longer than usual, and dropped from the satellite in what was known as a 'film bucket' – a capsule that plummeted 140 kilometres before the heat shield released at 18 kilometres above ground level, triggering a parachute. A plane was then sent out to catch the falling bucket mid-flight – if the plane was unsuccessful, searches were initiated on the ground or in the sea.

The satellites travelled at a speed equivalent to eight kilometres per second at ground level. Each image covered an area of 16 x 190 kilometres, and so the satellites took one photograph every other second – enabling the entire enemy territory to be photographed in just a day or two. The first roll of film contained images of sixty-four Soviet airports and twenty-six launch sites for anti-aircraft missiles. The Soviets launched their first spy satellite, *Zenit*, in 1962.

The Cold War made its mark on the period's maps. A Soviet map of the British city of Chatham, for example, clearly showed the dockyard where the Royal Navy was building submarines, while on the British map the same location was simply a blank space. The Soviet map also featured information about the size and load capacity of the bridges in the dockyard's immediate vicinity.

The two superpowers had different mapping strategies, which reflected the differences in their militaries. The Americans' command of the air meant that maps of areas of strategic interest showing more detail than

Next pages | A map of Montreal and the surrounding areas from 1972. The map provides an overview of the various soil types, where orange and yellow denote areas suitable for agriculture, green and white indicate less suitable areas and red areas are unsuitable. The turquoise areas are unidentified.

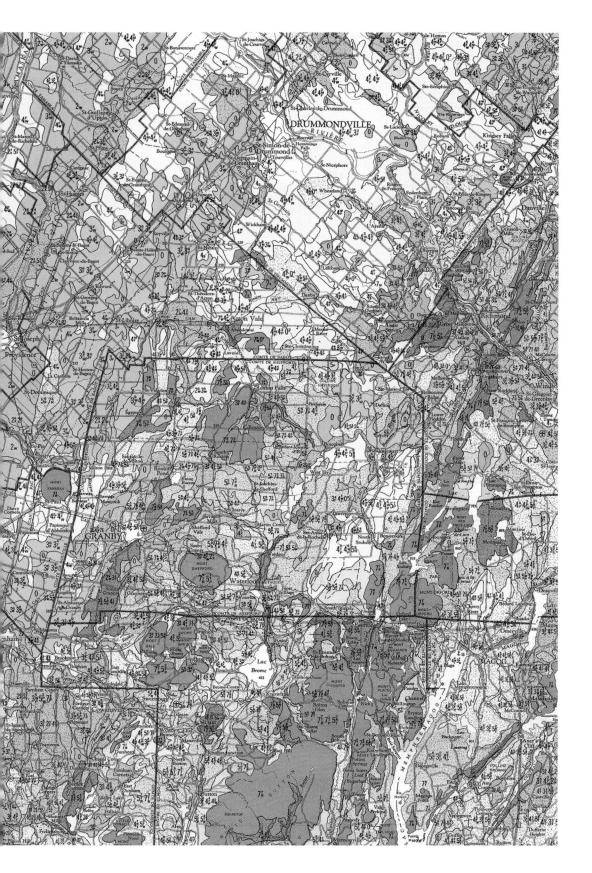

that provided at a scale of 1:250,000 were rarely necessary. The Soviet Union, on the other hand, was at the forefront of tank warfare and possessed the world's largest army, so required detailed maps that provided information such as road widths, the load capacity of bridges, river depths and forest topography. Many of them also featured meteorological information. The Soviets therefore mapped some parts of the world right down to building level, and Soviet military maps of western Europe and American terrain were often more detailed than those possessed by the countries themselves. They were also fiercely guarded – personnel were required to sign out any maps needed for exercises, and if a map was destroyed, the pieces had to be returned. At the same time, the Soviet Union's civil maps were almost useless – not only did they lack detail, but they were also deliberately distorted using a special projection process that resulted in random variations. Famous landmarks such as rivers and cities were included, but the specified coordinates, directions and distances were completely wrong. The point was to prevent western spies from being able to get hold of an accurate map of Soviet territory from any local newsagents or kiosk. The cartographer who developed this system received an award from Stalin for his efforts.

After Stalin's death in 1953 the Soviet military had global ambitions – Khrushchev saw fertile ground for communism in a world where former European colonies were becoming independent states. The Soviet military therefore dispatched cartographers to survey and map a broad range of developing countries, and here too they were extremely thorough in their activities – so thorough, in fact, that previously classified Soviet maps of these areas were purchased and used by telecommunications companies in setting up mobile networks. This work requires a topographical overview so that cell towers can be erected in appropriate locations, and the Soviet maps provided the best available overview of hilly regions in these parts of the world.

The Soviet Union used maps to systematise their knowledge of the globe. Their maps were like an analogue database – much like those of the Middle Ages – and provided more than geographical information alone. The Soviets presented extensive and varied information through the creation of a visual hierarchy, in which the most important aspects were emphasised and the less important remained in the background. Their maps prefigured the digital method, used today, of organising geographical information in several layers.

GIS | In the early 1960s, the Canadian authorities wanted to map over two and a half million square kilometres of land using similar techniques. Their aim was to create a map that provided an overview of agricultural areas, forests, areas rich in wildlife – and locations that could be promoted as tourist destinations and for other uses. A rough estimate indicated that the project would require 536 geographers, who would need to create 3,000 maps over a period of three years. The problem, however, was that Canada had a total of only sixty geographers. But in 1962, British geographer Roger Tomlinson set out a plan for how he thought the project could be completed nonetheless.

The Kenyan authorities had previously asked Tomlinson to find an area suitable for planting trees for a new paper factory. The plantation should preferably be located on a gradual incline in an area with an appropriate climate, which could be easily accessed by the plantation's workers. The area would also need to be free from monkeys, since they would eat the saplings, and be a safe distance from the routes taken by elephants. In order to identify such an area, Tomlinson would have to create several maps – meteorological, zoological, geological – and layer them on top of one another. This would be far too expensive, however, and so the project was dropped.

Later on, Tomlinson had the idea of using a computer to process the information – so that he could enter the elephants' routes on a map that showed both soil and weather conditions, for example. 'Computers,' said Tomlinson, 'could become information storage devices as well as calculating machines. The technical challenge was to put maps into these computers, to convert shape and images into numbers.' American cartographer Waldo R. Tobler had taken up this challenge three years earlier, when he programmed a computer to draw an outline of the United States in fifteen minutes using 343 punched cards – the first map ever to be drawn using a computer. 'Automation, it would seem, is here to stay,' wrote Tobler. 'It seems that some basic tasks, common to all cartography, may in the future be largely automated, and that the volume of maps produced in a given time will be increased while the cost is reduced.'

Tomlinson first tried to generate interest for digital maps among computer companies on his own initiative – without success. But he then met members of the team who were working on the Canadian mapping project. Tomlinson convinced them that the solution was to digitise the information, and together with computing company IBM, they developed a system through which the maps were converted into numerals and connected to information about conditions such as the surface area of fields, settlements, forestry matters and animal migration routes. Tomlinson called this a geographic information system – GIS – through which maps could provide a complete overview of the natural resources within a region or country.

Progress was slow – in 1970 there were still only forty people in the world using the methods – but weighty institutions, such as the American National Aeronautics and Space Administration (NASA), soon became adopters. In 1972, NASA sent up *Landsat 1*, the first satellite specially designed to monitor the Earth's surface. The satellite was equipped with cameras that had a poor resolution compared to those used by the military – 56 x 69 metres – but they were at least completely digital.

Norway was an active participant in the *Landsat* programme, and data from the satellite was used to study the ice around Svalbard, observe snow volumes in areas with hydroelectric power stations, perform geological surveys and monitor the environment. One day in 1973, *Landsat 1* photographed the Finnmarksvidda plateau in northern Norway, showing areas of birch forest and moorland covered with heathers and reindeer moss. An image of the same area taken six years later showed that the areas of bare rock and destroyed vegetation had grown in size due to increasing pollution from the nearby Russian nickel works. Using the satellite images, it was possible to monitor the natural destruction of the plateau year by year.

'Continuous satellite coverage may also be used in the monitoring and mapping of Norwegian areas. [...] The technological aids used in mapping and surveying activities are currently undergoing significant developments, characterised by new measuring instruments, the automation of cartographic processes and the extensive use of electronic data processing techniques,' stated an official report in 1975. The study emphasised that for Norway, with its responsibility for large areas in remote regions such as the Arctic and Antarctic, and recently increased activities at sea due to North Sea oil production, satellite images would be especially useful in monitoring oil spills from ships and leaks from drilling platforms and pipelines. Images showing the temperatures in coastal areas and out at sea would also be of interest for the fishing industry.

The geographic surveying of Norway was gradually digitised, and in 1981 computing company Norsk Data supplied four computer systems to the county mapping offices in Møre og Romsdal, Hedmark, Telemark and Rogaland. The other county offices were linked to the systems via the Datex public data network operated by Televerket, the state-owned telecommunications company, and were able to share just 543 megabytes of information – a tiny fraction of the capacity of today's mobile phones. The aim was to build up a geographic information system that could be combined with the authorities' data-based registers. By connecting houses on the map to the Building and Housing Register and National Registry, for example, the computers would be able to find out who lived at a certain location and their respective ages, and automatically create a map of households with children due to start at school in the autumn term.

www | In the 1400s, the art of printing enabled the Europeans to produce far greater numbers of books than previously; in the same way, digitisation meant that many more maps could be produced. The conversion of maps into computer code made it easy to connect them to other information and create thematic maps, statistical maps, topographical maps, vegetation maps or other types of maps – and to update them with no more than a few keystrokes. It also became easy to share maps between networked computers.

During the work with the Canadian maps, Tomlinson allowed his thoughts to wander – wouldn't it be something if there was a GIS database that everyone could connect to? One that covered the entire world down to the smallest detail? And he wasn't the only person to be thinking along these lines – with the benefit of the increased computing power that accompanied transistors and microchips, several data engineers were working to develop computer programs that could share information with each other using an electronic network of users across the world – an Internet.

The Internet of today is the result of work that was started by the United States Department of Defense in the late 1960s. The aim was to develop a communications network that would withstand a Soviet nuclear attack. Such a network couldn't be based on a single master station, but must be able to function even if one of its parts was destroyed, and was therefore constructed using a flat structure in which everyone could send information to each other. Four computers in the states of California and Utah comprised the world's first computer network when they were connected on 1 September 1969; two years later, the first email was sent using the @ symbol. In 1978, the invention of the modem meant that private individuals could send information to one another without having to go via the military network, and in 1994 the foundations for the World Wide Web, www, were laid when http (hypertext transfer protocol) made it possible to organise content into websites, and url (uniform resource locator) standardised web addresses, so that any computer anywhere in the world would reach the same location when typing in an address such as http://www.verdensteater.net. The world's first online map service, mapquest.com, was launched in 1996, with Streetmap, Mappy, Multimap and Hot Maps following shortly after.

In 1998, Vice President of the United States Al Gore took Tomlinson's dream one step further. He started a speech by highlighting how a 'new wave of technological innovation is allowing us to capture, store, process and display an unprecedented amount of information about our planet and a wide variety of environmental and cultural phenomena. Much of this information will be "georeferenced" – that is, it will refer to some specific place on the Earth's surface.' Gore imagined collating all this information using a single computer program that he called Digital Earth – 'a three-dimensional representation of the planet, into which we can embed vast quantities of geo-referenced data.' He asked his audience to imagine a child using the program: 'After donning a head-mounted display, she sees Earth as it appears from space. Using a data glove, she zooms in, using higher and higher levels of resolution, to see continents, then regions, countries, cities, and finally individual houses, trees, and other natural and man-made objects.' Gore admitted that this scenario might sound somewhat far-fetched – but that, if it was possible, he imagined such a program being able to help with diplomacy, the reduction of crime, the preservation of natural diversity, climate change predictions and increased global food production. Gore believed that enough pieces of the puzzle were already in place to start planning such a project – 'we should endeavour to develop a digital map of the world at one meter resolution.'

One existing piece of the 'Digital Earth' puzzle was a method of locating any place in the world digitally. The Transit system had been a success, but so had 621B, Secor and Timation – positioning systems developed by other branches of the United States military independently of the navy's programme. In 1973 it was agreed that the best aspects of all the systems would be combined to create a new one – the Global Positioning System (GPS) – for which the first satellite was launched in 1978. The Norwegian Mapping and Cadastre Authority tested the new system in 1986, and concluded that the results provided by GPS exceeded all expectations. 'It is not a question of *if* satellite positioning will become a part of land surveyors' everyday activities, but *when*,' they wrote enthusiastically; and just a short time later, in 1991, the positioning equipment that had been used more or less since the time of Johan Jacob Rick and Ditlev Wibe was put away for good.

The Global Positioning System was completed in 1994, with a total of twenty-four satellites in orbit around the Earth. The United States military, however, was nervous about allowing others –particularly the country's

Next pages | Google Maps' map of Manhattan from 2007. The colours are somewhat different from those used today – here, all the buildings are grey, while in 2016 some of them began to be coloured a light shade of orange, initially causing confusion. What did it mean? The difference between residential and commercial areas, perhaps? No. Google had decided that 'interesting areas' should be highlighted. It is also interesting to note that the 2007 version features no advertising.

enemies – to access the same location information, and so launched a civ-il version containing deliberate inaccuracies of several hundred metres. Many protested – including the Federal Aviation Administration, Department of Transportation and Coast Guard – and on the night before 1 May in the year 2000, President Bill Clinton made GPS open for everyone, bringing Gore's vision of a Digital Earth yet another step closer.

ONLINE MAPS | Computing company Silicon Graphics had been working on a program that would allow people to view and zoom in on Earth from space since long before Al Gore's speech. They achieved this using a smart technology called 'clipmapping', which permits a large image, such as a map of Europe measuring 420,000 x 300,000 pixels, to be displayed in a smaller version on a computer screen with a resolution of just 1024 x 768 pixels. Each of the pixels on the screen corresponds to a far greater number of pixels below it. First the entire continent is presented on screen, but if you click on the magnifying glass or plus symbol, or double-click on the area you would like to view in more detail, such as the north-west, this part of the map is then enlarged while the rest of the map is clipped away. Click – you see the British Isles; click, south-east England; click, Greater London; click, Camden Town; click, Chalk Farm Road; click, the statue of Amy Winehouse and Camden Market. Every time you drill down into the image, the technology clips away everything you're not interested in, so that you finally end up down in the smallest details of an image that in reality is far larger than the screen.

Inspired by Gore's speech, Silicon Graphics launched their Earth-viewer software in 2001. Those who purchased it could fly above a three-dimensional, digital version of the world at a speed and resolution never seen before. Countries other than the USA were fairly poorly reproduced, however – the company simply didn't have enough money to purchase all the necessary satellite images. But the software was good enough that American TV channels used it when the war against Iraq broke out in March 2003. In-Q-Tel, a company financed by the CIA, invested in Earthviewer just a few weeks before the invasion, and are said to have used it to assist the troops. Six versions of the software were published before Google acquired Earthviewer for an undisclosed sum in 2004, just a few weeks after acquiring digital mapping company Where2.

It was logical that the makers of the Google search engine would be interested in maps – around 30 per cent of Internet searches are about *where* something is. As early as 2002, Google had started purchasing satellite images from DigitalGlobe – a company with two satellites that photographed one million square kilometres of the Earth's surface at a half-metre resolution every single day. These images, worth several hundred million dollars, were added to Earthviewer to create Google Earth, which was launched in June 2005 – 'a valuable addition to Google's efforts to organize the world's information and make it universally accessible and useful,' as Google described the project. Google Maps had also been launched online just a few months earlier.

GOOGLE EARTH | When the program opens, Google Earth presents the day side of the Earth in blue, green, white and brown from a distance of 11,000 kilometres, like a lit globe against the pitch darkness of space. This is not only an image of the globe as it was described by Socrates, Cicero, Macrobius and von Braun in a digital and two-dimensional form, but also a geographic information system containing over twenty petabytes of data – equivalent to a textbook with ten thousand billion pages. All this information is drawn on in just seconds as the user navigates around the Earth or down towards it – the images are updated fifty times a second. In the menu to the left you can choose which map you'd like to layer over the terrain, depending on whether you're most interested in viewing the world with or without national borders, roads and place names; you can also select or deselect a number of functions that show various aspects of the globe. Selecting 'Global awareness' displays a range of symbols that you can click on to obtain more information, and which provide details of projects such as the World Wide Fund For Nature (WWF) panda conservation programme in the Qinling Mountains in China. Selecting 'Gallery' and 'Rumsey Historical Maps' displays a number of circles; clicking on these allows you to browse historical maps from the collection of American map collector David Rumsey – including a map of Scandinavia from 1794.

We are able to interact with Google Earth and Google Maps in a way that would never be possible using a paper-based map or atlas. Selecting 'Images' presents thousands of images, uploaded by users across the world, from Jerusalem to the beaches of Malibu. The system is also open to user participation – when a Slovenian city incorrectly ended up on the Italian side of the border, a user corrected the error; the fact that someone had written 'No Human Rights Here' in Tibet, which was occupied by China in 1965, resulted in extensive debate. Inaccuracies sometimes occur; a completely erroneous name was once entered for a bridge in Prague, and someone might upload an image at an incorrect location – but there is no doubt that Google Earth allows people to influence the image created of their surroundings in a way that would never have been possible at any previous point in cartographic history. Four hundred years ago, it might have been possible to send a map of Tuscany to Abraham Ortelius so that he could more accurately reproduce the area in his next edition of the *Theatrum orbis terrarum* – but how many people had the opportunity to do so? And regardless, it was then up to Ortelius to decide whether or not he wished to update his map.

Google Earth is a fantastic tool for getting to know our planet – using it, we can explore the historic cities of Angkor Wat, Machu Picchu and Pompeii, travel to the highest mountaintops, visit the Arctic and Antarctic and take a tour of the Amazon rainforest, Alaska, Alexandria, Bangkok or Chicago ... and yet there is also a search field into which I may type, for example, 'Pizza near Ullevål, Oslo'. And if I type 'pizza' into Google's search engine online, the top of the results page features a paid advertisement for a company offering pizza home delivery, and below this a map from Google Maps shows the locations of three pizza restaurants directly north, east and south of where I live.

This detail confirms what Waldo Tobler called the First Law of Geography: 'Everything is related to everything else, but near things are more related than distant things.' Google has understood that maps are primarily everyday tools – something we use to find a new store or the home of someone selling a used bicycle online – and much more rarely a starting point for daydreams of distant journeys. And this is exactly why Google is able to provide us with maps for free – by selling advertising to pizza restaurants and others in our local surroundings. As English cartographic historian Jerry Brotton states, Google Maps 'is partly a tool for delivering ads.'

This is a reminder that maps are not created in isolation. Ptolemy I Soter established the museum and library in Alexandria because knowledge generated trade; the Italian nautical charts that paved the way for more accurate medieval maps were created for travelling merchants; Abraham Ortelius got the idea for his atlas from a seaman who needed more practical maps; the Dutch East India Company paid two generations of the Blaeu family to create maps of the valuable Spice Islands; the pizza restaurants who pay for ads on Google Earth and Google Maps help to pay for the next round of satellite images that will produce even more accurate maps. 'Where maps and their makers are motivated by the apparently disinterested pursuit of geographical information, its acquisition requires patronage, state funding or commercial capital to make it viable. Mapping and money have always gone hand in hand and have reflected the vested interests of particular rulers, states, businesses or multinational corporations, but this does not necessarily negate the innovations made by the map-makers they have financed,' Brotton believes.

But now the question is whether Google has become too dominant a force. Competing map services – even those created by large corporations such as Apple, Microsoft and Yahoo – are squeezed by Google's huge 70 per cent market share. 'It is vital that regulators work fast to reinstate mapping plurality and avert the steady disappearance of Google's competitors in this sector,' wrote ICOMP, an organisation that works to ensure free and fair trade online, in a report in 2012. Simon Greenman, founder of mapquest.com, believes that although Google 'have done a wonderful job with Earth,' they also 'have the potential to dominate world mapping on a scale that is historically unprecedented. If we fast forward ten to twenty years Google will own global mapping and geospatial applications.'

THE FUTURE | The first rocket shot into space by Wernher von Braun and his employees on 3 October 1942 was decorated with Mrs Luna, a personified pin-up style image of the Moon and nod to the German film

Frau im Mond (*Woman in the Moon*) from 1929, which showed cinema audiences how a modern rocket worked for the very first time. In 2008, private satellite company GeoEye sent up a rocket featuring Google's logo to denote that the tech giant had already placed an order for all the photographs that would be taken by the new satellite. Google had purchased a permanent seat in Greek god Apollo's chariot – and six years later bought their own chariot when they acquired the company Skybox Imaging and its seven satellites.

The only limiting factor in how much information can be added to Google Earth and Google Maps is the available data storage capacity – and this is currently increasing faster than the data can be collected. Does this mean that we are now finally in a position to create the perfect map that cartographers have dreamed of since the dawn of time? Is it now possible to create a map of the world on our computers at a scale of 1:1? Ed Parsons, a geotechnologist at Google, says yes: 'If you talk to most people involved in Internet mapping and doing what we do we completely accept the fact that you could build a one-to-one map.'

The usefulness of such a map – whether anyone is really interested in being able to see holes in the tarmac on Fifth Avenue in New York from their home computer – is one thing. Another issue is that, like every other map created throughout history, the project would have to tackle the problem of reproducing a spherical globe on a flat surface. As soon as you pulled back from the 1:1 perspective – as would often be necessary, as only so much can be displayed on a computer screen – the problem of projection would once again rear its head. Google is already forced to manipulate its images to simulate the curvature of the Earth, and runs into difficulties in the regions to the north and south where the lines of latitude pull together – and the mathematical solution to this problem involves a number of compromises.

Maps are images of the world – representations of a world view. All the maps described in this book represent various ways of seeing the world, from the speculations of the ancient Greeks to the religious faith of the Middle Ages; from the scientific experimentation and objective mapping of the Renaissance to the collection of enormous volumes of data in today's digital age. Common to the cartographers of every age throughout history is that the ways in which they choose to present the world say much about what they consider important – and the opportunities that their age affords them.

The world is a theatre in which our history is constantly being played out. Ortelius described the maps of his time as enabling people to 'see that which was done, and where it was done, as if it were happening in the present' – which sounds rather prophetic looking back from an age in which digital maps are able to update users on the current traffic situation almost in real time. Since the age of Ortelius, the duration for which maps remain relevant has been drastically reduced. Ortelius's works were set aside after thirty years – might we eventually create maps that are updated minute by minute, showing houses being built and torn down; the progress of landslides and floods; the number of people strolling along the promenade at Alexandria, ships on their way to Indonesia and planes flying across the American continent – so that we will truly be able to see the entire world 'in the present'? In terms of technology, such a map is not necessarily such a long way off. Even now, digital maps are updated with four new satellite images per day. What we can be sure of is that the maps of the future will seem as strange to us as our hand-held mobile maps would have seemed to Ptolemy, Mercator and Ortelius – and in 400 years' time, our extraordinary digital maps will seem as simple as the *Theatrum orbis terrarum* does today.

The history of maps has been told in various ways by several others before me. The standard work is *The History of Cartography*, a multivolume project started by J. B. Harley and David Woodward at the University of Chicago in 1987, and which is still to be completed. All the volumes, with the exception of the most recent, have generously been made available for download at press.uchicago.edu/books/HOC/index.html. Just be aware that some of the details included in the first volumes are now outdated.

Another book I have found extremely useful is *A History of the World in Twelve Maps* by Jerry Brotton. Fridtjof Nansen's book *In Northern Mists* discusses Norway and the Nordic region as depicted through old texts and maps. This and many more of the books I have referenced have been scanned and made available on the National Library of Norway's website. A good overview, together with many reproductions of old maps, can be found in *Printed Maps of Scandinavia and the Arctic, 1482–1601* and *Maps and Mapping of Norway, 1602–1855* by William B. Ginsberg. *Soundings* by Hali Felt is an excellent biography of Marie Tharp; *Arctic Labyrinth: The Quest for the Northwest Passage* by Glyn Williams is a unique and useful book; *Imagined Corners* by Paul Binding is a fascinating read about Abraham Ortelius and the city of Antwerp in Ortelius's time; both Nicholas Crane and Andrew Taylor have written good biographies about Gerard Mercator, and *The World Map 1300–1492* by Evelyn Edson should be read by everyone.

I understand neither Greek nor Latin, nor any other languages apart from English to any great extent, and have therefore been forced to translate primary sources unavailable in Norwegian from the English where necessary.

PREFACE

'Oh, my God!' | '*Apollo 8* Onboard
Voice Transcription', NASA, Houston,
1969. William Anders was also the U.S.
Ambassador to Norway from 1976 to 1977.
Ortelius | The original poem is as follows:
'Ortelius, quem quadrijugo super aera curru
Phæbus Apollo vehi secum dedit, unde
jacentes Lustraret terras, circumfusumque
profondum.' Translated into Norwegian by
Tor Ivar Østmoe.

PAGE X:
'All the world's a stage' | Shakespeare.

THE FIRST IMAGES OF
THE WORLD

PAGE 1:
A large, advanced rock carving | Craig,
366–7.
'Next, in order' | Strabo, book 4, chapter 6,
section 8.

PAGE 2:
Italian archaeologist Alberto Marretta |
Schellenberg, 05:45.
Norwegian archaeologist | Marstrander, 247.

PAGE 3:
Minusinsk, Russia | Smith (1994), 3.

PAGE 4:
Humans also acquired | Lewis, 51.

PAGES 8–9:
In 1967, British archaeologist | Jennings, 7.
Seven years later | sci-news.com.
At Talat N'lisk | Smith (1987), 17.

PAGE 10:
'As a rule' | Cited in Smith (1987), 85.

PAGES 10–11:
In the Sahara | Smith (1987), 89.
A painstakingly crafted cave painting | Smith
(1994), 14.
In the early 1700s | Gabrielsen, 8.

PAGE 12:
At first there was only darkness | From A. L.
Basham's translation of the *Rig Veda* (1954).

PAGES 12–13:
Every place and time | Bringsværd &
Braarvig, 9.
'That which at some points in time' |
Bringsværd & Braarvig, 10.
'This ash is the best' | Snorri Sturluson, *The
Younger Edda*. Translated by Rasmus B.
Anderson (1901).
'Of Ymir's flesh' | *The Elder Edda of Saemund
Sigfusson*. Translated by Benjamin Thorpe
(1866).

PAGE 17:
'There earth, there heaven' | Homer, *The Iliad*.
Translated by Alexander Pope (1715).
A similar problem | Thank you to Benedicte
Gamborg Briså for providing me with
information about the classical view of the
world and the challenges of translation.

PAGE 19:
Babylon is at the centre | Brotton, 1.

PAGE 20:
Before the Babylonians, the Sumerians |
Millard, 107.

PAGE 21:
One such example | Nemet-Nejat, 95.
They used a measuring rope | Nemet-Nejat,
93.

PAGE 25:
Like the Sumerians and the Babylonians |
Shore, 117.
In his *Histories* | Translated by A. D. Godley
(1920)

PAGE 26:
Around the year 1150 BC | Harrell.
Amennakhte did not sign the map, but
we know that he drew it because his
handwriting is recognisable from other
works.

LIKE FROGS ABOUT A POND

PAGE 29:
During antiquity, Alexandria | The description of Alexandria and its library is based on 'Science' in Jerry Brotton's *A History of the World in Twelve Maps* and *Ancient Libraries* by Oikonomopoulou & Woolf.
'a tower of great height' | Caesar, *The Civil War*

PAGE 30:
'building[s] upon building[s]' | Strabo, book 17, chapter 1, section 8.

PAGES 31–32:
In their country is an immense mountain called Saevo | Pliny, book 4, chapter 27.
'But there is a consensus' | Cited in Berggren & Jones, 79.

PAGE 32:
'but since the setting out' | Cited in Berggren & Jones, 19.
'through drawing […] the entire' | Cited in Berggren & Jones, 3.

PAGE 36:
Later Greek writers | Aujac, 134.

PAGES 37–38:
Hecataeus of Miletus | Aujac, 134.
Hecataeus was probably | Roller, 3.
But we can point to | Aujac, 136.

PAGES 38–39:
Diogenes wrote that Pythagoras | Pythagoras was right in thinking that the Earth was inhabited 'all the way round' – people lived in Australia at the time.
And I laugh to see | Herodotus, *The Histories*. Translated by A. D. Godley (1920).
Democritus | Aujac, 137.

PAGE 40:
'as the Lacedaemonians report' | Herodotus, *The Histories*. Translated by A. D. Godley (1920).
The account is one of the earliest | Brotton, 32.
A scene in Aristophanes' | Aristophanes, *The Clouds*, Translated by Peter Meineck (1998).

PAGE 41:
'Secondly,' said he, | Plato, *Phaedo*. Translated by Harold North Fowler (1966).

PAGE 42:
After passing between the Pillars of Hercules | Nansen, 33.

PAGE 46:
Aristotle (384–322 BC) summarised | Aujac, 144.

PAGE 47:
'There are two inhabitable sections' | Aristotle, *Meteorology*. The Revised Oxford Translation of Aristotle (1984).
'They draw maps of the earth' | Aristotle.
Alexander had learned | Aujac, 149.
Around the year 250 BC | Aujac, 154, Brotton, 35.

PAGES 52–53:
Shortly after this, Crates of Mallus | Aujac, 162.
Hipparchus of Nicaea | Aujac, 164.
'Hipparchus,' Strabo wrote | Cited in Brotton, 39.
'If the people who visited' | Cited in Berggren & Jones, 62.

PAGE 53:
'Marinus of Tyre seems to be' | Cited in Berggren & Jones, 23.

PAGE 58:
'East of the Cimbrian' | Ptolemy, book 2, chapter 10.

Holy geography

PAGE 63:
Snorri Sturluson paces | Eskeland, 158.
The world was divided | Snorri Sturluson, *The Prose Edda*. Translated by Jean I. Young (1966).

PAGE 64:
'I shall now wander' | Orosius, 42.
Scholars preferred textual descriptions | It is telling that there is an entire book about medieval geographical knowledge, *The Earth is Our Book* by Natalia Lozovsky – which has nothing to do with maps.
Snorri's description is a perfectly adequate map | Schöller, 42.

PAGE 65:
It is characteristic that | Elliott, 101. The map's estimated original size is 8.5 metres. The western part of it has not survived, so today the map measures 'only' seven metres long.

PAGE 66:
Look at all the different zones | Cicero, *Republic*. Translated by Richard Hooker (1993).
Roman orator Eumenius | Albu, 113.
The map that opens | Lozovsky (2008), 170–1.
World maps played such | Albu, 112.

PAGES 67–68:
Christianity, however, took another view | Albu, 114.
Information about the world | Lozovsky (2000), 11.
'any competent man' | Augustine of Hippo, *On Christian Doctrine*. Translation from the Select Library of Nicene and Post-Nicene Fathers.
Jerome (AD 347–420) took up this challenge | Brotton, 92–3.
Augustine's advice | Edson & Savage-Smith, 24.
'Our ancestors' | Orosius, 36.

PAGE 68:
Legend has it | Catholic Online.

PAGE 72:
'Asia is named' | Isidore of Seville, 285.

PAGE 72:
'But as to the fable' | Augustine of Hippo, *City of God*. Translation from the Select Library of Nicene and Post-Nicene Fathers.
'though it be bare' | Augustine of Hippo, *City of God*. Translation from the Select Library of Nicene and Post-Nicene Fathers.
'Apart from these' | Isidore of Seville, 293.

PAGE 73:
'let us seek if we can' | Augustine of Hippo, *City of God*. Translation from the Select Library of Nicene and Post-Nicene Fathers.
Noah had three sons | The Bible, Genesis x, 5.
Ultima Thule | Isidore of Seville, 294.

PAGE 75:
This religious shift | Williams, 217.
in the east he drew Paradise | There is much discussion about what Beatus actually drew on his original map; I have tried to stick to a safe minimum. Information about that being discussed can be found here: myoldmaps. com/early-medieval-monographs/207-the-beatus-mappamundi/207-beatus-copy.pdf

PAGE 78:
From the 800s | Brotton, 102.
Since the decline | Gosch & Stearns, 135.
Dante, however, | Eriksen, 345.
Only towards the end | Edson, 90.

PAGES 78–79:
Ohthere of Hålogaland | Sandved, 643. The original text opens as follows: 'Ohthere sæde his hlaforde, Ælfrede cyninge, ðæt he ealra Norðmonna nordmest bude . . .'
'Ohthere told his lord' | Translation from *Two Voyagers at the Court of King Alfred*, translated by Christine E. Fell (York, 1984)

PAGE 80:

As Nortmannia is | Adam of Bremen, *History of the Archbishops of Hamburg-Bremen*. Translated by Francis J. Tschan.
'It starts in the east' | *Historia Norwegie*, 19. That Norway starts at the 'Great River' in the east is a guess, since the letters before 'River' are unreadable. Gustav Storm suggested the River Albia in accordance with an addendum from Adam of Bremen.

PAGE 81:

The Christianisation | Kyrkjebø & Spørck, 8.
'Paradise is located in the eastern part' | Kyrkjebø & Spørck, 77.
'The country from *Vegistafr*' | Kyrkjebø & Spørck, 81.
'Thus pilgrims travelling' | Kyrkjebø & Spørck, 83.

PAGE 82:

Books such as | Kyrkjebø & Spørck, 8.
'It is said that the earth's circle' | Snorri Sturluson, *Heimskringla*. Translated by Samuel Laing (1844).
'*Kringla heimsins*' is Snorri's translation of the Latin '*Orbus terrarum*', which means 'the round earth', and not, as is the case in Storm's Norwegian translation of Snorri, 'the earth's round disk'. Benedicte Gamborg Briså believes that the choice of word results from Storm believing that Snorri thought the Earth was flat – but this was false. Like all medieval scholars, Snorri knew that the Earth was round. The original opens as follows: '*Kringla heimsins, sú er mannfólkit byggir, er mjök vágskorin; ganga höf stór or útsjánum inn í jörðina …*'

PAGE 83:

The country surrounding the Vanaquisl | Snorri Sturluson, *Heimskringla*. Translated by Samuel Laing (1844).
Around the same time, King Henry III of England | La Porte, 31.

PAGE 88:

While *mappæ mundi* were | Edson, 33.

PAGES 89–90:

'This region of Norway is' | An English translation of the texts of the Catalan Atlas can be found here: cresquesproject.net/catalan-atlas-legends.
In Venice in the mid-1400s | This scene featuring Fra Mauro and Pietro Querini is pure conjecture, but it is highly probable that they met; they both lived in the same city at the same time, Fra Mauro spoke with many seamen as he worked, and Querini's landing is clearly marked on Fra Mauro's map.
Fra Mauro lives | Edson, 141.

PAGE 91:

But if we look at | Transcriptions, 1011.
'Those who are knowledgeable' | Transcriptions, 960.

PAGES 91–92:

'many cosmographers and' | Transcriptions, 1043.
'In this province' | Transcriptions, 2674.

PAGE 93:

This work | Edson, 164.

THE FIRST ATLAS

PAGE 95:

With her brush, Anne Ortel | This scene is also pure conjecture. It is not certain that Anne Ortel coloured this map, but nor is it improbable that she did so.
The Antwerp of Ortel's time | Binding, 7–11.

PAGES 96–97:

Anne Ortel was named | Binding, 19–24.
As early as the year 1500 | Binding, 39.

PAGES 97–98:
Abram and his sisters | Binding, 37.
Perhaps Leonard had hoped | Jan
Radermacher's letter is reproduced in
Binding, 67.
Another friend wrote | Broecke, Krogt &
Meurer, 30.
What books might Abram | Binding, 30, 35–
6.

PAGE 99:
In the Middle Ages, the Europeans |
Lozovsky, 8–10.

PAGE 99:
We don't know exactly | Dalché, 292.

PAGE 102:
After a church meeting | Dalché, 310.
Of the map, Fillastre wrote | Cited in Edson,
125.

PAGES 103–104:
Greenland is again located | cartographic-
images.net/Cartographic_Images/258_
Behaim_Globe. html
In his log, Columbus | Columbus, 35.

PAGE 104:
Vespucci's book | Herbermann, 88.

PAGE 107:
In the summer of 1527 | Miekkavaara, 1–15.

PAGE 112:
The quote allocated to the Norwegian king |
The quote is taken from Revelation 3:11.

PAGES 113–114:
an earnest young man | Binding, 28.
In 1547, Abram became | Binding, 39–41.
Twice every year | Binding, 88; Crane, 162.

PAGE 114:
It was in Frankfurt | Binding, 90.

PAGE 116:
The first map Mercator created | Bartlett, 37;
Crane, 83.

PAGES 121–122:
In 1554, Jan Rademacher | Binding, 73–9.
Plantin was French | Binding, 116–7.

PAGES 122–123:
The oldest known map | Binding, 129–131.
But in 1567 | Binding, 152.

PAGES 123 and 126:
'I therefore send you' | Lhuyd's letter is
reproduced in Binding, 167.
It was a huge undertaking | Binding, 175.
After Ortelius had drawn | Binding, 176.

PAGE 127:
'Abrahamus Ortelius' | Parts of the preface
are reproduced in Binding, 222–4.
To make this connection | Matei-Chesnoiu,
13.
At the top, Europe | But Ortelius was
not unaware of what was happening in
America. In a later edition, for a map of
New Spain (Mexico), he writes: 'This
province was in 1518 taken by force by the
Spanish authorities, commanded and led
by Fernando Cortez; who by sending many
of his own men to their deaths, but also
by killing far more of the inhabitants who
fought for their freedom, conquered it.'
Binding, 244.

PAGE 129:
'Quid ei potest' | Cicero, 150.

PAGES 129–30:
Ortelius therefore encourages | Binding,
256–8.
The atlas sold well | Binding, 254–5.
In May 1571 | Broecke, Krogt & Meurer, 82.

PAGE 131:
In December three years later | Binding,
292–3.

PAGE 131:
With his life's work | Binding, 194.

Venturing out

PAGES 135–136:
This is where the journey | Nissen (19 October 1960), 79.
Scavenius notes down distances | The place names are taken from Janssonius's map.

PAGE 136:
In 'Joan and Cornelius Blaeu printed the map': 'S. S' stands for *Superintendens* (bishop) *Stavangriensis* (in Stavanger).
The Diocese of Bergen | Nissen (14 October 1960), 92.

PAGE 138:
Joan and Cornelius made up | Brotton, 266.
The Republic of the Seven United Netherlands | European borders and place names were fluid during this period. For the sake of simplicity, I have chosen to use 'the Netherlands' when referring to the area that covers parts of the modern Netherlands and Belgium.

PAGE 138:
During the 1500s, the production and sale | Schilder & van Egmond; Nissen, 1949.

PAGE 140:
Blaeu was not the only | Brown, 170.

PAGE 140:
One day in 1597 | Hagen, 64.

PAGE 144:
Mercator's life's work | Crane, 193; Taylor, 185.
In 1569 he published | Crane, 204; conversation with Bengt Malm.

PAGE 146:
'The priest [. . .] related to the King' | Mercator's letter translated into Norwegian by Asgaut Steinnes. Cited in Ingstad.

PAGE 148:
In the autumn of 1585 | Crane, 260.
Mercator also wrote a preface | Crane, 275.
In later narratives | Mauretania must not be confused with today's Mauritania, which is located further south.

PAGES 149–150:
Not long after completing | Crane, 279.
Hondius the Elder understood | Barber, Peter in Clarke, 09:30.
Mercator would probably | Crane in Clarke, 11:00.

PAGE 150:
Blaeu was ecstatic | Brotton, 276.

PAGE 155:
But it was also a statue | Brotton, 286.

PAGE 156:
While Blaeu and Janssonius were caught up | Koeman & van Egmond, 1271.
Isaac van Geelkerck, a cartographer's son | Widerberg, 108.

PAGE 157:
The border between Norway and Sweden had always been | Nissen & Kvamen, XII.

PAGE 157:
The border disputes at Finnmark | Nissen, 1943 and 1963–1964.
'in all the places where any dispute' | Cited in Nissen & Kvamen, xv.
'compose a complete map' | Cited in Nissen & Kvamen, XVI.

PAGE 161:
It is difficult to overemphasise | Nissen & Kvamen, XIIX.

PAGES 161–162:
During the work on the border | Hanekamhaug, 12; Sinding-Larsen, 1.
In 1756, Norwegian officer | Ginsberg, 101.

PAGE 163:
It was also clearly more accurate | Schøning, 351–2.

PAGES 163–164:
During his work, Wangensteen | Aanrud, 97–101.
The task of drawing | Nissen, 1938, 126.
The forestry commission never | Aanrud, 97–101.

THE GREAT SURVEYS

PAGE 167:
The story of the modern | Rastad, 274–5; Pettersen (2009), 70–1.

PAGE 168:
The initiative to survey | Harsson (2009), 4.
'These maps will now' | Cited in de Seue, 11. Translated into Norwegian by Astrid Sverresdotter Dypvik.
The Border Survey of Norway was allocated premises | Harsson (2009), 4.
and the new institution's first task | Thank you to archivist Sidsel Kvarteig at the Norwegian Mapping Authority for showing me this map.

PAGES 169–170:
Details such as churches | Andressen, 45 in Andressen & Fladby.
Sometimes, as much as | Harsson & Aanrud, 108.
At the same time, the actions | Harsson & Aanrud, 109.
In the summer of 1763 | Nørlund, 59. All the Danish quotes are also sourced from here.

PAGE 172:
Dutch mathematician Gemma Frisius | Haasbroek, 8.
Danish astronomer Tycho Brahe was among | Haasbroek, 16.

PAGE 173:
In Prague, Brahe | Haasbroek, 59.

PAGES 174–175:
France was the first | Brotton, 295; O'Connor and Robertson.
'to agriculture, to commerce or manufacture' | Cited in Brotton, 300.
In 1679, King Louis XIV | Quoted on fr.wikipedia.org/wiki/Carte_de_Cassini

PAGES 176–177:
The first expedition set out | Nystedt.
Luckily, the journey to Sápmi | Brotton, 309; Nystedt.

PAGE 177:
Orry also took it upon | Brotton, 311.

PAGE 181:
'I want the map of my kingdom' | Reproduced in Brotton, 318.

PAGES 181–182:
'My poor Cassini' | Reproduced in Brotton, 321.
But at the same time, what was | Brotton, 325.

PAGE 183:
'His map may be good' | Reproduced in Brotton, 328.
'They took it away from me' | Reproduced in Godlewska, 77.
'If we had stuck to' | Reproduced in Brotton, 330.

PAGE 186–187:
'The survey shall hereafter' | Reproduced in de Seue, 17.
Throughout the autumn | Pettersen (2014), 97.
Equipped with a large officers' tent | de Seue, 31; Pettersen (2009), 71.

PAGE 188:
'the survey, which was undertaken by Captain' | Pontoppidan, 2.
in 1785 a royal decree | Hoem, 63.
'When Trondheim's meridian' | Reproduced in Pettersen (2014), 98.

PAGES 189 and 192:
The transit of Venus that | Clark.
Bugge obtained results | Pettersen (2014), 98.
The next transit of Venus | Johansen, 40.

PAGE 192:
Hell and a colleague | Johansen, 48.
'That the locations of many places' |
Reproduced in Johansen, 50.

PAGES 193 and 196:
The Wibe brothers triangulate | Heltne.
The king expressed | Reproduced in
the Dansk biografisk Lexikon (Danish
Biographical Encyclopedia), 210.

PAGE 196:
'Our farms, which we' | Cited in Paule, 7.

PAGE 198:
The increasing accuracy | Enebakk and
Pettersen, 263.

PAGE 200:
The subject was formalised | fagsider.org/
kirkehistorie/lover/1860_skole.htm
'If we were able' | Jensen, 57–8.

PAGE 204:
For a handwritten | Munch, at the back of
the book.

PAGE 204:
Since the country had for many | Kristiansen.

PAGE 206:
Continually reprinted | Sætre, 26.

WHITE SPACES IN THE NORTH

PAGE 209:
One September morning in 1896 | Sverdrup,
translated by Ethel Harriet Hearn (1904)

PAGES 210–211:
'Gunerius Ingvald Isachsen' | Sverdrup,
translated by Ethel Harriet Hearn (1904)
The expedition possessed | Isachsen
On Wednesday 14 September | Sverdrup,

translated by Ethel Harriet Hearn (1904)
'quite expected them to do' | Sverdrup,
translated by Ethel Harriet Hearn (1904)
'In such circumstances' | Sverdrup, translated
by Ethel Harriet Hearn (1904)

PAGES 211–212:
'The work first on' | Sverdrup, translated by
Ethel Harriet Hearn (1904)
'The orders I received' | Sverdrup, translated
by Ethel Harriet Hearn (1904)

PAGE 212:
'take lessons from the two races' | Sverdrup,
translated by Ethel Harriet Hearn (1904)
'very intelligent for a' | Sverdrup, translated
by Ethel Harriet Hearn (1904)

PAGES 213–214:
'from which it was evident' | Reproduced in
Ingstad, 24.
Skippers, seamen and farmers would gather
| Ingstad, 32.
So say wise men | Ingstad, 296.

PAGE 215:
An Icelandic map from | Ingstad, 205.

PAGE 218:
The Icelandic Annals | Reproduced in
Ingstad, 168.

PAGES 218 and 220:
'beyond Norway, which is the' | Adam of
Bremen, 214.
Roger Barlow | Williams, 8.
On a globe dating | The 'Lenox' globe. Its
creator is unknown.

PAGES 221–222:
The lack of reliable | Williams, 11.
Best had been a member of | Williams, 17.
The next day they encountered | De Veer,

PAGE 223:
The map shows a Mare Magnum | Hessel, 81.

PAGES 223–224:
Along the way, Baffin discovered | Williams, 42–4.
In 1619, three years after | Williams, 55.

PAGES 224–225:
'a revelation of that' | Cited in Williams, 59.
The Russians explored | Lainema & Nurminen, 104–129.
Three years later | Lainema & Nurminen, 113–114.

PAGE 228:
'it is always much better to omit' | Cited in Williams, 120.

PAGES 228–229:
In a letter dated October | Williams, 147.
'a Map that the most illiterate' | Cited in Williams, 146.
'We may consider Hudson's-Bay' | Cited in Williams, 53.

PAGE 229:
The sentiments of the two | Williams, 177.

PAGE 233:
Surgeon John Rae | Williams, 331–2.

PAGES 236–237:
'More than 40,000 miles' | Cited in Williams, 345.
What might not these four | Sverdrup
'Tuesday, March 20' | Sverdrup

PAGES 237–238:
'Early in the morning' | Sverdrup, translated by Ethel Harriet Hearn (1904)
'When I got back' | Sverdrup, translated by Ethel Harriet Hearn (1904)
One day, Sverdrup | Sverdrup, translated by Ethel Harriet Hearn (1904)

PAGES 238–239:
Isachsen Land | According to the Canadian authorities, Isachsen has the worst weather in Canada, scoring 99 points out of 100 on the severe weather index.
'When we look at the map' | polarhistorie.no/personer/Gunnar%20Isachsen

PAGE 239:
'justified sovereignty …' | Cited in Drivenes, 2004, 176.

PAGES 240–241:
'On Norwegian expeditions …' | Isachsen (1934).
'The difficulties for …' | Isachsen (1934).
'On these maps, which …' | Isachsen (1934).

AS SEEN FROM ABOVE

PAGE 243:
'The earth shook' | Cited in Sass.

PAGE 244:
'My table is covered' | Cited in Finnegan, 49.
The photographs were placed | Finnegan, 49.

PAGE 245–246:
During a demonstration | youtube.com/watch?v=q3beVhDiyio
'This arrangement has, of course' | Flight.

PAGES 246–247:
'I hope none of you' | Cited in Hylton, 16.
Members of the cavalry | Finnegan, 39.
The first British reconnaissance planes | Finnegan, 17.
In September 1914 | Finnegan, 25.
'I discovered the positions' | Cited in Finnegan, 28.

PAGES 247–248:
But despite this, nobody | Finnegan, 34.
'Our intelligence show was' | Cited in Finnegan, 49–50.

PAGES 248–249:
'I had had a camera as a boy' | Cited in Finnegan, 432.
'Photography again' | Cited in Finnegan, 431.
'Photography is a good job' | Cited in Finnegan, 438.
'It was something hugely satisfying' | Cited in Finnegan, 432.

PAGE 252:
'The reading and interpretation' | Cited in Finnegan, 445.

PAGES 252–253:
'The First World War paved the way' | Ween, 521.
'We have flown above' | Skappel & Widerøe, 83–7.

PAGE 254:
'Military conquests require' | Cited in Paule, 9.

PAGE 255:
In the summer of 1932 | Luncke, 347–61.
On 21 June | Ween, 530.

PAGE 256:
In 1936, Arild Widerøe | Skappel & Widerøe, 88–93.

PAGE 257:
That same year, Viggo Widerøe | Skappel & Widerøe, 111.
'Many people are indifferent' | Skappel & Widerøe, 128.

PAGE 258:
'The importance of this new' | Skappel & Widerøe, 101–2.

PAGE 263:
The Norwegian Armed Forces submitted | Gleditsch, 407–410.

PAGES 264–265:
'As far as possible' | Gleditsch, 410.
'We could discuss the farm symbol' | Gleditsch, 412.
'But the post-war period' | Cited in Paule, 5.
In 1964, the Norwegian Parliament | Paule, 76.

PAGE 265:
'Never before had a survey' | Paule, 13.

PAGE 266:
'In 1969, Kristian Gleditsch' | Balle, 438.
'When presenting plans' | NOU 1975: 26, 80.

'Today, there is a particular need . . .' | NOU 1975: 26, 80.
In a matter-of-fact and | NOU 1975: 26, 81–9.

BLUE PLANET

PAGE 271:
On 1 February | Felt, 115.

PAGES 272–273:
Tharp had started work | Felt, 93.
'Girl talk' | Cited in Felt, 99.

PAGE 273:
In his doctoral thesis | Hestmark, 76.

PAGE 275:
Nor is measuring the depth | Kunzig, 31.
In the wake of | Dahl, 33–8.

PAGE 278:
Norway became a leading | Hausken, Kristoffersen & Svendsen, 99.

PAGE 279:
Two differing views | Kunzig, 34–6.
Two professors | Wille, 6–9.

PAGE 280:
Second, the expedition | Wille, 4.
The steamship DS *Vøringen* | Wille, 19–22.

PAGE 282:
'One of the scientific tasks' | Nansen (vol. 2).
'I presupposed' | Nansen (vol. 1).

PAGES 282–283:
In March 1894 | Nansen, (vol. 1).
'I do not think we shall talk' | Nansen, (vol. 1).
Nansen wrote a pioneering work | Hestmark, 87.
The sonar system emitted | Kunzig, 39–42.

PAGE 283–284:
While the German ship | Felt, 20.
In 1930, American geologist | Felt, 56.

PAGE 288:
The Second World War had given American women | Felt, 38.

PAGE 289:
Marie Tharp's first geology tutor | Felt, 71.

PAGE 294:
But Tharp and Heezen didn't dare | Felt, 113.

PAGES 294–295:
The star of the conference | Felt, 128–130.
That same year, French planes | Meland.

PAGES 295–296:
Few were convinced | Carstens.
In Denmark, exploratory drilling | Sellevold, 8.
In the application made | Sellevold, 18.
In 1963, the Norwegian Geological Survey | Åm, 49–51.
On a 'Bathymetric Chart | Lervik, appendix 18.

PAGES 296–297:
An increasing number of foreign | Johansen, 158.
At around the same time | Felt, 169.

PAGE 298:
We can imagine them leaning | Felt, 224.

PAGE 299:
The panorama is not | Kunzig, 60–4.

PAGES 300–301:
But satellites have also | Kunzig, 64–9.
Sandwell and Smith continued | NASA.
'The fact is we can learn how this planet' | Cited in Kunzig, 75.

THE DIGITAL WORLD

PAGE 305:
'Until two days ago' | CBS News: 'Special Report', 6 October 1957. youtube.com/watch?v=dO33bvFbuCU
It was only 58 centimetres | Eisman & Hardesty, 71–3.

PAGE 306:
On Monday morning | Guier & Weiffenbach, 15; Warren & Worth, 3.

PAGE 307:
'Man must rise above the Earth' | Cited in Andersen, Brånå & Lønnum, 227.
The first person to imagine | en.wikipedia.org/wiki/ Newton%27s_cannonball

PAGE 308:
The missiles were first | Eisman & Hardesty, 1–7
In the 1920s, the lead architect | Eisman & Hardesty, 11–14.

PAGES 309 and 312:
'You must understand' | Cited in Cadbury, 90.
Both von Braun and Korolev | Warren & Worth, 2.

PAGES 312–313:
In 1955, the American | Eisman & Hardesty, 58, 96.
'a new moon' | Cited in Cadbury, 147.
His idea was approved at the highest level | Everest, episode 2, 18:20.
The Strela computer | computer-museum.ru.
'If the base 2 is used' | Cited in Brotton, 411.

PAGES 313–314:
Late in the evening | Eisman & Hardesty, 74; Cadbury, 165.
'This is music' | Cited in Cadbury, 166.

PAGES 314–315:
On the evening of Sputnik's launch | Everest, episode 2, 39:00.
Millions watched the events | Everest, episode 2, 43:50.

PAGES 315–316:
The navy and APL launched | Warren & Worth, 9 & 124.
Norway was one of the system's | Blankenburgh, 93; Danchik, 25.

PAGE 317:
The Cold War made its | Miller.

PAGE 321:
In the early 1960s | Brotton, 413; Greiner.
American cartographer Waldo R. Tobler had
taken up| Tobler, 137.

PAGES 322–323:
'Continuous satellite coverage' | NOU 1975, 6
& 103.
The geographic surveying of Norway |
Østensen, 407.

PAGE 324:
In 1998, Vice President | Cited in Brotton,
419.

PAGE 329:
'a valuable addition' | Cited in Brotton, 422.

PAGE 331:
'Where maps and their makers' | Brotton, 431.

PAGES 331–332:
'It is vital that regulators . . .' Icomp, 2012.
'have done a wonderful job' | Cited in
Brotton, 436.
'If you talk to most people' | Cited in Brotton,
427.

PAGE 333:
Even now, digital maps are updated | Meyer,
mars 2016.

LIST OF ILLUSTRATIONS

I am extremely grateful to the National Library of Norway, the Norwegian Mapping Authority, David Rumsey, the library of the Norwegian Directorate of Fisheries, the Norwegian Polar Institute, the National Archives of Norway, the National Library of Sweden, the Scripps Institution of Oceanography, the University of Texas, the Canadian Soil Information Service and the City Archaeological Park of Seradina and Bedolina for their assistance in providing the images for this book.

Front page: National Library of Sweden, Stockholm.
Page ii: Library of Congress, Washington; page vi–vii: Library of Congress; page viii; NASA, Washington; page xiii: Stiftsbibliothek, St. Gallen.

THE FIRST IMAGES OF THE WORLD
Page xvi: © Marretta Alberto for the City Archaeological Park of Seradina and Bedolina, Capo di Ponte; pages 6–7: Anati, Emmanuel: Civiltà Preistorica della Valcamonica (1964), figure 65; pages 14–15: National Archives of Norway *EA-4056, Samlinger til kildeutgivelse, Kjeldeskriftfondets avskriftsamling, serie F, eske 38 – Kjeldeskriftfondets manuskript nr. 222–235, mappenr. 233 (Primary source collections, Kjeldeskriftfondet's collection of certified copies, series F, box 38 – Kjeldeskriftfondet's manuscript no. 222–235, map no. 233)*, Oslo; pages 22–23: University of Toledo website.

LIKE FROGS ABOUT A POND
Page 28: davidrumsey.com; pages 34–35: davidrumsey.com; pages 44–45: National Library of Sweden; pages 50–51: Library of Congress; pages 56–57: davidrumsey.com; page 61: davidrumsey.com.

HOLY GEOGRAPHY
Page 62: British Museum, London; pages 70–71: davidrumsey.com; pages 76–77: Library of Congress; pages 86–87: Wikimedia Commons.

THE FIRST ATLAS
Page 94: Museum Plantin-Moretus, Antwerp; pages 100–101: National Library of Norway; pages 110–111: National Library of Sweden; pages 118–119: Library of Congress; pages 124–125: National Library of Norway; page 133: archive.org.

VENTURING OUT
Page 134: National Library of Norway; pages 142–143: Wikimedia Commons; pages 152–153: Geheugen van Nederland, Koninklijke Bibliotheek, Den Haag; pages 158–159: National Library of Norway.

THE GREAT SURVEYS
Page 166: Norwegian Mapping and Cadastre Authority, Hønefoss; page 171: archive.org; pages 178–179: Library of Congress; pages 190–191: Norwegian Mapping and Cadastre Authority; pages 194–195: Norwegian Mapping and Cadastre Authority; pages 202–203: National Library of Norway.

WHITE SPACES IN THE NORTH
Page 208: National Library of Norway; pages 216–217: National Library of Norway; pages 226–227: National Library of Norway; pages 234–235: National Library of Norway.

AS SEEN FROM ABOVE
Page 242: Alamy; pages 250–251: National Library of Norway; pages 260–261: National Library of Norway; page 269: Norwegian Polar Institute, Tromsø.

BLUE PLANET
Page 270: Library of Congress; pages 276–277: Norwegian Directorate of Fisheries Library, Bergen; pages 286–287: Norwegian Petroleum Directorate, Stavanger; pages 292–293: Library of Congress; page 303: Scripps Institution of Oceanography, San Diego.

THE DIGITAL WORLD
Page 305: NASA; pages 310–311: The University of Texas Libraries, Austin; pages 318–319: Canadian Soil Information Service/Service d'information sur les sols du Canada, Ottawa; pages 326–327: Google Maps.

Aanrud, Roald: 'Generalforstamtet og norsk kartografi. Et 200-års minne om Johann Georg von Langen' ['The Forestry Commission and Norwegian cartography: A 200-year anniversary remembrance of Johann Georg von Langen'] in *Norsk Geografisk Tidsskrift* [Norwegian Journal of Geography], vol. 31, 1977.

Adam of Bremen: *Beretningen om Hamburg stift, erkebiskopenes bedrifter og øyrikene i Norden*, Thorleif Dahls kulturbibliotek/ Aschehoug, Oslo, 1993. Translated by Bjørg Tosterud Danielsen and Anne Katrine Frihagen.

——: *History of the Archbishops of Hamburg-Bremen*, translated by Francis J. Tschan, Columbia University Press, 2002.

Albu, Emily: 'Rethinking the Peutinger Map' in Talbert & Unger, 2008.

Åm, Knut: *Aeromagnetic Investigation on the continental Shelf of Norway, Stad–Lofoten (62–69°N)*, Norges geologiske undersøkelse [Geographical Survey of Norway]/Universitetsforlaget, Oslo, 1970.

Andersen, Øystein; Brånå, Geir & Lønnum, Svein Erik: *Fotogrammetri* [*Photogrammetry*], NKI, Bekkestua, 1990.

Andressen, Leif T. & Fladby, Rolf (eds.): *Våre gamle kart* [*Our Old Maps*], Universitetsforlaget, Oslo, 1981.

Anonymous article from *Skilling-Magazin*, Saturday 17 December 1870, in Hausken, Kristoffersen & Svendsen (eds.): *Norges sjøkartverk. Kystens historie i kart og beskrivelser 1932–1982* [*Nautical Charts of Norway: The history of the coast in maps and descriptions 1932–1982*], Norges sjøkartverk, Stavanger, 1983.

Anonymous: 'A brief history of satellite navigation', news.stanford.edu/ pr/95/950613Arc5183.html

Anonymous: 'Çatalhöyük "Map" Mural May Depict Volcanic Eruption 8,900 Years Ago'. sci-news.com/archaeology/ science-catalhoyuk-map-mural-volcanic-eruption-01681.html

Anonymous: 'Chronological History of IBM', www 03.ibm.com/ibm/history/history/ decade_1950.html

Anonymous: 'How Google Monopolised Online Mapping & Listings Services', i-comp.org/wp-content/ uploads/2013/07/Mapping_ and_ Listing_Services.pdf

Anonymous: 'New Seafloor Map Helps Scientists Find New Features', earthobservatory.nasa.gov/IOTD/view. php?id=87276&src=ve

Anonymous: 'Paris Aero Show' at flightglobal.com/pdfarchive, pages 1355 and 1356.

Anonymous: 'Remote Sensing' at earthobservatory.nasa.gov/Features/ RemoteSensing/

Anonymous: 'Strela Computer', computer-museum.ru/english/strela.htm

Anonymous: 'Transit 1A NSSDCA ID: TRAN1', nssdc.gsfc.nasa.gov/nmc/ spacecraftDisplay.do?id=TRAN1

'*Apollo 8* Onboard Voice Transcription', NASA, Houston, 1969.

Aristophanes: *Skyene* [*The Clouds*], Aschehoug, Oslo, 1977. In a Norwegian retelling by Knut Kleve.

——: *The Clouds*, translated by Peter

Meineck, Hackett Publishing Company, Inc., Indianapolis/Cambridge, 1998.

Aristotle: *Meteorologien* [*Meteorology*], Vidarforlaget, Oslo, 2016. Translated by Mette Heuch Berg.

Aristotle: *The Complete Works of Aristotle: The Revised Oxford Translation*. Edited by Jonathan Barnes, 1984.

Augustine of Hippo: *De doctrina christiana. Om kristen opplæring* [*On Christian Doctrine*], Det Norske Samlaget, Oslo, 1998. Translated by Hermund Slaattelid.

——: *On Christian Doctrine*. The Select Library of Nicene and Post-Nicene Fathers http://faculty.georgetown.edu/jod/augustine/

——: *City of God.* The Select Library of Nicene and Post-Nicene Fathers http://faculty.georgetown.edu/jod/augustine/

——: *Gudsstaten* [*City of God*], Pax Forlag, Oslo, 1998. Translated by Reidar Aasgaard.

Aujac, Germaine: 'The Foundations of Theoretical Cartography in Archaic and Classical Greece' in Harley, J. B. & Woodward, David (eds.), 1987.

——: 'The Growth of an Empirical Cartography in Hellenistic Greece' in Harley, J. B. & Woodward, David (eds.), 1987.

Bäärnhielm, Göran: 'Förlaga till Bureus' Lapplandskarta' ['A Copy of Bureus's Lapland Map'], goran.baarnhielm.net/Kartor/Bureus-forlaga.html

Baker, Chris: 'The Battle of Neuve Chapelle', longlongtrail.co.uk/battles/battles-ofthe-western-front-in-france-and-flanders/the-battle-of-neuve-chapelle/

Barlaup, Asbjørn: *Widerøes flyveselskap gjennom 25 år* [*25 Years of the Widerøe Airline*], Widerøe, Oslo, 1959.

Bartlett, John R.: 'Mercator in the Wilderness' in Becking, Bob & Grabbe, Lester: *Between Evidence and Ideology*, Brill, Leiden, 2011.

Barton, Cathy: 'Marie Tharp, oceanographic cartographer, and her contributions to the revolution in the Earth sciences' in *The Earth Inside and Out: Some Major*

Contributions to Geology in the 20th Century by Oldroyd, David R. (ed.), Geological Society Special Publication, London, 2002.

Baumann, Paul R.: 'History of Remote Sensing, Satellite Imagery, part II' at oneonta.edu/faculty/baumanpr/geosat2/RS%20History%20II/RS-History-Part-2.html

Berggren, J. Lennart & Jones, Alexander: *Ptolemy's Geography: An Annotated Translation of the Theoretical Chapters*, Princeton University Press, Princeton, 2000.

Binding, Paul: *Imagined Corners: Exploring the World's First Atlas*, Review, London, 2003.

Bjørsvik, Elisabeth: *En festning i utvikling og forandring. Bergenhus 1646–1996* [*A fortress undergoing development and change: Bergenhus 1646–1996*], Bryggens museum, Bergen, 1996.

Blado, Antonio: 'Monstrum in Oceano', Roma, 1537. Translated by A. Boxer on the blog idolsoftecave.com. I have also found a translation of Magnus's '*Scandia. Peninsvla qvam …*' here.

Blankenburgh, Jan Christian: 'Geodesi med stjerner og satellitter i Norge' ['Geodesy with stars and satellites in Norway] in Kulvik, Kåre (ed.): *Kartografi i 50 år. Kartografisk forening 1937–1987, bilag til Kart og Plan nummer 1* [*Fifty Years of Cartography: The Cartographic Society 1937–1987, supplement to Maps and Plans number 1*], 1987.

Borre, Kai: 'Fundamental triangulation networks in Denmark' in *Journal of Geodetic Science*, vol. 4, Aalborg, 2014. cct.gfy.ku.dk/publ_others/JGS-S-13-00034.pdf

Bowen, Karen L. & Imhof, Dirk: *Christopher Plantin and Engraved Book Illustrations in Sixteenth-Century Europe*, Cambridge University Press, Cambridge, 2008.

Bratrein, Håvard Dahl: 'Ottar' in *Norsk biografisk leksikon* [*Norwegian Biographical Encyclopedia*], nbl.snl.no/Ottar

Brinchmann, Christian: *National-forskeren P.A. Munch. Hans liv og virke* [*National Researcher P. A. Munch: His Life and Work*], J.W. Cappelens Forlag, Oslo, 1910.

Bringsværd, Tor Åge & Braarvig, Jens: *I begynnelsen. Skapelsesmyter fra hele verden* [*In the Beginning: Creation Myths from Across the World*], De norske bokklubbene, Oslo, 2000.

Briså, Benedicte Gamborg: 'Hvordan ble Norge kartlagt? Fra omtrentlig geografi til detaljerte veikart' ['How was Norway mapped? From rough geography to detailed road maps'], Nasjonalbiblioteket and Universitetsbiblioteket, Oslo, 2014.

Broch, Ole Jørgen: *Norges Geografiske Opmålings virksomhet gjennem 150 år* [The activities of the Geographical Survey of Norway over 150 years], Grøndahl & Søns Forlag, Kristiania, 1923.

Broecke, Marcel van den: 'Ortelius' Theatrum Orbis Terrarum (1570-1641) Characteristics and development of a sample of on verso map texts', Koninklijk Nederlands Aardrijkskundig Genootschap, Faculteit Geowetenschappen Universiteit Utrecht, Utrecht, 2009. bmgn-lchr.nl/articles/abstract/10.18352/bmgn-l-chr.7350/

Broecke, Marcel van den; van der Krogt, Peter; Meurer, Peter (eds.): *Abraham Ortelius and the First Atlas: Essays commemorating the quadricentennial of his death*, H&S Publishers, Utrecht, 1998.

Brotton, Jerry: 'Introduction' in *A History of the World in Twelve Maps*, Allen Lane, London, 2012.

——: 'Money' in *A History of the World in Twelve Maps*, Allen Lane, London, 2012.

——: 'Science' in *A History of the World in Twelve Maps*, Allen Lane, London, 2012.

Brown, Lloyd A.: *The Story of Maps*, Dover Publications, New York, 1949.

Cadbury, Deborah: *Space Race*, Fourth Estate, London, 2005.

Caesar, Gaius Julius: *Borgerkrigen* [*The Civil War*], Thorleif Dahls kulturbibliotek/Aschehoug, Oslo, 1994. Translated by Oskar Fjeld.

Carstens, Halfdan: 'Et mye omtalt brev' ['A much discussed letter'] at geo365.no, 3 July 2014. geo365.no/oljehistorie/et-mye-omtalt-brev

Catholic Online has a biography of Isidore of Seville here: catholic.org/saints/saint.php?saint_id=58

Christensen, Lars: *Min siste ekspedisjon til Antarktis* [*My last expedition to the Antarctic*], Johan Grundt Tanum, Oslo, 1938.

Cicero, Marcus Tullius: *Om staten* [*Republic*], Thorleif Dahls kulturbibliotek/Aschehoug, Oslo, 1990. Translated by Oskar Fjeld.

——: *Republic*, translated by Richard Hooker, 1993. http://www.public.asu.edu/~mjwhite/Cicero,%20The%20Dream%20of%20Scipio.htm

——: *Samtaler på Tusculum* [*Tusculan Disputations*], Thorleif Dahls kulturbibliotek/Aschehoug, Oslo, 2000. Translated by Oskar Fjeld.

Clark, Stuart: 'Transit of Venus: Measuring the heavens in the 18th century' in the *Guardian*, 29 May 2012. theguardian.com/science/ blog/2012/may/29/transitvenus-measuring-heavens

Clarke, Stevens: *The Beauty of Maps*, episode 4: 'Atlas Maps – Thinking Big', Tern/BBC, 2010.

Collett, John Petter & Røberg, Ole Anders: *Norwegian Space Activities 1958–2003*, ESA Publications Division, Noordwijk, 2004.

Columbus, Christopher: *Journal of the First Voyage of Columbus*, The Hakluyt Society, London, 1893. Translated by Clements R. Markham. archive.org/details/journalofchristoo0colurich

Craig, Alexander: 'The Bedolina Map – An Exploratory Network Analysis' in *Layers of Perception*, pp. 366–72, CAA, Berlin, 2007. archiv.ub.uni-heidelberg.de/propylaeumdok/512

Crane, Nicholas: *Mercator: The Man Who Mapped the Planet*, Weidenfeld & Nicolson, London, 2002.

Daae, Ludvig: *Historiske Skildringer, Tillægshefte til Folkevennen* [*Historical descriptions: Supplementary booklet to the People's Friend journal*], Selskabet for Folkeoplysningens Fremme, Kristiania, 1878.

Dahl, Bjørn Westerbeek: 'Ophavsmanden til Dania-Norvegia-kortet i Det kongelige biblioteks kortsamling' ['The creator of the Denmark-Norway map in the royal library's collection'] in *Fund og Forskning*, vol. 26, 1982. tidsskrift.dk/index.php/fundogforskning/article/viewFile/1632/2714

Dahl, Chr. A.: *Norges Sjøkartsverks historie* [The History of Norway's Nautical Charts], Grøndahl & Søns Boktrykkeri, Kristiania, 1914.

Dalché, Patrick Gautier: 'The Reception of Ptolemy's Geography (End of the Fourteenth to Beginning of the Sixteenth Century)' in Woodward, David (ed.): *The History of Cartography Volume Three: Cartography in the European Renaissance*, The University of Chicago Press, Chicago, 2007.

Danchik, Robert J.: 'An Overview of Transit Development' in *Johns Hopkins APL Technical Digest*, vol. 19, no. 1 1998.

Djønne, Eirik: '"Polarfarerens ABC". Suksessfaktorene for de geografiske oppdagelsene og det kartografiske arbeidet på den andre norske polarferden med *Fram*', master's dissertation at the Institute for Archaeology, Conservation and History, University of Oslo, 2015.

Drivenes, Einar-Arne: 'Ishavsimperialisme' ['Arctic Ocean Imperialism'] in Drivenes, Einar-Arne & Jølle, Harald Dag (eds.): *Norsk polarhistorie II. Vitenskapene* [Norwegian Polar History II: The Sciences], Gyldendal, Oslo, 2004.

——: 'Svalbardforskning og Svalbardpolitikk 1870–1925' ['Svalbard research and policy] in *Nordlit* 29, UiT Norges arktiske universitet, Tromsø, 2012.

Duzer, Chet van: 'Waldseemüller's World Maps of 1507 and 1516: Sources and Development of his Cartographical Thought' in *The Portolan*, Winter 2012. academia.edu/2204120/Waldseem%C3%BCller_s_World_Maps_of_1507_and_1516_Sources_and_Development_of_his_Cartographical_Thought_

Edson, Evelyn: *The World Map, 1300–1492*, The Johns Hopkins University Press, Baltimore, 2007.

Edson, Evelyn & Savage-Smith, Emilie: *Medieval Views of the Cosmos*, Bodleian Library, Oxford, 2004.

Eisman, Gene & Hardesty, Von: *Epic Rivalry. The Inside Story of the Soviet and American Space Race*, National Geographic, Washington DC, 2007.

Ekrem, Inger: *Nytt lys over Historia Norwegie* [A new light on Historia Norwegiæ], Universitetet i Bergen, IKRR, Seksjon for gresk, latin og egyptologi, Bergen, 1998.

Eliassen, Finn-Einar: 'Generalforstamtet – vårt første skogdirektorat' ['The Forestry Commission – our first Directorate of Forestry'] on the National Archive's blog: dokumenteneforteller.tumblr.com/page/8

Elliott, Tom: 'Constructing a digital edition for the Peutinger Map' in Talbert & Unger, 2008.

Enebakk, Vidar: 'Kartlegging i tid og rom' ['Mapping in time and space'] in Bagge, Sverre; Collett, John Petter & Kjus, Audun (eds.): *P.A. Munch: Historiker og nasjonsbygger* [P. A. Munch: Historian and Nation Builder], Dreyer, Oslo, 2012.

Enebakk, Vidar & Pettersen, Bjørn Ragnvald: 'Christopher Hansteen and the Observatory in Christiania', *Monuments and Sites*, vol. 18, 2009.

Enterline, James Robert: *Erikson, Eskimos, and Columbus: Medieval European Knowledge of America*, The Johns Hopkins University Press, Baltimore, 2002.

Eriksen, Trond Berg: *Reisen til helvete. Dantes Inferno* [*Journey to Hell: Dante's*

Inferno], Universitetsforlaget, Oslo, 1993.

Eskeland, Ivar: *Snorri Sturluson. Ein biografi* [*Snorri Sturluson: A Biography*], Grøndahl Dreyer, Oslo, 1992.

Everest, Mark: *Space Race*, BBC series in four episodes, London, 2005.

Farman, Jason: 'Mapping the Digital Empire: Google Earth and the Process of Postmodern Cartography' in Dodge, Kitchin and Perkins: *The Map Reader*, Wiley-Blackwell, Chichester, 2011.

Felt, Hali: *Soundings. The Story of the Remarkable Woman Who Mapped the Ocean Floor*, Picador, New York, 2013.

Finnegan, Terrence J.: *Shooting the Front. Allied Aerial Reconnaissance and Photographic Interpretation on the Western Front – World War I*, National Defense Intelligence College Press, Washington DC, 2007.

Fløttre, Nils H.: *Satellitter og miljøovervåkning* [*Satellites and Environmental Surveillance*], Universitetsforlaget, Oslo, 1995.

Fra Mauro: My Old Maps has an English translation of Fra Mauro's texts: myoldmaps.com/late-medieval-maps-1300/249-fra-mauros-mappamundi/fra-mauro-transcriptions.pdf

Fryjordet, Torgeir: *Generalforstamtet 1739–1746* [*The Forestry Commission 1739–1746*]. Norsk Skogbrukmuseum, Elverum, 1968.

Gabrielsen, Trond: 'Thomas von Westens runebomme 1723' ['Thomas von Westen's Sami magic drum'] in *Ságat* no. 252, 2009. finnmarkforlag.no/09_16.html

Geller, Tom: 'Imaging the World: The State of Online Mapping' in Dodge, Kitchin and Perkins: *The Map Reader*, Wiley-Blackwell, Chichester, 2011.

Gerritsz, Hessel: *Detectio Freti Hudsoni*, Frederik Muller & Co., Amsterdam, 1878. Translated to English by Fred. John Millard.

Ginsberg, William: *Maps and Mapping of Norway, 1602–1855*, Septentrionalium

Press, New York, 2009.

——: 'Route Maps from the 1860s into the Early Twentieth Century: Competition, Evolution, and Specialization' in Ginsberg, William: *Maps and Mapping of Norway, 1602–1855*, Septentrionalium Press, New York, 2009.

Gjurd: Review of Albert Cammermeyers 'Reisekart over det sydlige Norge' (Travel map of southern Norway) and 'Lomme-Reisekart over Norge' ('Pocket travel map of Norway') in *Fedraheimen* magazine, no. 39, 1884.

Godlewska, Anne: *Geography Unbound: French Geographic Science from Cassini to Humboldt*, The University of Chicago Press, Chicago, 1999.

Gosch, Stephen S. & Stearns, Peter N.: *Premodern Travel in World History*, Routledge, New York, 2008.

Greiner, Lynn: 'Putting Canada on the map', *Globe and Mail*, Toronto, 17 December 2007: theglobeandmail.com/technology putting-canada-on-themap/article1092101/

Grove, G.L.: 'Grove, Carl Frederik' in *Dansk biografisk Lexikon* [*Danish Biographical Encyclopedia*], Gyldendalske Boghandels Forlag, Copenhagen, 1887–1905. runeberg.org/dbl/6/0212.html

Guier, William H. & Weiffenbach, George C.: 'Genesis of Satellite Navigation' in *Johns Hopkins APL Technical Digest*, vol. 19, no 1, Baltimore, 1998.

Haasbroek, N.D.: 'Gemma Frisius, Tycho Brahe and Snellius and their triangulations', *Rijkscommissie voor geodesie*, Delft, Netherlands, 1968.

Hagen, Rune Blix: 'Det kongelige kysttoktet til nordområdene i 1559' ['The royal coastal voyage to the northern regions in 1559'] in Briså, Benedicte Gamborg & Lavold, Bente (eds.): *Kompassrosen* [The Compass Rose], Nasjonalbiblioteket, Oslo, 2009.

Hanekamhaug, Hans Joachim (ed.): *Krigsskolen 1750–1950, Forsvarets undervisnings og velfærdskorps* [*The Military Academy 1750–1950: The Armed Forces' Education and Welfare*

Corps], Pressetjenesten, Oslo, 1950. Appendix: *Militær Orientering* [Military Orientation] 24.

Harrell, James: 'Turin Papyrus Map From Ancient Egypt' at eeescience. utoledo. edu/faculty/harrell/egypt/Turin%20 Papyrus/Harrell_Papyrus_Map_text. htm

Harsson, Bjørn Geirr: 'Historien bak Statens kartverk og kartleggingens historie' ['The story behind the Norwegian Mapping Authority and the history of mapping']
in *Lokalhistorisk magasin* [Local History Magazine], Trondheim, 01 2009. lokalhistoriskmagasin.no/utgivelser/ pdf/lokalhistorisk-magasin-2009-01

Harsson, Bjørn Geirr & Aanrud, Roald: *Med kart skal landet bygges. Oppmåling og kartlegging av Norge 1773–2016* [Building the Country with Maps: The Surveying and Mapping of Norway 1773–2016], Statens kartverk, Hønefoss, 2016.

Harsson, Margit: 'Stedsnavn – til lede og glede' ['Place names – to guide and give joy], apollon.uio.no/artikler/1996/sted. html

Harwood, Jeremy: *World War II From Above. An Aerial View of the Global Conflict*, Zenith Press, Minneapolis, 2014.

Heltne, Gunnar: 'Bruk av sunnmørske utsiktspunkt' ['Use of lookout points in Sunnmøre'] in Årbok for Sunnmøre Historielag 2009 [Sunnmøre Historical Society Yearbook 2009], Ålesund, 2009. sunnmore-historielag.no/?p=1132.

Herbermann, Charles George (ed.): *The Cosmographiæ Introductio of Martin Waldseemüller in Facsimile. Followed by the Four Voyages of Amerigo Vespucci, with their Translation into English; to which are added Waldseemüller's Two World Maps of 1507*, The United States Catholic Historical Society, New York, 1907. archive.org/details/ cosmographiaeint-00walduoft

Herodotus: *Historie* [*The Histories*], Thorleif Dahls kulturbibliotek/Aschehoug, Oslo, 1998. Translated by Henning Mørland.

——: *The Histories*, Perseus Digital Library, perseus.tufts.edu. English translation by A. D. Godley. Cambridge, Harvard University Press, 1920

Hestmark, Geir: 'Kartleggerne' ['The map-makers'] in Drivenes, Einar-Arne & Jølle, Harald Dag (eds.): *Norsk polarhistorie II. Vitenskapene* [*Norwegian Polar History II: The Sciences*], Gyldendal, Oslo, 2004. The section from *Historia Norwegiæ* was translated by Astrid Salvesen in Thorleif Dahls kulturbibliotek/Aschehoug, Oslo, 1969.

Hoel, Per: 'Kartografi og reproteknikk i kartverket. Utviklingen gjennom de siste 50 år' ['Cartography and reproduction techniques in the map series: developments over the past 50 years'] in Kulvik, Kåre (ed.), *Kartografisk forening 1937–1987, bilag til Kart og Plan nummer 1* [*Fifty Years of Cartography: The Cartographic Society 1937–1987, supplement to Maps and Plans number 1*], 1987.

Hoem, Arne I.: 'Utviklingen av sjøkartene over norskekysten til 1814' [The development of nautical charts of the Norwegian coast up to 1814] in Hausken, Kristoffersen & Svendsen (eds.): *Norges sjøkartverk. Kystens historie i kart og beskrivelser 1932–1982* [Nautical Charts of Norway: The History of the Coast in Maps and Descriptions 1932–1982], Norges sjøkartverk, Stavanger, 1983.

Hollingham, Richard: 'V2: The Nazi rocket that launched the space age' at bbc.com/ future/story/20140905-the-nazis-space-age-rocket

Holm, Knut Ragnar: 'Trekk fra fotogrammetriens historie i Norge' ['Aspects of the history of photogrammetry in Norway'], *Kart og plan 74*, Fagbokforlaget, Ås, 2014.

Holm-Olsen, Ludvig (trans.) *Edda-dikt*, J. W. Cappelens Forlag, Oslo, 1993.

Homer: *Iliaden* [*The Iliad*], Aschehoug, Oslo, 2004. Translated by Peter Østbye, edited by Øivind Andersen.

Howe, Nicholas: *Writing the Map of Anglo-*

Saxon England, Yale University Press, New Haven, 2008.

Ingstad, Helge: *Landet under leidarstjernen* [*The Land Under the Pole Star*], Gyldendal, Oslo, 1999.

Isachsen, Gunnar: '*Norvegia*' rundt sydpollandet. Norvegia-ekspedisjonen 1930–1931 [*'Norvegia' around the South Pole: The Norvegia Expedition 1930– 1931*], Gyldendal, Oslo, 1934.

——: 'Astronomical and Geodetical Observations' in *Report of the Second Norwegian Arctic Expedition in the 'Fram' 1898–1902*. vol. 2, Videnskabs-Selskabet i Kristiania, Kristiania, 1907.

Isidore of Seville: *The Etymologies*, Cambridge University Press, Cambridge, 2006. Translated by Stephen A. Barney, W. J. Lewis, J. A. Beach & Oliver Berghof.

Jennings, Ken: *Maphead*, Scribner, New York, 2011.

Jensen, Peter Andreas: *Læsebog for Folkeskolen og Folkehjemmet* [*Reader for Primary School and Home*], J. W. Cappelens Forlag, Oslo, 1863.

Johansen, Nils Voje: 'In ultimo fine Europae. Astronomen Maximilian Hell på besøk i Vardø' ['In ultimo fine Europae. Astronomer Maximilian Hell visits Vardø'] in Briså, Benedicte Gamborg & Lavold, Bente (eds.): *Kompassrosen* [*The Compass Rose*], Nasjonalbiblioteket, Oslo, 2009.

——: 'Caspar Wessel' in *Norsk biografisk leksikon* [*Norwegian Biographical Encyclopedia*], nbl.snl.no/Caspar_Wessel

Johansen, Terje: 'Seismikkbåtene som startet oljeeventyret' ['The seismic vessels that started the oil age'] in Årbok 2013, Arbeidernes Historielag i Rogaland [Yearbook of the Workers' Historical Society 2013], Stavanger, 2013, arbeiderhistorie.net/onewebmedia/ Seismikkb%C3%A5tene%20som%20 startet%20oljeeventyret.pdf

Jones, Michael: 'Tycho Brahe (Tyge Ottosen Brahe) 1546–1601' in Withers, Charles

W. J. & Lorimer, Hayden: *Geographers: Biobibliographical Studies*, vol. 27, Continuum, London, 2008.

Jorda sett med nye øyne [*The Earth Seen through New Eyes*], Norsk Romsenter [Norwegian Space Centre], 1999

Knudsen, Anders Leegaard: 'Geografi og topografi i *Gesta Danorum*' ['Geography and topography in *Gesta Danorum*'] in *Renæssanceforum* 3, 2007, renaessanceforum.dk

Koeman, Cornelis & van Egmond, Marco: 'Surveying and Official Mapping in the Low Countries, 1500–ca. 1670' in Woodward, David: *The History of Cartography Volume Three: Cartography in the European Renaissance*, The University of Chicago Press, Chicago, 2007.

König, Jason; Oikonomopoulou, Katerina; Woolf, Greg: *Ancient Libraries*, Cambridge University Press, Cambridge, 2013.

Konvitz, Josef: *Cartography in France, 1660–1848: Science, Engineering, and Statecraft*, University of Chicago Press, Chicago, 1987.

Kostka, Del: 'Air Reconnaissance in World War One', 2011, militaryhistoryonline. com/wwi/articles/airreconinwwi.aspx

Kristiansen, Nina: 'De kartla og navnga landet' ['They mapped and named the country'], forskning.no, 24 October 2012, forskning. no/historie-kulturhistorie-sprak/2012/10/de-kartlaog-navnga-landet

Kulvik, Kåre (ed.): *Kartografi i 50 år, Kartografisk forening, bilag til Kart og Plan nummer 1* [*Fifty Years of Cartography: The Cartographic Society, supplement to Maps and Plans number 1*], 1987.

Kunzig, Robert: *Mapping the Deep. The Extraordinary Story of Ocean Science*, Norton, New York, 2000.

Kyrkjebø, Rune & Spørck, Bjørg Dale (trans.): *Norrøn verdenshistorie og geografi* [*Norse World History and Geography*], Thorleif Dahls kulturbibliotek/Aschehoug, Oslo, 2012.

La Porte, Melissa: 'A Tale of Two *Mappae Mundi*: The Map Psalter and its Mixed-Media Maps', The University of Guelph, Ontario, 2012. atrium. lib.uoguelph.ca/xmlui/bitstream/ handle/10214/3662/LaPorte-final-05-09. pdf?sequence=6

Lainema, Matt & Nurminen, Juha: *Ultima Thule. Oppdagelsesreiser i Arktis* [*Ultima Thule: Journeys of Discovery in the Arctic*], Schibsted, Oslo, 2010.

Lervik, Arne: 'Geologien på den norske kontinentalsokkel nord for den 62. breddegrad' ['The geology of the Norwegian continental shelf above 62 degrees north], Oljedirektoratet (Norwegian Petroleum Directorate), Oslo, 1972. media.digitalarkivet.no/ view/49584/250?indexing=

Lewis, G. Malcolm: 'The Origins of Cartography' in Harley, J. B. & Woodward, David (eds.): *The History of Cartography Volume One: Cartography in Prehistoric, Ancient, and Medieval Europe and the Mediterranean*, The University of Chicago Press, Chicago, 1987.

Lozovsky, Natalia: 'The Earth is Our Book'. *Geographical Knowledge in the Latin West ca. 400–1000*, The University of Michigan Press, Michigan, 2000.

——: 'Maps and panegyrics' in Talbert & Unger, 2008.

Luncke, Bernhard: 'Norges Svalbard og Ishavsundersøkelsers luftkartlegning i Eirik Raudes land 1932' ['Aerial photography in Erik the Red's land by Norway's Svalbard and Arctic Ocean Survey']. Special printing of *Norsk Geografisk Tidsskrift* [*The Norwegian Journal of Geography*], vol. 4, issue 6, Oslo, 1933

MacLeod, Roy (ed.): *The Library of Alexandria*, I.B. Tauris Publishers, London, 2000.

McPhail, Cameron: 'Reconstructing Eratosthenes' Map of the World: A Study in Source Analysis', master's dissertation from the University of Otago, Dunedin, 2011. ourarchive.otago.

ac.nz/bitstream/handle/10523/1713/ McPhailCameron2011MA.pdf

Magnus, Olaus: *Historia om de nordiska folken* [*History of the Nordic People*], Michaelisgillet og Gidlunds förlag, Hedemora, 1909–1951. litteraturbanken. se/#!/forfattare/OlausMagnus

Marstrander, Sverre: Østfolds jordbruksristninger [Østfold's Agricultural Rock Carvings], Universitetsforlaget, Oslo, 1963.

Matei-Chesnoiu, Monica: *Re-imagining Western European Geography in English Renaissance Drama*, Palgrave Macmillan, Hampshire, 2012. pp. 13–14.

Meece, Stephanie: 'A bird's eye view – of a leopard's spots. The Çatalhöyük "map" and the development of cartographic representation in prehistory' in *Anatolian Studies*, no. 56 pp. 1–16, 2006. jstor.org/stable/20065543.

Meland, Trude: 'Tidslinje (1962– 1965)' ['Timeline (1962 –1965)'] at kulturminne-frigg.no

Mercator's projection: conversation with Bengt Malm at the Norwegian Maritime Museum.

Meyer, Robinson: 'A New 50-Trillion-Pixel Image of Earth, Every Day' at theatlantic.com/technology/ archive/2016/03/terra-bel-la-planet-labs/472734/

——: 'Google's Satellite Map Gets a 700-Trillion-Pixel Makeover' at theatlantic.com/technology/ archive/2016/06/ google-maps-gets-a-satellite-makeover-mosaic-700-trillion/488939/

Miekkavaara, Leena: 'Unknown Europe: The mapping of the Northern countries by Olaus Magnus in 1539' in Belgeo 3–4 2008. belgeo.revues.org/7677

Millard, Alan Ralph: 'Cartography in the Ancient Near East' in Harley, J. B. & Woodward, David (eds.): *The History of Cartography Volume One: Cartography in Prehistoric, Ancient, and Medieval Europe and the Mediterranean*, The University of Chicago Press, Chicago, 1987.

Miller, Greg: 'Inside the Secret World of Russia's Cold War Mapmakers' at wired.com/2015/07/secret-coldwar-maps/

Munch, Peter Andreas: *Indberetning om hans i somrene 1842 og 1843 med Stipendium foretagne Reiser gjennem Hardanger, Numedal, Thelemarken m.m. Hermed et Kart* [Report on his summers of 1842 and 1843 spent taking scholarship-funded journeys through Hardanger, Numedal, Telemark, etc. Including a Map], handwritten manuscript, 1844, Nasjonalbiblioteket (National Library of Norway), Oslo.

Myre, Olav (ed.): *For hundre år siden. P.A. Munch og mennene omkring ham* [*One hundred years ago: P. A. Munch and the people around him*], Olaf Norlis Forlag, Oslo, 1944.

Nansen, Fridtjof: *Fram over Polhavet. Første og anden del*, Aschehoug, Kristiania, 1897.

——: *Farthest North*, volumes I and II, Harper & Brothers Publishers, New York and London, 1898.

——(ed.): *The Norwegian North Polar Expedition 1893–1896. Scientific Results.* vol. IV, Christiania, Jacob Dybwad, 1904

——: *Nord i tåkeheimen. Utforskningen av Jordens nordlige strøk i tidlige* [*In Northern Mists: Arctic Exploration in Early Times*], Jacob Dybwads Forlag, Oslo, 1911.

——: *In Northern Mists: Arctic Exploration in Early Times.* Frederick A. Stokes Company, New York, 1911. Translated by Arthur G. Chater.

Nemet-Nejat, Karen Rhea: *Daily Life in Ancient Mesopotamia*, Greenwood Press, Westport, 1998.

Neugebauer, Otto: *A History of Ancient Mathematical Astronomy*, Springer-Verlag, New York, Heidelberg, Berlin, 1975.

Nissen, Kristian: 'Norlandia-kartet i Den Werlauffske gave og Andreas Heitmans kart over Nordlandene fra 1744–45 samt dermed beslektede karter' ['The Nordlandia Map and Andreas Heitman's map of the northern regions from 1744–45 and related maps] in *Norsk Geografisk Tidsskrift* [*The Norwegian Journal of Geography*] , vol. 7, 1938.

——: 'Melchior Ramus, en av den nasjonale kartografis grunnleggere' ['Melchior Ramus, a founder of national cartography'], speech made at 'Det Norske Geografiske Selskab' 24 February 1943, printed in *Norsk Geografisk Tidsskrift* [*The Norwegian Journal of Geography*], vol. 9, issue 5, Oslo, 1943.

——: 'Randsfjorden og Land på gamle karter' ['Randsfjorden and Land in old maps'] in Kolsrud, Oluf & Christensen, Reidar Th. (eds.): *Boka om Land. Bind 1* [*The Book of Land: Volume 1*], Lererlagene og Cammermeyers Boghandel, Oslo, 1948.

——: 'Hollendernes innsats i utformingen av de eldste sjøkarter over Nordsjøen og Norges kyster' ['How the Dutch shaped the oldest nautical maps of the North Sea and the coasts of Norway'] in *Bergens Sjøfartsmuseums årshefte 1949* [*Bergen Shipping Museum Yearbook 1949*], Bergen, 1950.

——: 'Det eldste kart over det gamle Stavanger stift.' ['The oldest map of the old Diocese of Stavanger']. Presentation at Rogaland Akademi 19 October 1960, printed in *Stavanger museum: Årbok 1960* [*Stavanger Museum: Yearbook 1960*], Dreyer, Stavanger, 1961.

——: 'Det eldste Vestlandskart.' ['The oldest map of Vestlandet'] Presentation at Selskapet til vitenskapens fremme 14 October 1960, printed in *Bergens historiske forening: Skrifter nr. 63 1960* [Bergen Historical Society: Journal no. 63], Bergen, 1961.

——: 'Nytt av og om Melchior Ramus' ['News of and about Melchior Ramus'] in *Norsk Geografisk Tidsskrift* [*The Norwegian Journal of Geography*], vol. 19, issues 5–6, Oslo, 1963–4.

Nissen, Kristian & Kvamen, Ingolf (eds.): *Major Peter Schnitlers grenseeksaminasjonsprotokoller*

1742–1745. [Major Peter Schnitler's border examination logs 1742–1745] vol. 1, Kjeldeskriftfondet, Norsk historisk kjeldeskriftinstitutt, Oslo, 1962.

Nørbeck, Torbjørn: 'Bruk av satellittbilder i kartframstilling' ['The use of satellite images in the presentation of maps'] in *Kart og Plan nummer 2*, 1986.

Nørlund, Niels Erik: *Danmarks kortlægning. En historisk fremstilling. Første bind. Tiden til afslutningen af Videnskabernes Selskab opmaaling* [The Mapping of Denmark: A historical presentation. Volume I], Ejnar Munksgaard, Copenhagen, 1942.

Norris, Pat: *Spies in the Sky*, Springer/Praxis Publishing, Chichester, 2008.

NOU 1975: 26, *Om norsk kart og oppmålingsvirksomhet* [On Norwegian Maps and Surveying], Miljøverndepartementet og Universitetsforlaget, Oslo, 1975.

Nunn, George E.: *Origin of the Strait of Anian Concept*, private publication, Philadelphia, 1929.

Nystedt, Lars: 'En expedition till vetgirighetens gräns' ['An expedition to the limits of curiosity'] in *Svenska Dagbladet*, 29 May 2006, svd.se/en-expediti-on-till-vetgirighetens-grans

O'Connor, John Joseph & Robertson, Edmund Frederick: 'Giovanni Domenico Cassini', history.mcs.st-and.ac.uk/Biographies/Cassini. html, St. Andrews, 2003.

Ohthere of Hålogaland's description is translated by Arthur O. Sandved from The Old English Orosius and retrieved from NOU 1984:18: 'Om samenes rettsstilling', Oslo, 1984, pp. 643–4.

Orosius, Paulus: *Seven Books of History Against the Pagans*, Liverpool University Press, Liverpool, 2010. Translated by Andrew T. Fear.

Ortelius, Abraham: *Theatrum orbus terrarum*, self-published, Antwerp, 1570.

Østensen, Olaf: 'EDB-utstyr til fylkeskartkontorene' ['Electronic data processing equipment for the county mapping offices'] in *Kart og Plan nummer 4* [*Maps and Plans number 4*], 1981.

Øverås, Eirik: *Snorre Sturlason*, Noregs Boklag, Oslo, 1941.

Paule, Torbjørn: *Den økonomiske kartleggingens historie i Norge* [*The History of Economic Mapping in Norway*].

Pettersen, Bjørn Ragnvald: 'Astronomy in service of shipping: Documenting the founding of Bergen Observatory in 1855' in *Journal of Astronomical History and Heritage* no. 8 (2), 2005.

——: 'The first astro-geodetic reference frame in Norway, 1779–1815' in *Acta Geod. Geoph. Hung.*, vol. 44, Budapest, 2009.

——: 'Jakten på Norges nullmeridian' ['The hunt for Norway's prime meridian'] in *Posisjon* [*Position*] no. 3, 2013.

——: 'Astronomiske bestemmelser av Norges første nullmeridian' ['Astronomical determinations of Norway's first prime meridian'] in *Kart og plan nr. 1.* [Maps and Plans number 1] 2014.

Pettersen, Bjørn Ragnvald & Harsson, Bjørn Geirr: 'Noen trekk fra geodesiens utvikling i Norge de siste 200 år' ['Some aspects of the development of geodesy in Norway over the past 200 years'] in *Kart og plan nr. 1* [*Maps and Plans number 1*], Oslo, 2014.

Plato: *Faidon* [*Phaedo*], Vidarforlaget, Oslo, 2001. Translated by Egil Kraggerud.

Plato: *Plato in Twelve Volumes, Vol. 1*, Perseus Digital Library, perseus.tufts. edu, translated by Harold North Fowler, 1966.

Pliny the Elder: *The Natural History*, Perseus Digital Library, perseus.tufts. edu, Medford, 1855. Translated by John Bostock and H.T. Riley.

Pontoppidan, Christian Jochum: *Geographisk Oplysning til Cartet over det sydlige Norge i trende Afdeelinger. Uddragen og samlet af de bedste, til Cartet brugte, locale Efterretninger og Hiel-pe-Midler* [*Geographical information to accompany the map of* southern Norway in three parts. Collated excerpts from the best local information and aids], printed by August Friederich Stein, Copenhagen, 1785.

Ptolemy, Claudius: *Geography*, translated by Edward Luther Stevenson, New York Public Library, New York, 1932, modified by Bill Thayer at penelope. uchicago.edu/Thayer/E/ Gazetteer/ Periods/Roman/_Texts/Ptolemy/home. html

The story of Pietro Querini can be read on the University of Tromsø website: ub.uit. no/northernlights/ nor/querini.htm

Randers, Kristofer: *Søndmøre. Reisehaandbog* [*Søndmøre Travel Handbook*], Aalesund-Søndmøre Turistforening and Albert Cammermeyer, Kristiania, 1890.

Rastad, Per Erik: *Kongsvinger festnings historie. Vakten ved Vinger – Kongsvinger festning 1682–1807* [*The Story of Kongsvinger Fortress: The Guard at Vinger – Kongsvinger Fortress 1687– 1807*], Hovedkomiteen for Kongsvinger festnings 300-årsjubileum (Lead committee for Kongsvinger Fortress's 300-year anniversary), 1992.

Reite, Arild: 'Digitale fylkeskart' ['Digital county maps'] in *Kart og Plan nummer 2* [Maps and Plans number 2], 1986.

Richelson, Jeffrey T.: 'U.S. Satellite Imagery, 1960–1999', nsarchive.gwu.edu/ NSAEBB/NSAEBB13/

Rogan, Bjarne: *Mellom tradisjon og modernisering. Kapitler av 1800-tallets samferdselshistorie* [*Between Tradition and Modernisation: Chapters from the transport history of the 1800s*], Novus forlag, Oslo, 1998.

Roller, Duane W.: *Eratosthenes' Geography*, Princeton University Press, Princeton, 2010.

Rytter, Olav: *Rigveda. Femtifem veda-hymnar* [The Rigveda: Fifty-five Veda hymns], Det Norske Samlaget, Oslo, 1976.

Sætre, Per Jarle: 'Ivar Refsdals skoleatlas. Atlasets innhold og betydning for samtiden' ['Ivar Refsdal's school atlas: its

content and contemporary significance'] in *Nordidactica* no. 2, 2014, kau.diva-portal.org/smash/get/diva2:765232/ FULLTEXT01.pdf

Sass, Erik: 'WWI Centennial: Battle of Neuve Chapelle', 2015, mentalfloss.com/ article/62119/wwi-centennial-battle-neuve-chapelle

Schellenberg, Rosie: *Maps: Power, Plunder and Possession*, episode 1: 'Windows on the World', BBC Productions, London, 2007.

——: *Maps: Power, Plunder and Possession*, episode 2: 'Spirit of the Age', BBC Productions, London, 2007.

Schilder, Günter & van Egmond, Marco: 'Maritime Cartography in the Low Countries during the Renaissance' in Woodward, David: *The History of Cartography Volume Three: Cartography in the European Renaissance*, The University of Chicago Press, Chicago, 2007.

Schöller, Bettina: 'Transfer of Knowledge: *Mappae Mundi* Between Texts and Images' in *Peregrinations: Journal of Medieval Art & Architecture*, vol. 4, no. 1 spring 2013. digital. kenyon.edu/cgi/viewcontent. cgi?article=1107&context=perejournal

Schøning, Gerard: 'Nogle Anmærkninger og Erindringer ved det, over Norge nylig udkomne, Kart' ['Some comments and changes on the new map of Norway'] in *Det Trondheimske Selskabs Skrifter. Anden Deel*, Copenhagen, 1763. ntnu. no/ojs/index.php/ DKNVS_skrifter/ article/view/699

Scott, Sheila: *On Top of the World*, Hodder and Stoughton, London, 1973.

Seip, Anne-Lise: 'P.A. Munch (1810–1863)', presentation at annual meeting, 3 May 2013.

Sellevold, Markvard Armin: 'Vitskapelege undersøkingar på den norske kontinental-sokkel 1960–1965: Resultat og problem' ['Scientific investigations on the Norwegian continental shelf 1960– 1965: Results and problems'] in Årbok 1996, Norsk Oljemuseum [*Norwegian*

Petroleum Museum Yearbook 1996], Stavanger, 1996.

Seue, Christian Martini de: *Historisk Beretning om Norges geografiske Opmaaling fra dens Stiftelse i 1773 indtil Udgangen af 1876* [*Historical account of the Geographical Survey of Norway from its establishment in 1773 until the end of 1876*], Kristiania, NGO, 1878.

Shakespeare, William: *As You Like It*, Oxford University Press, Oxford, 2008.

Shore, Arthur Frank: 'Egyptian Cartography' in Harley, J. B. & Woodward, David (eds.): *The History of Cartography Volume One: Cartography in Prehistoric, Ancient, and Medieval Europe and the Mediterranean*, The University of Chicago Press, Chicago, 1987.

Siebold, Jim: 'When America was part of Asia for 270 years', myoldmaps.com

Siewers, H.: *Geografi. Efter Rektor O.E.L. Dahm* [Geography], P.T. Mallings Forlagsboghandel, Kristiania, 1868.

Sinding-Larsen, Fredrik: *Den norske krigsskoles historie i ældre tider* [*The Early History of the Norwegian Military Academy*], Albert Cammermeyers Forlag, Oslo, 1900.

Skappel, Helge & Widerøe, Viggo: *Pionertid. 10 års sivilflyging i Norge* [*The Age of Pioneers: Ten years of civil flight in Norway*], Gyldendal Norsk Forlag, Oslo, 1946.

Skoleloven 1860 (Education Act 1860): fagsider.org/kirkehistorie/lover/1860_skole.htm

Smelror, Morten: 'Banebrytende geologiske oppdagelser' ['Groundbreaking geological discoveries'] at geo365.no/geoforskning/banebrytende-geologiske-oppdagelser

Smith, Catherine Delano: 'Cartography in the Prehistoric Period in the Old World: Europe, the Middle East, and North Africa' in Harley, J. B. & Woodward, David (eds.): *The History of Cartography Volume One: Cartography in Prehistoric, Ancient, and Medieval Europe and the Mediterranean*, The University of Chicago Press, Chicago, 1987.

——: 'Prehistoric Cartography in Asia' in Harley, J. B. & Woodward, David (eds.): *The History of Cartography Volume Two, Book Two: Cartography in the Traditional East and Southeast Asian Societies*, The University of Chicago Press, Chicago, 1994.

Smith, Catherine Delano & Ingram, Elizabeth Morley: *Maps in Bibles 1500–1600: An Illustrated Catalogue*, Librarie Droz, Geneva, 1991.

Strabo: *Geographica*, Harvard University Press, Cambridge, 1918–32. Translated by Horace Leonard Jones & John Robert Sitlington Sterrett.

Stubhaug, Arild: 'Christopher Hansteen' in *Norsk biografisk leksikon* [Norwegian Biographical Encyclopedia], nbl.snl.no/Christopher_Hansteen_-_1

Sturluson, Snorri: *Edda*, Cammermeyers Boghandel, Oslo, 1950. Translated by Anne Holtsmark.

——: *The Prose Edda*, translated by Jean I. Young, University of California Press, 1966.

——: *Heimskringla*, Translated by Samuel Laing, Longman, Brown, Green and Longmans, London, 1844.

——: *Kongesagaer* [*Kings' Sagas*], J. M. Stenersens Forlag, Oslo, 2009. Translated by Gustav Storm.

Sverdrup, Otto: *Nyt Land. Fire Aar i arktiske Egne* [New Land. Four Years in the Arctic Regions], Aschehoug, Kristiania, 1903.

——: *New Land. Four Years in the Arctic Regions*. Translated by Ethel Harriet Hearn, 1904.

Talbert, Richard J.A. & Unger, Richard W. (eds.): *Cartography in Antiquity and the Middle Ages*, Brill, Leiden, 2008.

Taylor, Andrew: *The World of Gerard Mercator*, Harper Perennial, London, 2004.

Taylor, E.G.R.: 'A Letter Dated 1577 from Mercator to John Dee' in *Imago Mundi*, vol. 13, 1956. jstor.org/stable/1150242. Norwegian translation of Mercator's letter to Dee by Asgaut Steinnes.

Tharp, Marie & Frankel, Henry: 'Mappers of the Deep' in *Natural History*, October 1986. faculty.umb.edu/anamarija.frankic/files/ocean_sp_09/MidAtlantic%20ridge%20discovery.pdf.gz

Tollin, Clas: 'When Sweden Was Put on the Map' in Palang, Hannes; Sooväli, Helen; Antrop, Marc & Setten, Gunhild (eds.): *European Rural Landscapes*, Kluwer, Dordrecht, 2004.

Trager, Leslie: 'Mysterious Mapmakers: Exploring the Impossibly Accurate 16th Century Maps of Antarctica and Greenland', newyorkmapsociety.org/LTMysteriousMapmakers.html, 2007.

Transit: Three Decades of Helping the World Find Its Way, JHU Applied Physics Laboratory, 1996: youtube.com/watch?v=HpYdvPtPTBI

Transit Satellites for Navigation: The Navy Navigation Satellite System, US Navy, 1967: youtube.com/ watch?v=HoTU_iKEFU8

Unikoski, Ari: 'The War in the Air – Observation and Reconnaissance', 2009, firstworldwar.com/airwar/observation.htm

Veer, Gerrit de: *Willem Barentsz' siste reise* [*The Last Voyage of Willem Barentsz*], Thorleif Dahls kulturbibliotek/Aschehoug, Oslo, 1997.

Wærdahl, Randi: 'Snorre Sturlason' i *Norsk biografisk leksikon* [Norwegian Biographical Encyclopedia] at nbl.snl.no/Snorre_Sturlason

Warren, Mame & Worth, Helen: *Transit to Tomorrow. Fifty Years of Space Research at The Johns Hopkins University Applied Physics Laboratory*, JHU/APL, Baltimore, 2009.

Ween, Thorolf: 'Kartlegging fra luften' ['Mapping from the air'] in *Norsk Geografisk Tidsskrift* [*The Norwegian Journal of Geography*] no. 8, 1933.

Welle-Strand, Erling & Helland-Hansen, Eigil: 'Smukke utsikter og kulturhistoriske minnesmerker' ['Beautiful views and historic cultural statues'] in Johnsen, Egil Børre & Eriksen, Trond Berg: *Norsk litteraturhistorie. Sakprosa fra 1750 til 1995, bind II* [*The History of Norwegian Literature: Non-fiction from 1750 to 1995, volume 2*], Universitetsforlaget, Oslo, 1998.

Widerberg, C.S.: Norges første militæringeniør Isaac van Geelkerck og hans virke 1644–1656 [Norway's first military engineer Isaac van Geelkerck and his work 1644–1656], Videnskapsselskapets skrifter. II. Hist.–filos. klasse. 1923. No. 2, printed by Jacob Dybwad, Kristiania, 1924.

Wille, Carl Fredrik: *Den norske Nordhavs-Expedition 1876–1878, IV, 1. Historisk Beretning* [*The Norwegian North-Atlantic Expedition 1876–1878, IV, 1. Historical account*], Grøndahl & Søns Bogtrykkeri, Christiania, 1882.

Williams, Glyn: *Arctic Labyrinth. The Quest for the Northwest Passage*, Penguin, London, 2010.

Williams, John: 'Purpose and Imagery in the Apocalypse Commentary of Beatus of Liébana' in Emmerson, Richard K. & McGinn, Bernard (eds.): *The Apocalypse in the Middle Ages*, Cornell University Press, Ithaca, 1992.

Woodman, Jenny: 'Wrangling a Petabyte of Data to Better View the Earth' at landsat.gsfc.nasa.gov/?p=9691

Ziegler, Georgianna: 'En-Gendering the World: the Politics and Theatricality of Ortelius's Titlepage' in Szönyi, György E. (ed.): *European Iconography. East and West*, E. J. Brill, Leiden/New York/Cologne, 1996.

INDEX OF NAMES